T0332526

# CURRENT ISSUES IN PARSING TECHNOLOGY

# THE KLUWER INTERNATIONAL SERIES IN ENGINEERING AND COMPUTER SCIENCE

## NATURAL LANGUAGE PROCESSING AND MACHINE TRANSLATION

*Consulting Editor*

**Jaime Carbonell**

**Other books in the series:**

EFFICIENT PARSING FOR NATURAL LANGUAGE: A FAST ALGORITHM
FOR PRACTICAL SYSTEMS, M. Tomita
ISBN 0-89838-202-5

A NATURAL LANGUAGE INTERFACE FOR COMPUTER AIDED DESIGN,
T. Samad
ISBN 0-89838-222-X

INTEGRATED NATURAL LANGUAGE DIALOGUE: A COMPUTATIONAL
MODEL, R.E. Frederking
ISBN 0-89838-255-6

NAIVE SEMANTICS FOR NATURAL LANGUAGE UNDERSTANDING,
K. Dahlgren
ISBN 0-89838-287-4

UNDERSTANDING EDITORIAL TEXT: A Computer Model of Argument
Comprehension, S.J. Alvarado
ISBN: 0-7923-9123-3

NATURAL LANGUAGE GENERATION IN ARTIFICIAL
INTELLIGENCE AND COMPUTATIONAL LINGUISTICS
Paris/Swartout/Mann
ISBN: 0-7923-9098-9

# CURRENT ISSUES IN PARSING TECHNOLOGY

edited by

**Masaru Tomita**
Carnegie Mellon University

**KLUWER ACADEMIC PUBLISHERS**
**Boston/Dordrecht/London**

**Distributors for North America:**
Kluwer Academic Publishers
101 Philip Drive
Assinippi Park
Norwell, Massachusetts 02061 USA

**Distributors for all other countries:**
Kluwer Academic Publishers Group
Distribution Centre
Post Office Box 322
3300 AH Dordrecht, THE NETHERLANDS

**Library of Congress Cataloging-in-Publication Data**

Current issues in parsing technology / edited by Masaru Tomita.
     p.  cm. — (Kluwer international series in engineering and
computer science ; SECS 126. Natural language processing and machine
translation)
    Rev. papers of the International Workshop on Parsing Techniques
-IWPT 89, held at the Carnegie-Mellon University and Hidden Valley
Resort on Aug. 28-31, 1989.
    Includes index.
    ISBN 0-7923-9131-4 (alk. paper)
    1. Natural language processing (Computer science)
2. Computational linguistics.   3. Artificial intelligence.
I. Tomita, Masaru.  II. International Workshop on Parsing Techniques
(1989 : Carnegie-Mellon University)  III. Series: Kluwer
international series in engineering and computer science ; SECS
126.  IV. Series: Kluwer International series in engineering and
computer science. Natural language processing and machine
translation.
QA76.9.N38C87   1991
006.3 ′5—dc20               90-49805
                                 CIP

**Copyright** © 1991 by Kluwer Academic Publishers

All rights reserved. No part of this publication may be reproduced, stored in a retrieval system or transmitted in any form or by any means, mechanical, photocopying, recording, or otherwise, without the prior written permission of the publisher, Kluwer Academic Publishers, 101 Philip Drive, Assinippi Park, Norwell, Massachusetts 02061.

*Printed on acid-free paper.*

Printed in the United States of America

# Contents

# List of Figures

# List of Tables

# Contributing Authors

Robert C. Berwick, Artificial Intelligence Laboratory, Massachusetts Institute of Technology, 545 Technology Square, Cambridge MA 02139.

E. Black, IBM Thomas J. Watson Research Center, P.O. Box 704, Yorktown Heights, NY 10598.

Harry Bunt, Institute for Language Technology and Artificial Intelligence ITK, P.O. Box 90153, 5000 LE Tilburg, The Netherlands.

Kenneth Church, Bell Laboratories.

J. Cocke, IBM Thomas J. Watson Research Center, P.O. Box 704, Yorktown Heights, NY 10598.

Sandiway Fong, Artificial Intelligence Laboratory, Massachusetts Institute of Technology, 545 Technology Square, Cambridge MA 02139.

T. Fujisaki, IBM Thomas J. Watson Research Center, P.O. Box 704, Yorktown Heights, NY 10598.

William Gale, Bell Laboratories.

Eva Hajičová, Faculty of Mathematics and Physics, Charles University, Prague, Malostranské n. 25, 118 00 Praha 1, Czechoslovakia.

Patrick Hanks, Oxford University Press.

Donald Hindle, Bell.

Ajay N. Jain, School of Computer Science, Carnegie Mellon University, Pittsburgh, PA 15213.

F. Jelinek, IBM Thomas J. Watson Research Center, P.O. Box 704, Yorktown Heights, NY 10598.

Karen Jensen, IBM.

Mark Johnson, Brown University.

Aravind K. Joshi, Department of Computer and Information Science, University of Pennsylvania, Philadelphia, PA 19104-6389, joshi@linc.cis.upenn.edu.

Ronald M. Kaplan, Xerox Palo Alto Research Center.

Bernard Lang. INRIA, B. P. 105, 78153 Le Chesnay, France, lang@inria.inria.fr.

John T. Maxwell III, Xerox Palo Alto Research Center.

Anton Nijholt, Faculty of Computer Science, University of Twente, P.O. Box 217, 7500 AE Enschede, The Netherlands.

T. Nishino, Tokyo Denki University.

Yves Schabes, Department of Computer and Information Science, University of Pennsylvania, Philadelphia, PA 19104-6389, schabes@linc.cis.upenn.edu.

Brian M. Slator, Department of Computer Science, North Dakota State University, Fargo, ND 58105-5075.

Mark Steedman, Department of Computer and Information Science, University of Pennsylvania, Philadelphia, PA 19104-6389.

Henry S. Thompson, Human Communication Research Centre, Department of Artificial Intelligence, Centre for Cognitive Science, University of Edinburgh.

Masaru Tomita, School of Computer Science and Center for Machine Translation Carnegie Mellon University, Pittsburgh, PA 15213.

K. Vijay-Shanker, Department of Computer & Information Science, University of Delaware, Delaware, DE 19716.

Alex H. Waibel, School of Computer Science, Carnegie Mellon University, Pittsburgh, PA 15213.

Robert E. Wall, University of Texas at Austin.

David J. Weir, Department of Electrical Engineering & Computer Science, Northwestern University, Evanston, IL 60208.

Yorick Wilks, Computing Research Laboratory, New Mexico State University, Las Cruces, NM 88003-0001.

Kent Wittenburg, MCC.

# Acknowledgments

Earlier versions of the papers in this book were originally presented at *International Workshop on Parsing Technologies — IWPT-89*, held at the Carnegie Mellon University and Hidden Valley Resort on August 28-31, 1989. The members of the workshop committee were: Masaru Tomita (chair), Bob Berwick, Harry Bunt, Aravind Joshi, Ron Kaplan, Bob Kasper, Mitch Marcus, Eva Hajicova, Makoto Nagao, Martin Kay, Jaime Carbonell, and Yorick Wilks.

45 papers were presented at the workshop, and 18 papers were selected and published in this volume based on recommendation by the programming committee. All papers concerning Generalized LR Parsing (Tomita algorithm) form another book, *Generalized LR Parsing*, M. Tomita (Ed.). Kluwer Academic Publishers.

I would like to thank Jeff Schlimmer and See-Kiong Ng for their help I received in preparing the final manuscript of this book.

*Masaru Tomita*

# CURRENT ISSUES IN PARSING TECHNOLOGY

# 1. Why Parsing Technologies?

## Masaru Tomita

*School of Computer Science and Center for Machine Translation*
*Carnegie Mellon University*

Natural languages are messy and difficult to parse with computers. It is clearly the case, and everybody agrees, that good linguistic theories are required to cope with the messy languages. Many linguistic theories and formalisms have been developed and discussed in the area of Computational Linguistics last couple of decades. On the other hand, there have been many practical systems that involve natural language parsing, such as machine translation, but only a few of them take full advantage of advances in linguistic theories. This is not because system builders are too lazy to learn new theories. I think there are two reasons. First, some linguistic theories and formalisms do not take implementation into account, and therefore cannot be implemented in a reasonable time with reasonable space. Second, there are too many other non-linguistic problems to worry about, and these problems (which are often underappreciated by theoreticians) more directly affect the system's performance. Thus, it would not make sense to adopt more sophisticated theories until better solutions to the non-linguistic problems are found.

Clearly, there is a big gap between linguistic theories and practical natural language applications. What we are lacking most is bridges between theories and practical applications. Those bridges include efficient parsing algorithms, software engineering for linguistic knowledge, implementation of linguistic theories/formalisms, and stochastic/probabilistic approaches.

This book is designed to make contributions to fill the gap between theories and practical systems. In the next section, the gap between linguistic theories and practical applications is highlighted.

## 1.1 The gap between theory and application

This section identifies two kinds of sentences: "linguistic" sentences and "real" sentences. The former is a kind of sentences that are often discussed in linguistic theory literatures, such as those in Table 1.1. The latter, on the other hand, is a kind of sentences that appear in practical applications, such as those in Table 1.2. Whereas both are grammatical English sentences, they appear to be significantly different. In this section, we discuss the characteristics of

Table 1.1. "Linguistic" sentences.

---

John hit Mary.
Every man who owns a donkey beats it.
I saw a man with a telescope.
The horse raced past the barn fell.
Time flies like an arrow.
The mouse the cat the dog chased ate died.
John persuaded Mary to expect that he believes that she likes an
     apple.

---

Table 1.2. "Real" sentences.

---

All processes (programs) in the destroyed window (or icon) are
killed (except *nohuped* processes; see *nohup(1)* in the *HP-UX Reference*); therefore, make sure you really wish to destroy a window
or an icon before you perform this task.

This window contains an HP-UX shell (either a Bourne shell or
C-shell, depending on the value of the SHELL environment variable; for details, see the "Concepts" section of the "Using Commands" chapter).

---

those two kinds of sentences.

It seems that problems in parsing sentences can be classified into two categories: linguistically "interesting" problems and linguistically "uninteresting"
problems. Linguistically "interesting" problems are those for which there
are no obvious solutions, and reasonably sophisticated theories are required
to solve them, or those behind which there are general linguistic principles,
and a small number of general rules can cope with them (e.g., relativization,
causativization, ambiguity, movement, garden-path, etc.). On the other hand,
linguistically "uninteresting" problems are those for which there exist obvious
solutions, or those behind which there is no general linguistic principle, and it
is just a matter of writing and adding rules to cope with these problems (e.g.,
punctuation, date and time expressions, idioms, etc.).

Tables 1.3 and 1.4 show example "interesting" and "uninteresting" problems, respectively. While one could give an elegant explanation of why the
second sentence in Table 3 is ungrammatical, there is no particular reason why
"15th July" is ungrammatical, other than that it is simply not English.

"Linguistic" sentences usually contain one or more linguistically interesting problems, with few or no linguistically uninteresting problems. "Real"
sentences, on the other hand, contain many uninteresting problems, but fewer
interesting problems. In (computational) linguistic literatures, uninteresting

Table 1.3. An interesting problem.

---

   John expects Mary to kiss herself.
\* John expects Mary to kiss himself.
   John expects Mary to kiss him.

---

Table 1.4. An uninteresting problem.

---

   on July 15th
   on the fifteenth of July
   on 7/15
\* on 15th July
\* in July 15th

---

problems can be ignored, as long as everybody agrees that there are obvious solutions for them. In practical applications, on the other hand, we cannot ignore uninteresting problems, or systems simply do not work.

There often exist reasonable approximate solutions to interesting problems in practical applications; for example, it is quite acceptable to assume that there are no embedded relative clauses in computer manuals, in order to simplify the (interesting) problem of relativization. On the other hand, there are no quick solutions to uninteresting problems other than writing a batch of rules. We can never anticipate and prepare for all of these uninteresting problems in advance. It seems as if there will be always these problems no matter how carefully and how many times we test and debug the system and its grammar. The quantity of the knowledge sources (i.e., grammars/rules) has to be very large; unlike interesting problems, rules for uninteresting problems can hardly generalized into a smaller number of rules, as each of them represents an uninteresting problem with no general linguistic principles behind it. This means that it is more difficult for humans to test, debug, and maintain a larger amount of knowledge sources accurately and consistently. And also it is more difficult for a system to access a larger amount of knowledge sources efficiently.

## 1.2  About this book

In the previous section, we highlighted some practical problems that are often overlooked by theoretical work. They are only a few of many non-linguistic problems in natural language processing. There are many other non-linguistic research problems that need to be solved in practical applications. This research area, which I call *Parsing Technologies*, is essential to bring down novel linguistic theories into practical applications.

Chapter 2, *The Computational Implementation of Principle-Based Parsers*, by Sandiway Fong and Robert C. Berwick, explores the abstract computational properties of principles to build more efficient parsers. In particular, they show how a parser can re-order principles under purely computational notions of "filters" and "generators" to avoid doing unnecessary work. A logical-based parser called the Principle-Ordering Parser (PO-PARSER) was built to investigate and demonstrate the effects of principle-ordering.

Chapter 3, *Parsing with Lexicalized Tree Adjoining Grammar*, by Yves Schabes and Aravind K. Joshi, defines a natural and general two-step parsing strategy for lexicalized grammars. The first step selects the set of structures corresponding to each word in the input sentence. The second step parses the sentence with respect to the selected structures. Tree Adjoining Grammars are chosen as an instance of lexicalized grammars, and the effects of the two-step strategy are investigated for several main types of parsing algorithms. The first step selects a relevant subset of the entire grammar, since only the structures associated with the words in the input sentence are selected for the parser. It also enables the parser to use non-local bottom-up information to guide its search. The strategy makes the search space of pure top-down parsers finite and prevents looping on left-recursive rules. Experimental data show that the performance of an Earley-type parser for TAGs is improved. Both in theory and in practice, the performances of the parsing algorithms are drastically improved.

Chapter 4, *Parsing with Discontinuous Phrase Structure Grammar*, by Harry Bunt, deals with discontinuous linguistic constituents — a fairly common phenomena in natural language. In order to represent syntactic structures with discontinuous constituents, the concept of discontinuous tree is introduced, as well as the notion of adjacency sequence. Based upon these concepts, a new class of grammars called Discontinuous Phrase-Structured Grammars (DPSGs) is defined. DPSG rules are generalizations of GPSG or HPSG rules, so DPSG rules can be added directly to a set of GPSG or HPSG rules to account for bounded discontinuity. The author also describes a matrix-driven DPSG parser based on active chart parsing concept. The parser is obtained by some enhancements of an ordinary phrase-structured grammar (PSG) parser to handle bounded discontinuity.

In Chapter 5, *Parsing with Categorial Grammar in Predictive Normal Form*, Kent Wittenburg and Robert E. Wall propose an alternate predictive normal form of categorial grammar which eliminates the problem of spurious ambiguity in parsing. The predictive normal form of a grammar can be obtained by replacing each composition rule with two predictive variants. The language generated by the resulting grammar subsumes that by the original grammar, and parsing problem occasioned by spurious ambiguity (that is, multiple semantically equivalent derivations) are eliminated at the expense of the slight profligacy of the recast grammar over the original.

The marriage of parsing and lexicography is investigated in Chapter 6, *PREMO: Parsing by Conspicuous Lexical Consumption*, by Brian M. Slator and Yorick Wilks. Semantic information obtained from a machine-readable dictionary is treated as a lexical resource used in directing the parsing process.

This chapter describes an architecture called PREMO (PREference Machine Organization), which is modeled as an operating system, for parsing natural language using preference semantics. PREMO is therefore a knowledge-based preference semantics parser with access to a large lexical semantic knowledge base. Parsing is performed as a best-first search within a large-scale application.

Chapter 7, *Parsing, Word Associations, and Typical Predicate-Argument Relations*, by Kenneth Church, William Gale, Patrick Hanks, and Donald Hindle, studies how several types of collocational constraints in natural language can be addressed with syntactic methods without requiring semantic interpretation. Co-occurrence relations such as word association and predicate-argument relation can be identified by computing summary statistics over a large corpus. The parser can then take advantage of such relations in syntactic analysis.

Chapter 8, *Parsing Spoken Language Using Combinatory Grammars*, by Mark Steedman, discusses the theory of Combinatory Categorial Grammar (CCG) and explores the possibility of merging phonology and parsing into a single unitary process in the theory. The problem of spurious ambiguity in CCG parsing can be resolved, to a large extent, by prosody in spoken language, since intonation largely determines which of the many possible bracketings permitted by the combinatory syntax is intended.

The topic-focus articulation of an utterance can affect the semantic interpretation of a given utterance. In Chapter 9, *A Dependency-Based Parser for Topic and Focus*, Eva Hajičová proposes parsing procedures for automatic identification of topic and focus of utterances. The main attention is on parsing written utterances in a "free word order" language (as in Czech). By paying attention to certain suprasegmental features like intonation center, the algorithm can be applied to the spoken form of the language. Parsing procedures for the written and spoken forms of languages that are not of free word order (as in English) are also investigated. The output structure of the analysis is a dependency-based labeled W-rooted tree which represents a (literal) meaning of the parsed utterance. This form of meaning representation is comparatively compact in depicting structural characteristics and deep word order of the sentence.

In order to employ probability to quantify language ambiguities, a hybrid model for natural language processing which comprises linguistic expertise and its probabilistic augmentation for approximating natural language is proposed in Chapter 10, *A Probabilistic Parsing Method for Sentence Disambiguation*, by T. Fujisaki, F. Jelinek, J. Cocke, E. Black, and T. Nishino. A completely automatic probabilistic augmentation process is described, together with a probabilistic parsing algorithm based on the Cocke-Kasami-Young algorithm. Empirical results in disambiguation of English and Japanese parsing are given in this chapter to illustrate the capabilities of the modeling method.

In Chapter 11, *Towards a Uniform Formal Framework for Parsing*, Bernard Lang takes on the task of providing a common ground on which the computational aspects of syntactic phenomena within the continuum of Horn-like formalisms which are used to define natural language syntax can be understood and compared. This can be achieved by considering all formalisms as special cases of Horn clauses and by expressing all parsing strategies with a unique operational device, namely the pushdown automaton. This chapter presents systematic study of two formalisms at both ends of the continuum (context-free grammar at the lower end and first order Horn clauses at the higher end) in this framework.

Chapter 12, *A Method for Disjunctive Constraint Satisfaction*, by John T. Maxwell, III and Ronald M. Kaplan, describes an algorithm for solving the disjunctive systems that arise in processing grammatical specifications involving feature equality constraints. Solving disjunctive constraints is exponentially difficult in the worst case. Maxwell and Kaplan obtain a better average time performance by exploiting a particular locality property of natural language, namely, that disjunctions that arise from different parts of a sentence tend to be independent. They propose a sound and complete method for solving disjunctive systems by embedding disjunctions from different parts of a sentence under different attributes in the feature structure. This method avoids multiplying the disjunctions together into a top-level disjunctive normal form, reducing the required parsing time by an exponential amount when the independence assumption holds.

In Chapter 13, *Polynomial Parsing of Extensions of Context-free Grammars*, K. Vijay-Shanker and David J. Weir present a general scheme for polynomial-time recognition of languages generated by certain extensions of context-free grammars, which include Linear Indexed Grammars(LIG), Combinatory Categorial Grammars (CCG) and Tree Adjoining Grammars (TAG). A full algorithm for LIG is presented, and those for CCG and TAG are obtained by adapting the algorithm using the grammar-mapping constructions which are used in showing the equivalence of these formalisms.

Chapter 14, *Overview of Parallel Parsing Strategies*, by Anton Nijholt, surveys various characteristic approaches to the problem of parallel parsing in a natural language processing context. Approaches such as the usage of multiple serial parsers, the application of parallelism in resolving parsing conflicts and the configuration of grammar into a network of process are described. Parsing strategies which are adapted from traditional algorithms such as CYK and Earley's algorithm, and strategies involving connectionist models are also discussed.

Loosely coupled parallel systems, that is, systems in which processors do not share memory, have become a common parallel system architecture. In Chapter 15, *Chart Parsing for Loosely Coupled Parallel Systems*, Henry S. Thompson investigates the computation-communication trade-off in parallel chart parsing under such system architecture. The author reports that the associated communication costs under current hardware is unfavorably high. To allow for wider comparisons between a variety of parallel systems, a portable parallel parser based on abstract parallel agenda mechanism is also presented in this chapter.

Connectionist modeling is a current prominent parallel architecture in Artificial Intelligence. Chapter 16, *Parsing with Connectionist Networks*, by Ajay N. Jain and Alex H. Waibel, describes a connectionist model which learns to parse sentences from sequential word input by acquiring its own grammar rules through training on example sentences. The trained network boasts of predictive ability, a certain degree of error tolerance, and some generalization capability. The application of this system to speech processing is considered, and encouraging empirical results are obtained.

Chapter 17, *A Broad-Coverage Natural Language Analysis System*, by Karen Jensen, reports about a highly experimental and data-driven system which is not modeled along the lines of any currently accepted linguistic theory. The work intends to achieve a broad coverage goal by building a robust and flexible natural language processing base which is both linguistically and computationally competent. This chapter discusses the three components of the system, namely the PNLP English Grammar, the reattachment component and the paragraph modeling component which happen to coincide with three linguistics levels: syntax, semantics and discourse.

The notion of 2-dimensional context-free grammar (2D-CFG) for 2-dimensional input text is introduced in Chapter 18, *Parsing 2-Dimensional Language*, by Masaru Tomita. 2D-CFG contains both horizontal and vertical productions. Parsing of 2-dimensional text input is done by combining rectangular regions of the input text to form larger regions using 2-dimensional phrase structure rule until the entire text is engulfed. Two efficient 2-dimensional parsing algorithms are provided in this chapter, namely 2D-Earley and 2D-LR, which are based on Earley's algorithm and Generalized LR algorithm respectively.

# 2. The Computational Implementation of Principle-Based Parsers

Sandiway Fong and Robert C. Berwick

*Artificial Intelligence Laboratory, Massachusetts Institute of Technology*

## 2.1 Introduction

Recently, there has been some interest in the implementation of grammatical theories based on the principles and parameters approach (Correa, 1988; Dorr, 1987; Johnson; Kolb & Thiersch, 1988; and Stabler, 1989). In this framework, a fixed set of universal principles parameterized according to particular languages interact deductively to account for diverse linguistic phenomena. Much of the work to date has focused on the not inconsiderable task of formalizing such theories. The primary goal of this chapter is to explore the computationally-relevant properties of this framework. In particular, we address the hitherto largely unexplored issue of how to organize linguistic principles for efficient processing. More specifically, this chapter examines if, and how, a parser can re-order principles to avoid doing unnecessary work. Many important questions exist: for example, (1) What effect, if any, does principle-ordering have on the amount of work needed to parse a given sentence? (2) If the effect of principle-ordering is significant, then are some orderings much better than others? (3) If so, is it possible to predict (and explain) which ones these are?

By characterizing principles in terms of the purely computational notions of "filters" and "generators," we show how principle-ordering can be utilized to minimize the amount of work performed in the course of parsing. Basically, some principles, like Move-$\alpha$ (a principle relating 'gaps' and 'fillers') and Free Indexing (a principle relating referential items) are "generators" in the sense that they build more hypothesized output structures than their inputs. Other principles, like the $\theta$-Criterion which places restrictions on the assignment of thematic relations, the Case Filter which requires certain noun phrases to be marked with abstract Case, and Binding Theory constraints, act as filters and weed-out ill-formed structures.

A novel, logic-based parser, the Principle-Ordering Parser (PO-PARSER), was built to investigate and demonstrate the effects of principle-ordering. The PO-PARSER was deliberately constructed in a highly-modular fashion to allow for maximum flexibility in exploring alternative orderings of principles. For

9

instance, each principle is represented separately as an atomic parser operation. A structure is deemed to be well-formed only if it passes all parser operations. The scheduling of parser operations is controlled by a dynamic ordering mechanism that attempts to eliminate unnecessary work by eliminating ill-formed structures as quickly as possible. (For comparison purposes, the PO-PARSER also allows the user to turn off the dynamic ordering mechanism and to parse with a user-specified (fixed) sequence of operations; see Section 2.3 for examples.)

Although we are primarily interested in exploiting the (abstract) computational properties of principles to build more efficient parsers, the PO-PARSER is also designed to be capable of handling a reasonably wide variety of linguistic phenomena. The system faithfully implements most of the principles contained in Lasnik and Uriagereka's (1988) textbook. That is, the parser makes the same grammaticality judgements and reports the same violations for ill-formed structures as the reference text. Some additional theory is also drawn from (Chomsky, 1981, 1986). Parser operations implement principles from Theta Theory, Case Theory, Binding Theory, Subjacency, the Empty Category Principle, movement at the level of Logical Form as well in overt syntax, and some Control Theory. This enables it to handle diverse phenomena including parasitic gaps constructions, strong crossover violations, passive, raising, and super-raising examples.

## 2.2   The principle ordering problem

This section addresses the issue of how to organize linguistic principles in the PO-PARSER framework for efficient processing. More precisely, we discuss the problem of how to order the application of principles to minimize the amount of 'work' that the parser has to perform. We will explain why certain orderings may be better in this sense than others. We will also describe heuristics that the PO-PARSER employs in order to optimize the ordering of its operations.

But first, is there a significant performance difference between various orderings? Alternatively, how important an issue is the principle ordering problem in parsing? An informal experiment was conducted using the PO-PARSER described in the previous section to provide some indication on the magnitude of the problem. Although we were unable to examine all the possible orderings, it turns out that order-of-magnitude variations in parsing times could be achieved merely by picking a few sample orderings.[1]

---

[1] The PO-PARSER has about twelve to sixteen parser operations. Given a set of one dozen operations, there are about 500 million different ways to order these operations. Fortunately, only about half a million of these are actually valid, due to logical dependencies between the various operations. However, this is still far too many to test exhaustively. Instead, only a few well-chosen orderings were tested on a number of sentences from the reference. The procedure involved choosing a default sequence of operations and 'scrambling' the sequence by moving operations as far as possible from their original positions (modulo any logical dependencies between operations).

## 2.2.1  Explaining the variation in principle ordering

The variation in parsing times for various principle orderings that we observed can be explained by assuming that overgeneration is the main problem, or bottleneck, for parsers such as the PO-PARSER. That is, in the course of parsing a single sentence, a parser will hypothesize many different structures. Most of these structures, the ill-formed ones in particular, will be accounted for by one or more linguistic filters. A sentence will be deemed acceptable if there exists one or more structures that satisfy every applicable filter. Note that even when parsing grammatical sentences, overgeneration will produce ill-formed structures that need to be ruled out. Given that our goal is to minimize the amount of work performed during the parsing process, we would expect a parse using an ordering that requires the parser to perform extra work compared with another ordering to be slower.

Overgeneration implies that we should order the linguistic filters to eliminate ill-formed structures as quickly as possible. For these structures, applying any parser operation other than one that rules it out may be considered as doing extra, or unnecessary, work (modulo any logical dependencies between principles).[2] However, in the case of a well-formed structure, principle ordering cannot improve parser performance. By definition, a well-formed structure is one that passes all relevant parser operations. Unlike the case of an ill-formed structure, applying one operation cannot possibly preclude having to apply another.

## 2.2.2  Optimal orderings

Since some orderings perform better than others, a natural question to ask is: Does there exist a 'globally' optimal ordering? The existence of such an ordering would have important implications for the design of the control structure of any principle-based parser. The PO-PARSER has a novel 'dynamic' control structure in the sense that it tries to determine an ordering-efficient strategy for every structure generated. If such a globally optimal ordering could be found, then we can do away with the run-time overhead and parser machinery associated with calculating individual orderings. That is, we can build an ordering-efficient parser simply by 'hardwiring' the optimal ordering into its control structure. Unfortunately, no such ordering can exist.

The impossibility of the globally optimal ordering follows directly from the "eliminate unnecessary work" ethic. Computationally speaking, an optimal ordering is one that rules out ill-formed structures at the earliest possible opportunity. A *globally* optimal ordering would be one that always ruled out every possible ill-formed structure without doing any unnecessary work. Consider the following three structures (taken from Lasnik's book):

(1)  a. *John$_1$ is crucial [$_{CP}$[$_{IP}$ $t_1$ to see this ]]

---

[2]In the PO-PARSER for example, the Case Filter operation which requires that all overt noun phrases have abstract Case assigned, is dependent on both the inherent and structural Case assignment operations. That is, in any valid ordering the filter must be preceded by both operations.

b. *$[_{NP}$John$_1$'s mother $][_{VP}$ likes himself$_1]$

c. *John$_1$ seems that he$_1$ likes $t_1$

Example (1) violates the Empty Category Principle (ECP). Hence the optimal ordering must invoke the ECP operation before any other operation that it is not dependent on. On the other hand, Example (1b) violates a Binding Theory principle, 'Condition A.' Hence, the optimal ordering must also invoke Condition A as early as possible. In particular, given that the two operations are independent, the optimal ordering must order Condition A before the ECP and vice-versa. Similarly, Example (1c) demands that the 'Case Condition on Traces' operation must precede the other two operations. Hence a globally optimal ordering is impossible.

### 2.2.3   Heuristics for principle ordering

The principle-ordering problem can be viewed as a limited instance of the well-known conjunct ordering problem (Smith & Genesereth, 1985). Given a set of conjuncts, we are interested in finding all solutions that satisfy all the conjuncts simultaneously. The parsing problem is then to find well-formed structures (i.e., solutions) that satisfy all the parser operations (i.e., conjuncts) simultaneously. Moreover, we are particularly interested in minimizing the cost of finding these structures by re-ordering the set of parser operations.

This section outlines some of the heuristics used by the PO-PARSER to determine the minimum cost ordering for a given structure. The PO-PARSER contains a dynamic ordering mechanism that attempts to compute a minimum cost ordering for every phrase structure generated during the parsing process.[3] The mechanism can be subdivided into two distinct phases. First, we will describe how the dynamic ordering mechanism decides which principle is the most likely candidate for eliminating a given structure. Then, we will explain how it makes use of this information to re-order parser operation sequences to minimize the total work performed by the parser.

**Predicting failing filters**

Given any structure, the dynamic ordering mechanism attempts to satisfy the "eliminate unnecessary work" ethic by predicting a "failing" filter for that structure. More precisely, it will try to predict the principle that a given structure violates on the basis of the simple structure cues. Since the ordering mechanism cannot know whether a structure is well-formed or not, it assumes that all structures are ill-formed and attempts to predict a failing filter for every

---

[3] In their paper, Smith and Genesereth drew a distinction between "static" and "dynamic" ordering strategies. In static strategies, the conjuncts are first ordered, and then solved in the order presented. By contrast, in dynamic strategies the chosen ordering may be revised between solving individual conjuncts. Currently, the PO-PARSER employs a dynamic strategy. The ordering mechanism computes an ordering based on certain features of each structure to be processed. The ordering may be revised after certain operations (e.g., movement) that modify the structure in question.

structure. In order to minimize the amount of work involved, the types of cues
that the dynamic ordering mechanism can test for are deliberately limited.
Only inexpensive tests such as whether a category contains certain features
(e.g., ±anaphoric, ±infinitival, or whether it is a trace or a non-argument) may
be used. Any cues that may require significant computation, such as searching
for an antecedent, are considered to be too expensive. Each structure cue is
then associated with a list of possible failing filters. (Some examples of the
mapping between cues and filters are shown below.) The system then chooses
one of the possible failing filters based on this mapping.[4]

(2)

| STRUCTURE CUE | POSSIBLE FAILING FILTERS |
|---|---|
| trace | Empty Category Principle, and Case Condition on traces |
| intransitive | Case Filter |
| passive | Theta Criterion Case Filter |
| non-argument | Theta Criterion |
| +anaphoric | Binding Theory Principle A |
| +pronominal | Binding Theory Principle B |

The correspondence between each cue and the set of candidate filters may
be systematically derived from the definitions of the relevant principles. For
example, Principle A of the Binding Theory deals with the conditions under
which antecedents for anaphoric items, such as "each other" and "himself,"
must appear. Hence, Principle A can only be a candidate failing filter for
structures that contain an item with the +anaphoric feature. Other corre-
spondences may be somewhat less direct: for example, the Case Filter merely
states that all overt noun phrase must have abstract Case. Now, in the PO-
PARSER the conditions under which a noun phrase may receive abstract Case
are defined by two separate operations, namely, Inherent Case Assignment and
Structural Case Assignment. It turns out that an instance where Structural
Case Assignment will not assign Case is when a verb that normally assigns
Case has passive morphology. Hence, the presence of a passive verb in a given
structure may cause an overt noun phrase to fail to receive Case during Struc-
tural Case Assignment — which, in turn may cause the Case Filter to fail.[5]

---

[4] Obviously, there are many ways to implement such a selection procedure. Currently, the
PO-PARSER uses a voting scheme based on the frequency of cues. The (unproven) underlying
assumption is that the probability of a filter being a failing filter increases with the number
of occurrences of its associated cues in a given structure. For example, the more traces there
are in a structure, the more likely it is that one of them will violate some filter applicable to
traces, such as the Empty Category Principle (ECP).

[5] It is possible to automate the process of finding structure cues simply by inspecting the
closure of the definitions of each filter and all dependent operations. One method of deriving
cues is to collect the negation of all conditions involving category features. For example, if
an operation contains the condition "not (Item has_feature intransitive)," then we can
take the presence of an intransitive item as a possible reason for failure of that operation.
However, this approach has the potential problem of generating too many cues. Although,
it may be relatively inexpensive to test each individual cue, a large number of cues will
significantly increase the overhead of the ordering mechanism. Furthermore, it turns out

The failing filter mechanism can been seen as an approximation to the Cheapest-first heuristic in conjunct ordering problems. It turns out that if the cheapest conjunct at any given point will reduce the search space rather than expand it, then it can be shown that the optimal ordering must contain that conjunct at that point. Obviously, a failing filter is a "cheapest" operation in the sense that it immediately eliminates one structure from the set of possible structures under consideration.

Although the dynamic ordering mechanism performs well in many of the test cases drawn from the reference text, it is by no means foolproof (see Section 2.3 for an example.) There are also many cases where the prediction mechanism triggers an unprofitable re-ordering of the default order of operations. (We will present one example of this in the next section.) A more sophisticated prediction scheme, perhaps one based on more complex cues, could increase the accuracy of the ordering mechanism. However, we will argue that it is not cost-effective to do so. The basic reason is that, in general, there is no *simple* way to determine whether a given structure will violate a certain principle.[6] That is, as far as one can tell, it is difficult to produce a cheap (relative to the cost of the actual operation itself), but effective approximation to a filter operation. For example, in Binding Theory, it is difficult to determine if an anaphor and its antecedent satisfies the complex locality restrictions imposed by Principle A without actually doing some searching for a binder. Simplifying the locality restrictions is one way of reducing the cost of approximation, but the very absence of search is the main reason why the overhead of the present ordering mechanism is relatively small.[7] Hence, having more sophisticated cues may provide better approximations, but the tradeoff is that the prediction methods may be almost as expensive as performing the real operations themselves.

## Logical dependencies and re-ordering

Given a candidate failing filter, the dynamic ordering mechanism has to schedule the sequence of parser operations so that the failing filter is performed as early as possible. Simply moving the failing filter to the front of the operations queue is not a workable approach for two reasons.

Firstly, simply fronting the failing filter may violate logical dependencies between various parser operations. For example, suppose the Case Filter was

---

that not all cues are equally useful in predicting failure filters. One solution may be to use "weights" to rank the predictive utility of each cue with respect to each filter. Then an adaptive algorithm could be used to "learn" the weighting values, in a manner reminiscent of (Samuels, 1967). The failure filter prediction process could then automatically eliminate testing for relatively unimportant cues. This approach is currently being investigated.

[6] If such a scheme can be found, then it can effectively replace the definition of the principle itself.

[7] We ignore the additional cost of re-ordering the sequence of operations once a failing filter has been predicted. The actual re-ordering can be made relatively inexpensive using various tricks. For example, it is possible to "cache" or compute (off-line) common cases of re-ordering a default sequence with respect to various failing filters, thus reducing the cost of re-ordering to that of a simple look-up.

chosen to be the failing filter. To create the conditions under which the Case Filter can apply, both Case assignment operations, namely, Inherent Case Assignment and Structural Case Assignment, must be applied first. Hence, fronting the Case Filter will also be accompanied by the subsequent fronting of both assignment operations — unless, of course, they have already been applied to the structure in question.

Secondly, the failing filter approach does not take into account the behavior of "generator" operations. A generator may be defined as any parser operation that always produces one output, and possibly more than one output, for each input. For example, the operations corresponding to $\bar{X}$ rules, Move-$\alpha$, Free Indexing and LF Movement are the generators in the PO-PARSER. (Similarly, the operations that we have previously referred to as "filters" may be characterized as parser operations that, when given $N$ structures as input, pass $N$ and possibly fewer than $N$ structures.) Due to logical dependencies, it may be necessary in some situations to invoke a generator operation before a failure filter can be applied. For example, the filter Principle A of the Binding Theory is logically dependent on the generator Free Indexing to generate the possible antecedents for the anaphors in a structure. Consider the possible binders for the anaphor "himself" in "John thought that Bill saw himself" as shown below:

(3)  a. *John$_i$ thought that Bill$_j$ saw himself$_i$

     b. John$_i$ thought that Bill$_j$ saw himself$_j$

     c. *John$_i$ thought that Bill$_j$ saw himself$_k$

Only in Example (3b), is the antecedent close enough to satisfy the locality restrictions imposed by Principle A. Note that Principle A had to be applied a total of three times in the above example in order to show that there is only one possible antecedent for "himself." This situation arises because of the general tendency of generators to overgenerate. But this characteristic behavior of generators can greatly magnify the extra work that the parser does when the dynamic ordering mechanism picks the wrong failing filter. Consider the ill-formed structure "*John seems that he likes t" (a violation of the principle that traces of noun phrase cannot receive Case). If however, Principle B of the Binding Theory is predicted to be the failure filter (on the basis of the structure cue "he"), then Principle B will be applied repeatedly to the indexings generated by the Free Indexing operation. On the other hand, if the Case Condition on Traces operation was correctly predicted to be the failing filter, then Free Indexing need not be applied at all. The dynamic ordering mechanism of the PO-PARSER is designed to be sensitive to the potential problems caused by selecting a candidate failing filter that is logically dependent on many generators.[8]

---

[8] Obviously, there are many different ways to accomplish this. One method is to compute the "distance" of potential failure filters from the current state of the parser in terms of the number of generators yet to be applied. Then the failing filter will be chosen on the basis of some combination of structure cues and generator distance. Currently, the PO-PARSER uses

## 2.2.4  Linguistic filters and determinism

In this section we describe how the characterization of parser operations in terms of filters and generators may be exploited further to improve the performance of the PO-PARSER for some operations. More precisely, we make use of certain computational properties of linguistic filters to improve the backtracking behavior of the PO-PARSER. The behavior of this optimization will turn out to complement that of the ordering selection procedure quite nicely. That is, the optimization is most effective in exactly those cases where the selection procedure is least effective.

We hypothesize that linguistic filters, such as the Case Filter, Binding Conditions, ECP, and so on, may be characterized as follows:

(4) **Hypothesis**: Linguistic filters are side-effect free conditions on configurations

In terms of parser operations, this means that filters should never cause structure to be built or attempt to fill in feature slots.[9] Moreover, computationally speaking, the parser operations corresponding to linguistic filters should be deterministic. That is, any given structure should either fail a filter or just pass. A filter operation should never need to succeed more than once, simply because it is side-effect free.[10] By contrast, operations that we have characterized as generators, such as Move-$\alpha$ and Free Indexing, are not deterministic in this sense. That is, given a structure as input, they may produce one or more structures as output.

Given the above hypothesis, we can cut down on the amount of work done by the PO-PARSER by modifying its behavior for filter operations. Currently, the parser employs a backtracking model of computation. If a particular parser

---

a slightly different and cheaper scheme. The failure filter is chosen solely on the basis of structure cues. However, the fronting mechanism is restricted so that the chosen filter can only move a limited number of positions ahead of its original position. The original operation sequence is designed such that the distance of the filter from the front of the sequence is roughly proportional to the number of (outstanding) operations that the filter is dependent on.

[9]So far, we have not encountered any linguistic filters that require either structure building or feature assignment. Operations such as $\theta$-role and Case assignment are not considered filters in the sense of the definition given in the previous section. In the PO-PARSER, these operations will never fail. However, definitions that involve some element of 'modality' are potentially problematic. For example, Chomsky's definition of an *accessible SUBJECT*, a definition relevant to the principles of Binding Theory, contains the following phrase "... *assignment to $\alpha$ of the index of $\beta$ would not violate the (i-within-i) filter* $*[_{\gamma_i}...\delta_i...]$." A transparent implementation of such a definition would seem to require some manipulation of indices. However, Lasnik (p. 58) points out that there exists an empirically indistinguishable version of *accessible SUBJECT* without the element of modality present in Chomsky's version.

[10]It turns out that there are situations where a filter operation (although side-effect free) could succeed more than once. For example, the linguistic filter known as the "Empty Category Principle" (ECP) implies that all traces must be "properly governed." A trace may satisfy proper government by being either "lexically governed" or "antecedent governed." Now consider the structure $[_{CP}$ $What_1$ $did$ $you$ $[_{VP}$ $read$ $t_1]]$. The trace $t_1$ is both lexically governed (by the verb *read*) and antecedent governed (by its antecedent *what*). In the PO-PARSER the ECP operation can succeed twice for cases such as $t_1$ above.

operation fails, then the default behavior is to attempt to re-satisfy the operation that was called immediately before the failing operation. In this situation, the PO-PARSER will only attempt to re-satisfy the preceding operation if it happens to be a generator. When the preceding operation is a filter, then the parser will skip the filter and, instead, attempt to resatisfy the next most recent operation and so on.[11] For example, consider the following calling sequence:

Suppose that a structure generated by generator $G_2$ passes filters $F_1$ and $F_2$, but fails on filter $F_3$. None of the three filters could have been the cause of the failure by the side-effect free hypothesis. Hence, we can skip trying to resatisfy any of them and backtrack straight to $G_2$.

Note that this optimization is just a limited form of dependency-directed backtracking. Failures are traced directly to the last generator invoked, thereby skipping over any intervening filters as possible causes of failure. However, the backtracking behavior is limited in the sense that the most recent generator may not be the cause of a failure. Consider the above example again. The failure of $F_3$ need not have been caused by $G_2$. Instead, it could have been caused by structure-building in another generator further back in the calling sequence, say $G_1$. But the parser will still try out all the other possibilities in $G_2$ first.

Consider a situation in which the principle selection procedure performs poorly. That is, for a particular ill-formed structure, the selection procedure will fail to immediately identify a filter that will rule out the structure. The advantages of the modified mechanism over the default backtrack scheme will be more pronounced in such situations — especially if the parser has to try several filters before finding a "failing" filter. By contrast, the behavior of the modified mechanism will resemble that of the strict chronological scheme in situations where the selection procedure performs relatively well (i.e., when a true failing filter is fronted). In such cases, the advantages, if significant, will be small. (In an informal comparison between the two schemes using about eighty sentences from the reference text, only about half the test cases exhibited a noticeable decrease in parsing time.)

---

[11] This behavior can be easily simulated using the 'cut' predicate in Prolog. We can route all calls to filter operations through a predicate that calls the filter and then cuts off all internal choice points. (For independent reasons, the PO-PARSER does not actually use this approach.)

## 2.3    Examples of parsing using the PO-PARSER

This section contains some examples of parsing using the implemented system. The 'core' portion of the PO-PARSER, consisting of a lexicon, various principle definitions, and a bottom-up $\bar{X}$-parsing machine, is written entirely in Prolog. The principle-ordering mechanism and user-interface portions are independently written in Lisp. The complete system runs on a Symbolics 3650 workstation.

The snapshot in Figure 2.1 shows the result of parsing the ambiguous sentence "John believes that Mary likes him." Since the parser recovers all possible parses, it returns two parses — one for the case where "John" and "him" are interpreted as being coreferential, and the other when "him" is coreferential with a third person, not named in this sentence. (In the second structure, the pronoun "him" has the same index (zero) as "John". For the first parse, the pronoun is given a separate index.) The list of parser operations on the right-hand-side of the screen provides useful statistics on the execution of the parse. (The panel is also used to provide an 'animated' display of the behavior of the system during parsing. The box surrounding each principle briefly 'flashes' each time the principle is invoked.) There are two numbers associated with each parser operation. The top number records how many times that operation was invoked during parsing. The bottom number indicates how many times the operation succeeded. For example, we can immediately trace the source of the referential ambiguity to the free indexation operation, because it is the only generator that produced two structures from one input. (As we will show later, the numbers will also serve to identify the failing principle in cases of ungrammatical input.)

The PO-PARSER allows the user to experiment with various orderings. The snapshot in Figure 2.2 below shows three distinct orderings. Each list of parser operations is just a permutation of the panel of operations shown in the snapshot above. Each list should be read in a 'top-down' fashion, that is, the topmost operation will be executed first, the operation immediately below the topmost will be executed next, and so on, down to the bottom operation. The leftmost list is the default ordering used in the previous example. In this session, we have created two alternative permutations as test orderings.

The pop-up menu shown above, allows the user to arbitrarily reorder parser operations, simply by 'moving' each operation around. (The system also keeps track of logical dependencies between the various operations — hence, it will prevent the construction of ill-formed orderings, for example, Inherent Case Assignment is never allowed to 'follow' the Case Filter.) For the purposes of the next example, the position of the Case Filter in the list will be the salient difference between the middle and the rightmost orderings. That is, the Case Filter appears as 'early' as possible in the middle, and as 'late' as possible in the rightmost ordering (as shown in the pop-up menu).

The snapshot in Figure 2.3 shows the result of running the parser using the rightmost ordering on the ungrammatical example "*It was arrested John."

Of course, the system returns no parses for this ungrammatical sentence. Note that the statistics collected for the Case Filter indicates that it was the

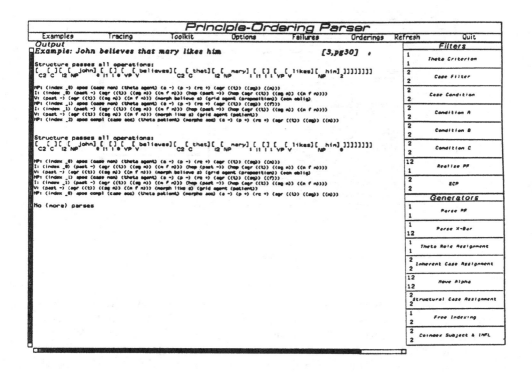

Figure 2.1. Snapshot of the result of parsing ambiguous sentence "John believes that Mary likes him."

failing filter in this case. (Every other operation succeeded at least once, only the Case Filter failed to pass a single structure.) The important to note about this diagram, is that every operation listed was 'exercised' at least once. The next snapshot in Figure 2.4 shows the result of parsing the same sentence, but using the middle ordering instead.

As before, the system returns no parses. (Of course, variations in ordering cannot affect the logic of the parser. That is, the parses produced in each case must be the same.) However, in this case the parser achieves the same result, but with much less work. That is, the ungrammatical sentence has been ruled out as early as possible. Observe that the statistics indicate that many fewer parser operations were invoked in this case.

Finally, the user can also allow the system to pick its own ordering via the dynamic ordering mechanism. The snapshot in Figure 2.5 shows the result of parsing the same example using dynamic ordering.

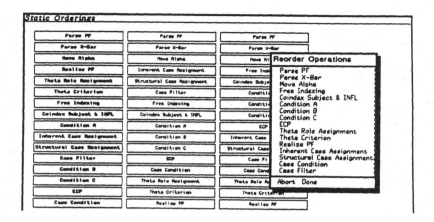

Figure 2.2. Snapshot of parsing showing three distinct orderings.

The snapshot in Figure 2.5 also contains information about any choices that the ordering mechanism made during execution. In this situation, the relevant structure cues are NONARG (from the non-argument "It") and PASSIVE (from "was arrested"). Since a nonargument cannot be assigned a theta-role, this suggests that the Theta Criterion may be the failing filter. Similarly, the presence of the passive element prevents "arrested" from assigning Case to its complement ("John"), which suggests the Case Filter as the failing filter. The passive element also prevents the external theta-role of "arrested" from being assigned to the noun phrase in subject position ("it"). Hence, there will be a total of two 'votes' for the Theta Criterion and one for the Case Filter. Thus, the ordering mechanism will pick the Theta Criterion as the most likely failing filter, and re-order the operations accordingly. Actually, it turns out, for the structure under consideration, that the Theta Criterion was not the optimal choice. The ordering mechanism then re-evaluates its choice, and collects votes in the same fashion as before. The outcome of the voting is unchanged, but the Theta Criterion has already been applied. Hence, the system picks the Case Filter as the most likely failing filter (the correct choice) on the second attempt.

## 2.4   Concluding remarks

In the framework of the PO-PARSER, dynamic principle-ordering can provide a significant improvement over any fixed ordering. Speed-ups varying from three- or four-fold to order-of-magnitude improvements have been observed in

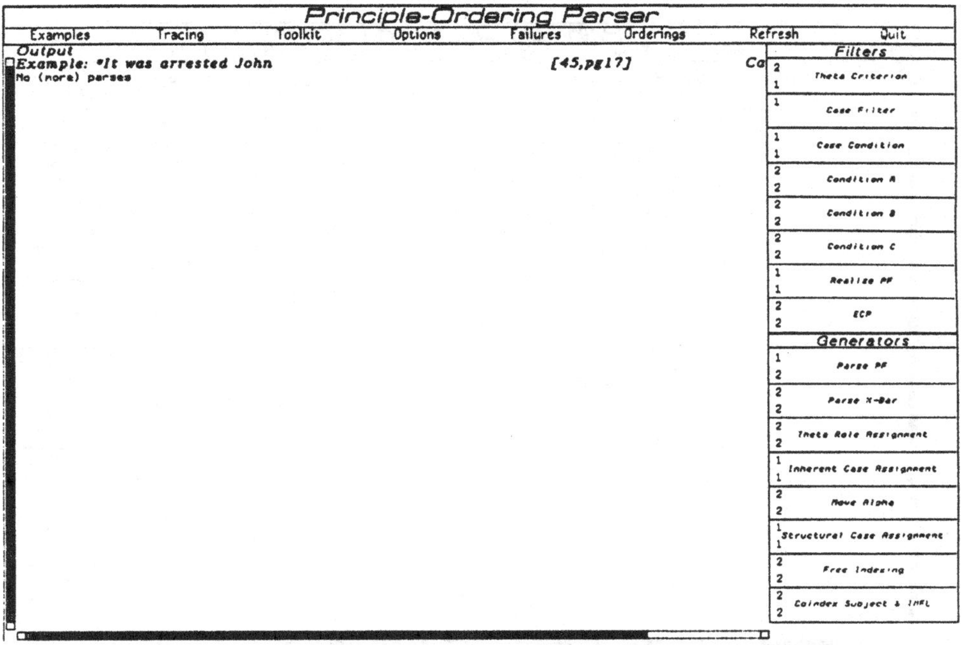

Figure 2.3. Running the parser using the rightmost ordering on the ungrammatical example "*It was arrested John."

many cases.[12]

The control structure of the PO-PARSER forces linguistic principles to be applied one at a time. Many other machine architectures are certainly possible. For example, we could take advantage of the independence of many principles and apply principles in parallel whenever possible. However, any improvement in parsing performance would come at the expense of violating the minimum (unnecessary) work ethic. Lazy evaluation of principles is yet another alternative. However, principle-ordering would still be an important consideration for efficient processing in this case. Finally, we should also consider principle-ordering from the viewpoint of scalability. The experience from building prototypes of the PO-PARSER suggests that as the level of sophistication of the parser increases (both in terms of the number and complexity

---

[12] Obviously, the speed-up obtained will depend on the number of principles present in the system and the degree of 'fine-tuning' of the failure filter selection criteria.

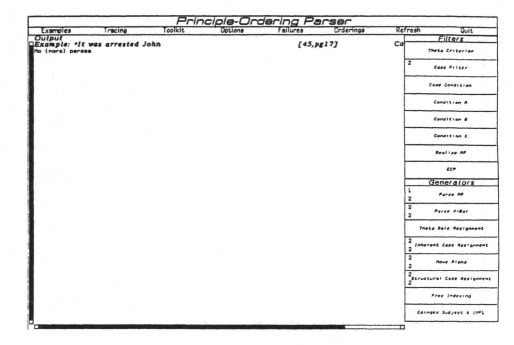

Figure 2.4. Running the parser using the middle ordering on the ungrammatical example "*It was arrested John."

of individual principles), the effect of principle-ordering also becomes more pronounced.

## Acknowledgments

The work of the first author is supported by an IBM Graduate Fellowship. R. C. Berwick is supported by NSF Grant DCR-85552543 under a Presidential Young Investigator's Award.

## References

Chomsky, N. A. (1981). *Lectures on government and binding: The Pisa lectures.* Foris Publications.

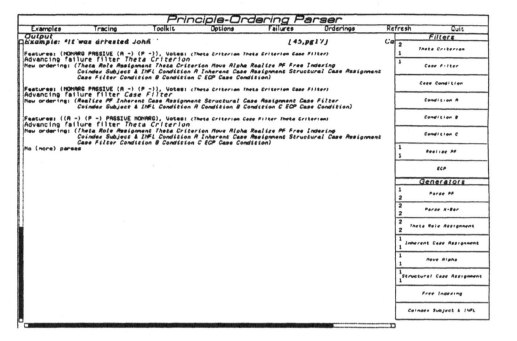

Figure 2.5. Running the parser using dynamic ordering on the ungrammatical example "*It was arrested John."

Chomsky, N. A. (1986). *Knowledge of language: Its nature, origin, and use.* Prager.

Correa, N. (1988). *Syntactic analysis of English with respect to government-binding grammar.* Unpublished doctoral dissertation. Syracuse University.

Dorr, B. J. (1987). *UNITRAN: A principle-base approach to machine translation* (Tech. Rep. No. 1000). Cambridge: Massachusetts Institute of Technology.

Johnson, M. *Knowledge as language.* M. I. T. Brain and Cognitive Sciences.

Kolb, H. P., & Thiersch, C. (1988). *Levels and empty categories in a principles and parameters approach to parsing.* Tilburg University.

Lasnik, H., & Uriagereka, J. (1988). *A course in GB syntax: Lectures on binding and empty categories.* MIT Press.

Samuels, A. L. (1967). Some studies in machine learning using the game of Checkers. II — Recent progress. *IBM Journal*, November.

Smith, D. E., & Genesereth, M. R. (1985). Ordering conjunctive queries. *Artificial Intelligence, 26*, 171–215.

Stabler, E. P., Jr. (1989). *The logical approach to syntax: Foundations, specifications and implementations of theories of government and binding.* University of Western Ontario.

# 3. Parsing with Lexicalized Tree Adjoining Grammar

## Yves Schabes and Aravind K. Joshi

*Department of Computer and Information Science, University of Pennsylvania*

## 3.1 Introduction

Most current linguistic theories give lexical accounts of several phenomena that used to be considered purely syntactic. The information put in the lexicon is thereby increased in both amount and complexity: see, for example, lexical rules in LFG (Kaplan & Bresnan, 1983), GPSG (Gazdar, Klein, Pullum, & Sag, 1985), HPSG (Pollard & Sag, 1987), Combinatory Categorial Grammars (Steedman, 1987), Karttunen's version of Categorial Grammar(Karttunen, 1986, 1988), some versions of GB theory (Chomsky, 1981), and Lexicon-Grammars (Gross, 1984).

We would like to take into account this fact while defining a formalism. We therefore explore the view that syntactical rules are not separated from lexical items. We say that a grammar is **lexicalized** (Schabes, 1990; Schabes, Abeillé, & Joshi, 1988) if it consists of:[1]

- a finite set of structures each associated with lexical items; each lexical item will be called the **anchor**[2] of the corresponding structure; the structures define the domain of locality over which constraints are specified;

- an operation or operations for composing the structures.

The notion of anchor is closely related to the word associated with a functor-argument category in Categorial Grammars. Categorial Grammar (as used for example by [Steedman, 1987]) are 'lexicalized' according to our definition since each basic category has a lexical item associated with it.

Lexicalized grammars are finitely ambiguous. A sentence (of finite length) selects a finite number of structures which can be combined in finitely many

---

[1]By 'lexicalized' we mean that in each structure there is a lexical item that is realized. We do not mean simply adding feature structures (such as head) and unification equations to the rules of the formalism.

[2]In previous publications, the term 'head' was used instead of the term 'anchor.' Henceforth, we will use the term anchor instead; the term 'head' introduces some confusion because the lexical items which are the source of the elementary trees need not be the same as the traditional syntactic head of those structures.

ways since each structure is associated with at least one lexical item. The finite ambiguity of lexicalized grammars is relevant for processing. For example, it ensures that the recognition problem of feature based lexicalized grammars is decidable.

There is a natural general two-step parsing strategy that can be defined for 'lexicalized' grammars. In the first stage, the parser selects a set of elementary structures associated with the lexical items in the input sentence, and in the second stage the sentence is parsed with respect to this set. The strategy is independent of the nature of the elementary structures in the underlying grammar. In principle, any parsing algorithm can be used in the second stage.

The first step selects a relevant subset of the entire grammar, since only the structures associated with the words in the input string are selected for the parser. The number of structures filtered during this pass depends on the nature of the input string and on characteristics of the grammar such as the number of structures, the number of lexical entries, the degree of lexical ambiguity, and the languages it defines.

Since the structures selected during the first step encode the morphological value of their anchor (and therefore its position in the input string), the first step also enables the parser to use non-local bottom-up information to guide its search. The encoding of the value of the anchor of each structure constrains the way the structures can be combined. This information is particularly useful for a top-down component of the parser.

This parsing strategy is general and any standard parsing technique can be used in the second step. Since in the worst case, the grammar filtering may select the entire grammar,[3] the strategy does not intrinsically lead to a better upper bound (worst case complexity) of the parsing problem. However, according to our intuition that words anchoring the structures may give useful information for parsing, we have experienced in practice an improvement of the performance of the parser when used on natural language grammars.

We consider Lexicalized Tree Adjoining Grammars as an instance of lexicalized grammars. We take three main types of parsing algorithms: purely top-down (as in definite clause parsing), purely bottom-up (as the CKY-algorithm) and bottom-up parsing with top-down information (as in the Earley-type parser). For each type, we investigate if the two-step strategy provides any improvement. For the Earley-type parser, we evaluate the two-step strategy with respect to two characteristics. First, the amount of filtering on the entire grammar is considered: once the first pass is performed, the parser uses only a subset of the grammar. Second, we evaluate the use of non-local information: the structures selected during the first pass encode the morphological value (and therefore the position in the string) of their anchor.

---

[3]There are grammars for which the two-step parsing strategy will not help at all. A grammar generating $\{a^*\}$ in which the elementary structures are anchored by $a$ is such an example.

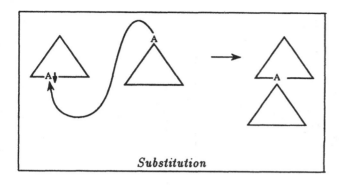

*Substitution*

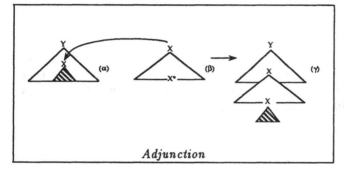

*Adjunction*

Figure 3.1. Combining operations.

## 3.2  Lexicalization of CFGs

In the process of lexicalizing a grammar, we require that the 'lexicalized' grammar produce not only the same language as the original grammar, but also the same structures (or tree set).

Not every grammar is in a 'lexicalized' form. Because of its restricted domain of locality, a CFG, in general, will not be in a 'lexicalized' form. The domain of locality of CFGs can be easily extended by using a tree rewriting grammar (Schabes, 1990; Schabes, Abeillé, & Joshi, 1988) that uses only substitution as a combining operation. This tree rewriting grammar consists of a set of trees that are not restricted to be of depth one (as in CFGs). Substitution can take place only on non-terminal nodes of the frontier of each tree. Substitution replaces a node marked for substitution by a tree rooted by the same label as the node (see Figure 3.1; the substitution node is marked by a down arrow ↓).

CFGs cannot be 'lexicalized,' if only tree substitution is used. Even when a CFG can be lexicalized with tree substitution, in general, there is not enough freedom to choose the anchor of each structure. This is important because we want the choice of the anchor for a given structure to be determined on purely linguistic grounds.

If adjunction is used as an additional operation to combine these structures,

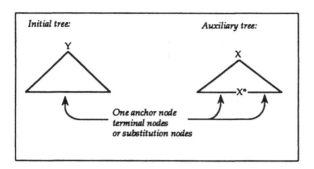

Figure 3.2. Schematic initial and auxiliary trees.

finitely ambiguous CFGs can be lexicalized. Adjunction builds a new tree from an auxiliary tree $\beta$ and a tree $\alpha$. It inserts an auxiliary tree in another tree (see Figure 3.1). Adjunction is more powerful than substitution. It can weakly simulate substitution, but it also generates languages that could not be generated with substitution.[4]

## 3.3 Lexicalized TAGs

Elementary structures of extended domain of locality (each associated with a lexical item) combined with substitution and adjunction yield Lexicalized TAGs. This system falls in the class of mildly context-sensitive languages (Joshi, 1985).

TAGs[5] were first introduced by Joshi, Levy and Takahashi (1975) and Joshi (1985). For more details on the original definition of TAGs, we refer the reader to Joshi (1985, 1988), Kroch and Joshi (1985), or Vijay-Shanker (1987). It is known that Tree Adjoining Languages (TALs) are mildly context sensitive. TALs properly contain context-free languages.

A Lexicalized Tree Adjoining Grammar is a tree-based system that consists of two finite sets of trees: a set of initial trees, $I$ and a set of auxiliary trees $A$ (see Figure 3.2). The trees in $I \cup A$ are called **elementary trees**. Each elementary tree is constrained to have at least one terminal symbol which acts as its anchor.

The **tree set** of a lexicalized TAG $G$, $\mathcal{T}(G)$ is defined to be the set of all derived trees starting from S-type[6] initial trees in $I$ (all substitution nodes

---

[4]It is also possible to encode a context-free grammar with auxiliary trees using adjunction only. However, although the languages correspond, the set of trees do not correspond.

[5]In some earlier work of Joshi (1969, 1973), the use of the two operations 'adjoining' and 'replacement' (a restricted case of substitution) was investigated both mathematically and linguistically. However, these investigations dealt with string rewriting systems and not tree rewriting systems.

[6]Trees whose root is labeled by $S$.

being filled). The **string language** generated by a TAG, $\mathcal{L}(G)$, is defined to be the set of all terminal strings of the trees in $\mathcal{T}(G)$.

By lexicalizing TAGs, we have associated lexical information to the 'production' system encoded by the TAG trees. We have therefore kept the computational advantages of 'production-like' formalisms (such as CFGs, TAGs) while allowing the possibility of linking them to lexical information (Abeillé, 1990). Formal properties of TAGs hold for Lexicalized TAGs.

As first shown by Kroch and Joshi (1985) and by Kroch (1989), the properties of TAGs permit us to encapsulate diverse syntactic phenomena in a very natural way. TAG's extended domain of locality and its factoring recursion from local dependencies enables us to localize most syntactic dependencies (such as filler-gap) as well as some semantic dependencies (such as predicate-arguments). Abeillé (1988) uses the distinction between substitution and adjunction to capture the different extraction properties between sentential subjects and complements. Abeillé (1988) makes use of the extended domain of locality and lexicalization to account for NP island constraint violations in light verb constructions; in such cases, extraction out of NP is to be expected, without the use of reanalysis. The relevance of Lexicalized TAGs to idioms has been suggested by Abeillé and Schabes (1989, 1990).

We will now give some examples of structures that appear in a Lexicalized TAG lexicon. In the following trees, ↓ is the mark for substitution nodes, ∗ is the mark for the foot node of an auxiliary tree, ◇ is the mark for the node under which the anchor is lexically inserted. We put numerical indices on some non-terminals to express semantic roles. The index shown on the empty string ($\epsilon$) and the corresponding filler in the same tree is for the purpose of indicating the filler-gap dependency.

Some examples of initial trees are (for simplicity, we have omitted unification equations associated with the trees):

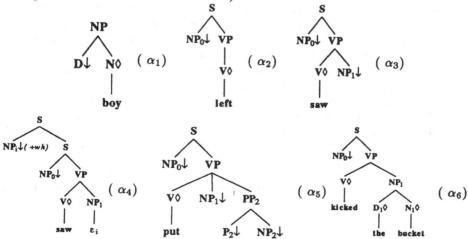

Examples of auxiliary trees (they correspond to predicates taking sentential complements or modifiers):

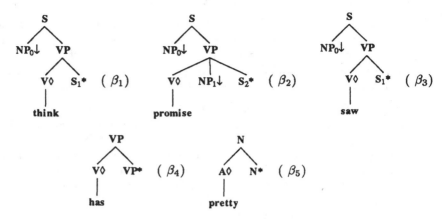

A Lexicalized TAG is organized into two major parts: a **lexicon** and **tree families** (sets of trees). Although it is not necessary to separate trees from their realization in the lexicon, we chose to do so in order to capture some generalities about the structures. TAG's factoring recursion from dependencies, the extended domain of locality of TAGs, and lexicalization of elementary trees make Lexicalized TAG an interesting framework for grammar writing. Abeillé (1988) discusses the writing of a Lexicalized TAG for French. Abeillé, Bishop, Cote, and Schabes (1990) similarly discuss the writing of a Lexicalized TAG grammar for English.

A **tree family** is essentially a set of sentential trees sharing the same argument structure abstracted from the lexical instantiation of the anchor. Because of the extended domain of locality of Lexicalized TAG, the argument structure need not be explicitly represented or explicitly enforced since it is implicitly stated in the topology of the trees in a tree family. The syntactic structure is constructed with the lexical value of the predicate and with all the nodes of its arguments. This fact eliminates the redundancy often noted between phrase structure rules and subcategorization frames.[7] Each tree in a family can be thought of as a possible syntactic 'transformation' of a given argument structure. Information (in the form of feature structures) that is valid independently of the value of the anchor is stated on the trees of the tree families. For example, the agreement between the subject and the main verb or auxiliary verb is stated on each tree of the tree family. Currently, the trees in a family are explicitly enumerated.

The following trees, among others, compose the tree family of verbs taking

---

[7] Optional arguments are stated in the structure.

one object (the family is named $np0Vnp1$):[8]

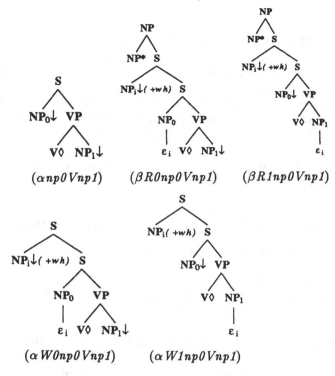

$$(\alpha np0Vnp1) \qquad (\beta R0np0Vnp1) \qquad (\beta R1np0Vnp1)$$

$$(\alpha W0np0Vnp1) \qquad (\alpha W1np0Vnp1)$$

$\alpha np0Vnp1$ is an initial tree corresponding to the declarative sentence, $\beta R0np0Vnp1$ is an auxiliary tree corresponding to a relative clause where the subject has been relativized, $\beta R1np0Vnp1$ corresponds to the relative clause where the object has been relativized, $\alpha W0np0Vnp1$ is an initial tree corresponding to a wh-question on the subject, $\alpha W1np0Vnp1$ corresponds to a wh-question on the object.

The **lexicon** associates a word with tree families. Words are not associated with basic categories as in a CFG-based grammar, but with tree-structures corresponding to minimal linguistic structures.

The lexicon also states some word-specific feature structure equations that have to be added to the ones already stated on the trees (such as the equality of the value of the subject and verb agreements).[9] In our approach the category of a word is not a non-terminal symbol but a multi-level structure corresponding to minimal linguistic structures: sentences (for predicative verbs, nouns and adjectives) or phrases (NP for nouns, AP for adjectives, PP for prepositions

---

[8] The trees are simplified. ◇ is the mark for the node under which the anchor word of the tree is attached.

[9] In practice, there is a morphological lexicon that associates the inflected forms of a word to its base form and to their morphological features. Then the syntax associates the base form of the word with tree families or individual trees. Attributes specific to the anchor are passed by unification to the node under which it is lexically inserted.

yielding adverbial phrases).

## 3.4    Parsing lexicalized TAGs

In order to evaluate the two-step parsing strategy, we divide the parsing algorithms in three main types: purely top-down (as in the usual definite clause parsing), purely bottom-up (as the CKY-algorithm), bottom-up with dynamic top-down information (as the Earley-type parser). We will also mention current work on bottom-up parsing with compiled top-down information (as LR-style parsing).

For each algorithm, we discuss the possible advantages provided by the two-step strategies.

### 3.4.1    Two ways to take advantage of lexicalization

An off-line parsing algorithm can take advantage of lexicalization in two ways.

- The trees corresponding to the input string are selected and then the parser parses the input string with respect to this set of trees. We will refer to this process as **grammar filtering**.

- The fact that, after the first pass, each structure encodes the morphological value (and therefore the positions in the string) of its anchor imposes constraints on the way the structures can be combined (the anchor positions must appear in increasing order in the combined structure). We will refer to this information as **bottom-up information**. It seems that this free bottom-up information is particularly useful in a top-down component of the parser.

For example, given the sentence:

> The $_1$ men $_2$ who $_3$ hate $_4$ women $_5$ that $_6$ smoke $_7$
> cigarettes $_8$ are $_9$ intolerant $_{10}$

the trees shown in Figure 3.3 are selected (among others) after the first pass.[10]

The fact that no adverbial or no bi-transitive trees will be selected after the first pass illustrates the filtering process on the grammar.

The anchor positions of each structure impose constraints on the way the structures can be combined (the anchor positions must appear in increasing order in the combined structure). The tree corresponding to men cannot be substituted at $NP_1$ in the tree selected by hate and smoke since the anchor positions would not be in the right order. This constitutes an example of the use of bottom-up information.

---

[10]The example is simplified to illustrate our point.

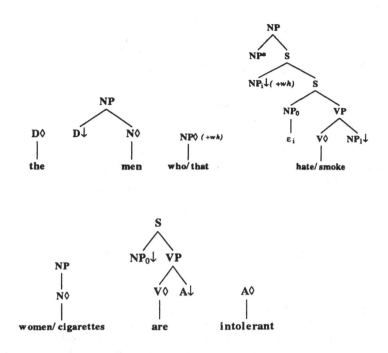

Figure 3.3. Trees selected by: **The men who hate women that smoke cigarettes are intolerant.**

## 3.4.2 Internal representation of lexicalized trees

The definition of lexicalized grammar does not imply a particular internal representation of a tree that a specific parsing algorithm may use. Each parsing algorithm may use the representation which is most efficient for it.

We present two ways (see Figure 3.4) according to which a parsing algorithm may internally represent a lexicalized tree. We will call a **parser-tree**, the internal representation that a parser has of a tree selected by an anchor in a given input string.

The first representation (first box in Figure 3.4) considers each tree with a pre-terminal node that corresponds to the anchor node. All lexical items that are anchoring a tree can be lexically inserted at the node below which the mark for the anchor appears, and the tree holds this information as part of its definition. This representation differentiates trees by their topology only. The representation is close to the usual notion of pre-terminals in CFGs. It does not violate the notion of lexicalization since the tree itself contains the information which specifies which lexical items can appear as anchor. If attributes in the form of feature structures are used, the tree will have attributes stated abstractly from the anchor and the anchor will specify attributes that will be passed through the anchor node (See section 3.4.7). This representation will be used for the CKY-type, the Earley-type and the LR-like parsers for Lexicalized

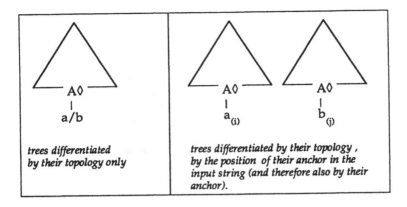

Figure 3.4. Internal representations of a lexicalized tree.

TAGs.

The second representation (second box in Figure 3.4) differentiates trees by their topology, by the value of their anchor and also by the position of the anchor in the input string. In this case, two identical words at different positions in the input sentence are not associated to the same parser-trees (since the position of the input differentiate them). This representation multiplies the number of trees (compared to the first one) by the number of terminals and by the length of the input sentence. However, this representation allows the parser to use a specific tree only once in the derivation since a tree corresponds to a specific word at a given position in the input string.[11] This representation will be used by the DCG-type parser for Lexicalized TAGs.

### 3.4.3   Bottom-up parsing

Vijay-Shanker and Joshi (1985) designed a CKY-type parser for TAGs. It is a pure bottom-up parser that uses dynamic programming techniques. Since this algorithm is data driven, the bottom-up information given by the first pass has no effect on the algorithm. However, the grammar filtering reduces the number of nodes put in the recognition matrix.

### 3.4.4   Top-down parsing

In a similar manner as CFGs, TAG can be axiomatized with definite clauses. Bernard Lang (1990) uses logical PDAs to interpret with dynamic programming techniques such axiomatization. Four indices instead are required for TAGs (instead of two for CFGs). The four positions correspond to the positions of the strings to the left and right of a foot node of an auxiliary tree (see

---

[11]Using it more then once would imply using the same word more then once in the parse.

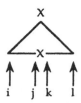

Figure 3.5. Four positions needed for an auxiliary tree.

Figure 3.5).

For example, the trees for *left* and *quickly* can be axiomatized as in Figure 3.6. `connects` axiomatizes the fact that a terminal spans the substring from position I to J. `aux_node(Cat,I,J,K,L)` axiomatizes the fact that an auxiliary tree spanning the substrings $a_i \cdots a_j$ and $a_k \cdots a_l$, can be adjoined at a node labeled by `Cat`. Initial trees span a contiguous substring $(a_i \cdots a_j)$ and auxiliary trees span two substrings $(a_i \cdots a_j$ and $a_k \cdots a_{l,})$.

The set of definite clauses can be interpreted in a top-down fashion. As in CFGs, this algorithm loops on left recursive rules. This problem is particularly acute for TAGs since left recursive rules are quite frequent.

However, the two-step parsing strategy enables us to define a top-down interpretation of the axiomatization of a lexicalized TAGs which will halt in all cases. Given an input sentence, the parser considers the trees selected by the first pass. If the parser internally distinguishes the trees by their topology and by the position of their anchor, each parser-tree should be used only once since it corresponds to a word at a unique position in the input string. Therefore each time the recognition of a parser-tree is attempted by the interpreter, this parser-tree is deleted from the set of parser-trees available. When backtracking is necessary, the parser-tree will be put back into the list of available parser-trees.

Since lexicalized grammar are finitely ambiguous, the search space of a top-down parser can be made finite. One can therefore design a pure top-down parser that will halt on all cases.

## 3.4.5   Bottom-up parsing with top-down information

An Earley-type parser for TAGs has been designed by Schabes and Joshi (1988) and by Schabes (1990).[12] As Earley's CFG parser, it is a bottom-up parser that uses top-down information provided by prediction. This parser can take advantage of lexicalization. It uses the structures selected after the first pass to parse the sentence. The parser is able to use the non-local information given by the first step to filter out prediction and completion states. It has been extended to deal with feature structures for TAGs as defined by Vijay-Shanker

---

[12] The system is available on Symbolics machines. It includes a graphical tree editor, the Earley-type parser for lexicalized feature-based TAGs and tools for developing lexicons.

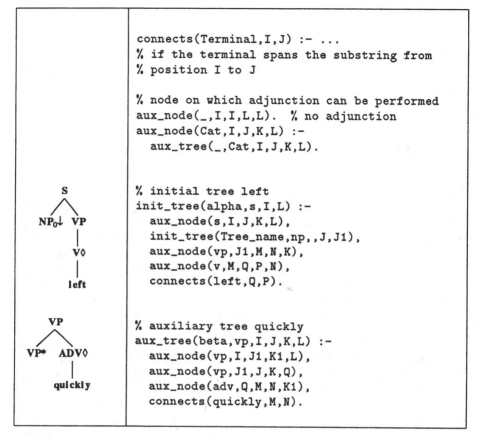

```
connects(Terminal,I,J) :- ...
% if the terminal spans the substring from
% position I to J

% node on which adjunction can be performed
aux_node(_,I,I,L,L).  % no adjunction
aux_node(Cat,I,J,K,L) :-
    aux_tree(_,Cat,I,J,K,L).


% initial tree left
init_tree(alpha,s,I,L) :-
    aux_node(s,I,J,K,L),
    init_tree(Tree_name,np,,J,J1),
    aux_node(vp,J1,M,N,K),
    aux_node(v,M,Q,P,N),
    connects(left,Q,P).


% auxiliary tree quickly
aux_tree(beta,vp,I,J,K,L) :-
    aux_node(vp,I,J1,K1,L),
    aux_node(vp,J1,J,K,Q),
    aux_node(adv,Q,M,N,K1),
    connects(quickly,M,N).
```

Figure 3.6. Axiomatization of a TAG.

and Joshi (1988). The extended algorithm we propose always halts when used on Lexicalized TAGs without special devices such as restrictors. Unification equations are associated with both extended linguistic structures and lexical information given by the anchor. This representation allows a more natural and more direct statement of unification equations.

### Taking advantage of lexicalization

An off-line version of the Earley-type parser for TAGs can be used with no modification for parsing Lexicalized TAGs. First, the trees corresponding to the input string are selected and then the parser parses the input string with respect to this set of trees.

However, Lexicalized TAGs simplify some cases of the algorithm. For example, since by definition each tree has at least one lexical item attached to it (its anchor), it will not be the case that a tree can be predicted for substitution and completed in the same states set. Similarly, it will not be the case that an auxiliary tree can be left predicted for adjunction and right completed in the same states set.

But most importantly, the algorithm can be extended to make crucial use of the two-stage parsing of Lexicalized TAGs. Once the first pass has been performed, a subset of the grammar is selected. Each structure encodes the morphological value (and therefore the positions in the string) of its anchor. Identical structures with different anchor values are merged together (by identical structures we mean identical trees and identical information, such as feature structures, stated on those trees).[13] This enables us to use the anchor position information while efficiently processing the structures. For example, given the previous sentence:

> The $_1$ men $_2$ who $_3$ hate $_4$ women $_5$ that $_6$ smoke $_7$
> cigarettes $_8$ are $_9$ intolerant $_{10}$

The trees in Figure 3.3 (among others) are selected after the first pass. The anchor positions of each structure impose constraints on the way that the structures can be combined (the anchor positions must appear in increasing order in the combined structure). This helps the parser to filter out predictions or completions for adjunction or substitution. For example, the tree corresponding to men will not be predicted for substitution in any of the trees corresponding to hates or smoke since the anchor positions would not be in the right order (see Figure 3.3).

We have evaluated the influence of the grammar filtering and the use of anchor position information on the behavior of the Earley-type parser. We have conducted experiments on a feature structure-based Lexicalized English TAG whose lexicon defines 200 entries associated with 130 different elementary trees (the trees are differentiated by their topology and their feature structures but not by their anchor value). Twenty five sentences of length ranging from 3 to 14 words were used to evaluate the parsing strategy. For each experiment, the number of trees given to the parser and the number of states were recorded.

In the first experiment (referred to as *one pass, OP*), no first pass was performed. The entire grammar (i.e., the 130 trees) was used to parse each sentence. In the second experiment (referred to as *two passes no anchor, NA*), the two-pass strategy was used but the anchor positions were not used in the parser. And in the third experiment (referred to as *two passes with anchor, A*), the two-pass strategy was used and the information given by the anchor positions was used by the parser.

The average behavior of the parser for each experiment is given in Table 3.1. The first pass filtered on average 85% (always at least 75%) of the trees. The grammar filtering alone decreased the number of states $((NA - OP)/OP)$ by 86%. The additional use of the information given by the anchor positions further decreased $((A - NA)/NA)$ the number of states by 50%. The decrease given by the filtering of the grammar and by the information of the anchor

---

[13] Unlike our previous suggestions (Schabes, Abeillé, & Joshi, 1988), we do not distinguish each structure by its anchor position since it increases unnecessarily the number of states of the Earley parser. The Earley parser enables us to process only once parts of a tree that are associated with several lexical items selecting the same tree.

Table 3.1. Empirical evaluation of the two-pass strategy.

|            | (NA-OP)/OP | (A-OP)/OP | (A - NA)/NA |
|------------|------------|-----------|-------------|
| # TREES    | -85%       | -85%      | 0%          |
| # STATES   | -86%       | -93%      | -50%        |

positions is even bigger on the number of attempts to add a state (not reported in the table).[14]

This set of experiments shows that the two-pass strategy can greatly increase the performance of the Earley-type parser for TAGs. The more significant factor is the filtering of the grammar. The information given by anchor position in the first pass allows further improvement of the parser's performance (50% reduction of the number of states). The bottom-up non-local information given by the anchor positions improves the top-down component of the Earley-type parser.

We performed our evaluation on a relatively small grammar and did not evaluate the variations across grammars. The lexical degree of ambiguity of each word, the number of structures in the grammar, the number of lexical entries, and the length (and nature) of the input sentences are parameters which certainly must be considered. Although it might appear easy to conjecture the influence of these parameters, the actual experiments are difficult to perform since statistical data on these parameters are hard to obtain. We hope to perform some limited experiments along those lines.

### 3.4.6   LR-style parsing

In LR-style parsing, a machine is driven by a parsing table built before run-time. Although this type of algorithm behaves purely bottom-up, it uses precompiled top-down information provided by the parsing table. However, in case of LR-parsing of lexicalized TAGs even when the table is built for the entire grammar before run-time, the two-step strategy may be useful to solve conflicts of moves if they occur.

LR-type parsers for TAGs have been recently proposed by Schabes and Vijay-Shanker (1990). The algorithm drives a machine called Bottom Up Embedded Automaton (a stack of stacks) in a bottom-up fashion. At run-time, before the point where a tree is reduced, two partial reductions can be performed (those partial reductions correspond to partial recognition of auxiliary trees). These partial reductions may occur at a point where the anchor has not yet be scanned. Therefore, the grammar filtering (and also the non-local bottom-up information) can be used to solve at run-time some conflicts of moves. We plan in the near future to collect empirical data to determine to what extent this two-step strategy is useful in solving conflicts of moves in parsing natural language grammars.

---

[14] A state is effectively added to a state set if it does not already exist in the set.

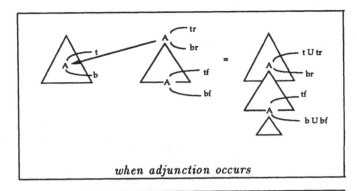

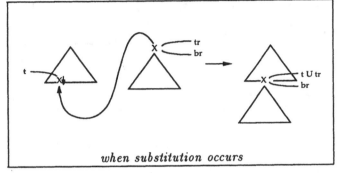

Figure 3.7. Updating of feature structures.

### 3.4.7 Parsing feature based lexicalized TAGs

As defined by Vijay-Shanker (1987) and Vijay-Shanker and Joshi (1988), feature-based TAGs attach two feature structures to each adjunction node in an elementary tree: a top and a bottom feature structure. When the derivation is completed, the top and bottom feature structures of all nodes are unified simultaneously. If the top and bottom feature structures of a node do not unify, then a tree must be adjoined at that node. This definition can be easily extended to substitution nodes. To each substitution node we attach one feature structure which acts as a top feature structure. The updating of feature structures in the cases of adjunction and substitution is shown in Figure 3.7.

### Unification equations

As in PATR-II (Shieber, 1984, 1986), we express with unification equations dependencies between DAGs[15] in an elementary tree. The extended domain of locality of TAGs allows us to state unification equations between feature structures of nodes that are not at the same level in the tree.

---

[15] Directed Acyclic Graphs which represent the feature structures.

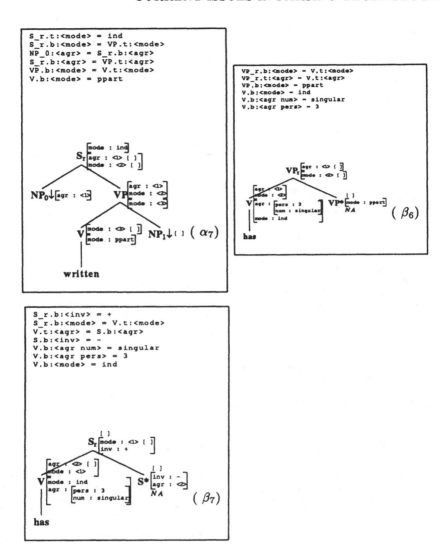

Figure 3.8. Examples of unification equations.

The system consists of a TAG and a set of unification equations on the DAGs associated with nodes in elementary trees. An example of the use of unification equations in TAGs is given in Figure 3.8.[16]

The coindexing may occur between feature structures associated with different nodes in the tree. Top or bottom feature structures of a node are referred

---

[16] In these examples we have merged the information stated on the trees and in the lexicon. We write unification equations above the tree to which they apply. We have also printed to the right of each node the matrix representation of the top and bottom feature structures.

to by a node name (e.g., $S_r$)[17] followed by *.t* (for top) or *.b* (for bottom). The semicolon states that the following path specified in angle brackets is relative to the specified feature structure. The feature structure of a substitution node is referred to without *.t* or *.b*. For example, *VP_r.t:<agr num>* refers to the path *<agr num>* in the top feature structure associated with the adjunction node labeled by $VP_r$ and *NP_0:<agr>* refers to the path *<agr>* of the substitution node labeled by $NP_0$.

The top and bottom feature structures of all nodes in the tree $\alpha_7$ (Figure 3.8) cannot be simultaneously unified: if the top and bottom feature structures of $S$ are unified, the *mode* will be *ind* which cannot unify with *ppart* (*VP* node). This forces an adjunction to be performed on $S$ (e.g., adjunction of $\beta_7$ to derive a sentence like *Has John written a book?*) or on *VP* (e.g., adjunction of $\beta_6$ to derive a sentence like *John has written a book*). The sentence *John written a book* is thus not accepted.

In the tree $\alpha_7$ agreement is checked across the nodes $NP_0$, $S$ and *VP*. These equations handle the two cases of auxiliary : $NP_0$ *has written* $NP_1$ and *has* $NP_0$ *written* $NP_1$ *?*. The corresponding derived trees are shown in Figure 3.9. $\alpha_8$ derives sentences like *John has written a book*. It is obtained by adjoining $\beta_6$ on the *VP* node in $\alpha_7$. $\alpha_9$ derives sentences like *Has John written a book?*. It is obtained by adjoining $\beta_7$ on the $S$ node in $\alpha_7$. The obligatory adjunction imposed by the mode feature structure has disappeared in the derived trees $\alpha_8$ and $\alpha_9$. However, to be completed, $\alpha_8$ and $\alpha_9$ need *NP*-trees to be substituted in the nodes labeled by *NP* (e.g., *John* and *a book*).

## Decidability of the recognition problem of feature-based lexicalized TAGs

As for context-free based unification based grammar, the problem of knowing whether a string is recognized by a unification-based TAG is undecidable. To make the system decidable, Vijay-Shanker and Joshi (1988) restrict the feature structures of each node to be of bounded size. The resulting system is more expressive than TAGs and is still weakly equivalent to TAGs.

Lexicalization of feature-based TAGs guarantees by itself the decidability of the recognition problem. Since lexicalized grammars are finitely ambiguous, for a given sentence only a finite number of structures must be considered as possible parses. Furthermore, the Earley-type parsing algorithm can be extended to handle feature-based lexicalized TAGs in a simple way without the use of special mechanisms.

## Extension to the Earley-type parser

The Earley-type algorithms for TAGs (Schabes, 1990; Schabes & Joshi, 1988) can be extended to parse Lexicalized TAG with unification equations on elementary trees. The extension is similar to the one proposed by Shieber (1985) for parsing the PATR-II formalism, but it does not require the use of restrictors.

---

[17]We implicitly require that each node have a unique name in an elementary tree. If necessary, subscripts differentiate nodes of the same category.

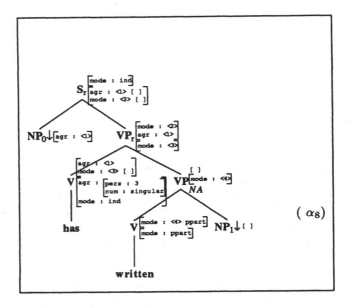

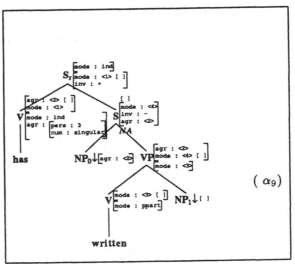

Figure 3.9. NP$_0$ *has written* NP$_1$ and *Has* NP$_0$ *written* NP$_1$ *?*.

For the recognition of a substituted tree, we check that unification constraints are compatible at the prediction step and pass information only at the completion step. For the recognition of an adjunction, we check only that unification constraints are compatible at the Left Predictor, Left Completer and Right Predictor steps and we pass information only at the Right Completer step.

What follows is an informal explanation of the extension to the Earley-type parsers. A new component $D$ is added to the states manipulated by the

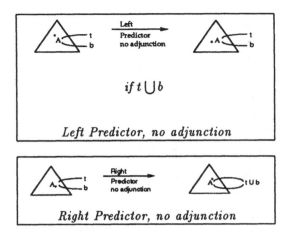

Figure 3.10. No adjunction.

Earley-type parsers. $D$ specifies a set of feature structures associated with the nodes of the tree represented by the state. The manipulation of the other components of a state remain the same. We will ignore these components of a state and focus our attention here on the manipulation of the set of feature structures $D$.

The Scanner, Move-dot-down and Move-dot-up processors behave as before and copy the DAG $D$ to the new state.[18] The Left Predictor predicts all possible adjunctions and also tries to recognize the tree with no adjunction. In case no adjunction is left predicted, the Left Predictor adds the new state only if the top and bottom feature structures are compatible (see Figure 3.10). If they are compatible, a new state is added but top and bottom feature structures are not unified. They will be unified in the Right Predictor. Then, if no adjunction has been left predicted, the Right Predictor moves the dot up and unifies top and bottom feature structures (see Figure 3.11).

The recognition of an adjunction with feature structures is shown in Figure 3.11.[19] At each step of the recognition of an adjunction, the compatibility of the feature structures is checked. The information is passed only at the Right Completer step.

For non-lexicalized TAGs, this approach does not guarantee that the algorithm halts (for similar reasons as CFG-based unification grammar). However for Lexicalized TAGs, even when recursion occurs, the termination of the algorithm is guaranteed since the recognition of a tree entails the recognition of at least one input token (its anchor) and since information is passed only when a tree is completely recognized. If information were passed before the Right Completer step (in case of adjunction), restrictors can be used to guarantee

---

[18] Identical states have identical components and identical feature structures $D$.

[19] A substituted tree is recognized in a similar way and is not explained here.

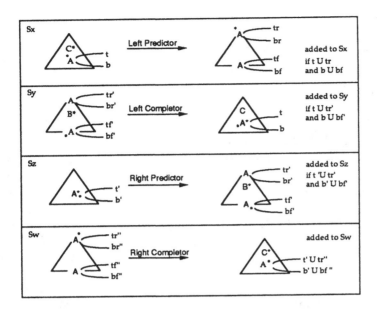

Figure 3.11. Recognition of an adjunction.

halting of the algorithm. However we believe that in practice (for the Lexicalized TAGs for French and English) passing information at an earlier step than the Right Completer step does not improve the performance.

## 3.5   Concluding remarks

In 'lexicalized' grammars, each elementary structure is systematically associated with a lexical anchor. These structures specify extended domains of locality (as compared to the domain of locality in CFGs) over which constraints can be stated. The 'grammar' consists of a lexicon in which each lexical item is associated with a finite number of structures for which that item is the anchor.

We have seen that lexicalized grammars suggest a natural two-step parsing strategy. The first step selects the set of structures corresponding to each word in the sentence. The second step tries to combine the selected structures.

Lexicalized grammars allow us to make the search space of a pure topdown parser (as DCG-type parser for TAGs) finite and prevent looping on left-recursive rules. Experimental data show that the performance of the Earley-type parser is drastically improved. The first pass not only filters the grammar used by the parser to produce a relevant subset but also enables the parser to use non-local bottom-up information to guide its search. Current work done in collaboration with Vijay-Shanker indicates that some conflicts of move of LR-type parsers for TAGs can be solved at run-time with this strategy. We plan to study in practice to what extend the strategy improves the performance of an LR-parser for TAGs used in a pseudo-parallel way.

Finally, we showed that lexicalization makes the recognition problem for feature-based TAGs decidable. Then we explained how constraints over these structures expressed by unification equations can be parsed by a simple extension of the Earley-type parsers for TAGs.

The organization of lexicalized grammars and the simplicity and effectiveness of the two-pass strategy are therefore attractive from both a linguistic and for processing point of view.

# Acknowledgments

This work is partially supported by Darpa grant N0014-85-K0018, ARO grant DAAL03-89-C-0031PRI NSF grant IRI84-10413 A02.

We have benefited from our discussions with Anne Abeillé, Bob Frank, Lauri Karttunen, Bernard Lang, Mitch Marcus, Stuart Shieber, Mark Steedman and K. Vijayshanker. We would also like to thank Ellen Hays.

# References

Abeillé, A. (1988a). *A lexicalized Tree Adjoining Grammar for French: The general framework* (Tech. Rep. No. MS-CIS-88-64). University of Pennsylvania.

Abeillé, A. (1988b). Light verb constructions and extraction out of NP in Tree Adjoining Grammar. *Papers from the 24th Regional Meeting of the Chicago Linguistic Society.* Chicago.

Abeillé, A. (1988c). Parsing French with Tree Adjoining Grammar: Some linguistic accounts. *Proceedings of the 12th International Conference on Computational Linguistics (COLING'88).* Budapest.

Abeillé, A. (1990). Lexical constraints on syntactic rules in a Tree Adjoining Grammar. *Proceedings of the 28th Meeting of the Association for Computational Linguistics (ACL'90).*

Abeillé, A., Bishop Kathleen, M., Cote, S, & Schabes, Y. (1990). *A lexicalized Tree Adjoining Grammar for English* (Tech. Rep. No. MS-CIS-90-24). University of Pennsylvania: Department of Computer and Information Science.

Abeillé, A., & Schabes, Y. (1989). Parsing idioms in Tree Adjoining Grammars. *Fourth Conference of the European Chapter of the Association for Computational Linguistics (EACL'89).* Manchester.

Abeillé, A., & and Schabes, Y. (1990). Non compositional discontinuous constituents in Tree Adjoining Grammar. *Proceedings of the Symposium on Discontinuous Constituents.* Tilburg, Holland.

Chomsky, N. (1981). *Lectures on government and binding.* Foris, Dordrecht.

Gazdar, G., Klein, E., Pullum, G. K., & Sag, I. A. (1985). *Generalized phrase structure grammars.* Oxford: Blackwell Publishing. Also published by Harvard University Press, Cambridge, MA.

Gross, M. (1984). Lexicon-grammar and the syntactic analysis of French. *Proceedings of the 10th International Conference on Computational Linguistics (COLING'84)*. Stanford, CA.

Joshi, A. K. (1969). Properties of formal grammars with mixed type of rules and their linguistic relevance. *Proceedings of the International Conference on Computational Linguistics*. Sanga Saby.

Joshi, A. K. (1973). A class of transformational grammars. In M. Gross, M. Halle, & M. P. Schutzenberger (Eds.), *The formal analysis of natural languages*. Mouton, La Hague.

Joshi, A. K. (1985). How much context-sensitivity is necessary for characterizing structural descriptions — Tree Adjoining Grammars. In D. Dowty, L. Karttunen, & A. Zwicky (Eds.), *Natural language processing — Theoretical, computational and psychological perspectives*. New York: Cambridge University Press. Originally presented in a Workshop on Natural Language Parsing at Ohio State University, Columbus, May 1983.

Joshi, A. K. (1988). An introduction to Tree Adjoining Grammars. In A. Manaster-Ramer (Ed.), *Mathematics of language*. Amsterdam: John Benjamins.

Joshi, A. K., Levy, L. S., & Takahashi, M. (1975). Tree adjunct grammars. *J. Comput. Syst. Sci.*, *10*, 1.

Karttunen, L. (1986). *Radical lexicalism* (Tech. Rep. No. CSLI-86-68). CSLI, Stanford University. Also in (1989) M. Baltin & A. Kroch (Eds.), *Alternative conceptions of phrase structure*. Chicago, University of Chicago Press.

Kroch, A. (1989). Asymmetries in long distance extraction in a TAG grammar. In M. Baltin & A. Kroch (Eds.), *Alternative conceptions of phrase structure*. University of Chicago Press.

Kroch, A., & Joshi, A. K. (1985). *Linguistic relevance of Tree Adjoining Grammars* (Tech. Rep. No. MS-CIS-85-18). University of Pennsylvania, Department of Computer and Information Science.

Lang, B. (1990). Towards a uniform formal framework for parsing. In M. Tomita (Ed.), *Current issues in parsing technologies*. Kluwer Academic.

Pollard, C., & Sag, I. A. (1987). *Information-based syntax and semantics: Fundamentals* (Vol. 1). CSLI.

Schabes, Y. (1990). *Mathematical and computational aspects of lexicalized grammars* (Tech. Rep. No. MS-CIS-90-48 LINC LAB 179). Unpublished doctoral dissertation. University of Pennsylvania, Department of Computer and Information Science.

Schabes, Y., Abeillé, A., & Joshi, A. K. (1988). Parsing strategies with 'lexicalized' grammars: Application to Tree Adjoining Grammars. *Proceedings of the 12th International Conference on Computational Linguistics (COLING'88)*. Budapest.

Schabes, Y., & Joshi, A. K. (1988). An Earley-type parsing algorithm for Tree Adjoining Grammars. *26th Meeting of the Association for Computational Linguistics (ACL'88)*. Buffalo.

Schabes, Y., & Vijay-Shanker, K. (1990). Deterministic left to right parsing of Tree Adjoining Languages. *Proceedings of the 28th Meeting of the Association for Computational Linguistics (ACL'90)*.

Shieber, S. M. (1984). The design of a computer language for linguistic information. *22nd Meeting of the Association for Computational Linguistics (ACL'84)*. Stanford.

Shieber, S. M. (1985). Using restriction to extend parsing algorithms for complex-feature-based formalisms. *23rd Meeting of the Association for Computational Linguistics (ACL'85)*. Chicago.

Shieber, S. M. (1986). *An introduction to unification-based approaches to grammar*. Stanford, CA: Center for the Study of Language and Information.

Steedman, M. (1987). Combinatory grammars and parasitic gaps. *Natural Language and Linguistic Theory, 5*, 403–439.

Vijay-Shanker, K. (1987). *A study of Tree Adjoining Grammars*. Unpublished doctoral dissertation. University of Pennsylvania, Department of Computer and Information Science.

Vijay-Shanker, K., & Joshi, A. K. (1985). Some computational properties of Tree Adjoining Grammars. *23rd Meeting of the Association for Computational Linguistics* (pp. 82–93).

Vijay-Shanker, K., & Joshi, A. K. (1988). Feature structure based Tree Adjoining Grammars. *Proceedings of the 12th International Conference on Computational Linguistics (COLING'88)*. Budapest.

# 4. Parsing with Discontinuous Phrase Structure Grammar

## Harry Bunt

*Institute for Language Technology and Artificial Intelligence ITK*

## 4.1 Introduction

Syntactic as well as semantic analysis, in theory as well as in practice, starts nearly always from the decomposition of sentences into smaller groups of words such as noun phrases, verb phrases, adjective phrases, prepositional phrases, etc. Syntactically, this is motivated by the assumption that a higher level of generalization in the description of natural language structures can be achieved in terms of such groups than in terms of individual words. Semantically, it is motivated by the compositionality principle, which entails the decomposition of sentences into meaningful parts in order to systematically derive sentence meanings from individual word meanings. Moreover, the smallest meaningful parts of a sentence are sometimes groups of words rather than individual words, as in the case of Sentence (1), where *woke up* is a meaningful part rather than each of these words separately:

(1) *Mary* woke up *at seven-thirty.*

More often then not, the relevant word groups ("constituents") are formed by words standing next to one another, as in (1). Sometimes, however, some other words are intervening. Sentence (2) provides an example:

(2) *Mary* woke *me* up *at seven-thirty.*

In such a case we speak of a *discontinuous constituent*.

Exactly which discontinuities a grammar has to deal with, depends on the general views on constituency which the grammar takes. Theories which recognize verb phrases for instance, as most theories do, will say that Sentence (2) displays a discontinuity in the VP *woke me up*. Verb phrases are in fact very often discontinuous, and in many theories of grammar discontinuous VPs are a major object of study (see e.g., Emonds, 1976, 1979; Hepple, 1990; Hoekstra, 1990; McCawley, 1982; Reape, 1990; and Ross, 1973).

Noun phrases are not so often discontinuous. But of course, relative clause extraction leads to discontinuous NPs, and so do the VP-discontinuities in NP-embedded VPs, as in premodifying relative clauses in Dutch or German. A genuine NP discontinuity can be formed using the Dutch complex determiner *Wat voor*, as in Sentence (3):

(3)    b. W̲a̲t̲ *heb jij* v̲o̲o̲r̲ a̲u̲t̲o̲ *gekocht?*

   *(*W̲h̲a̲t̲ *did you* c̲a̲r̲ *buy?,* meaning *What car did you buy?)*

Such discontinuities have been studied by Corver (1990).

   PPs and APs are mostly contiguous, but again, it is certainly not impossible for them to be discontinuous. Examples of discontinuous adjective- and adverbial phrases are presented in (4) and (5):

(4)  *This is a* b̲e̲t̲t̲e̲r̲ *movie* t̲h̲a̲n̲ ̲I̲ ̲e̲x̲p̲e̲c̲t̲e̲d̲.

*(5)  Leo is* h̲a̲r̲d̲e̲r̲ *gegaan* d̲a̲n̲ ̲o̲o̲i̲t̲ ̲t̲e̲v̲o̲r̲e̲n̲.

   *(Leo has been going faster than ever before.)*

   Moreover, phrases which are 'naturally' continuous can very often become discontinuous by the insertion of *metacomments,* such as parentheticals. Some examples:

*(6)  John* t̲a̲l̲k̲e̲d̲ *of course* a̲b̲o̲u̲t̲ ̲p̲o̲l̲i̲t̲i̲c̲s̲.

*(7)  Peter bought a house* o̲n̲, *at almost on,* A̲n̲g̲e̲l̲s̲ ̲B̲e̲a̲c̲h̲.

*(8)  Leo is going* f̲a̲s̲t̲e̲r̲, *I would say,* t̲h̲a̲n̲ ̲e̲v̲e̲r̲ ̲b̲e̲f̲o̲r̲e̲.

   It is not an exaggeration to say that discontinuities may arise almost everywhere; discontinuous constituents are obviously not rare or exceptional. Yet most grammar formalisms are quite clearly based on the idea of a constituent as a continuous sequence of words, being primarily designed to describe continuous constituents and having to take recourse to special operations for handling discontinuities. The reason for this is that rewrite rules, and therefore the notion of *adjacency,* play in important role in most grammars. The description of structures made up of non-adjacent elements therefore presents difficulties.

   The central idea of this paper is that constituents should not be regarded as sequences of words, but as *sets of words* with certain precedence relations amongst themselves and with other words. Central in the elaboration of this idea is the notion of a *discontinuous tree,* which is a tree-like structure describing discontinuous constituency.

   This idea is not new; e.g., McCawley (1982) has suggested to analyze Sentence (6) as having the constituent structure displayed in (9).

   Besides 'discontinuous trees,' a second important notion in our approach is that of *adjacency sequence,* which generalizes the notion of *adjacency pair* so as to apply to 'discontinuous sequences.' The use of adjacency sequences makes it possible to formulate rewrite rules which describe (generate, parse) discontinuous constituents. The grammar formalism described below, *Discontinuous Phrase-Structure Grammar (DPSG),* is intended to illustrate the feasibility and usefulness of this idea.

(9)

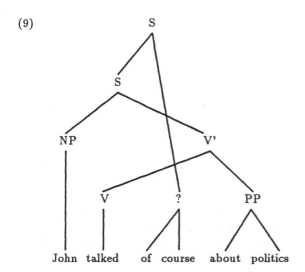

(10)

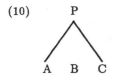

## 4.2    Trees with discontinuities

If we want to represent that a phrase P has constituents A and C, while there is an intervening phrase B, we must allow the node corresponding to P to dominate the A and C nodes without dominating the B node, even though this node is located between A and C; see (10). This will have the consequence that our structures get crossing branches, if we still want every node to be dominated by a higher node, as happens in (9).

In what respects exactly do such structures differ from ordinary trees? Mc-Cawley (1982) has tried to answer this question, suggesting a formal definition for trees with discontinuities by amending the definition of an ordinary tree. An ordinary tree is often defined as a set of elements, called NODES, on which two relations are defined, immediate dominance and linear precedence. These relations are required to have certain properties, to the effect that a tree has exactly one top node, which dominates every other node; that every node has exactly one mother node, etc. (see e.g., Wall, 1972).

McCawley's definition of trees with discontinuities is redundant at some points, and it unintentionally allows structures to be cyclic or unconnected;

(11)

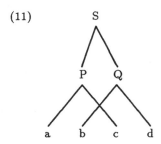

more importantly, it does not lead to notion of adjacency which can be used to formulate rules for generating or manipulating discontinuous trees.

An attractive alternative to the 'axiomatic' definition of tree-like structures is a recursive one. Ordinary trees are easily defined recursively since their building blocks are again trees, if we consider terminal nodes as atomic trees. Therefore, a tree can be defined as an ordered pair $< t, [X_1, .., X_n] >$ consisting of a top node $t$ and a sequence of subtrees. A terminal node is the top node in a tree $< t, [\,] >$, dominating zero subtrees.

A recursive definition of a tree with discontinuities, or DISCO-TREE, is not so easily given, since such a structure is built up of substructures which themselves are not necessarily (disco-)trees. Example (11) illustrates this.

The disco-tree S is made up of the substructures with top nodes P and Q which are not well-formed disco-trees since they contain 'loose' nodes (b and d), not connected to the rest of the structure. Therefore, we first define these substructures ('SUBDISCO-TREES') separately; this can be done recursively.

(12) Let N be a non-empty set whose elements are called NODES.

   (i) If $t \in N$, then the pair $<t,[\,]>$ is a subdisco-tree;

   (ii) If $x \in N$ and $X_1, .., X_k$ are subdisco-trees that share no subdisco-trees[1] then the pair $<x, [X_1, Y_2, .., Y_j, X_k]>$ is a subdisco-tree, where $Y_i = X_i$ or $Y_i$ is a sub-list of $\{X_2, ..,X_{k-1}\}$.

   (iii) No other structures than those defined by (i) and (ii) are subdisco-trees.

Instead of '$<x, [X_1, .., [..], .., X_k]>$,' we also write: '$x(X_1, X_2 ,.., [..] ,.., X_k).$' The idea is that a subdisco-tree consists of a top node x and a sequence of nodes dominated by x (daughter nodes), possibly interrupted by subsequences $[X_i, X_j,..]$ of nodes not dominated by x (so-called INTERNAL CONTEXT of x, or CONTEXT DAUGHTERS of x).

We define direct dominance in subdisco-trees as follows:

(13) Direct dominance ($D$):

---

[1] Two subdisco-trees X and Y share a subdisco-tree T if both X and Y contain a node dominating T.

      (i) in an atomic subdisco-tree <x, [ ]>, there is no node dominated by
         x;

      (ii) in a subdisco-tree <x, [$X_1$, $Y_1$, .., $Y_j$, $X_k$]> the node x directly
         dominates the top nodes of $X_1$, of $X_k$, and of every $Y_i$ that is a
         subdisco-tree, but *not* the top nodes of elements in lists [ ..,$X_j$,..] of
         subdisco-trees.

A discontinuous tree is now simply a subdisco-tree without any 'loose' nodes, nodes that are not connected to the rest of the structure through the dominance relation. In other words, every node should have a mother node.

    We now have a reliable definition of discontinuous tree structures. The next point to consider is their generation. We know that ordinary tree structures are generated by phrase-structure grammars; can discontinuous trees also can be produced by some sort of phrase-structure rules? This turns out to be far from trivial; to answer this question, we will have to look at linear precedence and adjacency in disco-trees.

## 4.2.1 Linear precedence and adjacency in discontinuous trees

A classical phrase-structure rule rewrites a constituent into a sequence of pairwise adjacent constituents. The formulation of phrase-structure rules for discontinuous trees thus requires a notion of adjacency in such structures. Since adjacency is a special case of linear precedence, we first have to define the precedence relation for disco-trees. We may try to do this in the same way as usual for ordinary trees (< denotes linear precedence, $D$ denotes direct dominance):

(14)   (i) In a tree A($X_1$,.., $X_n$), $X_i < X_j$ iff i < j .

       (ii) If P, Q, x and y are nodes in a tree such that P < Q, P $D$ x, and Q
          $D$ y, then x < y.

The obvious disco-counterpart of this definition is:

(15)   (i) In a subdisco-tree A($X_1$, .., [.., $X_i$, ..] ,.., $X_n$), $X_i < X_j$ iff $1 \leq i <$
          $j \leq n$ .

       (ii) If P, Q, x and y are nodes in a subdisco-tree such that P < Q, P $D$
          x, and Q $D$ y, then x < y.

Adjacency can subsequently be defined as precedence without intervening nodes. We shall write 'x + y' to indicate that x and y are adjacent.

    Unfortunately, this notion of adjacency is of no help for formulating grammar rules that do anything with internal context constituents. We turn to the issue of grammar rules for generating discontinuous trees in the next section.

(16)

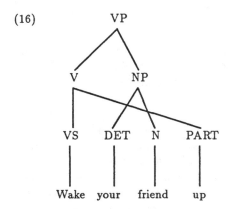

## 4.3   Disco-Trees in grammar rules

### 4.3.1   Adjacency and concatenation

The following example illustrates the inadequacy of the notion of adjacency introduced above. Suppose we are to generate the discontinuous tree structure (16). To achieve this, we need rules like those in (17), where square brackets indicate internal context elements.

(17) VP     → V + NP
     V      → VS + [DET] + [N] + PART
     NP     → DET + N
     VS     → wake
     DET    → your
     N      → friend
     PART   → up

According to the second clause in (15), however, the particle *up* precedes the determiner and the noun, so these rules generate the incorrect structure (18). This problem occurs generally when a discontinuous constituent is to be concatenated with some other constituent. We thus need a different precedence relation for discontinuous trees.

The source of the problem is that according to (15) a context daughter of a node P which is a 'real' daughter of another node Q, either precedes or is preceded by all the daughter nodes of P, depending on whether P precedes Q or Q precedes P. But characteristic of an internal context node is precisely that it is located in between the 'real' daughters of a node. We therefore relax the second clause in (15) to (19):

(18)

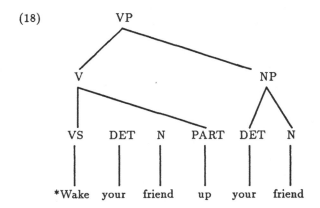

(19) if x and y are nodes in a subdisco-tree such that x < y, then x's leftmost
daughter precedes y's leftmost daughter.[2]

With this notion of precedence, and the notion of adjacency that follows
from it, the rules (17) give besides the incorrect structure (18), also the correct
possibility (16). To prevent the generation of the incorrect structure (18), we
define adjacency slightly differently:

(20) Two nodes x and y are adjacent iff:

    (i) x's leftmost daughter $L_m(x)$ precedes y's leftmost daughter $L_m(y)$;

    (ii) for every node z such that $L_m(x) < z < L_m(y)$, x D z.

In other words, x and y are neighbors if x precedes y and y's leftmost daughter
is the first node to the right of x's leftmost daughter which does not belong
to x. With this definition of adjacency the rules (17) do not generate the
structure (18), since the V and NP in that case are not adjacent.

## 4.3.2   Disco-Trees in phrase-structure grammar

Upon closer inspection, the adjacency relation as now defined is still unsatis-
factory, however. Example (21) illustrates this.

Suppose we want to generate the structure (21). To generate the S node, we
would like to have a phrase-structure rule that rewrites S into its constituents,
like (22):

(22) S → P + Q + E

But this rule would not apply here, since Q and E are not adjacent; according
to (20), Q has C as its right neighbor rather than E. Therefore, the correct
rule for generating (21) would be (23):

---

[2] The choice of leftmost rather than rightmost daughters is somewhat arbitrary. Limitations of space prevent us from motivating this choice here.

(21)

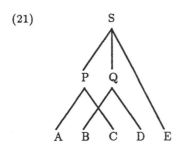

(23)  S → P + Q + [C] + [D] + E

This is ugly, and even uglier rules are required in more complex cases with discontinuities at different levels. Moreover, there seems to be something fundamentally wrong, since the C and D nodes are on the one hand internal context for the S node according to rule (23), while on the other hand they are also dominated by S. That is, these nodes are both 'real' constituents of S and internal context of S.

To remedy this we introduce the concept called ADJACENCY SEQUENCE, which generalizes the traditional notion of *sequence of adjacency pairs*. The definition goes as follows:

(24)  A sequence <a,..., n> is an adjacency sequence iff:

    (i) every pair <i,j> in the sequence is either an adjacency pair or is connected by a sequence of adjacency pairs of which all members are a constituent of some element in the subsequence <a,..., i>;

    (ii) the elements in the sequence do not share any constituents.

For example, in the structure (21) the triple <P, Q, E> is an adjacency sequence since <P, Q> is an adjacency pair and Q and E are connected by the sequence of adjacency pairs Q-C-D-E, with C and D constituents of P and Q, respectively. Moreover, P, Q, and E do not share any substructures. The triple <P, B, C>, on the other hand, is not an adjacency sequence since P and C share C.

This notion of adjacency sequence can now be used to define phrase-structure rules for discontinuous trees as prescriptions to rewrite a nonterminal into a set of constituents which forms an adjacency sequence, like (22), where some of the elements may be marked as internal context elements. A phrase-structure grammar consisting of rules of this kind we call *Discontinuous Phrase-Structure Grammar, or DPSG*.

It is worth emphasizing that this notion of phrase-structure rule is a generalization of the usual notion, since an adjacency sequence as defined by (24) subsumes the traditional notion of sequence of adjacency pairs. We have also seen that trees with discontinuities are a generalization of the traditional tree concept. Therefore, phrase-structure rules of the familiar sort coincide with

DPSG rules without discontinuous constituents, and they produce the familiar sort of trees without discontinuities. In other words, DPSG-rules can simply be added to an ordinary PSG (possibly augmented, generalized or head-driven), with the result that the grammar generates trees with discontinuities for sentences with discontinuous constituents, while doing everything else as before.

## 4.3.3   An ID/LP format for DPSG rules

Sofar, we have considered rewrite rules for disco-trees only in their classical form, where they state something about immediate dominance as well as about linear precedence. One of the important innovations of GPSG has been the decoupling of these aspects, which makes it possible to formulate rules that express much greater generalizations.

A rule that generates a discontinuous tree must by its very nature say something about immediate dominance as well as about linear precedence, so it seems, and an ID/LP format for such rules therefore seems strange.

This is a wrong impression, however. A rule like (25) is equivalent to the ID/LP-rules (26), where CD stands for (immediate) context daughters:

(25)  R → A + [B] + [C] + D

(26)  ID: R → {A, D}

     CD: {B, C}

     LP: A < B, B < C, C < D.

In this example, the ID/LP-like formulation clearly has no advantages over the traditional formulation; such advantages can only be expected if the same dominance rule allows various precedences. This is precisely what is often the case with discontinuities; for example, in Dutch an intervening adverb (phrase) can be placed on a variety of positions. If, in the case of example (25), the B and C constituents may appear in arbitrary order, we get an attractive ID/LP-like formulation:

(27)  ID: R → {A, D}

     CD: {B, C}

     LP: A < D.

The LP-rule is now very simple, since internal context elements by their nature can only occur in between the real daughters of the top node.

The exact ID/LP-like format of DPSG rules is rather complex, when features are taken into account and semantics is added.

# 4.4   Implementing DPSG: An enhanced chart parser

As part of the TENDUM dialogue system (see Bunt *et al.*, 1985) a parser-interpreter for DPSG has been designed and implemented which performs syntactic, semantic and pragmatic interpretation of Dutch input sentences. The output of the parser consists of one or more triples, each formed by (i) a syntactic analysis in the form of a disco-tree; (ii) a semantic analysis in the form of an expression of the logical language EL/F (a type-logic language based on ensemble theory, an extension of set theory; see [Bunt, 1985]); (iii) a pragmatic analysis in the form of a bundle of features relevant for the determination of illocutionary function. We will only consider the syntactic side of the parsing process here.

The parsing algorithm is based on the active chart parsing concept; it uses a special matrix-driven strategy for the application of rules, and it incorporates additional devices for the correct handling of context daughters and the n-ary adjacency-sequence relation of DSPG. For the sake of clarity, we first describe the algorithm with its matrix-driven strategy for a classical phrase-structure grammar, and subsequently turn to the extended algorithm for DPSG parsing.

## 4.4.1   A matrix-driven PSG parsing algorithm

The algorithm described below assumes its input sentences to be converted into lists of arcs by a preprocessor. The algorithm furthermore presupposes the presence of a PSG grammar $G$ which can be consulted using a function which, given a syntactic category $K$, delivers the subgrammar $G_K$ of all rules where the first rewriting element has category $K$. The parser uses an array RESULT for stacking arcs, with their vertex number as index in the array, and a matrix RULES (two dimensional array) for storing active rules, with syntactic categories as one dimension and vertex numbers as the other. These ingredients are used as shown in (28).

(28) *for*   every arc $A$ in the input
   *do*   process-arc($A$);


   *if*   there are arcs in RESULT spanning the entire input
   *then* hurray
   *else* bad luck


   *process-arc(A):*
      store $K$ in RESULT[vertex-number($A$)]
      *process-A-for-all-rules-in*($G_{cat(A)}$)
      *process-A-for-all-rules-in*(RULES[cat($A$),vertexno($A$)])

*process-A-for-all-rules-in(L):*

   *for* every rule $R$ in $L$

   *do* copy $R$ to $R'$

      mark $cat(A)$ in $R'$ as seen

      *if*   $R'$ is done, with resulting arc $N$

      *then process-arc(N)*

      *else* store $R'$ in RESULT[cat(next arc in $R'$),

                              vertexno(successor($A$))]

N.B. A rule is *done* if every rewriting constituent of the rule is processed; a resulting arc can then be built.

A very simple example:

Grammar $G$:
   rule $R_1$:   NP   $\Longrightarrow$ PROPERNAME
   rule $R_2$:   S    $\Longrightarrow$ NP + VERB
   rule $R_3$:   S    $\Longrightarrow$ S + ADSENT

Processing the input sentence *John walks fast*, preprocessed as the arc list: $_1$PROPERNAME$_2$VERB$_3$ADSENT$_4$, will at the end lead to the following results:

RESULT[1] :: $_1$S$_4$, $_1$S$_3$, $_1$NP$_2$, $_1$PROPERNAME$_2$

RESULT[2] :: $_2$VERB$_3$

RESULT[3] :: $_3$ADSENT$_4$

Only the arc $_1$S$_4$ spans the entire input. The matrix of active rules is at that moment:

RULES[VERB, 2] :: copy of rule $R_2$ with the NP linked to arc $_1$NP$_2$

RULES[ADSENT, 3] :: copy of rule $R_3$ with the rewriting S linked to arc $_1$S$_3$.

## 4.4.2   Enhancements for discontinuous PSG

In order to handle DPSG rules with discontinuities, the algorithm described above has to be enhanced in two respects. First, the algorithm should 'skip' internal context elements when looking for constituents, but come back to them at the appropriate moment in order to use them in building constituents; second, whereas a classical chart parser verifies adjacency relations in a trivial way by checking for successive vertex numbers, the verification of the DPSG adjacency-sequence relation requires a more elaborate bookkeeping.

    These enhancements are realized by means of additional clauses in the part of the algorithm called '*process-K-for-all-rules-in(L)*,' as shown below, and by an administration of which nodes already have a real mother and which don't to the arcs in the chart under construction by active rules. This leads to enhancements in the algorithm (29), where the additional clauses are indicated in boldface:

(29) *process-A-for-all-rules-in(L):*

> *for* every rule $R$ in $L$
>
> *do*  copy $R$ to $R'$;
>
>> mark $cat(A)$ in $R'$ as seen;
>>
>> *if*    $R'$ is done, with resulting arc $N$
>>
>> *then* **if**    $R'$ **has internal context elements**
>>
>>> **then mark RULES;**
>>>
>>> **process-arc(N);**
>>>
>>> **for each internal context element**
>>>> $C$ **in** $R'$
>>>
>>> **do process-C-for-all-rules-in**
>>>> **(RULES[cat($C$),vertexno($C$)])**
>>>> **added after the marking;**
>>>> **undo the marking**
>>
>> *else*   *process-arc(N)*
>>
>> *else* **if adjacency-sequence test succeeds**
>>
>> *then* store $R'$ in RESULT[cat(next arc in $R'$,
>>> vertexno(successor($A$)))]

We illustrate the extended algorithm with a simple example. Consider the input $_1$PROPERNAME$_2$AUX$_3$ADSENT$_4$VERB$_5$, for the sentence *John will not come*, and the following grammar:

| rule $R_1$: | NP | $\rightarrow$ | PROPERNAME |
|---|---|---|---|
| rule $R_2$: | S | $\rightarrow$ | NP + VERB |
| rule $R_3$: | VERB | $\rightarrow$ | AUX + [ADSENT] + VERB |
| rule $R_4$: | S | $\rightarrow$ | S + ADSENT |

The algorithm will go through the following steps:

- *process-arc($_1$PROPERNAME$_2$)*: rule $R_1$ is applicable; arc $_1$NP$_2$ is built; *process-arc($_1$NP$_2$)*: rule $R_2$ becomes active; a copy is added to RULES [VERB,2]

- *process-arc($_2$AUX$_3$)*: rule $R_3$ becomes active; a copy is added to RULES [ADSENT,3]

- *process-arc($_3$ADSENT$_4$)*: rule $R_3$ is further processed: a copy is added to RULES[VERB,4]

- *process-arc($_4$VERB$_5$)*: rule $R_3$ is applicable; arc $_2$VERB$_5$ is built; rule $R_3$ contains an internal context element, so all the rules in RULES are marked;

  - *process-arc$_2$ VERB$_5$*: rule $R_2$ is applicable; arc $_1$S$_5$ is built;
  - *process-arc$_1$S$_5$*: rule $R_4$ becomes active; a copy is added to RULES [ADSENT,3]
  - *process-arc$_1$ADSENT$_5$*: the context daughter is processed. Rule $R_4$ is applicable; arc $_1$S'$_5$ is built.
  - *process-arc$_1$S'$_5$*: rule $R_4$ becomes active, but successor($_1$S'$_5$) doesn't exist, so no effect is produced.

- *process-arc($_2$AUX$_3$)*: rule $R_3$ becomes active; a copy is added to RULES [ADSENT,3]

  RESULT[1] :: $_1$S$_4$, $_1$S$_3$, $_1$NP$_2$, $_1$PROPERNAME$_2$

  RESULT[2] :: $_2$VERB$_3$

  RESULT[3] :: $_3$ADSENT$_4$

Only the arc $_1$S$_4$ spans the entire input. The matrix of active rules at that moment is:

RULES[VERB, 2] :: copy of rule $R_2$ with the NP linked to arc $_1$NP$_2$

RULES[ADSENT, 3] :: copy of rule $R_3$ with the rewriting S linked to arc $_1$S$_3$.

All other stacks in the matrix are empty.

For the way in which the adjacency-sequence test is performed and for a more detailed description of the algorithm the reader is referred to (van der Sloot, 1990). The parsing algorithm is currently being redesigned in order to allow direct parsing of the ID/LP-like format mentioned in Section 4.3.

The use of DPSG in the generation of sentences starting from formal representations of semantic content and communicative function is also explored both theoretically and in an experimental implementation (see Bunt, 1987).

An interesting recent development is an attempt to express feature structures and DPSG rules in an extended version of the EL/F language, originally designed for semantic representation and used as such in the TENDUM system. This leads to a formal, model-theoretic interpretation of the syntactic part of the grammar and to the expression of syntactic and semantic information within one representation formalism.

## 4.5   Concluding remarks

In this chapter we have introduced the concept of a *discontinuous tree* for the natural, straightforward representation of syntactic structures with discontinuous constituents. The definition is such that ordinary trees are a special case of discontinuous trees.

In order to be able to describe the generation and concatenation of discontinuous trees the *adjacency sequence* concept was introduced, a generalization of the notion 'sequence of adjacency pairs.' This allows us to formulate rules in a form generalizing the classical phrase-structure rule. A *'Discontinuous Phrase-Structure Grammar' (DPSG)* consists of such rules. DPSG rules are able to describe discontinuous structures in their dominance- and precedence properties, as well as in the material that may separate the components of the structure; such rules are especially useful for describing *bounded* discontinuities. We have also introduced an ID/LP format for DPSG rules, which has the effect that DPSG rules are generalizations of GPSG or HPSG rules. DPSG rules can thus be added to a set of GPSG- or HPSG rules to account for bounded discontinuity, while everything else in the grammar can remain the same.

The DPSG parser we described has a similar relation to a parser for 'ordinary' PSG as a DPSG grammar to an 'ordinary' PSG: the parser has enhancements for dealing with discontinuities, such that when presented an 'ordinary' PSG it will only do a certain amount of not strictly necessary bookkeeping, but otherwise just work like a PSG parser.

## Acknowledgments

The parsing algorithm described in this chapter was designed and implemented by Ko van der Sloot, and was partly based on earlier work together with Jan Thesingh. I wish to thank them as well as Joop van Gent, Erik Aarts, Guido Minnen, and Masaru Tomita for many stimulating discussions on DPSG and related matters.

## References

Bunt, H. C. (1985). *Mass terms and model-theoretic semantics*. Cambridge, England: Cambridge University Press.

Bunt, H. C. (1987). Utterance generation from semantic representation augmented with pragmatic information. In G. Kempen (Ed.), *Natural language generation*. The Hague: Kluwer/Nijhoff.

Bunt, H. C., Beun, R. J., Dols, F. J. H., Linden, J. A. van der, & Schwartzenberg, G. O. thoe (1985). The TENDUM dialogue system and its theoretical basis. *IPO Annual Progress Report 19* (pp. 105–113).

Corver, N. (1990). Discontinuity and the 'wat voor'-construction in Dutch. *Proceedings of the Symposium on Discontinuous Constituency*. Tilburg.

Emonds, J. E. (1976). *A transformational approach to English syntax*. New York: Academic Press.

Emonds, J. E. (1979). Appositive relatives have no properties. *Linguistic Inquiry, 10*, 211–243.

Gazdar, G., Klein. E., Pullum, G. K. & Sag, I. A. (1985). *Generalized phrase-structure grammar*. Cambridge, MA: Harvard University Press.

Hepple, M. (1990). Verb movement in categorical grammar and the Dowty-Bach analysis of grammatical relations. *Proceedings of the Symposium on Discontinuous Constituency*. Tilburg.

Hoekstra, E. (1990). Discontinuity and the binding theory. *Proceedings of the Symposium on Discontinuous Constituency*. Tilburg.

Linden, E. J. van der (1989). Lambek theorem proving and feature unification. *Proceedings of the 4th EACL Conference*. Manchester.

McCawley, J. D. (1982). Parentheticals and discontinuous constituent structure. *Linguistic Inquiry, 13*, 91–106.

Reape, M. (1990). Getting things in order. *Proceedings of the Symposium on Discontinuous Constituency*. Tilburg.

Ross, J. R. (1973). Slifting. In M. Gross, M. Halle, & M. P. Schützenberger (Eds.), *The formal analysis of natural language*. The Hague: Mouton.

Sanfilippo, A. (1990). Thematic Accessibility in Discontinuous Dependencies. *Proceedings of the Symposium on Discontinuous Constituency*. Tilburg.

Sloot, K. van der (1990). *The TENDUM 2.7 parsing algorithm for DPSG* (ITK Research Memo). ITK, Tilburg.

Wall, R. E. (1972). *Introduction to mathematical linguistics*. Englewood Cliffs: Prentice-Hall.

# 5. Parsing with Categorial Grammar in Predictive Normal Form

Kent Wittenburg

*MCC*

Robert E. Wall

*University of Texas at Austin*

## 5.1 Introduction

Steedman (1985, 1987), Dowty (1987), Moortgat (1988), Morrill (1988), and others have proposed that Categorial Grammar, a theory of syntax in which grammatical categories are viewed as functional types, be generalized in order to analyze "noncanonical" natural language constructions such as wh-extraction and nonconstituent conjunction. A consequence of these augmentations is an explosion of semantically equivalent derivations admitted by the grammar, a problem we have characterized as spurious ambiguity from the parsing perspective (Wittenburg, 1986). In Wittenburg (1987), it was suggested that the offending rules of these grammars could take an alternate predictive form that would eliminate the problem of spurious ambiguity. This approach, consisting of compiling grammars into forms more suitable for parsing, is within the tradition of discovering normal forms for phrase structure grammars, and thus our title. Our approach stands in contrast to those which are attempting to address the spurious ambiguity problem in Categorial Grammars through the parsing algorithm itself rather than through the grammar (see Gardent & Bes, 1989; Pareschi & Steedman, 1987) and also to those addressing the problem by proof-theoretic means in the Lambek calculus tradition (Bouma, 1989; Hepple & Morrill, 1989; Koenig, 1989; Lambek, 1958; Moortgat, 1986, 1988). We follow the line of Steedman (1985, 1987), Dowty (1987), and various strains of Categorial Unification Grammar (Karttunen, 1986; Uszkoreit, 1986; Wittenburg, 1986; Zeevat, Klein, & Calder, 1987) in that we assume a finite number of combinatory rules and study the behavior of parsers that apply these rewrite rules in roughly the phrase-structure parsing tradition.

In Wittenburg (1987) it was conjectured that predictive forms for Categorial Grammars were equivalent to the source forms and that they did indeed

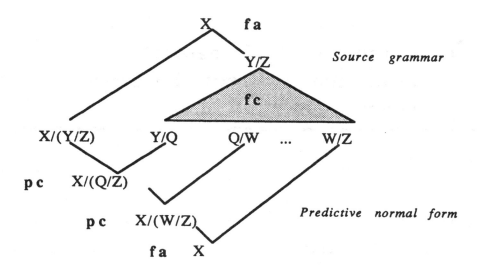

Figure 5.1. Derivational schema.

eliminate spurious ambiguity. Here we report on formal results that have en-
sued from these original conjectures. We have found that, on the whole, the
conjectures proved valid although we have discovered that the relationship between predictive normal forms for these grammars and their source forms are
more complicated than was implied by the earlier paper. As we will show, an
additional condition is necessary to ensure equivalence of these grammars and
eliminate spurious ambiguity from the picture.

## 5.2   Overview of predictive normal form

The use of function composition rules together with higher-order functional
types is the key for Categorial Grammars to analyze nonlocal dependencies
such as wh- movement and various forms of nonconstituent conjunction. In
the upper half of Figure 5.1 we show a scheme for one of the directional variants
of such derivations.

A right-looking higher-order functional type $X/(Y/Z)$ appears at the left
end of a category sequence. Such higher-order categories are assigned to
fronted wh- or topicalized phrases and also to (instantiations of) conjunctions.
The sequence to the right requires function composition (fc) to be reduced to
a single functional type $Y/Z$. The shaded area indicates that this part of the
sequence gives rise to spurious ambiguity — there are at least Catalan-number
of equivalent derivations possible (Wittenburg, 1986). The topmost reduction
then involves function application (fa) of the higher-order type to the reduced

category. If the higher-order category has been formed through type-raising, then this technique delivers analyses where the basic category appearing on one end of a sequence acts as argument to the function on the other extreme end — thus one can capture long-distance dependencies with only local combinations.

Predictive normal forms for these grammars give rise to derivations like that in the bottom half of Figure 5.1. The higher-order category acts as a contextual trigger for rules that, in effect, predict function composition. Since each application of predictive composition (pc) results in yet another higher-order category, the predictive rules can continue to apply, giving rise to the same unbounded dependencies. The difference is that the area of equivalence among derivations has been eliminated. From grammars that give rise to derivations that can branch multiple ways to yield equivalent results, predictive normal form grammars produce derivations that branch uniformly (either leftward or rightward, depending on category directionality) from the site of the higher-order category.

## 5.3   Source grammar (G)

In this work we focus on the role of basic function composition as a way of illustrating the effects of predictive normal forms. For this discussion then, we assume a form of Categorial Grammar that is considerably more restricted than those advocated by Steedman (1987), Moortgat (1988), Morrill (1988), and others. As the work of these authors shows, the simple Categorial Grammars we assume here are not linguistically adequate. We do not consider the effects of type-raising nor of generalized conjunction here, nor do we address the issue of generalized composition. While we intend to address these points in future work, the simplifications we assume here allow us to uncover an initial set of properties associated with the use of predictive combinators.

We assume for our source grammar G the following combinatory rules together with a lexically assigned system of categories of the usual recursive sort. That is, we assume a set of basic categories, say, {S, NP, N}. If X and Y are categories, so are X/Y and Y\X. Our notation follows Steedman (1987) and Dowty (1985) in that the domain type appears consistently to the right of a slash and a range type to the left. Left directionality is then indicated by a left-leaning slash, and right directionality by a right-leaning slash. Semantically, we assume that lexical categories introduce functional constants in lambda terms where the arity of the functions bears an obvious and direct relation to the syntactic type.[1] Here are example lexical entries.

| | | | |
|---|---|---|---|
| eats: S\NP/NP | John: S/(S\NP) | a: NP/N | quiche: N |
| $\lambda x \lambda y$ ((eats x) y) | $\lambda f(f$ john) | $\lambda x(a\ x)$ | quiche |

---

[1] Although we use the term semantics here to describe the relevant issues of derivational ambiguity, it should be understood that we dealing with a syntactic domain. Our "semantics" then defines the syntactic structures yielded by derivations using these grammars. See (Wittenburg & Aone, 1989) for a defense of the position that this level of representation is properly construed as syntactic.

We assume the following set of combinatory rules:

Forward function application (fa>)
$$X/Y \quad Y \quad \longrightarrow \quad X$$
$$f \qquad a \qquad\qquad f(a)$$

Backward function application (fa<)
$$Y \quad X\backslash Y \quad \longrightarrow \quad X$$
$$a \qquad f \qquad\qquad f(a)$$

Forward function composition (fc>)
$$X/Y \quad Y/Z \quad \longrightarrow \quad X/Z$$
$$f \qquad g \qquad\qquad \lambda x(f(g(x))) = Bfg$$

Backward function composition (fc<)
$$Y\backslash Z \quad X\backslash Y \quad \longrightarrow \quad X\backslash Z$$
$$g \qquad f \qquad\qquad \lambda x(f(g(x))) = Bfg$$

Given these semantics, G yields equivalence classes of derivations, where equivalence is defined modulo $\beta$-conversion of semantic terms.[2] The two sources of spurious ambiguity in G are summarized by the following equivalences generalized over directional variants of the rules:

(apply (compose X Y) Z) = (apply X (apply Y Z))

(compose X (compose Y Z)) = (compose (compose X Y) Z)

An example illustrating the first of these equivalences follows:[3]

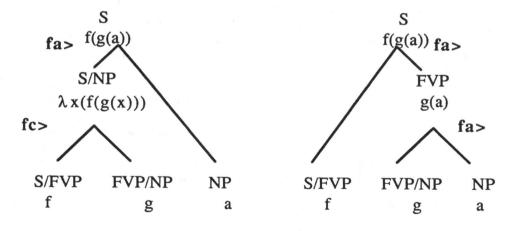

---

[2]This definition of equivalence does not take quantifier scope differences into account. It is more in harmony with the predictive normalization techniques to assume that scoping structure is not necessarily isomorphic to the derivation tree, a position also advocated by Steedman (1987) and Moortgat (1988).

[3]FVP is used as a notational convenience for the category S\NP.

The terminal string "John eats a quiche" would yield the equivalent derivational terms ((eats (a quiche)) John) given that either tree above could be involved in an analysis. Note that the use of function composition here does not match the pattern evident in Figure 5.1. There are, in fact, no long-distance dependencies in this example. Such uses of function composition are, in fact, "optional" and predictive normal form grammars rule out the use of composition in such cases.

## 5.4   Predictive normal form (G')

A predictive normal form version of G replaces each composition rule with two predictive variants.[4]

> Forward-predictive forward function composition (fpfc>)
> X/(Y/Z)      Y/W      $\longrightarrow$   X/(W/Z)
> $\quad$ f $\qquad\quad$ g $\qquad\qquad\qquad\qquad$ $\lambda h(f(Bgh)) = \lambda h(f(\lambda x(g(h(x)))))$

> Backward-predictive forward function composition (bpfc>)
> W/Z      X\(Y/Z)      $\longrightarrow$   X\(Y/W)
> $\quad$ g $\qquad\quad$ f $\qquad\qquad\qquad\qquad$ $\lambda h(f(Bhg)) = \lambda h(f(\lambda x(h(g(x)))))$

> Backward-predictive backwards function composition (bpfc<)
> Y\W      X\(Y\Z)      $\longrightarrow$   X\(W\Z)
> $\quad$ g $\qquad\quad$ f $\qquad\qquad\qquad\qquad$ $\lambda h(f(Bgh)) = \lambda h(f(\lambda x(g(h(x)))))$

> Forward-predictive backwards function composition (fpfc<)
> X/(Y\Z)      W\Z      $\longrightarrow$   X/(Y\W)
> $\quad$ f $\qquad\quad$ g $\qquad\qquad\qquad\qquad$ $\lambda h(f(Bhg)) = \lambda h(f(\lambda x(h(g(x)))))$

We will now consider, first, the question of ambiguity in G'. Second, we will take up the question of whether G and G' are equivalent.

## 5.5   Ambiguity in G'

Is there ambiguity in G'? We will consider first cases that are analogous to the derivations in G known to give rise to spurious ambiguity followed by a discussion of remaining cases.

### 5.5.1   Cases of spurious ambiguity in G

In G, spurious ambiguity arises from the use of composition. Consider any maximal subtree of fc> in a derivation in G, i.e.,

---

[4] These rules are derivable in the Lambek calculus (Lambek, 1958).

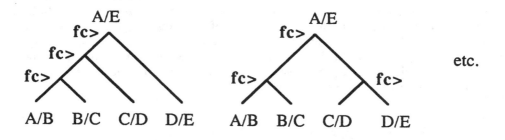

These subtrees must feed into an instance of fa at the top (either as functor or as argument) — if it fed into fc, this tree would not be a maximal fc tree.

So subderivations in G with fc> must be of one of the following forms:

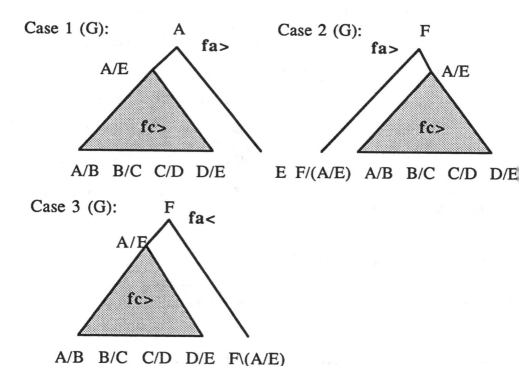

In either case, there is one and only one derivation in G' each of these sequences.

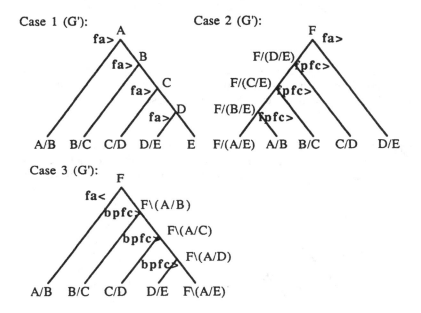

The cases of fc< are parallel. Either the maximal fc< tree in G feeds a final application of fa< as functor, in which case only fa< will be involved in G', or else the fc< tree in G will feed a higher-order functor as argument, in which case one of the two predictive backward composition rules will be involved in G'. And since fc> and fc< cannot appear together in a maximal fc tree because of directionality clash, all cases are accounted for. We have shown here that cases of spurious ambiguity in G do not give rise to analogous spurious ambiguity in G', but of course there may be new sources of ambiguity in G' that we have not yet considered.

## 5.5.2   Remaining cases of ambiguity

Can there be any cases of derivational ambiguity in G'? That is, can there be derivation trees of the form

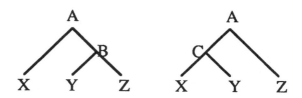

for (possibly complex) categories A, B, C, X, Y, Z, where mothers are derived from daughters using just the rules of fa and predictive function composition? An exhaustive list of all the combinatory possibilities reveals just two types:

**Type I:** $X = Y/Y$ and $Z = Y\backslash Y$. The central category Y can combine first by fa with Y/Y to its left or with $Y\backslash Y$ to its right, to yield Y in either case. This Y can then combine with the remaining category by fa to give Y again:

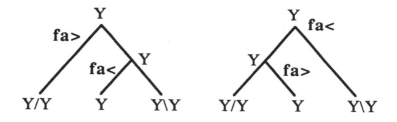

But this is a genuine ambiguity, not a spurious one, for the topmost Y can be assigned different semantic values by the two derivations. If $[[Y/Y]] = f$, $[[Y]] = a$, and $[[Y\backslash Y]] = g$, the left derivation yields $f(g(a))$ and the right one $g(f(a))$.

In the more general case, we might have $m$ instances of Y/Y to the left of the Y and $n$ instances of $Y\backslash Y$ to the right. In such a situation the number of syntactically and semantically distinct derivations would be the $(m + n)$th Catalan number. And since only fa> and fa< are used, the same ambiguity, if it is present, will be found in both G and in G'.

**Type II:** A predictive combination rule is involved in the derivation. We will illustrate with just one case; the others are similar, differing only the directions of the slashes and the order of constituents.

Consider the derivation tree

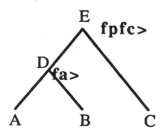

in which each mother node is derived from its daughters by the indicated rule. Since E is derived by fpfc>, D must be of the form X/(Y/Z) and C of the form Y/W; hence E is of the form X/(W/Z). Then because D is derived by fa>, it follows that A must be of the form (X/(Y/Z))/B. That is, the derivation tree is of the form

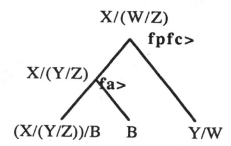

for (possibly complex) categories B, W, X, Y, Z.

Given the rules of fa and predictive composition, there is a distinct derivation tree yielding X/(W/Z) from the category sequence (X/(Y/Z))/B, B, Y/W; namely,

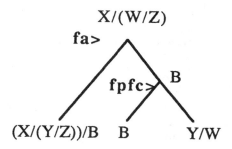

assuming we can solve for B. Now because $(X/(Y/Z))/B$ becomes $X/(W/Z)$ by fa>, it follows that $X/(Y/Z) = X/(W/Z)$, and so $Y = W$. Further, B combines with $Y/W$ (i.e., $Y/Y$) to give B again, so B is required to be of the form $R/(Y/Y)$, for some R. (Note that $R/(Y/Y)$ could also combine with $Y/Y$ by fa>, but nothing prevents fpfc> from applying here as well.) In summary, G' allows the following sort of derivational ambiguity (and others symmetrical to it):

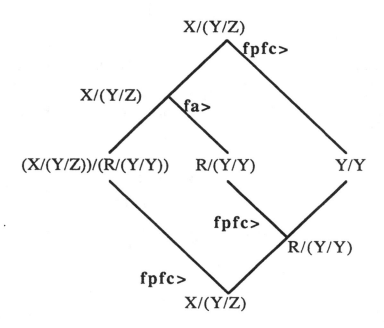

Is this a spurious or a genuine ambiguity? Letting the three leaf constituents have semantic values f, g, and h, respectively, we obtain $\lambda i[f(g)(Bhi)]$ for the root node of the top tree and $f[\lambda i[g(Bhi)]]$ for the root of the tree on the bottom. (Bhi denotes the composition of functions h and i.) These expressions are certainly non-equivalent for arbitrary functions f, g, h. At any rate, we might ask if this sort of ambiguity can lead to an explosion of combinatorial possibilities like the one we were trying to rid ourselves of in the first place. The worst case would be when there is a sequence of n categories $Y/Y$ extending rightward, thus:

$$(X/(Y/Z))/(R/(Y/Y))    R/(Y/Y)    Y/Y    Y/Y    \ldots    Y/Y$$

Now $R/(Y/Y)$ can combine with $Y/Y$'s by fpfc, yielding $R/(Y/Y)$ each time, then combine with the large category on the left by fa> to give $X/(Y/Z)$, which can then combine with any remaining $Y/Y$'s by fpfc> to give $X/(Y/Z)$ back again. The lone instance of fa> can thus occur at any point in the derivation, and if there are n $Y/Y$'s, there will be n+1 distinct derivation trees. Thus, the number of derivations grows only linearly with the number of occurrences of Y/Y, not with a Catalan growth rate.

# 5.6 Equivalence of G and G'

The previous discussion should give an indication of the results concerning equivalence of G and G'. We first take up the question of whether L(G) is a subset of L(G') followed by the question of whether L(G') is a subset of L(G).

## 5.6.1 Subsumption of L(G) by L(G')

Proof sketch: By induction on the depth of derivation trees, we show that any derivation in G has a derivation in G'.

Any derivation of category S in G must end in fa> or fa<. Consider the immediate daughters of a derivation tree produced by fa. Either they are lexical or have been produced by another fa rule, in which case G' also shares this derivation, or else they have been produced by fc. As shown in Section 5.5.1, any maximal fc tree feeding into fa in G has a corresponding derivation in G'.

## 5.6.2 Subsumption of L(G') by L(G)

Does the language of G include the language of G'? Consider the following derivation in G':

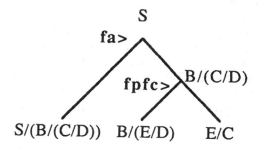

There is no corresponding derivation in G. (Neither fa> nor fc> is applicable to the given categories.) Thus, in general, L(G) does not include L(G') and the grammars are not equivalent.

What can be done about the non-equivalence of G' and G?

1. **Restrict rule application in G'**: One may stipulate that the result category of a predictive rule cannot serve as argument in any other rule. (In function application X/Y Y ⇒ Z we take Y to be the argument category. In predictive rule X/(Y/Z) Y/W ⇒ X/(W/Z) we take the Y/W to be the argument. For backwards rules, the argument category is the leftmost term.) In the derivation just above, the predictive rule

fpfc> "feeds" fa> as argument. If derivations in G' are restricted in this way, L(G') is provably included in L(G), and the grammars are weakly equivalent.

Proof sketch: By induction on the depth of derivation trees, we show that any derivation in the restricted G' has a derivation in G.

Any derivation of category S in G' must end in fa> or fa<. Consider the immediate daughters of a node produced by fa. Either they are lexical or have been produced by another fa rule, in which case G also shares this derivation, or else they have been produced by pfc. The only maximal pfc trees possible are those which consist of repeated applications of a single pfc rule — the rule restriction above and directionality clashes exclude all others. Again because of the rule restriction, we need consider only those subderivations with maximal fpc trees in which the highest node feeds into fa as functor. As is evident from Section 5.5.1, any such subtree in G' has a corresponding derivation in G.

Note that this same restriction banishes all cases of Type II ambiguity noted in Section 5.5.2 above. Observe that Type II ambiguity depends on predictive rules in G' being able to "feed" the arguments of further instances of predictive rules. Thus, G' becomes free of any ambiguity not already present in G, a result we should expect since the two grammars have now been made weakly equivalent.

This restriction on rule application might be thought to be reminiscent of Pareschi and Steedman (1987), where spurious ambiguity is addressed through procedural means in parsing. Yet our proposal actually need not constrain the parsing algorithm at all. A node formed by a predictive rule can be flagged by a feature, while those formed by fa would not be. All combinatory rules could then have a feature on their "argument" categories that would block the rule's application when encountering this flag. This rather minimal addition to the grammar could easily be accommodated in the parsing strategy of one's choice: top-down, bottom-up, left-right, breadth-first, or whatever.

2. **Grin and bear it**: Recasting the grammar in "predictive normal form" eliminates all cases of spurious ambiguity occasioned by sequences of function composition, a problem which is known to crop up very frequently in actual applications and to cause serious delays in parsing times. On the other hand, because of the complexity and the rather specific forms of the categories which give rise to the ambiguities and the new derivations of G' that are outside of G, it seems reasonable to suppose that such cases are unlikely to be encountered in ordinary applications. In any event, as we noted above, the number of Type II ambiguous derivations in G' grows only linearly and not in Catalan fashion with increasing string length and would not be expected to lead to intolerable parsing times. The slight profligacy of G' over G might, therefore, present no serious practical problem.

For those still inclined to worry, we offer the following reassurance: a predictive normal form grammar can misbehave only if categories of sufficient "complexity" can be derived from the given set of categories in the lexicon, e.g., a category of the form $S/(X/(W/Z))$ in the case of non-equivalence above and of the form $(X/(Y/Z))/(R/(Y/Y))$ in the instances of Type II ambiguity. But given such a grammar and the lexical categories it is a decidable question (see Appendix) whether any categories of the undesired complexity can arise during a derivation. (We wish to thank Jim Barnett for suggestions on how to prove this.) Thus one can tell whether a particular G' is equivalent to G and is free from spurious ambiguity.

## 5.7   Concluding remarks

The main result of this chapter is that we have shown that Categorial Grammars with predictive variants of function composition rules can satisfy the requirements for normalization, namely, that the "compiled" grammars can preserve equivalence and that they do so with the benefit of eliminating the parsing problem occasioned by spurious ambiguity. We have also enumerated decidability proofs of interest. Our next task is to explore the predictive normal form strategy with more expressive, and more nearly adequate, Categorial systems such as those that incorporate some form of generalized composition and conjunction, type-raising, etc. What we expect to find is that if predictive normalization techniques are applicable at all, the predictive grammars will have a relationship to their source forms that parallels the one we have uncovered here. In other words, we expect the restriction on the use of predictive rules is in general necessary for preserving equivalence when using predictive combinators.

## Acknowledgments

This work has been carried out within the research program of the Interface Languages project in the Human Interface Laboratory of the Advanced Computer Technology Program at MCC. We are indebted to Jim Hollan and Bill Curtis for their support of this work.

## References

Bouma, G. (1989). Efficient processing of flexible categorial grammar. *Proceedings of the Fourth Conference of the European Chapter of the Association for Computational Linguistics* (pp. 19–26).

Dowty, D. (1987). Type raising, functional composition, and non-constituent conjunction. In R. Oehrle, E. Bach, & D. Wheeler (Eds.), *Categorial grammars and natural language structures*. Dordrecht: Reidel.

Gardent, C., & Bes, G. (1989). Efficient parsing for French. *Proceedings of the 27th Annual Meeting of the Association for Computational Linguistics* (pp. 280–287). Vancouver.

Hepple, M., & Morrill, G. (1989). Parsing and derivational equivalence. *Proceedings of the Fourth Conference of the European Chapter of the Association for Computational Linguistics* (pp. 9–18). Manchester, England.

Karttunen, L. (1986). *Radical lexicalism* (Tech. Rep. No. CSLI-86-68). CA: Stanford University, Center for the Study of Language and Information.

Koenig, E. (1989). Parsing as natural deduction. *Proceedings of the 27th Annual Meeting of the Association for Computational Linguistics* (pp. 272–286). Vancouver, British Columbia.

Lambek, J. (1958). The mathematics of sentence structure. *American Mathematical Monthly, 65*, 154–170.

Moortgat, M. (1986). Lambek categorial grammar and the autonomy thesis. *The ZWO Symposium "Morphology and Modularity."* Utrecht. Also available as INL Working Paper No. 87-03. Instituut voor Nederlandse Lexicologie, Leiden, Netherlands.

Moortgat, M. (1988). *Categorial investigations: Logical and linguistic aspects of the Lambek calculus.* Foris.

Morrill, G. (1988). *Extraction and coordination in phrase structure grammar and categorial grammar.* Unpublished doctoral dissertation. University of Edinburgh, Centre for Cognitive Science.

Pareschi, R., & Steedman, M. (1987). A lazy way to chart-parse with categorial grammars. *Proceedings of the 25th Annual Meeting of the Association for Computational Linguistics* (pp. 81–88). Stanford, CA.

Steedman, M. (1985). Dependency and coordination in the grammar of Dutch and English. *Language, 61*, 523–568.

Steedman, M. (1987). Combinatory grammars and parasitic gaps. *Natural Language and Linguistic Theory, 5*, 403–440.

Uszkoreit, H. (1986). Categorial unification grammars. *Proceedings of COLING* (pp. 187–194).

Wittenburg, K. (1986). *Natural language parsing with combinatory categorial grammars in a graph-unification-based formalism.* Unpublished doctoral dissertation. University of Texas at Austin.

Wittenburg, K. (1987). Predictive combinators: A method for efficient parsing of combinatory categorial grammars. *Proceedings of the 25th Annual Meeting of the Association for Computational Linguistics* (pp. 73–80). Stanford, CA.

Wittenburg, K., & Aone, C. (1989). *Aspects of a categorial syntax/semantics interface* (Tech. Rep. No. ACT-HI-143-89). TX: MCC.

Zeevat, H., Klein, E., & Calder, J. (1987). Unification categorial grammar. In N. Haddock, E. Klein, & G. Morrill (Eds.), *Edinburgh working papers in cognitive science: Categorial grammar, unification grammar, and parsing* (Vol. 1). Centre for Cognitive Science, University of Edinburgh.

# Appendix: Proofs of decidability

The rules of G':

1.  fpfc> X/(Y/Z) + Y/W $\longrightarrow$ X/(W/Z)
2.  bpfc> W/Z + X\(Y/Z) $\longrightarrow$ X\(Y/W)
3.  bpfc< Y\W + X\(Y\Z) $\longrightarrow$ X\(W\Z)
4.  fpfc< X/(Y\Z) + W\Z $\longrightarrow$ X/(Y\W)
5.             fa> X/Y + Y $\longrightarrow$ X
6.             fa< Y + X\Y $\longrightarrow$ X

**Definition:** We define the **degree** of a category expression to be the number of slashes it contains without regard to direction or grouping by parentheses.

For example: A/(B\(C\D)) is of degree 3; A/B is of degree 1; B is of degree 0.

**Definition:** We define the **numerator** (resp, **denominator**) of a category of degree $\geq$ 1 to be the category to the left (resp, right) of its principal connective slash.

For example: The numerator of A\B is A and the denominator is B. The numerator and denominator of (A/(B\A))/C are A/(B\A) and C, respectively. The category A has neither numerator nor denominator.

We will refer also to the **denominator's numerator** and the **denominator's denominator** (abbreviated **dn** and **dd**, respectively) in the obvious way. Neither is defined unless the denominator is of degree $\geq$ 1.

**Definition:** We call a category expression **uniform** if its principal connective slash and the principal connective slash of its denominator are in the same direction. If these are in opposite directions, the expression is **mixed**. A category of degree 0 or whose denominator is of degree 0 is neither uniform nor mixed.

For example: A/(B/D) and A\(B\D) are uniform; A\(B/D) and A/(B\D) are mixed. (A/B)\(C\D) is uniform (the "/" in the numerator is irrelevant), and (A/B)/(C\(D\E)) is mixed. A and A/B are neither uniform nor mixed.

**Definition:** In the pfc rules above, we call the category denoted by all three variables X, Y, and Z the **functor** category. The other category on the left of the arrow is the **argument** category. In the fa rules, the X, Y category is the functor and the Y is the argument.

**Remark:** The rules of bpfc> and fpfc< require a mixed category as functor and produce a mixed category as output.

The rules of fpfc> and bpfc< require a uniform category as functor and produce a uniform category as output.

In the rules of fa> and fa<, since their functors may be of degree 1 and their arguments of degree 0, the notions of mixed or uniform are not immediately relevant.

**Remark:**  All four of the pfc rules preserve the numerator of the functor in the numerator of the output category. Thus no new numerators are created by the application of these rules. Similarly, in both the fa rules the numerator of the functor category is the output category. If the output category is itself of degree $\geq 1$, i.e., of the form A/B or A\B, then its numerator may also be produced by an fa rule (A/B + B $\longrightarrow$ A), and so on. Thus, given a grammar G' with an initial (finite) stock of categories in its lexicon, no derived category can have a numerator which does not already appear as a numerator in the lexicon, or as a numerator of a numerator ... of a numerator of a lexical category.

Thus, the maximum degree for any numerator in any category derivable in G' is given by the maximum degree of a numerator among the lexical categories. Call this number N.

**Remark:**  The mixed categories derived in the rules of bpfc> and fpfc< inherit the denominator's numerator (dn) from the functor category. Therefore, a dn in a mixed category cannot grow larger by the application of one of these rules. Mixed categories are never produced by the other two pfc rules, bpfc< and fpfc>. A mixed category may, however, be produced by an application of fa — for example, (X/(Y\Z))/Q + Q $\longrightarrow$ X/(Y\Z), but in such a case it arises from the numerator of some larger expression and is therefore of degree at most N. Thus if DN is the maximum degree of a denominator's numerator in a mixed expression in the lexicon, the maximum degree of a dn in a mixed expression produced by G' is given by max(N, DN), a constant.

**Remark:**  A mixed expression formed by the rules of bpfc> or fpfc< gets its denominator's denominator from the numerator of the argument category. Mixed categories derived by rules of fa arise from numerators, and, as before, their degree — and thus the degree of the dd — is no greater than N. If DD is the maximum degree of a dd in a mixed expression in the lexicon, the maximum degree of a dd in a mixed expression produced by G' is given by max(N, DD), a constant.

**Lemma:**  In a grammar G' with a finite set of lexical categories the producible mixed categories are of degree no greater than N + max(N, DN) + max(N, DD) + 2 and are therefore finite in number.

**Remark:**  The uniform categories produced by rules fpfc> and bpfc< inherit the denominator's denominator from the functor category. Uniform categories are not produced by the rules of fpfc< and bpfc>. If a uniform category is the output of fa, e.g., (X/(Y/Z))/Q + Q $\longrightarrow$ X/(Y/Z), it arises from the numerator of a larger expression, and therefore its dd is of degree at most N. If DD' is the maximum degree of a dd in a uniform expression in the lexicon, then the maximum degree of any dd in a uniform expression produced by G' is max(N, DD').

**Remark:**  The denominator's numerator of a uniform expression can grow arbitrarily large. For example:

$$\begin{array}{ccccc} & & \text{fpfc>} & & \\ A/(A/B) & + & A/(A/B) & \longrightarrow & A/((A/B)/B) \\ X\ Y\ Z & & Y\ W & & X\ W\ Z \end{array}$$

The resulting category can then become an argument in fpfc> with A/(A/B) again as functor:

$$\begin{array}{ccccc} A/(A/B) & + & A/((A/B)/B) & \longrightarrow & A/(((A/B)/B)/B) \\ X\ Y\ Z & & Y\ W & & X\ W\ Z \end{array}$$

Corresponding examples can be constructed with bpfc< and left-leaning slashes.

**Lemma:** Let K be the maximum degree of any lexical category in G'. If a uniform category has a dn of degree greater than K, then this category can only be used as argument in the rule of fpfc> or bpfc<.

**Proof:** Let X/(Y/Z) be a uniform category with degree(Y) > K. (The argument holds *mutatis mutandis* for X\(Y\Z).)

X/(Y/Z) cannot be the functor in fa>

$$X/(Y/Z) + Y/Z \rightarrow X$$

since this would require a category Y/Z with numerator of degree >K (therefore >N), which cannot be produced in G'.

X/(Y/Z) cannot be the argument in fa>

$$Q/(X/(Y/Z)) + X/(Y/Z) \rightarrow Q$$

since this would require a category Q/(X/(Y/Z)) with dd of degree >K (therefore > max(N, DD')), which cannot be produced in G'. Similarly, serving as argument in fa< would require Q\(X/(Y/Z)), with dd of degree >K (therefore > max(N, DD)), which is likewise unproducible in G'.

X/(Y/Z) cannot be the functor in bpfc> or fpfc< since it is not a mixed category.

X/(Y/Z) cannot be the argument in bpfc> (or fpfc< with reversed slashes)

$$\begin{array}{c} \text{bpfc>} \\ X/(Y/Z) + Q\backslash(R/(Y/Z)) \longrightarrow Q\backslash(R/X) \end{array}$$

since this would require a mixed category Q\(R/(Y/Z)) with dd of degree >K (therefore > max(N, DD)), which cannot be produced in G'.

X/(Y/Z) cannot be the functor in fpfc>

$$\begin{array}{c} \text{fpfc>} \\ X/(Y/Z) + Y/W \longrightarrow X/(W/Z) \end{array}$$

since this would require a category Y/W with numerator of degree
>K (therefore >N), which cannot be produced in G'.

Thus, the only remaining possibility is for X/(Y/Z) to be the argument in fpfc>

$$Q/(X/R) + X/(Y/Z) \longrightarrow Q/((Y/Z)/R)$$

to produce another uniform category Q/((Y/Z)/R) with a dn of
even greater degree, which can therefore only be used as an argument in fpfc>, etc. Note that degree (Y/Z) > degree (X), since if
degree(X) were larger than K, Q/(X/R) could not serve as functor in fpfc>, as shown just above, nor could it be a numerator in
X/(Y/Z).

**Theorem:** Given a grammar G' with a finite set of lexical categories, the set
of producible categories is decidable.

**Proof:** By the first Lemma above, the set of producible mixed categories
is finite. The set of all producible categories of degree 0 or 1 is finite, since
each either (1) appears in the lexicon or (2) is derived by a rule of fa and is a
numerator of some category X|Y, or (3) is a numerator of a numerator ... of a
numerator (e.g., (((... (A/B)/C)/D) ... Q) and is derived from a succession
of fa's with categories Q, ..., D, C, B, to give A), where Q, ...,D, C, B are
of degree less than N. The set of all producible uniform categories with dn of
degree at most K is finite. Therefore, if a category C is mixed, or of degree 1
or 0, or uniform with degree(dn) ≤ K, we can see if C is produced by simply
enumerating all the members of this finite set of categories. If C is uniform
with degree (dn) > K, we take all uniform categories in the previous set with
degree(dn) ≤ K and let them be arguments to all possible functors (a finite
set) by the rule of fpfc> (resp., bpfc<). Let all the newly produced uniform
categories again be arguments to all possible functors, and continue in this
way until all such categories with degree (dn) equal to that of category C have
been produced and see if C is among them. In any case after a finite number
of steps we see whether G' produces C.

**Corollary:** For a given grammar G', the number of "useful" categories, i.e.,
those which can appear in some derivation resulting in S, the sentence category,
is finite.

**Proof:** No uniform category with dn of degree > K can appear in a derivation
resulting in S since no rule of fa can be applied to it.

Thus, we see that derivations in G' are possible for arbitrarily long strings
only because the derivation trees themselves can be arbitrarily wide (and deep).
The categories appearing in these trees do not themselves grow without limit:
their length is, in fact, bounded.

**Corollary:** The question whether there can be any "spurious" ambiguity in
the derivations of a given G' is decidable.

**Proof:**   Search for all categories of the forms which give rise to such ambiguity among the finite set of "useful" categories.

**Corollary:**   The question whether there can be any genuinely ambiguous derivations in G' is decidable.

**Proof:**   As for the previous corollary.

**Corollary:**   The question whether G' is weakly equivalent to G is decidable.

**Proof:**   All instances of non-equivalence in G' arise from an application of fa to an argument resulting from a pfc rule and a functor with this argument as denominator.   Search for all such pairs among the finite set of "useful" categories.

# 6. PREMO: Parsing by conspicuous lexical consumption

## Brian M. Slator

*Department of Computer Science, North Dakota State University*

## Yorick Wilks

*Computing Research Laboratory, New Mexico State University*

## 6.1 Introduction

In recent years there has been a renewed emphasis on *scale* in computational linguistics, and a certain disillusionment with the so-called "toy systems" of linguistic and AI models. Recent years have also seen rising interest in the computational analysis of machine-readable dictionaries as a lexical resource for parsing. These two trends are neither accidental nor independent of each other; an obvious place to look for large-scale linguistic information is in existing dictionaries.

However, this marriage of parsing and lexicography is a troubled one. In the worst case, parsing reduces to enumerating structures and choosing one, and there are well-known combinatorial results concerning the potential size of this search space, just as there are well-known anecdotes in AI about systems that failed to "scale-up" very well. The addition of large-scale lexical knowledge bases does nothing towards solving this problem. If anything, machine-readable dictionary analysis adds another dimension of difficulty to an already hard problem.

PREMO: The PREference Machine Organization, was designed with this troubled marriage in mind. The system is, we believe, the first to take semantic information directly from a dictionary via computational means in order to apply that information to parsing. The system architecture was specifically chosen because it allows consistent handling of lexical objects in an environment where nearly every word is defined in terms of multiple senses. The algorithm implements a "best-first" heuristic because in a large-scale system such as this, virtually anything else is out of the question. In PREMO, dictionary analysis and text analysis are independent processes that are directly coupled to each other. The design of PREMO was uniquely informed by the structure of information in the dictionary, and by the process involved in extracting that information.

PREMO is a knowledge-based Preference Semantics parser with access to

85

a large, lexical semantic knowledge base. The system is organized along the lines of an operating system. The state of every partial parse is captured in a structure called a *language object*, and the control structure of the preference machine is a priority queue of these language objects. The language object at the front of the queue has the highest score as computed by a preference metric that weighs grammatical predictions, semantic type matching, and pragmatic coherence. The highest priority language object is the intermediate reading that is currently most preferred (the others are still "alive," but not actively pursued); in this way the preference machine avoids combinatorial explosion by following a "best-first" strategy for parsing. The system has clear extensions into parallel processing.

## 6.2   The preference machine

PREMO is an architecture, modeled as an operating system, for parsing natural language. Each "ready" process in the system captures the state of a partial parse in a "process control block" structure called a *language object*. The control structure is a priority queue of competing parses, with priority given to each parse "process" on the basis of a preference semantics evaluation. The "time-slice" for each process is whatever is needed to move forward one word in a local process sentence buffer (where each process operates on a private copy of the current sentence). After every time slice, the preference/priority for the currently "running" parse is re-computed and the language object for that process is returned to the priority queue. The first process to emerge from the queue with its sentence buffer empty is declared the winner and saved. This strategy is both a run-time optimization and an application of the "Least Effort Principle" of intuitively plausible language processing. The parsing is robust in that some structure is returned for every input, no matter how ill-formed or "garden-pathological" it is.

### 6.2.1   Language object structures

The basic data structure manipulated by the preference machine is called a *language object*. Each language object is a complex structure containing at least the following attributes:

- **Name and Type:** every object *name* is a word from the text. Object *type* defaults to *word* until a word is found to be part of phrase, then that object is changed to type *phrase*. The *head* of a phrase is the language object with its co-members subordinated to it.

- **Score:** see Section 6.4.1, *Computing Preferences*, below.

- **Lexical Frame:** see Section 6.3.1, *Text Lexicon*, below.

- **Predictions and Requirements:** grammatical predictions and constraints, both as found in the language object itself and as synthesized from subordinated language objects (see Section 6.3.1 *Text Lexicon*, below).

- **Preceding and Remaining Text**: the sentential context, or local sentence buffers; (preceding words are needed to check on grammatical predictions and requirements that can be either forward or backward in the sentence). When the *remaining text* is exhausted, the language object is a candidate sentence representation.

- **Subordinated Language Objects**: subordination refers to the way an NP is subordinated to a PP, an AP is subordinated to an NP, and a phrase element is subordinated to the phrase head. A corresponding label list holds labels associated with each stack element.

## 6.2.2 Preference machine control

PREMO receives two inputs: a text to be parsed, and a lexicon of semantic objects specific to that text. The algorithm of the preference machine, after loading the priority queue with scored language objects for every sense of the first word in the sentence, is as follows (Figure 6.1):

1. **Delete-Max** — retrieve the highest priority language object in the queue. (If the sentence buffer for that object is empty then go to Step 8).

2. **Get-Lexical** — retrieve the list of sense frames associated with the first word in the sentence buffer within the current language object.

3. **Make-Language-Object(s)** — instantiate a new language object for every sense of the new word, with an appropriate initial preference score.

4. **Copy-Language-Object** — create a copy of the current high priority language object to pair with each new language object.

5. **Coalesce** — If more than a single grammar rule applies to the pair, copies of the pair are made. Combine the pairs of language objects, subordinating one to the other.

6. **Compute-Preference** — assign a new priority score to each of the language objects resulting from coalescing pairs.

7. **Enqueue** — insert the coalesced language objects onto the priority queue in preference score order. Go to Step 1.

8. **Inter-sentential Processes** — save the language object at the front of the priority queue and flush the queue. If there are no more sentences, return; otherwise, read the next sentence in the text and load the priority queue with scored language objects for every sense of the first word in the new sentence. Go to Step 1.

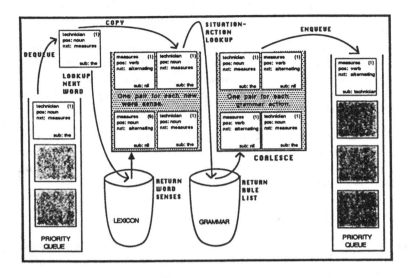

Figure 6.1. PREMO: The PREference Machine Organization.

## 6.3   Global data

Global system data structures include a *text-specific lexicon*, and a *context structure* derived from Longman's Dictionary of Contemporary English (LDOCE; Procter *et al.*, 1978), and a *phrase grammar*.

### 6.3.1   Text lexicon

LDOCE is a full-sized dictionary in machine-readable form, designed for learners of English as a second language, and containing several non-standard features (grammar, type, and pragmatic codes). A PREMO sub-system produces text-specific lexicons from selected machine-readable dictionary definitions (Wilks, Fass, Guo, McDonald, Plate, & Slator, 1987, 1988, 1989). The input to this sub-system is unconstrained text; the output is a collection of lexical semantic objects, one for every *sense* of every word in the text. Each lexical semantic object in this lexicon contains grammatical and sub-categorization information, often with general (and sometimes specific) grammatical predictions; content word objects also have semantic selection codes; and many have contextual (pragmatic) knowledge as well. As a natural side-effect of the lexicon construction, a relative contextual score is computed for each object that bears such a code; these scores provide a simple metric for comparing competing word senses for text-specific contextual coherence, and so directly address the problem of lexical ambiguity. Besides exploiting those special encodings supplied with the dictionary entries, the text of selected dictionary definitions are analyzed, through parsing and pattern matching, to further enrich the

Table 6.1. The gloss for a generic grammar rule: if given a language object of phrase-type-A, whose top-of-stack language object is of phrase-type-B, and confronting a new language object of grammatical category-C, then for each i from 1 to n, make a copy of the pair, change the new language object copy into phrase-type-$D_i$, and perform $operation_i$ (either Sub, Push, or Subto), at $location_i$ (within the New, Old, or Old-Sub language object).

---

(phrase-type-A phrase-type-B category-C)

$\Rightarrow$ (phrase-type-$D_1$ $operation_1$ $location_1$)

$\Rightarrow$ (phrase-type-$D_2$ $operation_2$ $location_2$)

$\Rightarrow \ldots$

$\Rightarrow$ (phrase-type-$D_n$ $operation_n$ $location_n$)

---

resulting representation (Slator, 1988a, 1988b; Slator & Wilks 1987, 1989).

## 6.3.2 Syntactic structures

The PREMO grammatical formalism is non-standard, being not a phrase-structured production system of rewrite rules but rather a phrase-triggered system of situation-action rules. The **Coalesce** procedure lies at the heart of the PREMO algorithm. This routine accepts a pair of language objects:

1. the current high priority language object as retrieved (and perhaps copied) from the priority queue, and

2. a new language object representing a single word sense of the next word in the sentence buffer of the current high priority language object.

Every language object that is retrieved from the priority queue is of type *phrase*, and every new language object created from the sentence buffer of the currently running parse is of type *word*. The rules of the phrase grammar have a triple of symbols on the left hand side representing: (1) the phrase type of the current high priority language object; (2) the phrase type of the language object on the top of the stack of the current high priority language object; and (3) the syntactic category of the newly created language object. There are one or more triples of symbols on the right hand side of each grammar rule specifying: (1) the phrase type of the new language object; (2) the action to be performed on the new language object; and, (3) the location where the action is to take place (Table 6.1).

The set of possible phrase types is limited, at present, to these five: Adjective phrase, Noun phrase, Prepositional phrase, Verb phrase, and Clause (a generic Other phrase type). Although several action triples (all of which get executed), could appear on the right hand side of a rule, in the current implementation no rule exceeds five action triples and most are three or less.

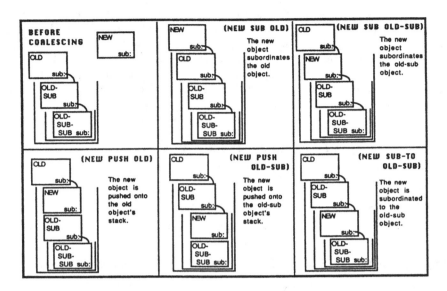

Figure 6.2. PREMO coalesce operations.

Further, the part of speech set in the lexicon derived from LDOCE has 10 members: adjective, adverb, conjunction, determiner, interjection, noun, predeterminer, preposition, pronoun, and verb. These three facts conspire to give a limiting factor to the total size of the grammar rule set.

This grammar is a phrase (or constituent) grammar and not a sentence grammar. The parser posits a sentence analysis only when its sentence buffer is consumed; until that point phrases are constructed and coalesced with each other as they are encountered, without regard to sentence level structure. The **Coalesce** decision is a syntactic one, with the resulting superordinate language object effectively assuming the status of the *head* of the entire existing structure. Either the new language object is inserted somewhere within the highest priority language object as a subordinate, or the highest priority object is subordinated to the new object (Figure 6.2). In the second case the new object is effectively elevated to the status of superordinate, and it is this coalesced language object that is inserted into the priority queue (with a suitably computed preference score).

At any given point in a parse, there will always be a language object construed as the *head* of the parse. Whatever language object has the superordinate status, of the pair being coalesced, will become the head as per the rules of the grammar (where status is generally a reflection of the usual syntactic dominance, with PP's dominating NP's, and VP's dominating everything).

## 6.4   Preference semantics

PREMO is a knowledge-based Preference Semantics parser (Wilks 1972, 1975a, 1975b, 1978), with access to the large, lexical semantic knowledge base created by the PREMO lexicon-provider subsystem. Preference Semantics is a theory of language in which the meaning for a text is represented by a complex semantic structure that is built up out of smaller semantic components; this compositionality is a fairly typical feature of semantic theories. The principal difference between Preference Semantics and other semantic theories is in the explicit and computational treatment of ambiguous, metaphorical, and non-standard language use.

The links between the components of the semantic structures are created on the basis of semantic preference and coherence. In text and discourse theory, coherence is generally taken to refer to the meaningfulness of text. Fass (1987) suggests that in NLP work such as Preference Semantics the notions of "satisfaction" and "violation" (of selection restrictions or preferences) and the notion of "semantic distance" (across structured type hierarchies) are different ways of characterizing the meaningfulness of text; they capture different coherence relations. The original systems of Preference Semantics (Wilks 1972, 1975a, 1975b, 1978), were principally based on the coherence relation of "inclusion" (semantic preferences and selection restrictions); the emphasis in PREMO is more on the coherence relation based on semantic distance, although the original notions of coherence also survive.

In Preference Semantics the semantic representation computed for a text is the one having the most semantically *dense* structure among the competing "readings." Semantic density is a property of structures that have preferences regarding their own constituents, and satisfied preferences create density. Density is compared in terms of the existence of preference-matching features, the lack of preference-breaking features, and the length of the inference chains needed to justify each sense selection and constituent attachment decision. The job of a Preference Semantics parser, then, is to consider the various competing interpretations, of which there may be many, and to choose among them by finding the one that is the most semantically dense, and hence preferred.

### 6.4.1   Computing preferences

When a new language object is first created it receives a preliminary preference score. An initial value is given between 1.0 and 2.0 that depends on the word's sense number (the lower the word sense, the higher, closer to 2.0, the score). Immediately thereafter, various attributes of the language object are evaluated and the initial score is adjusted. Adjustments to scores are either "minor," "standard," or "major" (in the current implementation these are 2%, 10%, and 50% respectively), and can be in either direction. In the current implementation preliminary scores are *decreased* in the case of an "interjection" part of speech, or for an LDOCE time-and-frequency code of "archaic" or "rare." Preliminary scores are *increased* if the language object is for a phrasal definition (such as "alternating current"), or is for a closed class word, or if it makes a grammatical prediction, or if it is a word with only a single sense definition. Finally, scores are strongly influenced, in either direction, by the position of the word with respect to a restructured pragmatic hierarchy computed for the text. For example, if the text has a scientific orientation then the scientific senses of words are given preferential increases and the other senses of those words are given decreased scores (such as the scientific senses, as opposed to the political and musical senses, of "measure").

After the **Coalesce** decision has been made, and one language object has been subordinated to the other, a new score is assigned to the result. These scores are computed according to the following criteria:

**Predictions and Requirements:** The lexical semantic frames have GRAMMAR slots that contain predictions and requirements: some general and some specific. Some general codes mark nouns as "a countable noun followed by the infinitive with *to*," and others mark verbs as "ditransitive and followed by a *that* clause" (such as *attempt* in "an attempt to climb the mountain," and *warn* in "He warned her (that) he would come.").

There are also specific predictions: particular senses of "sat" and "lay" predict an adverb or preposition, and particularly "down." And there are some absolute requirements: one sense of "earth" requires the article "the." These are collected and checked as language objects are being coalesced, and subordinate predictions are "synthesized" into their superordinate language object. Naturally, when a prediction is fulfilled the preference/priority is increased; and when a prediction is made but not fulfilled, scores are decreased. The degree to which scores are changed is still being experimented with, the currently implemented heuristic is to effect larger changes for more specific predictions.

**Subordination:** When language objects are coalesced the current implementation awards minor increases to pairings that follow a notion of natural order; for example, a Verb phrase subordinating a Noun phrase is a natural event to expect, but an Adjective phrase subordinating a Verb phrase less so. Both must be permitted, since it is possible to construct an example of either.

**Semantic Matching:** Content words in the text lexicon have semantic codes placing them in the LDOCE type hierarchy (types like **abstract, concrete**, or **animate**). Nouns and adjectives have a single code identifying their place in the hierarchy; verbs have 1, 2, or 3 codes identifying selection restrictions on their arguments. Semantic matching is done, and scores are adjusted for semantic coherence, whenever a pair of language objects are coalesced such that (1) an adjective (or a nominal) modifies a noun phrase head, or (2) a noun phrase is being attached as an argument to a verb, or (3) a noun phrase is being attached as the object of a preposition, or (4) a prepositional phrase is being attached as an argument to a verb. In the current implementation increases (but not decreases) are computed as a function of distance in the type hierarchy.

If a head prefers, say, an **animate** argument and is presented with an **abstract** word sense, the increase will be quite small as opposed to being presented with a competing **human** word sense.

### 6.4.2   Semantic structures

When the **Coalesce** decision is being made, PREMO looks to see if one language object is being subordinated to the other with a "push" operation. If so, a new constituent is being started and it is appropriate to affix a semantic label onto the subordinate object, since it is about to disappear under the new top-of-stack. These labels identify the functional or semantic relations that hold between a language object and its superordinate. The LDOCE hierarchies, in conjunction with the lexical semantic frame contained within each language object, and the "frame enriching" procedures developed for the lexicon are brought to bear at this point (Slator & Wilks, 1987, 1989); as well as the hand-coded definitions for prepositions that we must admit to creating since LDOCE, from our point of view, does not include useful case information in their preposition definitions.

Every sentence in a text is eventually represented by a single language object. These language objects are named for the word seen to be the head of the dominating phrase in the sentence, and are of type *phrase* (and presumably of phrase type VP, in the usual grammatical case). Each of the subordinated phrases in the sentence is stacked within this superordinate language object, along with a corresponding relation label.

## 6.5   PREMO example

Consider the following sentence:

(1) *The technician measures alternating current with an ammeter.*

First PREMO loads the lexicon specific to this text, which contains 26 frames for content words. These 26 frames are: *alternate* (3 adjective senses, 1 verb sense), *ammeter* (1 noun sense), *current* (3 adjectives, 4 nouns), *measure* (8 nouns, 3 verbs, 1 adjective), *technician* (1 noun sense), and the phrase "alternating current" (1 noun sense). LDOCE defines about 7,000 phrases. PREMO performs a contextual analysis by appeal to the pragmatic codes as organized into a specially restructured hierarchy. This results in the various Science and Engineering word senses receiving increased preference/priority scores while most other word senses receive decreased scores. This context setting mechanism is discussed at length in Slator (1988a, 1988b), Slator and Wilks (1987, 1989) and Fowler and Slator (1989).

Then, PREMO initializes the priority queue (PQ) with language objects for both the adverbial and definite determiner senses of *The* (the first word in the sentence), at which point the loop of the algorithm in Section 6.2.2, *Preference Machine Control* is entered. In the first iteration the determiner is instantiated as an Adjective phrase [AP:*The*], as is the adverb reading, according to the rules of the grammar. The analysis of Sentence (1) requires a total of 12 iterations through this loop. Notice that Sentence (1) is 336-way ambiguous if just the number of senses of polysemous content words are multiplied out (*alternate*=4, times *current*=7, times *measure*=12, equals 336), and that number grows to 1008 if the three cases of *with* are included.

**Iteration 2:**  The PQ contains three language objects for *The*, of which the definite determiner is slightly preferred. This object is popped from the queue, and the next word in its sentence buffer, *technician* is retrieved from the lexicon and instantiated as a language object. There is only a single sense of *technician* and only a single grammar rule action for the situation:

1. (AP nil noun) $\Rightarrow$ (NP sub old).

This means *technician* becomes an NP with the determiner *The* subordinated to it [NP:*technician*, *The*]. This act of coalescing results in a minor increase being assigned to [NP:*technician*, *The*], and it returns to the priority queue.

**Iteration 3:**  The language object [NP:*technician*, *The*] is popped from the queue and the 11 senses of the next word in its sentence buffer, *measure*, are instantiated; then 11 copies of [NP:*technician*, *The*] are created and paired with them. The two major grammar competitors during this iteration are:

2. (NP AP noun) $\Rightarrow$ (NP sub old)

3. (NP AP verb) $\Rightarrow$ (VP sub old)

that is, *measures* as a noun becoming the new head of [NP:*technician*, *The*], as opposed to *measures* as the head of a verb phrase taking [NP:*technician*, *The*] as an argument.

The criteria for comparing these readings (and the fact that PREMO prefers the second, VP, analysis), reduces to the fact that the noun *measures* carries an **abstract** semantic code which does not match well with the **human** semantic code carried by *technician*; while the verb *measures* carries a **human** selection restriction for its first argument, which matches exactly with the semantic code carried by *technician*.

**Iteration 4:**  The language object [VP:*measures*] with its subordinated language object [NP:*technician*, *The*] on the top of its stack, is popped from the queue and the 4 senses of *alternate*, along with the language object for the phrasal *alternating current*, are instantiated; 5 copies of [VP:*measures*] are then created and paired with them. Phrasal objects are preferred by PREMO, and nothing occurs to outweigh that preference. The question to be decided is which of these two readings should be preferred:

4. (VP NP noun) $\Rightarrow$ ((NP push old) <or> (NP sub old-sub))

that is, does *alternating current* represent the start of a new NP constituent, or is it the new head of the ongoing top-of-stack NP constituent (in this case [NP:*technician*, *The*]). The semantic code carried by *alternating current* is **abstract-physical-quality** which is a poor match with the **human** of [NP:*technician, The*] but a good match with the second argument code of [VP:*measure*], which is **abstract**. Therefore the new NP constituent reading receives the better preference/priority score and assumes the position at the head of the PQ. However, first a label must be attached to the NP constituent that is about to disappear from the top-of-stack as a result of the "push" operation. In this case, since the verb prefers and receives a **human** subject, this NP is labeled "Agentive."

**Iterations 5-11:** The high priority language object on the front of the PQ is [VP:*measures*] which now subordinates both [NP:*technician, The*] and [NP:*alternating current*]. The continuation of the sentence buffer in [VP:*measures*] is now *with an ammeter*. The next several iterations are concerned with pushing a PP onto the subordinate stack of [VP:*measures*] and then subordinating [NP:*ammeter, an*] as the object of the PP. The current implementation recognizes 3 senses of the preposition *with* representing the ACCOMPANIMENT, POSSESSION, and INSTRUMENT cases. Each of these is coalesced with [NP:*ammeter, an*] and pushed onto the subordinate stack of [VP:*measures*]. The INSTRUMENT reading is preferred on the basis of semantic matching between the selection restriction code on the object of the preposition, which is **concrete**, and the semantic code for *ammeter*, which is **movable-solid**.

**Iteration 12:** The final iteration retrieves the language object for the [VP:*measures*] from the front of the PQ and finds the sentence buffer is empty. It is at this point that the case label marking the top-of-stack element (which is [PP:*with,*[NP:*ammeter, an*]]), as the INSTRUMENT case is actually affixed. This language object is then saved as the interpretation of Sentence (1), the queue is flushed and PREMO reads whatever sentence text follows, or if none follows, PREMO ends.

## 6.5.1   Towards solving a hard old problem

Two contrasting methods of word sense selection have been described here. The earlier method was first explored by the Cambridge Language Research Unit, beginning in the mid-1950s. This method performed a global analysis, (Masterman, 1957, as described in Wilks, 1972), that relied on a thesaural resource. This method was good at choosing word senses coherent with the other words in the text, by using a system of looking to the sets of words found under common thesaural heads, and performing set intersections. The problem is that the less "coherent" word senses are missed and so, for example, in a physics text only the scientific sense of *mass* will chosen and, therefore, the word *mass* in the phrase *mass of data* will come out wrong in that text.

The other method is Preference Semantics that performs a local analysis that relies on semantic type markers. This method is good at choosing word senses that best fit with other words in a sentence, by using a system of matching and comparing among the various primitive elements that make up the meanings of words. The problem is that this can be fooled into preferring

word senses that only seem to be best. The standard example, attributed to
Phil Hayes, is the following.

(2) *A hunter licked his gun all over and the stock tasted good.*

In this example, the challenge is to choose the correct sense of *stock*. The
problem is that the local evidence supplied by the verb *to taste* points towards
the "stock as soup" reading, which is wrong. Granted, this is something of
a pathological example, but it is famous, and it captures the flavor of the
objection.

PREMO attempts to tackle these contrasting analysis problems by bringing
together both global and local information. To demonstrate this, consider the
analysis of the following two short texts. The first is familiar from the example
in Section 6.5, above.

(3) *Current can be measured.*

   The technician measures alternating current with an ammeter.

The following text is intended to parallel the first one.

(4) *Current can be measured.*

   The geographer measures river basin flow near a lake.

The point at issue is choosing the correct sense of *current* in each case.
In Text (3) it is the **engineering/electrical** sense that should be chosen. In
Text (4), however, it is the **geology-and-geography** sense of *current* that is
correct. In the absence of other evidence, the **geology-and-geography** sense
is the one most systems would choose, since this is the more common usage
of the word in the language (and the lowest numbered word sense in LDOCE,
which reflects this notion of default preference). And since most systems have
no notion of global text coherence, most would get the wrong sense of *current*
in Text (3) at first reading. It is conceivable that the sense selection for *current*
could be corrected after further text has been processed, but few if any systems
attempt this, and it is far from obvious how this should be done in general.
PREMO gets both of these texts right, by choosing the correct sense of *current*
in each case, and making all of the other word sense and attachment decisions
(see Table 6.2).

In Table 6.2, each line element represents a condensation of a language
object. Language objects are complex items which this display merely summarizes. The form of these displays is as follows:

   (<name>  <phrase-type>  <score>  <part-of-speech>  <sense-
   number>  <stack-labels>)

and the lower language objects are on stacks, as indicated by their indentations.
And so, the first language object reads as this: the third sense of the verb
*measure* (the linking verb sense), has two elements on its subordinate stack,
one marked as a verb inflection (the language object for *be*, which itself has

a language object on its internal stack marking verb inflection, the language object for *can*), and the other stack element (note, the second sense of *current*), marked as the subject of the measuring. The third language object in Table 6.2 has the identical interpretation, except that the subject of the measuring is the first sense of *current* rather than the second.

The other two language objects displayed both show the first sense of *measure* each with three language objects on the subordinate stack. In each case these subordinate language object constituents represent the AGENT (*technician* and *geographer*), and the OBJECT (*alternating current* and *river basin flow*), of the measuring action. Text (3) also has a prepositional phrase attached in the INSTRUMENT case while Text (4) has a prepositional phrase attached in the LOCATIVE case.

In spite of this success, the problem of mediating the tension between global and local sources of information is still not solved. PREMO assumes text coherence and so, while Preference Semantics provides a naturally local sort of analysis procedure, these local effects can be overcome by appeal to global context. However, it is still possible to find examples, such as Text (2) above, that do not have any context (a common situation in the computational linguistics literature, where space constraints and custom preclude long examples). And in the absence of this global information, PREMO will not perform any better than any other system of analysis. That is, if Text (2) were embedded in a longer exposition about hunters and guns, then the probability is high that the correct sense of *stock* would be chosen. If however, Text (2) were embedded in an exposition about food and cooking, PREMO would almost certainly get this wrong. And in the absence of context PREMO will choose the "soup stock" reading because the notion of gun stocks having a taste is not one that finds much support in a system of semantic analysis.

## 6.6   Comparison to other work

The original Preference Semantics implementations (Wilks 1972, 1975a, 1975b, 1978), operated over a hand-coded lexicon of semantic formulae. Input strings were segmented into phrases beforehand, and coherence was essentially a matter of counting "semantic ties" inferred by pattern matching between formulae. PREMO operates over a machine-readable lexicon that is at once much broader and shallower than the original. To make up for this, preference scoring in PREMO is much more finely grained and takes more into account (grammatical predictions, pragmatic context, etc.). If anything, PREMO is grammatically weaker than the original work, while being more robust in the sense that syntactic anomalies and ill-formed input are processed the same as anything else.

A group at Martin Marietta (Johnson, Kim, Sekine, & White, 1988; White 1988), built a language understander based on Preference Semantics, but modified by their own interpretation of Wilks, Huang, and Fass (1985). Their NLI system is frame-based and much of the system's knowledge resides in the lexicon, which is constructed by hand. The parsing process is separated into three

Table 6.2. PREMO analyses for Texts (3) and (4).

---

PREMO analysis for Text (3) *Current can be measured.*

((*measured* VP 4.855569S0 "v" "0300" (INFL SUBJECT))
 (((*be* VP 4.197S0 "v" "0008" (INFL))
   ((*can* VP 3.174081S0 "v" "0100" nil)))
  (*Current* NP 2.985294S0 "n" "0200" nil)))

PREMO analysis for *The technician measures alternating current with an ammeter.*

((*measures* VP 4.68685S0 "v" "0100"
   (INSTRUMENT OBJECT1 AGENTIVE))
 (((*with* PP 3.726117S0 "prep" "0000" (OBJECT1))
    (((*ammeter* NP 2.814706S0 "n" "0000" (DET))
      ((*an* AP 1.815S0 "indef" "0000" nil)))))
  (*alternating*current* NP 3.838235S0 "n" "0000" nil)
  ((*technician* NP 0.8368717S0 "n" "0000" (DET))
   ((*The* AP 0.9982499S0 "definite" "0100" nil)))))

PREMO analysis for Text (4) *Current can be measured.*

((*measured* VP 4.757666S0 "v" "0300" (INFL SUBJECT))
 (((*be* VP 4.077573S0 "v" "0008" (INFL))
   ((*can* VP 3.028026S0 "v" "0100" nil)))
  (*Current* NP 2.763158S0 "n" "0100" nil)))

PREMO analysis for *The geographer measures river basin flow near a lake.*

((*measures* VP 4.354593S0 "v" "0100"
   (LOCATIVE OBJECT1 AGENTIVE))
 (((*near* PP 2.406232S0 "prep" "0000" (OBJECT1))
    (((*lake* NP 2.719298S0 "n" "0000" (DET))
      ((*a* AP 0.9075S0 "indefinite" "0100" nil)))))
  ((*flow* NP 1.433986S0 "n" "0500" (KIND-OF))
   (((*river*basin* NP 2.178159S0 "n" "0000" (DET))
     ((*the* AP 0.9982499S0 "definite" "0100" nil)))))
  ((*geographer* NP 1.693873S0 "n" "0000" (DET))
   ((*The* AP 0.9982499S0 "definite" "0100" nil)))))

---

autonomous modules: BuildRep (a constituent parser), Validate (a sort of constituent filter), and Unify (which incrementally builds a semantic structure from validated constituents). The principle differences between their system and PREMO lies in their criteria for abandoning non-productive paths (their domain constraints allow them to prune on the basis of semantic implausibility), and in their lack of a high level control structure (it is possible in their system for every parse to be abandoned and nothing returned).

Preference Semantics has also been used for parsing by Boguraev (1979), Carter (1984, 1987), and Huang (1984, 1988). However, that work uses a conventional parsing strategy in which syntax drives the parsing process depth-first and Preference Semantics is used within a semantics component that provides semantic verification of syntactic constituents. PREMO has a more flexible, more breadth-first parsing strategy in which syntax, semantics, and pragmatics interact more freely. The Meta5 semantic analyzer of Fass (1986, 1987, 1988), based on the system of Collative Semantics, which extends Preference Semantics, operates over a rich hand-coded lexicon comprised of a network of "sense frames." The principal goal of this system is to identify and resolve metaphorical and metonymous relations and, with its rich semantic knowledge base, Meta5 is able to produce deep semantic analyses which are quite impressive.

## 6.7   Concluding remarks

PREMO employs a uniform representation at the word, phrase, and sentence levels. Further, at every step in the process there is a dominating language object visible; that is, there is always a "well-formed partial parse" extant. This gives an appealing processing model (of a language understander that stands ready to accept the next word, whatever it may be), and a real-time flavor, where the next word is understood in the context of existing structure. PREMO intentionally exploits everything that LDOCE offers, particularly in the area of grammatical predictions, and also in terms of the TYPE hierarchy as given, and the PRAGMATIC hierarchy as restructured, as well as extracting semantic information from the text of definitions.

One of the PREMO design principles is "always return something" and that policy is guaranteed by keeping every possibility open, if unexplored. (This is the PREMO approximation to back-tracking.) Another design principle is to cut every conceivable corner by making "smart" preference evaluations. The potential remains however, for worst case performance, where the preference/priority scores work out so that every newly coalesced pair immediately is placed at the bottom of the priority queue. If this happens the algorithm reduces to a brute search of the entire problem space.

By exploiting the operating system metaphor for control, PREMO inherits some very attractive features. First, PREMO avoids combinatorial explosion by ordering the potential parse paths and only pursuing the one that seems the best. This is antithetical to the operating system principle of "fairness," a point where the metaphor is intentionally abandoned in favor of a scheme that has some faint traces of intuitive plausibility. The competition between parses, based as it is on the tension between the various preference/priority criteria is vaguely reminiscent of a "spreading activation" system where the various interpretations "fight it out" for prominence. The PREMO architecture is, of course, utterly different in implementation detail, and it is not at all obvious how it could be equivalently converted, or that this metaphor is even a fruitful one. Second, the operating system metaphor is an extensible one; that is, it is possible to conceive of PREMO actually being implemented on a dedicated machine. Further, since the multiplication factor at each cycle through the algorithm is small (in the 40-60 range for the near-worst case of 10-12 word senses times 4-5 applicable grammar rules), and since each of these pairings is independent, it is easy to imagine PREMO implemented on a parallel processor (like a Hypercube). Each of the pairs would be distributed out to the (cube) processing elements where the coalescing and preference/priority scoring would be done in parallel.

# Acknowledgments

This work was supported in part by ASEND/EPSCoR Grant 4248-3341, administered by the North Dakota Board of Higher Education, and by the New Mexico State University Computing Research Laboratory - grateful acknowledgement is accorded to the members of the CRL Natural Language Group for their continuing interest and support.

# References

Boguraev, B. K. (1979). *Automatic resolution of linguistic ambiguities* (Tech. Rep. No. 11). Cambridge, UK: University of Cambridge Computer Laboratory.

Carter, D. M. (1984). An approach to general machine translation based on preference semantics and local focussing. *Proceedings of the 6th European Conference on AI (ECAI-84)* (pp. 231–238). Pisa, Italy.

Carter, D. M. (1987). *Interpreting anaphors in natural language texts.* Chichester, UK: Ellis Horwood.

Fass, D. C. (1986). *Collative semantics: An approach to coherence* (Lab. Memo. No. MCCS-86-56). Las Cruces, NM: New Mexico State University, Computing Research Laboratory.

Fass, D. C. (1987). Semantic relations, metonymy, and lexical ambiguity resolution : A coherence-based account. *Proceedings of the 9th Annual Cognitive Science Society Conference* (pp. 575–586). Seattle, WA: Lawrence Erlbaum.

Fass, D. C. (1988). An account of coherence, semantic relations, metonymy, and lexical ambiguity resolution. In S. L. Small, G. W. Cottrell, & M. K. Tanenhaus (Eds.), *Lexical Ambiguity Resolution in the Comprehension of Human Language.* San Mateo, CA: Morgan Kaufmann.

Fowler, R. H., & Slator, B. M. (1989). Information retrieval and natural language analysis. *Proceedings of the 4th Annual Rocky Mountain Conference on Artificial Intelligence (RMCAI-89)* (pp. 129–136). Denver, CO.

Huang, X. (1984). A computational treatment of gapping, right node raising and reduced conjunction. *Proceedings of the 10th International Conference on Computational Linguistics (COLING-84)* (pp. 243–246). Stanford, CA.

Huang, X. (1988). *XTRA: The design and implementation of a fully automatic machine translation system* (Lab. Memo. No. MCCS-88-121). Las Cruces, NM: New Mexico State University, Computing Research Laboratory.

Johnson, H., Kim, G., Sekine, Y., & White, J. S. (1988). Application of natural language interface to a machine translation problem. *Proceedings of the Second International Conference on Theoretical and Methodological Issues in Machine Translation.* Pittsburgh, PA.

Masterman, M. (1957). The thesaurus in syntax and semantics. *Mechanical Translation, 4,* 1–2.

Procter, P., *et al.* (1978). *Longman dictionary of contemporary English (LDOCE).* Harlow, Essex, UK: Longman Group Limited.

Slator, B. M. (1988a). Constructing contextually organized lexical semantic knowledge-bases. *Proceedings of the Third Annual Rocky Mountain Conference on Artificial Intelligence* (pp. 142–148). Denver, CO.

Slator, B. M. (1988b). *Lexical semantics and a preference semantics analysis* (Lab. Memo. No. MCCS-88-143). Unpublished doctoral dissertation. Las Cruces, NM: New Mexico State University, Computing Research Laboratory.

Slator, B. M. (1988c). PREMO: The PREference Machine Organization. *Proceedings of the Third Annual Rocky Mountain Conference on Artificial Intelligence* (pp. 258–265). Denver, CO.

Slator, B. M., & Wilks, Y. A. (1987). Towards semantic structures from dictionary entries. *Proceedings of the Second Annual Rocky Mountain Conference on Artificial Intelligence* (pp. 85–96). Boulder, CO.

Slator, B. M., & Wilks, Y. A. (Forthcoming-1990). Towards semantic structures from dictionary entries. In A. Kunz & U. Schmitz (Eds.), *Linguistic Approaches to Artificial Intelligence.* Frankfurt: Peter Lang Publishing House. (Revision of RMCAI-87.)

White, J. S. (1988). Advantages of modularity in natural language interfaces. *Proceedings of the Third Annual Rocky Mountain Conference on Artificial Intelligence* (pp. 248–257). Denver, CO.

Wilks, Y. A. (1972). *Grammar, meaning, and the machine analysis of language.* London: Routledge and Kegan Paul.

Wilks, Y. A. (1975a). An intelligent analyzer and understander of English. *Communications of the ACM, 18,* 264–274. Reprinted in (1986) B. J. Grosz, K. Sparck-Jones, & B. L. Webber (Eds.), *Readings in natural language processing.* San Mateo, CA: Morgan Kaufmann.

Wilks, Y. A. (1975b). A preferential pattern-seeking semantics for natural language inference. *Artificial Intelligence, 6,* 53–74.

Wilks, Y. A. (1978). Making preferences more active. *Artificial Intelligence*, *11*, 75–97.

Wilks, Y. A., Fass, D. C., Guo, C., Mcdonald, J. E., Plate, T., & Slator, B. M. (1987). A tractable machine dictionary as a resource for computational semantics. *Proceedings of the Workshop on Natural Language Technology Planning*. Blue Mountain Lake, NY. Reprinted in (1990) B. K. Boguraev & T. Briscoe (Eds.), *Computational lexicography for natural language processing*. Harlow, Essex, UK: Longman.

Wilks, Y. A., Fass, D. C., Guo, C., Mcdonald, J. E., Plate, T., & Slator, B. M. (1988). Machine tractable dictionaries as tools and resources for natural language processing. *Proceedings of the 12th International Conference on Computational Linguistics (COLING-88)* (pp. 750–755). Budapest, Hungary.

Wilks, Y. A., Fass, D. C., Guo, C., Mcdonald, J. E., Plate, T., & Slator, B. M. (Forthcoming-1990). Providing machine tractable dictionary tools. In J. Pustejovsky (Ed.), *Theoretical and computational issues in lexical semantics*. Dordrecht, Holland: Kluwer.

Wilks, Y. A., Huang, X., & Fass, D. C. (1985). Syntax, preference, and right attachment. *Proceedings of Ninth International Joint Conference on Artificial Intelligence* (pp. 779–784). Los Angeles, CA: Morgan Kaufmann.

# 7. Parsing, Word Associations, and Typical Predicate-Argument Relations

## Kenneth Church, William Gale
*Bell Laboratories*

## Patrick Hanks
*Oxford University Press*

## Donald Hindle
*Bell Laboratories*

## Abstract

There are a number of collocational constraints in natural languages that ought to play a more important role in natural language parsers. Thus, for example, it is hard for most parsers to take advantage of the fact that *wine* is typically *drunk, produced,* and *sold,* but (probably) not *pruned.* So too, it is hard for a parser to know which verbs go with which prepositions (e.g., *set up*) and which nouns fit together to form compound noun phrases (e.g., *computer programmer*). This chapter will attempt to show that many of these types of concerns can be addressed with syntactic methods (symbol pushing), and need not require explicit semantic interpretation. We have found that it is possible to identify many of these interesting co-occurrence relations by computing simple summary statistics over millions of words of text. This chapter will summarize a number of experiments carried out by various subsets of the authors over the last few years. The term *collocation* will be used quite broadly to include constraints on SVO (subject verb object) triples, phrasal verbs, compound noun phrases, and psycholinguistic notions of word association (e.g., *doctor/nurse*).

## 7.1 Mutual information

Church and Hanks (1989) discussed the use of the mutual information statistic in order to identify a variety of interesting linguistic phenomena, ranging from semantic relations of the doctor/nurse type (content word/content word) to lexico-syntactic co-occurrence constraints between verbs and prepositions (content word/function word). (Jelinek (1985) has also found mutual information to be an extremely useful statistic for modeling language constraints for applications in speech recognition.) Mutual information, $I(x; y)$, compares

Table 7.1. Associations with "Doctor" in the 1987 AP Corpus (N = 15 million; w = 6).

| INTERESTING ASSOCIATIONS | | | | | |
|---|---|---|---|---|---|
| I(x; y) | F(x, y) | F(x) | x | F(y) | y |
| 8.0 | 2.4 | 111 | honorary | 621 | doctor |
| 8.0 | 1.6 | 1105 | doctors | 44 | dentists |
| 8.4 | 6.0 | 1105 | doctors | 241 | nurses |
| 7.1 | 1.6 | 1105 | doctors | 154 | treating |
| 6.7 | 1.2 | 275 | examined | 621 | doctor |
| 6.6 | 1.2 | 1105 | doctors | 317 | treat |
| 6.4 | 5.0 | 621 | doctor | 1407 | bills |
| 6.4 | 1.2 | 621 | doctor | 350 | visits |
| 6.3 | 3.8 | 1105 | doctors | 676 | hospitals |
| 6.1 | 1.2 | 241 | nurses | 1105 | doctors |
| LESS INTERESTING ASSOCIATIONS | | | | | |
| -1.3 | 1.2 | 621 | doctor | 73785 | with |
| -1.4 | 8.2 | 284690 | a | 1105 | doctors |
| -1.4 | 2.4 | 84716 | is | 1105 | doctors |

the probability of observing word $x$ and word $y$ *together* (the joint probability) with the probabilities of observing $x$ and $y$ *independently* (chance).

$$I(x; y) = \log_2 \frac{P(x, y)}{P(x)P(y)}$$

If there is a genuine association between $x$ and $y$, then the joint probability $P(x, y)$ will be much larger than chance $P(x)P(y)$, and consequently $I(x; y) \gg 0$, as illustrated in Table 7.1. If there is no interesting relationship between $x$ and $y$, then $P(x, y) \approx P(x)P(y)$, and thus, $I(x; y) \approx 0$. If $x$ and $y$ are in complementary distribution, then $P(x, y)$ will be much less than $P(x)P(y)$, forcing $I(x; y) \ll 0$. Word probabilities, $P(x)$ and $P(y)$, are estimated by counting the number of observations of $x$ and $y$ in a corpus, $f(x)$ and $f(y)$, and normalizing by $N$, the size of the corpus. Joint probabilities, $P(x, y)$, are estimated by counting the number of times that $x$ is followed by $y$ in a window of $w$ words, $f_w(x, y)$, and normalizing by $N(w - 1)$.[1]

## 7.2  Phrasal verbs

Church and Hanks (1989) also used the mutual information statistic in order to identify phrasal verbs, following up a remark by Sinclair:

---

[1]The window size parameter allows us to look at different scales. Smaller window sizes will identify fixed expressions (idioms), noun phrases, and other relations that hold over short ranges; larger window sizes will highlight semantic concepts and other relationships that hold over larger scales.

"How common are the phrasal verbs with *set*? *Set* is particularly rich in making combinations with words like *about, in, up, out, on, off*, and these words are themselves very common. How likely is *set off* to occur? Both are frequent words; [*set* occurs approximately 250 times in a million words and] *off* occurs approximately 556 times in a million words.... [T]he question we are asking can be roughly rephrased as follows: how likely is *off* to occur immediately after *set*? .... This is $0.00025 \times 0.00055$ $[P(x)P(y)]$, which gives us the tiny figure of $0.0000001375$ .... The assumption behind this calculation is that the words are distributed at random in a text [at chance, in our terminology]. It is obvious to a linguist that this is not so, and a rough measure of how much *set* and *off* attract each other is to compare the probability with what actually happens... *Set off* occurs nearly 70 times in the 7.3 million word corpus $[P(x,y) = 70/(7.3 \times 10^6) \gg P(x)P(y)]$. That is enough to show its main patterning and it suggests that in currently-held corpora there will be found sufficient evidence for the description of a substantial collection of phrases... (Sinclair 1987, pp. 151–152).

It happens that *set ... off* was found 177 times in the 1987 AP Corpus of approximately 15 million words, about the same number of occurrences per million as Sinclair found in his (mainly British) corpus. Quantitatively, $I(set; off) = 3.7$, indicating that the probability of *set ... off* is $2^{3.7} \approx 13$ times greater than chance. This association is relatively strong; the other particles that Sinclair mentions have scores of: *about* (-0.9), *in* (0.6), *up* (4.6), *out* (2.2), *on* (1.0) in the 1987 AP Corpus of 15 million words.

## 7.3  Preprocessing the corpus with a part of speech tagger

Phrasal verbs involving the preposition *to* raise an interesting problem because of the possible confusion with the infinitive marker *to*. We have found that if we first tag every word in the corpus with a part of speech using a method such as Church (1988) or DeRose (1988), and then measure associations between tagged words, we can identify interesting contrasts between verbs associated with a following preposition *to/in* and verbs associated with a following infinitive marker *to/to*. (Part of speech notation is borrowed from Francis and Kucera (1982); in = preposition; to = infinitive marker; vb = bare verb; vbg = verb + ing; vbd = verb + ed; vbz = verb + s; vbn = verb + en.) The score identifies quite a number of verbs associated in an interesting way with *to*; restricting our attention to pairs with a score of 3.0 or more, there are 768 verbs associated with the preposition *to/in* and 551 verbs with the infinitive marker *to/to*. The ten verbs found to be most associated before *to/in* are:

- *to/in*: alluding/vbg, adhere/vb, amounted/vbn, relating/vbg, amounting/vbg, revert/vb, reverted/vbn, resorting/vbg, relegated/vbn

Table 7.2. Objects of verb *drink* occurring at least two times in a sample of six million words of text.

| Object | Frequency | Mutual Information |
|---|---|---|
| <quantity> beer | 2 | 12.34 |
| tea | 4 | 11.75 |
| Pepsi | 2 | 11.75 |
| champagne | 4 | 11.75 |
| liquid | 2 | 10.53 |
| beer | 5 | 10.20 |
| wine | 2 | 9.34 |
| water | 7 | 7.65 |
| anything | 3 | 5.15 |
| much | 3 | 2.54 |
| it | 3 | 1.25 |
| <quantity> | 2 | 1.22 |

- *to/to*: obligated/vbn, trying/vbg, compelled/vbn, enables/vbz, supposed/vbn, intends/vbz, vowing/vbg, tried/vbd, enabling/vbg, tends/vbz, tend/vb, intend/vb, tries/vbz

Thus, we see there is considerable leverage to be gained by preprocessing the corpus and manipulating the inventory of tokens.

## 7.4 Preprocessing with a syntactic parser

Hindle has found it useful to preprocess the input with the Fidditch parser (Hindle, 1983) in order to ask about the typical arguments of verbs. Thus, for any of verb in the sample, we can ask what nouns it takes as subjects and objects. Table 7.2 shows the objects of the verb *drink* that appeared at least two times in a sample of six million words of AP text, in effect giving the answer to the question "what can you drink?" Calculating the co-occurrence weight for *drink*, shown in the third column, gives us a reasonable ranking of terms, with *it* near the bottom. This list of drinkable things is intuitively quite good.

A standard alternative approach to the classification of entities is in terms of a hierarchy of types. The biological taxonomy is the canonical example: a penguin is a bird is a vertebrate and so on. Such "is-a" hierarchies have found a prominent place in natural language processing and knowledge representation because they allow generalized representation of semantic features and of rules. There is a wide range of problems and issues in using "is-a" hierarchies in natural language processing, but two especially recommend that we investigate alternative classification schemes like the one reported here. First, "is-a" hierarchies are large and complicated and expensive to acquire by hand. Attempts to automatically derive these hierarchies for words from

Table 7.3. Significant bigrams ending with *potatoes.*

| T | X | Y |
|-----|--------|----------|
| 4.6 | sweet | potatoes |
| 4.3 | mashed | potatoes |
| 4.3 | , | potatoes |
| 4.0 | and | potatoes |
| 3.8 | couch | potatoes |
| 3.3 | of | potatoes |
| 3.3 | frozen | potatoes |
| 2.8 | fresh | potatoes |
| 2.8 | small | potatoes |
| 2.1 | baked | potatoes |

existing dictionaries have been only partially successful (Chodorow, Byrd, & Heidorn, 1985). Yet without a comprehensive hierarchy, it is difficult to use such classifications in the processing of unrestricted text. Secondly, for many purposes, even knowing the subclass-superclass relations is insufficient; it is difficult to predict which properties are inherited from a superclass and which aren't, and what properties are relevant in a particular linguistic usage. So for example, as noted above, despite the fact that both potatoes and peanuts are edible foods that grow underground, we typically *bake potatoes*, but *roast peanuts*. A distribution-based classification, if successful, promises to do better at least on these two problems.

# 7.5 Significance levels

If the frequency counts are very small, the mutual information statistic becomes unstable. This is the reason for not reporting objects that appeared only once with the verb *drink.* Although these objects have very large mutual information scores, there is also a very large chance that they resulted from some quirk in the corpus, or a bug in the parser. For some purposes, it is desirable to measure confidence rather than likelihood. Gale and Church have investigated the use of a t-score instead of the mutual information score, as a way of identifying "significant" bigrams.

Table 7.3 shows a few significant bigrams ending with *potatoes*, computed from 44 million words of AP news wire from 2/12/88 until 12/31/88. The numbers in the first column indicate the confidence in standard deviations that the word sequence is interesting, and cannot be attributed to chance. These numbers were computed by the following formula:

$$t = \frac{E(P(xy)) - E(P(x)P(y))}{\sqrt{\sigma^2(P(xy)) + \sigma^2(P(x)P(y))}}$$

where $E(P(xy))$ and $\sigma^2(P(xy))$ are the mean and variance of the probability of seeing word $x$ followed by word $y$. The means and variances are

Table 7.4. Words that take sentential complements.

| T | X | Y |
|------|-----------|------|
| 74.0 | said | that |
| 50.9 | noted | that |
| 43.3 | fact | that |
| 41.9 | believe | that |
| 40.7 | found | that |
| 40.1 | is | that |
| 40.0 | reported | that |
| 39.5 | adding | that |
| 38.6 | Tuesday | that |
| 38.4 | Wednesday | that |

computed by the Good-Turing method (Good, 1953).

Let $r$ be the number of times that the bigram $xy$ was found in a corpus of $N$ words, and let $N_r$ be the frequencies of frequences (the number of bigrams with count $r$). Then $r*$, the estimated expected value of $r$ in similar corpus of the same size, is $r* = N \times E(P(xy)) = (r+1)\frac{N_{r+1}}{N_r}$ and the variance of $r$ is $\sigma^2(r) = N^2\sigma^2(P(xy)) = r*(1 + (r+1)* -r*)$.

## 7.6   Just a powerful tool

Although it is clear that the statistics discussed above can be extremely powerful aids to a lexicographer, they should not be overrated. We do not aim to replace lexicographers with self-organizing statistics; unlike (Jelinek, 1985), we merely hope to provide a set of tools that could greatly improve their productivity. Suppose, for example, that a lexicographer wanted to find a set of words that take sentential complements. Then it might be helpful to start with a table of t-scores such as in Table 7.4.

It might be much quicker for a lexicographer to edit down this list than to construct the list from intuition alone. It doesn't take very much time to decide that *Tuesday* and *Wednesday* are less interesting than the others. Of course, it might be possible to automate some of these decisions by appropriately preprocessing the corpus with a part of speech tagger or a parser, but it will probably always be necessary to exercise some editorial judgment.

## 7.7   Practical applications

The proposed statistical description has a large number of potentially important applications, including:

- enhancing the productivity of lexicographers in identifying normal and conventional usage,

Table 7.5. Probabilities for eight bigrams where "farm" and "form" are equally likely and the concept is either "federal __ credit" or "some __ of."

| X | Y | Observations Per Million Words |
|---|---|:---:|
| federal | farm | 0.500 |
| federal | form | 0.039 |
| farm | credit | 0.130 |
| form | credit | 0.026 |
| some | form | 4.100 |
| some | farm | 0.630 |
| form | of | 34.000 |
| farm | of | 0.810 |

- enhancing the productivity of computational linguists in compiling lexicons of lexico-syntactic facts,

- providing disambiguation cues for parsing highly ambiguous syntactic structures such as noun compounds, conjunctions, and prepositional phrases,

- retrieving texts from large databases (e.g., newspapers, patents), and

- constraining the language model both for speech recognition and optical character recognition (OCR).

Consider the optical character recognizer (OCR) application. Suppose that we have an OCR device such as (Kahan, Pavlidis, & Baird, 1987), and it has assigned about equal probability to having recognized "farm" and "form," where the context is either: (1) "federal __ credit" or (2) "some __ of." We doubt that the reader has any trouble specifying which alternative is more likely. By using the probabilities in Table 7.5 for the eight bigrams in this sequence, a computer program can rely on an estimated likelihood to make the same distinction.

The probability of the tri-grams can be approximated by multiplying the probabilities of the two constituent bigrams. Thus, the probability of *federal farm credit* can be approximated as $(0.5 \times 10^{-6}) \times (0.13 \times 10^{-6}) = 0.065 \times 10^{-12}$. Similarly, the probability for *federal form credit* can be approximated as $(0.039 \times 10^{-6}) \times (0.026 \times 10^{-6}) = 0.0010 \times 10^{-12}$. The ratio of these likelihoods shows that "farm" is $(0.065 \times 10^{-12})/(0.0010 \times 10^{-12}) = 65$ times more likely than "form" in this context. In the other context, "some __ of," it turns out that "form" is 273 times more likely than "farm." This example shows how likelihood ratios can be used in an optical character recognition system to disambiguate among optically confusing words. Note that alternative disambiguation methods based on syntactic constraints such as part of speech are unlikely to help in this case since both "form" and "farm" are commonly used as nouns. In contrast, the tri-gram model (Jelinek, 1985) will have no difficulty with this example. Although the tri-gram model may be obviously flawed (Chomsky, 1957, p. 17), it does have its strengths.

## 7.8   Alternatives to collocation for recognition applications

There have been quite a number of attempts to use syntactic methods in speech recognition, beginning with the ARPA speech project and continuing on to the present. It might be noted, however, that there has not been very much success, perhaps because syntax alone is not a strong enough constraint on language use (performance). We believe that collocational constraints should play an important role in recognition applications, and attempts to ignore collocational constraints and use purely syntactic methods will probably run into difficulties.

Syntactic constraints, by themselves, though are probably not very important. Any psycholinguist knows that the influence of syntax on lexical retrieval is so subtle that you have to control very carefully for all the factors that really matter (e.g., word frequency, word association norms, etc.). On the other hand, collocational factors (word associations) dominate syntactic ones so much that you can easily measure the influence of word frequency and word association norms on lexical retrieval without careful controls for syntax.

There are many ways to demonstrate the relative lack of constraint imposed by syntax. Recall the old television game show, "The Match Game," where a team of players was given a sentence with a missing word, e.g., "Byzantine icons could murder the divine BLANK," and asked to fill in the blank the same way that the studio audience did. The game was 'interesting' because there are enough constraints in natural language so that there is a reasonably large probability of a match. Suppose, however, that we make our speech recognition device play the match game with a handicap; instead of giving the speech recognition device the word string, "Byzantine icons could murder the divine BLANK," we give the speech recognition device just the syntactic parse tree, [S [NP nn nns] [VP [AUX md ] v [NP at jj BLANK ]]], and ask it to guess the missing word. This is effectively what we are doing by limiting the language model to syntactic considerations alone. Of course, with this the handicap, the match game isn't much of a game; the recognition device doesn't have a fair chance to guess the missing word.

We believe that syntax will ultimately be a very important source of constraint, but in a more indirect way. As we have been suggesting, the real constraints will come from word frequencies and collocational constraints, but these questions will probably need to be broken out by syntactic context. How likely is it for this noun to conjoin with that noun? Is this noun a typical subject of that verb? And so on. In this way, syntax plays a crucial role in providing the relevant representation for expressing these very important constraints, but crucially, it does not provide very much useful constraint (in the information theoretic sense) all by itself.[2]

---

[2]Much of the work on language modeling for speech recognition has tended to concentrate

## 7.9   Concluding remarks

In any natural language there are restrictions on what words can appear together in the same construction, and in particular, on what can be arguments of what predicates. It is common practice in linguistics to classify words not only on the basis of their meanings but also on the basis of their co-occurrence with other words. Running through the whole Firthian tradition, for example, is the theme that "You shall know a word by the company it keeps" (Firth, 1957).

> "On the one hand, *bank* co-occurs with words and expressions such as *money, notes, loan, account, investment, clerk, official, manager, robbery, vaults, working in a, its actions, First National, of England,* and so forth. On the other hand, we find *bank* co-occurring with *river, swim, boat, east* (and of course *West* and *South*, which have acquired special meanings of their own), *on top of the,* and *of the Rhine.*" (Hanks 1987, p. 127)

Harris (1968) makes this "distributional hypothesis" central to his linguistic theory. His claim is that: "the meaning of entities, and the meaning of grammatical relations among them, is related to the restriction of combinations of these entities relative to other entities" (Harris, 1968, p. 12). Granting that there must be some relationship between distribution and meaning, the exact nature of such a relationship to our received notions of meaning is nevertheless not without its complications. For example, there are some purely collocational restrictions in English that seem to enforce no semantic distinction. Thus, one can *roast chicken* and *peanuts* in an oven, but typically *fish* and *beans* are *baked* rather than *roasted*: this fact seems to be a quirk of the history of English. Polysemy provides a second kind of complication. A *sentence* can be *parsed* and a *sentence* can be *commuted*, but these are two distinct senses of the word *sentence*; we should not be misled into positing a class of things that can be both *parsed* and *commuted*.

Given these complicating factors, it is by no means obvious that the distribution of words will directly provide a useful semantic classification, at least in the absence of considerable human intervention. The work that has been done based on Harris' distributional hypothesis (most notably, the work of the associates of the Linguistic String Project (see for example, Hirschman, Grishman, & Sager, 1975)) unfortunately does not provide a direct answer, since the corpora used have been small (tens of thousands of words rather than millions) and the analysis has typically involved considerable intervention by the researchers. However, with much larger corpora (10-100 million words) and robust parsers and taggers, the early results reported here and elsewhere appear extremely promising.

---

on search questions. Should we still be using Bates' island driving approach (Bates, 1975), or should we try something newer such as Tomita's so-called generalized LR(k) parser (Tomita, 1986)? We suggest that the discussion should concentrate more on describing the facts, and less on how they are enforced.

# Acknowledgments

The first author has benefited greatly from a 1982 course taught at MIT by Jelinek, Bahl and Mercer.

# References

Bates, M. (1975). *Syntactic Analysis in a Speech Understanding System* (Tech. Rep. No. 3116). BBN.

Chodorow, M., Byrd, R., & Heidorn, G. (1985). Extracting semantic hierarchies from a large on-line dictionary. *ACL Proceedings*.

Chomsky, N. (1957). *Syntactic structures*. The Hague: Mouton & Co.

Church, K. (1988). A stochastic parts program and noun phrase parser for unrestricted text. *Second Conference on Applied Natural Language Processing*. Austin, TX.

Church, K., & Hanks, P. (1989). Word association norms, mutual information, and lexicography. *ACL Proceedings*.

DeRose, S. (1988). Grammatical category disambiguation by statistical optimization. *Computational Linguistics, 14*.

Firth, J. (1957). A synopsis of linguistic theory 1930-1955. In *Studies in linguistic analysis*. Oxford: Philological Society. Reprinted (1988) in F. Palmer (Ed.), *Selected papers of J. R. Firth*. Harlow, Longman.

Francis, W., & Kucera, H. (1982). *Frequency analysis of English usage*. Boston: Houghton Mifflin Company.

Good, I. J. (1953). The population frequencies of species and the estimation of population parameters. *Biometrika, 40*, 237–264.

Hanks, P. (1987). Definitions and explanations. In J. Sinclair, P. Hanks, G. Fox, R. Moon, & P. Stock (Eds.), *Collins cobuild English language dictionary*. London and Glasgow: Collins.

Harris, Z. (1968). *Mathematical structures of language*. New York: Wiley.

Hindle, D. (1983). *User manual for Fidditch, a deterministic parser*. (Tech. Rep. No. 7590-142). Naval Research Laboratory.

Hirschman, L., Grishman, R., & Sager, N. (1975). Grammatically-based automatic word class formation. *Information Processing and Management, 11*, 39–57.

Jelinek, F. (1985). *Self-organized language modeling for speech recognition* (Tech. Rep.). IBM.

Kahan, S., Pavlidis, T., & Baird, H. (1987). On the recognition of printed characters of any font or size. *IEEE Transactions PAMI*, 274–287.

Sinclair, J. (1987). The nature of the evidence. In J. Sinclair (Ed.), *Looking up: An account of the COBUILD project in lexical computing*. London and Glasgow: Collins.

Tomita, M. (1986). *Efficient parsing for natural language*, Boston, MA: Kluwer.

# 8. Parsing Spoken Language Using Combinatory Grammars

Mark Steedman

*Department of Computer and Information Science, University of Pennsylvania*

## 8.1 Introduction

Combinatory Grammars are a generalization of Categorial Grammars to include operations on function categories corresponding to the combinators of Combinatory Logic, such as functional composition and type raising. The introduction of such operations is motivated by the need to provide an explanatory account of coordination and unbounded dependency. However, the associativity of functional composition tends to engender an equivalence class of possible derivations for each derivation permitted by more traditional grammars. While all derivations in each class by definition deliver the same function-argument relations in their interpretation, the proliferation of structural analyses presents obvious problems for parsing within this framework and the related approaches based on the Lambek calculus (cf. Moortgat, 1988).

This problem has been called the problem of "spurious ambiguity," (although it will become apparent that the term is rather misleading). A number of ways of dealing with it have been proposed, including "compiling" the grammar into a different form (Wittenburg, 1986), "normal form"-based parsing (Hepple & Morrill, 1989; Koenig, 1989), and a "lazy" chart parsing technique which may allow the properties of the combinatory rules themselves to be exploited to provide a unified treatment for "spurious" ambiguities and "genuine" attachment ambiguities (Pareschi & Steedman, 1987).

While no completely satisfactory solution to the problem has yet been found, recent work suggests that the very free notion of syntactic structure that is engendered by the theory is identical to the notion of structure that is required by recent theories of phrasal intonation and prosody. Intonational Structure is notoriously freer than traditional syntactic structure, and is commonly regarded as conveying distinctions of discourse focus and propositional attitude. The present chapter argues that the focussed entities, propositions, and abstractions that are associated with a given intonational structure can be identified with the interpretations that the grammar provides for the non-standard constituents that it allows under one particular derivation from an equivalence class. The constituent interpretations corresponding to each possible intonational tune belong to the same equivalence class, and therefore reduce to the same canonical function argument relations. However, it is apparent that the ambiguity between derivations in the same equivalence class is not spurious at all, but meaning-bearing.

Of course, not *all* structural ambiguities are resolved by distinctions of intonation. (An example is PP attachment ambiguity.) It follows that some of the techniques proposed for written parsing must be implicated as well. However, the theory opens the possibility of unifying phonological and syntactic processing, as well as simplifying the architecture required for integrating higher-level modules in spoken language processing.

## 8.2   Structure and intonation

Phrasal intonation is notorious for structuring the words of spoken utterances into groups which frequently violate orthodox notions of constituency. For example, the normal prosody for the answer (b) to the following question (a) imposes the intonational constituency indicated by the brackets (stress is indicated by capitals):

(1a) I know that brassicas are a good source of minerals,
       but what are LEGumes a good source of?

 (b) (LEGumes are a good source of) VITamins.

Such a grouping is orthogonal to the traditional syntactic structure of the sentence. The presence of two apparently uncoupled levels of structure in natural language grammar appears to complicate the path from speech to interpretation unreasonably, and to thereby threaten a number of computational applications.

Nevertheless, intonational structure is strongly constrained by meaning, and its function in discourses like the above seems to be to convey distinctions of focus, information, and propositional attitude towards entities in the discourse. These entities are more diverse than mere noun phrase or propositional referents. In particular, the include what E. Prince (1986) calls "open propositions." Open propositions are most easily understood as being that which is introduced into the discourse context by a Wh-question. So for example the question in (1), *What are legumes a good source of?* introduces an open proposition which, as Jackendoff (1972) pointed out, it is natural to think of as a functional *abstraction*. It would be written as follows in the notation of the λ-calculus:

(2) $\lambda x[good'(source'\ x)\ legumes']$

(Primes indicate interpretations whose detailed semantics is of no direct concern here.) When this function or concept is supplied with an argument *vitamins'*, it *reduces* to give a proposition, with the same function argument relations as the canonical sentence:

(3) $good'(source'\ vitamins')legumes'$

It is the presence of the above open proposition rather than some other that makes the intonation contour in (1) felicitous. (I am not claiming that its presence uniquely *determines* this response, nor that its explicit mention is necessary for interpreting the response.)

All natural languages include syntactic constructions whose semantics is also reminiscent of functional abstraction. The most obvious and tractable class are Wh-constructions themselves, in which exactly the same fragments that can be delineated by a single intonation contour appear as the residue of the subordinate clause. But another and much more problematic class are the fragments that result from coordinate constructions. While coordinate constructions have constituted another major source of complexity for natural language understanding by machine, it is tempting to think that this conspiracy between syntax and prosody might point to a unified notion of structure that is somewhat different from traditional surface constituency.

## 8.3 Combinatory grammars

Combinatory Categorial Grammar (CCG, Steedman, 1987) is an extension of Categorial Grammar (CG). Elements like verbs are associated with a syntactic "category" which identifies them as *functions*, and specifies the type and directionality of their arguments and the type of their result:

(4) *eats* :- (S\NP)/NP: eat'

The category can be regarded as encoding the semantic type of their translation. Such functions can combine with arguments of the appropriate type and position by functional application:

```
(5) Harry      eats      apples
    ------   ----------  ------
      NP     (S\NP)/NP     NP
             -------------------->
                    S\NP
             ------------------<
                      S
```

Because the syntactic functional type is identical to the semantic type, apart from directionality, this derivation also builds a compositional interpretation, *eats'apples'harry'*, and of course such a "pure" categorial grammar is context free. Coordination might be included in CG via the following rule, allowing any constituents of like type, including functions, to form a single constituent of the same type:

(6) $X \ conj \ X \Rightarrow X$

```
(7) I    cooked    and     ate    a frog
    --  ----------  ----  ----------  ------
    NP  (S\NP)/NP  conj  (S\NP)/NP    NP
```

```
-------------------------&
     (S\NP)/NP
```

(The rest of the derivation is omitted, being the same as in (5).) In order to allow coordination of contiguous strings that do not constitute constituents, CCG generalizes the grammar to allow certain operations on functions related to Curry's combinators (Curry & Feys, 1958). For example, functions may *compose*, as well as apply, under the following rule

(8) Forward Composition:
$$X/Y : F \; Y/Z : G \; \Rightarrow \; X/Z : \lambda x \; F(Gx)$$

The most important single property of combinatory rules like this is that they have an invariant semantics. This one composes the interpretations of the functions that it applies to, as is apparent from the right hand side of the rule.[1] Thus sentences like *I cooked, and might eat, the beans* can be accepted, via the following composition of two verbs (indexed as **B**, following Curry's nomenclature) to yield a composite of the same category as a transitive verb. Crucially, composition also yields the appropriate interpretation, assuming that a semantics is also provided for the coordination rule.

```
(9)   cooked    and  might     eat
     ---------  ---- ---------  -----
     (S\NP)/NP  conj (S\NP)/VP VP/NP
                     ---------------->B
                        (S\NP)/NP
     -------------------------&
           (S\NP)/NP
```

Combinatory grammars also include type-raising rules, which turn arguments into functions over functions-over-such-arguments. These rules allow arguments to compose, and thereby take part in coordinations like *I cooked, and you ate, the legumes*. They too have an invariant compositional semantics which ensures that the result has an appropriate interpretation. For example, the following rule allows the conjuncts to form as below (again, the remainder of the derivation is omitted):

(10) Subject Type-raising:
$$NP : y \; \Rightarrow \; S/(S\backslash NP) : \lambda F \; Fy$$

```
(11)    I       cooked   and  you        ate
      --------  --------- ---- --------  ---------
        NP      (S\NP)/NP conj   NP      (S\NP)/NP
      -------->T                -------->T
      S/(S\NP)                  S/(S\NP)
      ----------------->B       ----------------->B
```

---

[1] The rule uses the notation of the $\lambda$-calculus in the semantics, for clarity. This should not obscure the fact that it is functional composition itself that is the primitive, not the $\lambda$ operator.

```
S/NP                              S/NP
-------------------------------&
         S/NP
```

It should be obvious that, once subjects are allowed to become functions and to compose like verbs, the grammar allows unboundedly many such functions to combine, even across clause boundaries. The theory thus immediately captures the kind of fragments that are left as a result of "unbounded" constructions such as relative clause formation and "right node raising," as in

(12a)  bagels which *I believe that Harry eats*

 (b)  *I believe that Harry ate,* and *I know that he cooked,* the bagels.

# 8.4   Parsing with CCG

The basic apparatus sketched above has been applied to a respectable range of phenomena of extraction and coordination in a number of languages. However, combinatory grammars achieve this coverage at the cost of embodying an unusual view of surface structure, according to which strings like *I might eat, I believe that Harry eats,* and even *John, beans* are, quite simply, constituents. According to this view, surface structure is much more ambiguous than is generally realized, for such strings must also be possible constituents of canonical sentences like *I might eat the mushrooms, I believe that Harry eats bagels,* and *I gave John beans* as well. It follows that such sentences must have several surface structures, corresponding to different sequences of composition, type raising and application. (An entirely unconstrained combinatory grammar would in fact allow any bracketing on a sentence.)[2] For example, the following is only one among many surface structures that are allowed for the sentence in question:

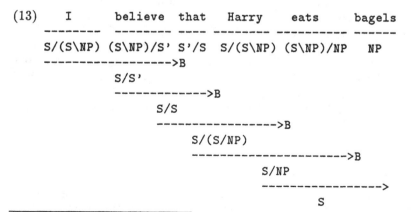

```
(13)      I       believe  that   Harry      eats     bagels
       --------   -------- ----  -------- ----------- ------
       S/(S\NP) (S\NP)/S' S'/S  S/(S\NP) (S\NP)/NP    NP
       ------------------->B
              S/S'
              ------------->B
                 S/S
                 ---------------->B
                    S/(S/NP)
                    --------------------->B
                             S/NP
                             ---------------->
                                       S
```

---

[2]The actual grammars we write for configurational languages like English are heavily constrained by local conditions. (An example would be a condition on the composition rule that is tacitly assumed here, forbidding the variable Y in the composition rule to be instantiated as NP, thus excluding constituents like *[eat the]$_{VP/N}$.)

Such families of derivations form equivalence classes, for of course they all deliver the same interpretation, determining the same function-argument relations. (It is assumed here that the level of interpretation in question is neutral with respect to non-argument-structure dependent aspects of meaning such as quantifier scope.) Indeed, there is a close relation between the canonical interpretation structures that they deliver according to the theory sketched above, and traditional notions of constituent structure.

However, the proliferation of surface analyses creates serious problems for parsing written text, because it compounds the already grave problems of local and global ambiguity in parsing by introducing numerous semantically equivalent potential derivations. The problem is acute: while it clearly does not matter which member of any equivalence class the parser finds, it has to find *some* member of *every* semantically distinct class of analyses. The danger is that the entire forest of possible analyses will have to be examined in order to ensure that all such analyses have been found. This problem has been referred to as the problem of "spurious" ambiguity by Wittenburg (1986).

It has already been noted that the associativity of functional composition ensures that all the derivations that arise from composing functions in different orders for a given set of given function-argument relations will produce the *same* interpretation. This fact both sanctions the coherence of the grammar itself, and points to a solution to the parsing problem: if these analyses are equivalent, it clearly doesn't matter *which* of them we find, just so long as we find *one*. A couple of simple strategies immediately suggest themselves as the basis for a parser that just finds one analysis in each equivalence class, paraphrasable as "combine as soon as you can," or "only combine when you have to." The first alternative, expressed as a "reduce first" strategy embodied in a shift-reduce parser, augmented by a means for handling non-determinism, is one basis for an algorithm to do this. This regime favors predominantly left-branching analyses like the above, where the grammar permits them, rather than the standard right-branching surface structures.[3] The problem for that common-sense parser, as for other left-to-right processors, arises from the non-determinism introduced by the presence of *backward modifiers*. There are a number of proposals for dealing with this problem, including Wittenburg (1986, 1987), Pareschi and Steedman (1987), and Hepple and Morrill (1989). However, none of these proposals are entirely satisfactory. In searching for alternatives, it is interesting to consider the relation of intonation to constituency in a CCG.

---

[3] In this respect, the processor resembles the one proposed by Hausser (1986). However, it is here the *parser* that is *as left-associative as the grammar permits*, not the grammar itself. The grammar is impartial with respect to left- and right- association. It is also interesting to note in connection with such parsers and derivations that the inclusion of type raised categories makes most combinations "function first." Such grammars may therefore be of a kind that is well-suited to "head-driven" (or rather, functor-driven) parsing, unlike grammars in general (cf. Kay, this volume).

## 8.5   Intonational structure

The claim of the present chapter is simply that particular surface structures
that are induced by the specific combinatory grammar that was introduced
to explain coordination in English are identical to the intonational structures
that are required to specify the possible intonation contours for those same
sentences of English.[4] More specifically, the claim is that in spoken utterance,
intonation largely determines *which* of the many possible bracketings permitted
by the combinatory syntax of English is intended, and that the interpretations
of the constituents are related to distinctions of focus among the concepts and
open propositions that the speaker has in mind. Thus, whatever problems for
parsing written text arise from the profusion of equivalent alternative surface
structures engendered by this theory, these "spurious" ambiguities seem to be
to a great extent resolved by prosody in spoken language. The theory therefore
offers the possibility that phonology and parsing can be merged into a single
unitary process.

The proof of this claim lies in showing that the rules of combinatory grammar can be annotated with intonation contour schemata, which limit their
application in spoken discourse, and to showing that the major constituents
of intonated utterances like (1b), under the analyses that these rules permit,
correspond to the focus structure of the context to which they are appropriate,
such as (1a).

I shall use a notation which is based on the theory of Pierrehumbert (1980),
as modified in more recent work by Selkirk (1984), Beckman and Pierrehumbert
(1986, Pierrehumbert & Beckman, 1989), and Pierrehumbert and Hirschberg
(1987). I have tried as far as possible to take my examples and the associated
intonational annotations from those authors.

I follow Pierrehumbert in assuming two abstract pitch levels, and three
types of tones, as follows. There are two phrasal tones, written H and L,
denoting high or low "simple" tones — that is, level functions of pitch against
time. There are also two boundary tones, written H% and L%, denoting an
intonational phrase-final rise or fall. Of Pierrhumberts six pitch accent tones,
I shall only be concerned with two, the H* accent and the L+H*. The phonetic
or acoustic realization of pitch accents is a complex matter. Roughly speaking,
the L+H* pitch accent that is extensively discussed below in the context of the
L+H* LH% melody generally appears as a maximum which is preceded by a
distinctive low level, and peaks *later* than the corresponding H* pitch accent
when the same sequence is spoken with the H* L melody that goes with "new"
information, and which is the other melody considered below.

In the more recent versions of the theory, Pierrehumbert and her colleagues
distinguish *two* levels of prosodic phrase that include a pitch accent tone. They
are the intonational phrase proper, and the "intermediate phrase." Both end in
a phrasal tone, but only intonational phrases have additional boundary tones
H% and L%. Intermediate phrases are bounded on the right by their phrasal tone

---

[4] There is a precedent for the claim that prosodic structure can be identified with the
structures arising from the inclusion of associative operations in grammar in the work of
Moortgat (1988) and Oehrle (1988), and in Steedman (1985).

alone, and do not appear to be characterized in $F_0$ by the same kind of final rise or fall that is characteristic of true intonational phrases. The distinction does not play an active role in the present account, but I shall follow the more recent notation of prosodic phrase boundaries in the examples, without further comment on the distinction.

There may also be parts of prosodic phrases where the fundamental frequency is merely interpolated between tones, notably the region between pitch accent and phrasal tone, and the region before a pitch accent. In Pierrehumbert's notation, such substrings bear no indication of abstract tone whatsoever.

A crucial feature of this theory for present purposes is that the position and shape of a given pitch accent in a prosodic phrase, and of its phrase accent and the associated right-hand boundary, are essentially invariant. If the constituent is very short — say, a monosyllabic noun phrase — then the whole intonational contour may be squeezed onto that one syllable. If the constituent is longer, then the pitch accent will appear some way to the left of the phrasal tone and boundary tone, if any. The latter will appear at its right edge, and the intervening pitch contour, as well as any part that precedes the pitch accent(s), will merely be interpolated. In this way, the tune can be spread over longer or shorter strings, in order to mark the corresponding constituents for the particular distinction of focus and propositional attitude that the melody denotes. Pierrehumbert and Hirschberg (1987) claim that this discourse meaning of the tune is determined compositionally, from invariant interpretations of the component pitch-accent, boundary tone and/or phrasal tone.

Consider for example the prosody of the sentence *Fred ate the beans* in the following pair of discourse settings, which are adapted from Jackendoff (1972, p. 260):

(14) Q: Well, what about the BEAns?
         Who ate THEM?
      A: FRED     ate the BEA-ns.
         H*L             L+H*LH%

(15) Q: Well, what about FRED?
         What did HE eat?
      A: FRED ate the BEAns.
         L+H* LH%       H* LL%

In these contexts, the main stressed syllables on both *Fred* and *the beans* receive a pitch accent, but a different one. In (14), the pitch accent contour on *Fred* is H*, while that on *beans* is L+H*. (I base these annotations on Pierrehumbert and Hirschberg's (1987, ex. 33) discussion of this example.)

In the second example (15) above, the pitch accents are reversed: this time *Fred* is L+H* and *beans* is H*. The assignment of these tones seem to reflect the fact that (as Pierrehumbert and Hirschberg point out) H* is used to mark information that the speaker believes to be *new to the hearer*. In contrast, L+H* seems to be used to mark information which the current speaker knows to be known to the hearer (for example because the current hearer mentioned it in a question), but which constitutes a novel topic of conversation for the speaker, standing in a contrastive relation to a previous topic, where this term is as used by Hajicova (this volume, Hajičová & Sgall, 1988). In the terms of Halliday (1967) this is a (marked) *theme*. (If the information were merely known to all, or "given" in Halliday's terms, it would receive *no* tone according to Pierrehumbert's theory — or be left out altogether.) Thus in (15), the L+H* LH% phrase including this accent is spread across the phrase *Fred ate*.[5] Similarly, in (14), the same tune is confined to the object of the open proposition *ate the beans*, because the intonation of the original question indicates that eating beans *as opposed to some other comestible* is the new topic.

## 8.6   A hypothesis

The L+H* LH% intonational melody in example (15) belongs to a phrase *Fred ate* ... which corresponds under the combinatory theory of grammar to a grammatical constituent, complete with a translation equivalent to the open proposition $\lambda x[(ate'\ x)\ fred']$. The combinatory theory thus offers a way to assign contours like L+H* LH% to such novel constituents, entirely under the control of independently motivated rules of grammar. I conjecture that it is possible to do this by making the rule of forward composition subject to a restriction (which is in the terms of Pierrehumbert's theory an extremely natural one), amounting to the injunction "Don't apply this rule across an intonational phrase or intermediate phrase boundary."[6] Such a restriction would still allow the following derivation for *Fred ate* ..., in which for once the semantic interpretation is included:[7]

```
(16)      Fred              ate         ...
       ---------------   ---------------
       NP:fred'          (S\NP)/NP:ate'
         L+H*                  LH%
       ---------------->T
       S/(S\NP): [P] P fred'
          L+H*
       ------------------------------->B
          S/NP: [X] (ate' X) fred'
             L+H*LH%
```

---

[5] An alternative prosody, in which the contrastive tune is confined to *Fred*, seems equally coherent, and may be the one intended by Jackendoff. I believe that this alternative is informationally distinct, and arises from an ambiguity as to whether the topic of this discourse is *Fred* or *What Fred ate*. It is accepted by the present rules.

[6] The device by which this restriction can be imposed goes beyond the scope of the present chapter, and is presented elsewhere (cf. Steedman, 1990a, 1990b).

[7] The application of the abstraction operator, as in $\lambda X$, appears in derivations as brackets, as in [X]. As usual, primes indicate interpretations whose details are of no concern here. It will be apparent from the derivations that the assumed semantic representation is at a level prior to the explicit representation of matters related to quantifier scope.

It is assumed here that the combinatory rules in all cases ensure that their result bears the concatenation of the tones on their inputs. (The rules will therefore allow the L+H* LH% tune to occur "spread" across any sequence that can be composed by repeated applications of the rule.) On the assumption that the grammar imposes a complementary restriction upon forward functional application, so that it can combine complete intonational phrases, again concatenating their tunes, the derivation of (15) could be completed as follows:

```
(17)    Fred           ate            the        beans
      ---------- ---------------- ---------- --------
      NP:fred' (S\NP)/NP:ate' NP/N: the' N:beans'
      L+H*            LH%                    H* LL%
      --------->T                   -------------------->
      S/(S\NP):                     NP:the' beans'
      [P]P fred'                        H* LL%
      L+H*
      ----------------------->B
      S/NP:[X](ate' X) fred'
          L+H* LH%
            ----------------------------------------->
           S: ate' (the' beans') fred'
              L+H* LH%  H* LL%
```

The division into contrastive/given open proposition versus new information is appropriate. On the assumption that the intonational restrictions on syntactic combination forbid even the forward application of functions bearing such incomplete rightmost fragments of intonational tunes as a bare phrasal tone or phrasal tone and boundary tone, no other derivation would be allowed, given this intonation contour.

In contrast, the intonation contour on (14) would not permit the composition rule to apply, because *Fred* ends with a L boundary intonation. The bracketing imposed above for (15) (and the formation of the corresponding open proposition) would therefore not be allowed. However, given the lesser restriction upon forward functional application, the following derivation of (14) *would* be allowed. Again, the derivation divides the sentence into new and given information consistent with the context given in the example:

```
(18)    Fred           ate            the        beans
      ---------- ---------------- ---------- --------
      NP:fred' (S\NP)/NP:ate' NP/N:the' N:beans'
      H* L                               L+H* LH%
      -------->T                    -------------------->
      S/(S\NP):                     NP:the' beans'
      [P]P fred'                       L+H* LH%
      H* L
            ----------------------------------------->
           S\NP:eat'(the' beans')
              L+H* LH%
```

```
------------------------------------------>
    S: eat'(the' beans') fred'
    H* L        L+H* LH%
```

This time, the effect of the rules would be to annotate the entire predicate as an **L+H\* LH%**. (This does not mean that the *tune* would be spread, but rather that the whole constituent would be marked for the corresponding discourse function – roughly, *topic* or *theme*). The finer grain information that it is the object that is contrasted, while the verb is given, resides in the tree itself. Similarly, the fact that boundary tones are associated with words at the lowest level of the derivation does not mean that they are *part of* the word, nor that the word is the entity that they are a boundary *of.* It is prosodic phrases that they bound, and these also are defined by the tree. No other analysis would be allowed for (18). Other cases considered by Jackendoff would also yield only contextually appropriate interpretations (cf. Steedman, 1990b).

## 8.7   Conclusion

The problem of so-called "spurious" ambiguity, or multiple semantically equivalent derivations, now appears in a quite different light. While the semantic properties of the rules (notably the associativity of functional composition that engenders the problem in the first place) do indeed guarantee that these analyses are semantically equivalent at the level of Argument Structure, they are nonetheless meaning-bearing at the level of Information Structure. To call them "spurious" is rather misleading. What is more, while there are usually a great many different analyses for any given sequence of words, intonation contour often limits or even eliminates the non-determinism arising from this source.

The significance of eliminating non-determinism in this way should not be under-estimated. Similar intonational markers are involved in coordinate sentences, like the following 'right-node-raised" example:

(19) I will, and you won't, eat mushrooms

In such sentences the local ambiguity between composing *won't* and *eat* and applying the latter to its argument first is a *genuine* local ambiguity, equivalent to a local attachment ambiguity in a more traditional grammar, for only *one* of the alternatives will lead to a parse at all. And the correct alternative is the one that is selected by the restriction against forward composition across prosodic phrase boundaries.

However, the extent to which intonation alone renders parsing deterministic should also not be over-stated. There still are sources of non-determinism in the grammar, which must be coped with somehow. Most obviously, there are sources common to all natural language grammars, such as the well-known PP-attachment ambiguities in the following example:

(20) Put the block in the box on the table.

While intonation *can* distinguish the two analyses, they do not seem to be *necessarily* so distinguished. There is also a residuum of so-called spurious ambiguity, because function categories bearing *no* tone are free to forward compose *and* to apply.

It is important to observe that this ambiguity is widespread, and that it is a true ambiguity in discourse interpretation. Consider yet another version of the example with which the chapter began, uttered with only an H* LL% tune on the last word:

(21) `Legumes are a good source of VItamins.`
                                  `H*    LL%`

Such an intonation contour is compatible with *all* the analyses that the unannotated CCG would allow. However, such an utterance is also compatible with a large number of contextual open propositions. For example, it is a reasonable response to the question *What can you tell me about legumes?* But it is similarly reasonable as an answer to *What are legumes?*, or to *What are legumes a good source of?* The ambiguity of intonation with respect to such distinctions is well-known, and it would simply be incorrect not to include it.

It is interesting that in the case of such examples, the occasions on which the intonation contour does *not* disambiguate the derivation seem to be exactly the occasions on which the disambiguating information is contextually available. That is, the null tone appears to go with information that is in Halliday's term, "given." This fact suggests that thwe human parser can use the presence of an open proposition in the context to resolve the local ambiguity between shifting and reducing.

However, if this information is available in parsing the spoken language, it would be surprising if it were not also available for the resolution of both "genuine" and "spurious" structural ambiguities during human parsing of the written language, as originally proposed by Winograd (1972) in connection with examples like (20), and subsequently by Crain and Steedman (1985), and Altmann and Steedman (1988).

# Acknowledgments

I am grateful to Julia Hirschberg, Aravind Joshi, Mitch Marcus, Janet Pierrehumbert, and Bonnie Lynn Webber for comments and advice. The research was supported by DARPA grant no. N0014-85-K0018, ARO grant no. DAAG29-84-K-0061, and NSF grant no. CER MCS 82-19196.

# References

Altmann, G., & Steedman, M. (1988). Interaction with context during human sentence processing. *Cognition, 30*, 191–238.

Beckman, M., & Pierrehumbert, J. (1986). Intonational structure in Japanese and English. *Phonology Yearbook, 3*, 255–310.

Chomsky, N. (1971). Deep structure, surface structure, and semantic interpretation. In D. Steinberg & L. Jakobovits (Eds.), *Semantics*, Cambridge: CUP.

Crain, S., & Steedman, M. (1985). On not being led up the garden path: The use of context by the psychological parser. In D. Dowty, L. Kartunnen, & A. Zwicky (Eds.), *Natural language parsing: Psychological, computational and theoretical perspectives* (ACL Studies in Natural Language Processing). Cambridge University Press.

Curry, H., & Feys, R. (1958). *Combinatory logic*. Amsterdam: North Holland.

Hajičová, E., & Sgall, P. (1988). Topic and focus of a sentence and the patterning of a text. In J. Petöfi (Ed.), *Text and discourse constitution*. Berlin: De Gruyter.

Halliday, M. (1967). *Intonation and grammar in British English*. The Hague: Mouton.

Hausser, R. (1986). *NEWCAT: Parsing natural language using left-associative grammar*. Berlin: Springer Verlag.

Hepple, M., & Morrill, G. (1989). Parsing and derivational equivalence. *Proceedings of the Fourth Conference of the European Chapter of the ACL* (pp. 10–18). Manchester.

Jackendoff, R. (1972). *Semantic interpretation in generative grammar*. Cambridge, MA: MIT Press.

König, E. (1989). Parsing as natural deduction. *Proceedings of the 27th Annual Conference of the ACL* (pp. 272–280). Vancouver, BC.

Marcus, M., Hindle, D., & Fleck, M. (1983). D-theory: Talking about talking about trees. *Proceedings of the 21st Annual Meeting of the Association for Computational Linguistics* (pp. 129–136). Cambridge, MA.

Moortgat, M. (1988). *Categorial investigations*. Dordrecht: Foris.

Oehrle, R. T. (1985). Paper to the *Conference on Categorial Grammar*. Tucson, AR. Also published in R. T. Oehrle, E. Bach, & D. Wheeler, (Eds.) (in press), *Categorial grammars and natural language structures*. Dordrecht: Reidel.

Pareschi, R., & Steedman, M. (1987). A lazy way to chart parse with categorial grammars. *Proceedings of the 25th Annual Conference of the ACL* (pp. 81–88). Stanford, CA.

Pierrehumbert, J. (1980). *The phonology and phonetics of English intonation*. Unpublished doctoral dissertation. Cambridge, MA: MIT. (Distributed by Indiana University Linguistics Club, Bloomington, IN.)

Pierrehumbert, J., & Beckman, M. (1989). *Japanese tone structure*. Cambridge, MA: MIT Press.

Pierrehumbert, J., & Hirschberg, J. (1987). *The meaning of intonational contours in the interpretation of discourse* (Tech. Rep.). Bell Labs.

Prince, E. F. (1986). On the syntactic marking of presupposed open propositions. *Papers from the Parasession on Pragmatics and Grammatical Theory at the 22nd Regional Meeting of the Chicago Linguistic Society* (pp. 208–222).

Selkirk, E. (1984). *Phonology and syntax*. Cambridge, MA: MIT Press.

Steedman, M. (1985). Dependency and coordination in the grammar of Dutch and English. *Language, 61*, 523–568.

Steedman, M. (1987). Combinatory grammars and parasitic gaps. *NL&LT, 5*, 403–439.

Steedman, M. (1990a). Intonation and syntax in spoken language systems. *Proceedings of the 28th Annual Conference of the ACL* (to appear). Pittsburgh, PA.

Steedman, M. (1990b). *Structure and intonation* (Tech. Rep.). University of Pennsylvania.

Winograd, T. (1972). *Understanding natural language.* Edinburgh University Press.

Wittenburg, K. B. (1986). *Natural language parsing with combinatory categorial grammar in a graph-unification based formalism.* Unpublished doctoral dissertation. Austin: University of Texas.

Wittenburg, K. B. (1987). Predictive combinators: A method for efficient processing of combinatory grammars. *Proceedings of the 25th Annual Conference of the ACL* (pp. 73–80). Stanford, CA.

# 9. A Dependency-Based Parser for Topic and Focus

Eva Hajičová

*Faculty of Mathematics and Physics, Charles University*

## 9.1 Introduction

A deepened interest in the study of suprasegmental features of utterances invoked by increasing attempts at a build-up of algorithms for speech recognition and synthesis quite naturally turned attention of the researchers to the linguistic phenomena known for decades under the terms of theme-rheme, topic-comment, topic-focus. In this chapter we propose a linguistic procedure for parsing utterances in a "free word order" language, the resulting structure of which is a labeled W-rooted tree that represents (one of) the (literal) meaning(s) of the parsed utterance. Main attention will be paid to the written form of language; however, due regard will be also paid to (at least some of) the suprasegmental features and additional remarks will be made with respect to parsing strategies for written and spoken English.

## 9.2 Dependency-based output structures

### 9.2.1

The procedure is based on the linguistic theory of functional generative description as proposed by Sgall (cf. Sgall 1964, 1967; Sgall *et al.*, 1986). The representation of the meaning(s) of the sentence — i.e., the output of the analysis — is a projective rooted tree with the root labeled by a complex symbol of a verb and its daughter nodes by those of the complementations of the verb, i.e., participants (or — in another terminology — the cases, theta-roles, valency), as well as adverbials. The relation between the governor (the verb) and the dependents (its daughter nodes) is a kind of dependency between the two nodes. The complementations of the daughter nodes (and their respective complementations, etc.) are again connected with their governors by an edge labeled by a type of dependency relation. The top-down dimension of the tree thus reflects the structural characteristics of the sentences. The left-to-right dimension represents the deep word order, see Section 9.3 below. Structures with coordination may be then represented by complex dependency structures (no longer of a tree character) with a third dimension added to the

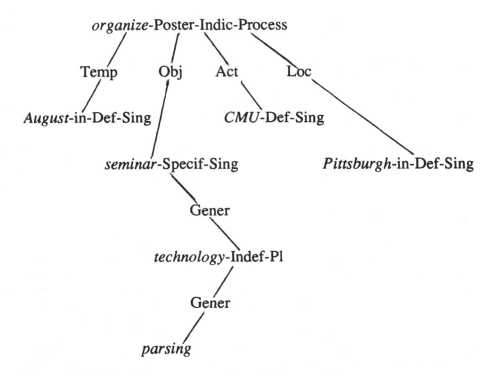

Figure 9.1. Underlying representation of Sentence (1).

tree structure (Plátek, Sgall & Sgall, 1984), or, alternatively, nodes of quite special properties can be added to the tree itself (Močkořová, 1989). Such a type of description can dispense with problems of constituency and "spurious" ambiguity and offers an effective and economic way of representing sentence meaning.

To illustrate (with several simplifications, some of which will be clarified in Section 9.3 below) the type of representations characterized till now, we present in Figure 9.1 an underlying representation of Sentence (1).

(1) In August, a seminar on parsing technologies will be organized by CMU in Pittsburgh.


## 9.2.2

A dependency oriented account of syntactic(o-semantic) relations offers a rather straightforward way for a formulation of a lexically-driven parsing procedure, since a great part of the relevant information is projected from the frames belonging to the lexical entries of the heads. In the description we subscribe to, valency slots are not understood just in the sense of obligatory or regular kinds of complementation, but are classified into

(i) inner participants (theta roles, each of which can be present at most once with a single head token) and free modifications;

(ii) obligatory and optional; this distinction can be made with both kinds of complementations quoted under (i) depending on the specific heads.

As for (i), five inner participants are being distinguished (for motivation, see Panevová, 1974; Hajičová & Panevová, 1984), namely deep subject (Actor), deep object (Patient, Objective), Addressee, Origin (Source) and Effect; among free modifications, there belong Instrument, Locative, Directional, Manner, several temporal adverbials, adverbials of cause, condition, regard, General relationship, etc. As for (ii), an operational test was formulated that helps to determine which of the complementations with a given lexical head is obligatory (although perhaps deletable) and which is optional; the test is based on judgements on the coherence of a simple dialogue (see Panevová, 1974).

Both (i) and (ii) are reflected in the valency frames of individual lexical entries in the lexicon. Thus, e.g., for the verb *to change*, the valency frame consists of two obligatory slots for Actor and Objective, two optional slots for Source and Effect (*to change something from something into something*) and a list of free modifications, which can be stated once for all the verbs. If one of the free modifications is obligatory with a certain head (e.g., Directional with *arrive*, Appurtanance with *brother*, Material with *full*), this has to be indicated in the valency frame of the relevant head.

## 9.2.3

Dependency can be operationally defined on the basis of endocentricity (cf. Sgall & Panevová, 1989, following Kulagina, 1958). If in a syntactic construction one of two members of the construction can be left out, while the other retains the distributional properties characteristic for the given pair, then the member that can be omitted is considered to depend on the other: e.g., in *Jim read a book* the sentence part *a book* can be omitted without the sentence losing its grammaticality; thus, the verb rather than *the book* is the head of the construction. The set of word classes that is determined on independent grounds can then be used to identify the "direction of dependency" in other (exocentric) constructions: though in *Jim bought a book* the sentence part *a book* cannot be omitted, *buy* and *read* are assigned a single word class (on independent morphemic and syntactic criteria) and thus it may be postulated that *bought* rather than *a book* is the governor (head) of the construction *bought a book*. In a similar vein, a construction such as *Jim read* can be substituted in its syntactic position (as constituting a sentence) by a subjectless verb in many languages (cf. Latin *Pluit*; also in English *It rains* the surface subject *it* has no semantic value: it cannot be freely substituted by a noun or by another pronoun and is equivalent to the Latin ending).

### 9.2.4

It is not our objective in the present contribution to contrast dependency structures with those of phrase structure grammar. Let us only mention in conclusion of this section, that among the main advantages of dependency trees there is the relatively small number of nodes; the basic syntactic hierarchy can be described without any non-terminal nodes occurring in the representations of sentences, although in their derivations non-terminals can be used without the limitations characteristic of Gaifman's approach to dependency. In addition, if function words are understood as mere grammatical morphemes having no syntactic autonomy, then their values can be treated as indices, i.e., parts of complex labels of nodes, as illustrated in Figure 9.1 above. In this way, the component parts of syntactically autonomous units can be represented correctly as having other syntactic properties than the autonomous units themselves, and the representations do not get necessarily complicated.

## 9.3  The semantic impact of topic-focus articulation

### 9.3.1

The topic-focus articulation of an utterance has an impact on the semantic interpretation of the given utterance. It is important to notice that (a) and (b) are two different sentences in (2) as well as in (3), though the semantic difference is much more important in (3) than in (2). With (2) the two sets of propositions to which the two sentences correspond assign the value "true" to the same subset of possible worlds, which is not the case with (3).[1]
(The intonation center is denoted by italics.)

(2) a. Mother is *coming*.

   b. *Mother* is coming.

(3) a. I do linguistics on *Sundays*.

   b. On Sundays, I do *linguistics*.

In the representations of meaning as characterized in Section 9.2, we distinguish:

(i) contextually bound (CB) and non-bound (CN) nodes, where "contextually" covers both verbal co-text and situational context;

(ii) the dichotomy of topic and focus;

(iii) the hierarchy of communicative dynamism (deep word order).

---

[1] With (2) as well as with (3) the presuppositions triggered by (a) and (b) differ, so that different subsets of possible worlds get the value 'false'; e.g., (2b) differs from (2a) in presupposing that someone is coming.

To illustrate Points (i) through (iii), let us take Sentence (5) if uttered after (4), as an example.

(4) How did John organize the books in his library?

(5) He arranged his books on nature in an alphabetic order in his bedroom. (In his library, philosophical books are arranged chronologically.)

(i) CB nodes: he, arranged, his, books, his
    NB nodes: nature, alphabetic, order, bedroom

(ii) topic: he arranged his books on nature
     focus: in an alphabetic order in his bedroom

(iii) deep word order (dots stand for the modifications of the nodes explicitly mentioned)
      he – ... books ... – arranged – order ... – ... bedroom

## 9.3.2

The impact of the three aspects (i) through (iii) can be illustrated by Examples (6) through (8), respectively:

(6) a. (You have just listened to our night concert.)
       The compositions of Chopin were played by S. *Richter.* We will devote to him also our next *programme.*
       him = Richter

    b. (You listen to our night concert.)
       Chopin's compositions were played by S. *Richter.* We will devote to him also our next *programme.*
       him = Chopin

(7) a. Staff only behind the *counter.*

    b. *Staff* only behind the counter.

(8) a. It was *John* who talked to few girls in many towns.

    b. It was *John* who talked in many towns to few girls.

The distinction between (a) and (b) in (6) consists in the different preference of anaphoric use of referring expressions if the possible referent is mentioned in the previous context by an NB or a CB element (as *Chopin* in (a) or in (b), respectively); in both cases, the anaphoric elements are in the topic part of the sentence.

Sentence (7a) differs from (7b) only in that *the counter* is in the focus part of (a), while *staff* is in the focus part of (b), which difference leads to a significant distinction in interpretation: (a) holds true if the members of the staff are (to stay) only behind the counter and nowhere else, while (b) holds true if the space behind the counter is (to be) occupied only by the members of the staff; in contrast to (b), the sentence (a) holds true also if there is somebody else than a member of the staff in that space. In (7), the relevant semantic distinction is rendered by a different placement of the intonation center; in (3) above, the same effect results from a word order change.

The clefting in (8) univocally points to *John* as the focus of the sentence, the rest being its topic; the two sentences (a) and (b) differ as to the (deep) order of Locative and Addressee. This distinction again has an important semantic impact: with (a), there was a group of girls who were few, and the same group was talked to in many towns, while with (b) John talked in each of the many towns with (maybe) a (different) small group of girls. This difference need not be reflected in the surface word order: the same effect is reached by a shift of intonation center, see (9a) and (9b).

(9) a. John talked to few girls in many *towns*.

     b. John talked to few *girls* in many towns.

## 9.4   Parsing procedure for topic and focus

### 9.4.1

The proposed procedure of automatic identification of topic and focus is based on two rather strong hypotheses:

(i) the boundary between topic and focus is always placed so that there is such an item A in the representation of meaning that every item of this representation that is less (more) dynamic than A belongs to the topic (focus); in the primary case the verb meets the condition on A and is itself included in the focus;

(ii) the grammar of the particular language determines an ordering of the kinds of complementations (dependency relations) of the verb, of the noun, etc., called 'systemic ordering' (SO). The deep word order within focus is determined by this ordering; with sentences comprising contextually bound items, these items stand to the left in the hierarchy of communicative dynamism and their order (with respect to their governors) is determined by other factors. An examination of Czech in comparison with English and several other languages has led to the conclusion that the SO of some of the main complementations is identical for many languages, having the form Actor – Addressee – Objective, As for Instrument, Origin, Locative, it seems that English differs from Czech in that these three complementations follow Objective in English, though they precede it in Czech. It need not be surprising that languages differ in such semantically relevant details of their grammatical structures as those concerning SO — similarly as they appear to differ in the semantics of verbal aspects, of the articles, of dual number, etc.

We assume further that every sentence has a focus, since otherwise it would convey no information relevant for communication; however, there are sentences without topic.

## 9.4.2

For an automatic recognition of topic, focus and the degrees of CD, two points are crucial:

(A) Either the input is a spoken discourse (and the recognition procedure includes an acoustic analysis), or written (printed) texts are analyzed.

(B) Either the input language has (a considerable degree of) the so-called free word order (as in Czech, Russian, Latin, Warlpiri) or its word order is determined mainly by the grammatical relations (as in English, French).

Since written texts usually do not indicate the position of intonation center and since the "free" word order is determined first of all by the scale of communicative dynamism, it is evident that the former cases in (A) and (B) do not present so many difficulties for the recognition procedure as the latter cases do.

A written "sentence" corresponds, in general, to several spoken sentences which differ in the placement of their intonation center, cf. Example (3) above. In languages with the "free" word order this fact does not bring about serious complications with written technical texts, since there is a strong tendency to arrange the sentences in such texts so that the intonation center falls on the last word of the sentence (if this word is not enclitical).

## 9.4.3

A procedure for the identification of topic and focus in Czech written texts can then be formulated as follows (we use the term 'complementation' or 'sentence part' to denote a subtree occupying the position of a participant or free modification as discussed in Section 9.2 above):

(i)   a. If the verb is the last word of the surface shape of the sentence (SS), it always belongs to the focus.

      b. If the verb is not the last word of the SS, it belongs either to the topic, or to the focus.

Note: The ambiguity accounted for by Rule (ib) can be partially resolved (esp. for the purposes of the practical systems) on the basis of the features of the verb in the preceding sentence: if the verb of the analyzed sentence is identical with the verb of the preceding sentence, or if a relation of synonymy or meaning inclusion holds between the two verbs, then V belongs to the topic. Also, a semantically weak, general verb such as *to be, to become, to carry out*, most often can be understood as belonging to the topic. In other cases the primary position of the verb is in the focus.

(ii) The complementations preceding the verb are included in the topic.

(iii) As for the complementations following the verb, the boundary between topic (to the left) and focus (to the right) may be drawn between any two complementations, provided that those belonging to the focus are arranged in the surface word order in accordance with the systemic ordering.

(iv) If the sentence contains a rhematizer (such as *even, also, only*), then in the primary case the complementation following the rhematizer belongs to the focus and the rest of the sentence belongs to the topic.

Note: This concerns such sentences as *Here even a device of the first type can be used.*; in a secondary case the rhematizer may occur in the topic, e.g., if it together with the sentence part in its scope is repeated from the preceding co-text.

## 9.4.4

Similar regularities hold for the analysis of spoken sentences with normal intonation. However, if a non-final complementation carries the intonation center (IC), then

(a) the bearer of the IC belongs to the focus and all the complementations standing after IC belong to the topic;

(b) rules (ii) and (iii) apply for the elements standing before the bearer of the intonation center;

(c) the rule (ib) is applied to the verb (if it does not carry the IC).

## 9.4.5

As for the identification of topic and focus in an English written sentence, the situation is more complicated due to the fact that the surface word order is to a great extent determined by rules of grammar, so that intonation plays a more substantial role and the written form of the sentence displays much richer ambiguity. For English texts from polytechnical and scientific domains the rules stated for Czech in Section 9.4.3 should be modified in the following ways:

(i)    a. holds, if the surface subject of the sentence is a definite NP; if the subject has an indefinite article, then it mostly belongs to the focus, and the verb to the topic; however, marginal cases with both subject and verb in the focus, or with subject (though indefinite) in the topic and the verb in the focus are not excluded;[2]

     b. holds, including the rules of thumb contained in the note;

(ii) holds, only the surface subject and a temporal adverbial can belong to the focus, if they do not have the form of definite NP's;

(iii) holds, with the following modifications:

---

[2]For the solution of such cases, it again is useful to "remember" the lexical units contained in the preceding utterance, cf. the Note to (ib) in Section 9.4.3 above.

a.  if the rightmost complementation is a local or temporal comple-
    mentation, then it should be checked whether its lexical meaning is
    specific (its head being a proper name, a narrower term, or a term
    not belonging to the subject domain of the given text) or general
    (a pronoun, a broader term); in the former case it is probable that
    such a modification bears the IC and belongs to the focus, while in
    the latter case it rather belongs to the topic;

b.  if the verb is followed by more than one complementation and if the
    sentence final position is occupied by a definite NP or a pronoun,
    this rightmost complementation probably is not the bearer of IC
    and it thus belongs to the topic;

c.  if (a) or (b) apply, then it is also checked which pair of comple-
    mentations disagreeing in their word order with their places under
    systemic ordering is closest (from the left) to IC (i.e., to the end of
    the focus); the boundary between the (left-hand part of the) topic
    and the focus can then be drawn between any two complementations
    beginning with the given pair;

(iv)  holds.

### 9.4.6

If a spoken sentence of English is analyzed, the position of IC can be determined
more safely, so that it is easier to identify the end of the focus than with
written sentences and the modifications to Rule (iii) are no longer necessary.
The procedure can be based on the regularities stated in Section 9.4.4.

Up to now, we have taken into account in our discussion on automatic
identification of topic and focus in spoken utterances only the position of the
intonation center; a question naturally arises whether other features of intonation patterns such as tune and phrasing (in terms of Pierrehumbert) can help as
clues for sentence disambiguation as for its topic and focus. Schmerling (1971)
was the first, to our knowledge, to propose that the different interpretations
of Chomsky's 'range of permissible focus' (which basically corresponds to our
'deep word order,' see Hajičová & Sgall, 1975) are rendered on the surface
by different intonation patterns; most recently, Pierrehumbert and Hirschberg
(1989, Note 5) express a suspicion that the accented word in such cases (within
an NP) need not have the same prominence in all the interpretations; they also
admit that similar constraints on the accenting of parts of a VP are even less
understood.

## 9.5    Parsing sentences in a text

To resolve some complicated issues such as the ambiguity of pronominal reference, a whole co-text rather than a single sentence should be taken into
account. Several heuristics have been proposed to solve this problem; e.g.,
Hobbs (1976) specifies as a common heuristics for pronominal resolution the

determination of the antecedent on the basis of the hearer's preference of the subject NP to an NP in the object position (in a similar vein, Sidner (1981) in her basic rule tests first the possibility of co-specification with what she calls 'actor focus'), the other strategy including inferencing and factual knowledge. Following up our investigation of the hierarchy of activation of items of the stock of knowledge shared by the speaker and the hearer (see Hajičová & Vrbová, 1982; Hajičová, 1987; Hoskovec, 1989; Hajičová & Hoskovec, 1989), we maintain that also this hierarchy should be registered for parsing sentences in a text. We propose to use a partially ordered storage space, reflecting the changes of the activation (prominence) of the elements of the information shared by the speaker and the hearer. The rules assigning the degrees of activation after each utterance take into account the following factors:

(i) whether the given item was mentioned in the topic part or in the focus part of the previous utterance: mentioning in the focus part gives the item the highest prominence, mentioning in the topic part is assumed to assign a one degree lower activation to the given item;

(ii) grammatical means by which the given item is rendered in the surface shape of the utterance: mentioning by means of a (weak) pronoun gives a lower prominence than mentioning by means of a noun;

(iii) association with the items explicitly mentioned in the utterance: items which are associated with the items explicitly mentioned in the preceding utterance get a certain level of prominence, though lower than those mentioned explicitly; it is assumed that the association relations can be classified according to the 'closeness' of the items in question so that some types of associations receive higher degrees of activation than others (e.g., is-a relation is 'closer' in this sense than the part-of relation);[3]

(iv) non-mentioning of a previously mentioned item: an item that has been introduced into the activated part of the stock of shared knowledge but is not mentioned in the subsequent utterances loses step by step its prominence;

(v) not only the immediate degree of activation after the given utterance is relevant for the assignment of reference but also the sequence of degrees of salience from the whole preceding part of the text; thus if an item is being mentioned subsequently for several times in the topic of the sentence, its salience is maintained on a high level and it is more likely an antecedent for pronominal reference than an item that appeared in the focus part (with no prominence history) and received thus the highest degree of activation.

---

[3] It is more exact to understand the association relationships in terms of natural language inferencing (concerning the occurrence of a single associated item) than in terms of the activation of the whole set of items associated with an occurrence of a possible 'antecedent.'

## 9.6    Concluding remarks

Since even in such languages as English or French, surface word order corresponds to the scale of communicative dynamism to a high degree (although such grammatical means as passivization, or the inversion of *make out of* to *make into*, etc., often are necessary here to achieve this correspondence), it is useful in automatic language processing to reflect the word order of the input at least in its surface form. If the effects of the known surface rules on the verb placement, on the position of adjectives, genitives, etc., before (or after) nouns, and so on, are handled,[4] and if the items mentioned in the preceding utterance are stored (to help decide which expressions are contextually bound), then the results may be satisfactory.

# References

Hajičová, E. (1987). Focussing - A meeting point of linguistics and artificial intelligence. In Ph. Jorrand & V. Sgurev (Eds.), *Artificial intelligence II - Methodology, systems, applications*. Amsterdam.

Hajičová, E., & Hoskovec, T. (1989). On some aspects of discourse modelling. *Fifth International Conference on Artificial Intelligence and Information-Control Systems of Robots*. Amsterdam.

Hajičová, E., & Panevová, J. (1984). Valency (case) frames of verbs. In P. Sgall (Ed.), *Contributions to functional syntax, semantics, and language comprehension*. Prague: Amsterdam.

Hajičová, E., & Sgall, P. (1975). Topic and focus in transformational grammar. *Papers in Linguistics*, *8*, 3–58.

Hajičová, E., & Vrbová, J. (1982). On the role of hierarchy of activation in the process of natural language understanding. *Coling 82 — Proceedings of the Ninth Int. Conf. on Computational Linguistics* (pp. 107–113). Prague: Amsterdam.

Hobbs, J. R. (1976). *Pronoun resolution* (Tech. Rep. No. 76-1). City University of New York, City College, Department of Computer Science.

Hoskovec, T. (1989). Modelling a pragmatical background of discourse. *AI '89* (pp. 289–296). Prague.

Kulagina, O. S. (1958). Ob odnom sposobe opredelenija grammatičeskich ponjatij. *Problemy Kibernetiki*, *1*, 203–214.

Močkořová, Z. (1989). *Generalizované podkladové závislostní struktury* (Generalized Underlying Dependency Structures). Unpublished diploma thesis.

Panevová, J. (1974). On verbal frames in functional generative description I. *Prague Bulletin of Mathematical Linguistics*, *22*, 3–40.

Panevová, J. (1975). On verbal frames in functional generative description II. *Prague Bulletin of Mathematical Linguistics*, *23*, 17–52.

---

[4] This has been done, at least to a certain degree, in the experimental systems of English-to-Czech and Czech-to-Russian translation, implemented in Prague.

Pierrehumbert, J. & Hirschberg, J. (1989). *The meaning of intonational contours in the interpretation of discourse.*

Plátek, M., Sgall, J., & Sgall, P. (1984). A dependency base for a linguistic description. In P. Sgall (Ed.), *Contributions to functional syntax, semantics, and language comprehension.* Prague: Amsterdam.

Schmerling, S. F. (1971). Presupposition and the notion of normal stress. *Papers from the Seventh Regional Meeting* (pp. 242–253). Chicago Linguistic Society.

Sgall, P. (1964). Generative beschreibung und die ebenen des sprachsystems. *The Second International Symposium in Magdeburg.* Printed in Zeichen und System der Sprache III (1966) (pp. 225–239) Berlin.

Sgall, P. (1967). Functional sentence perspective in a generative description. *Prague Studies in Mathematical Linguistics, 2,* 203–225.

Sgall, P. (1984) (Ed.), *Contributions to functional syntax, semantics, and language comprehension.* Prague: Amsterdam.

Sgall, P., Hajičová, E., Panevová, J. (1986). *The meaning of the sentence in its semantic and pragmatic aspects.* Prague: Dordrecht.

Sgall, P., & Panevová, J. (1989). Dependency syntax — A challenge. *Linguistics, 15.*

Sidner, C. L. (1981). Focusing for interpretation of pronouns. *American Journal of Computational Linguistics, 7,* 217–231.

# 10. A Probabilistic Parsing Method for Sentence Disambiguation

T. Fujisaki, F. Jelinek, J. Cocke, E. Black

*IBM Thomas J. Watson Research Center*

T. Nishino

*Tokyo Denki University*

## 10.1 Introduction

Constructing a grammar which can parse sentences selected from a natural language corpus is a difficult task. One of the most serious problems is the unmanageably large number of ambiguities. Pure syntactic analysis based only on syntactic knowledge will sometimes result in hundreds of ambiguous parses. Martin (1979) reported that his parser generated 455 ambiguous parses for the sentence:

> List the sales of products produced in 1973 with the products produced in 1972.

Through the long history of work in natural language understanding, semantic and pragmatic constraints have been known to be indispensable for parsing. These should be represented in some formal way and be referred to during or after the syntactic analysis process. AI researchers have been exploring the use of semantic networks, frame theory, etc. to describe both factual and intuitive knowledge for the purpose of filtering out meaningless parses and to aid in choosing the most likely interpretation. The SHRDLU system by Winograd (1972) successfully demonstrated the possibility of sophisticated language understanding and problem solving in this direction. However, to represent semantic and pragmatic constraints, which are usually domain sensitive, in a well-formed way is a very difficult and expensive task. To the best of our knowledge, no one has ever succeeded in doing so except in relatively small restricted domains.

Furthermore, there remains a basic question as to whether it is possible to formally encode all of the syntactic, semantic and pragmatic information needed for disambiguation in a definite and deterministic way. For example, the sentence

Print for *me* the sales of stair carpets.

seems to be unambiguous; however, in the ROBOT system pure syntactic
analysis of this sentence resulted in two ambiguous parses, because the "ME"
can be interpreted as an abbreviation of the state of Maine (Harris, 1979).
Thus, this simple example reveals the necessity of pragmatic constraints for
the disambiguation task. Readers may claim that the system which would
generate the second interpretation is too lax and that a human would never
be perplexed by the case. However, a reader's view would change if he were
told that the sentence below had been issued previous to the sentence above.

Print for *ca* the sales of stair carpets.

Knowing that the speaker inquired about the business in California in the
previous queries, it is quite natural to interpret "me" as the state of Maine in
this context. A problem of this sort usually calls for the introduction of an
appropriate discourse model to guide the parsing. Even with a sophisticated
discourse model beyond anything available today, it would be impossible to
take account all previous sentences: The critical previous sentence may always
be just beyond the capacity of the discourse stack.

Thus it is quite reasonable to think of a parser which disambiguates sentences by referring to statistics which encode various characteristics of the past
discourse, the task domain, and the speaker. For instance, the probability that
the speaker is referring to states and the probability that the speaker is abbre-
viating a name, are useful in disambiguating the example. If the probabilities
of the above are both statistically low, one could simply neglect the interpretation of the state of "Maine" for "me." Faced with such a situation, we propose,
in this paper, to employ probability as a device to quantify language ambiguities. In other words, we will propose a hybrid model for natural language
processing which comprises linguistic expertise, i.e., grammar knowledge, and
its probabilistic augmentation for approximating natural language. With this
framework, semantic and pragmatic constraints are expected to be captured
implicitly in the probabilistic augmentation.

Section 10.2 introduces the basic idea of the probabilistic parsing modeling
method and Section 10.3 presents experimental results arising from applications of this modeling method to the tasks of parsing sentences in English and
noun compounds in Japanese. Detailed description of the method is given
elsewhere.

## 10.2    Probabilistic context-free grammar

### 10.2.1    Extension to context-free grammar

A probabilistic context-free grammar is an augmentation of a context-free
grammar (Fu, 1974). Each of the grammar and lexical rules $\{r\}$, of form $\alpha \rightarrow \beta$,
is associated with a conditional probability $P(r) = P(\beta|\alpha)$. This conditional

Table 10.1. Probability of a derivation tree.

$$
\begin{aligned}
P(t) \;=\; & P(NP.VP.ENDM|S)\times \\
& P(DET.N|NP)\times \\
& P(\text{the}|det)\times \\
& P(\text{boy}|N)\times \\
& P(V.NP|VP)\times \\
& P(\text{likes}|V)\times \\
& P(DET.N|NP)\times \\
& P(\text{that}|det)\times \\
& P(\text{girl}|N)\times \\
& P(.|ENDM)
\end{aligned}
$$

probability denotes the probability that a non-terminal symbol $\alpha$, having appeared during the sentence derivation process, will be replaced with a sequence of terminal and/or non-terminal symbols $\beta$. Obviously $\sum_\beta P(\beta|\alpha) = 1$ holds.

Probabilistic context-free grammars generate sentences from the "Start" or "Sentence" symbol S, in just the same manner as non-probabilistic context-free grammars do. But the advantage of probabilistic grammars is that a probability can be computed for each derivation tree generated, which enables us to quantify sentence ambiguities as described below.

The probability of a derivation tree $t$ can be computed as the product of the conditional probabilities of the rules which are employed for deriving $t$.

$$
P(t) = \prod_{r \in D(t)} P(r)
$$

Here $r$ denotes a rule of the form $\alpha \rightarrow \beta$, and $D(t)$ denotes the ordered set of rules which are employed for deriving the tree $t$. Table 10.1 illustrates how the probability of a derivation tree $t$ can be computed as a product of rule probabilities.

An ambiguous grammar allows many different derivation trees for a given sentence to coexist. From the viewpoint of sentence parsing, we say that a sentence is ambiguous when more than two parse trees, say $t_1, t_2, \ldots$ are derived from the parsing process. Having a device to compute derivation tree probabilities as shown above, we can handle sentence ambiguity in a quantitative way. Namely, when a sentence $s$ is parsed ambiguously as derivation trees $t_1, t_2, \ldots$ and a probability $P(t_j)$ is computed for each derivation tree $t_j$, the sum of the probabilities $\sum_j P(t_j)$ can be regarded as the probability that a particular sentence $s$ will happen to be generated among infinite other possibilities. More interesting is the ratio denoting relative probabilities among ambiguous derivation trees:

$$
\frac{P(t_j)}{\sum_k P(t_k)}
$$

We can assume that it should denote the "likelihood" of each derivation tree. For example, consider the following English sentence "Reply envelopes are enclosed for your convenience." The sentence is ambiguous because it can be parsed in two different ways, the first being in the imperative mode, and the second in the declarative.

$t_1$ "Reply (that) envelopes are enclosed for your convenience." $\Rightarrow$ $\frac{P(t_1)}{(P(t_1)+P(t_2))}$

$t_2$ "Reply envelopes (A kind of envelopes) are enclosed for your convenience." $\Rightarrow$ $\frac{P(t_2)}{(P(t_1)+P(t_2))}$

These correspond to two different parse trees, $t_1$ and $t_2$. By computing $P(t_1) + P(t_2)$, we can estimate the probability that the specific sentence "Reply envelopes are ..." is generated from among an infinite number of possible sentences. On the other hand, $P(t_1)/(P(t_1)+P(t_2))$ and $P(t_2)/(P(t_1)+P(t_2))$ give measures of likelihood for interpretations $t_1$ and $t_2$.

## 10.2.2   Estimation of rule probabilities from data

The Forward/Backward Algorithm, described in (Jelinek *et al.*, 1976), popularly used for estimating transition probabilities for a given hidden Markov model, can be extended so as to estimate rule probabilities of a probabilistic context free grammar, in the following manner.

Assume a Markov model, whose states correspond to possible sentential forms derived via a context free grammar. Then each transition between two states of the Markov model corresponds to an application of a context-free rule that maps one sentential form into another. For example, the state $NP.VP$ can be reached from the state $S$ by applying the rule $S \rightarrow NP.VP$ to a start symbol $S$, the state $ART.NOUN.VP$ can be reached from the state $NP.VP$ by applying the rule $NP \rightarrow ART.NOUN$ to the first $NP$ of the sentential form $NP.VP$, and so on. Since each rule corresponds to a state transition between two states, parsing a set of sentences given as training data will enable us to count how many times each transition is traversed. In other words, a tally is obtained of the number of times each rule is fired when the given set of sentences is generated. For example, the transition from the state $S$ to the state $NP.VP$ may occur most frequently because the rule $S \rightarrow NP.VP$ is commonly used in almost every declarative sentence. A transition such as that from the state $ART.NOUN.VP$ to the state **every**$..NOUN.VP$ may happen fairly infrequently. And so forth. In a context-free-grammar, each replacement of a non-terminal symbol occurs independently of the context. Therefore, counts of all transitions between states $\alpha.A.\beta$ to $\alpha.B.C.\beta$, with arbitrary $\alpha$ and $\beta$, are tied together.

Counting the transitions in the manner just delineated, for thousands of sentences, will enable us to estimate the rule probabilities $\{P(\beta|\alpha)\}$, which are the probabilities that left hand side non-terminal symbols $\alpha$ will be replaced with right hand side patterns $\beta$. The actual iteration procedure to estimate these probabilities from $N$ sentences $\{B^i\}$ is shown below.

1. Make an initial guess of $\{P(\beta|\alpha)\}$ such that $\sum_\beta P(\beta|\alpha) = 1$ holds.

2. Parse each output sentence $B^i$. Assume that the grammar is ambiguous and that in particular, more than one derivation path exists which generate the given sentence $B^i$. In such cases, we denote as $D^i_j$ the $j$th derivation path for the $i$th-sentence.

3. Compute the probability of each derivation path $D^i_j$ in the following way:

$$P(D^i_j) = \prod_{r \in D^i_j} P(r)$$

This computes $P(D^i_j)$ as a product of the probabilities of the rules $\{r\}$ which are employed to generate derivation path $D^i_j$.

4. Compute the Bayes *a posteriori* estimate of the count $C^i_\alpha(\beta)$ which represents how many times the rule $\alpha \rightarrow \beta$ was used for generating sentence $B^i$.

$$C^i_\alpha(\beta) = \sum_j \left( \frac{P(D^i_j)}{\sum_k P(D^i_k)} \times n^i_j(\alpha, \beta) \right)$$

Here, $n^i_j(\alpha, \beta)$ denotes the number of times the rule $\alpha \rightarrow \beta$ is used in derivation path $D^i_j$.

5. Normalize the count so that the total count for rules with the same left hand side non-terminal symbol $\alpha$ becomes 1.

$$f_\alpha(\beta) = \sum_i \frac{C^i_\alpha(\beta)}{\sum_\gamma C^i_\alpha(\gamma)}$$

6. Replace $\{P(\beta|\alpha)\}$ with $\{f_\alpha(\beta)\}$ and repeat from Step 2.

Through this procedure, $\{P(\beta|\alpha)\}$ will approach the actual transition probability (Baker, 1982; Jelinek, 1983). This algorithm has been proven to converge (Baum, 1970).

## 10.2.3 Parsing procedure which computes probabilities

To find the most likely parse — that is, the parse tree which has the highest probability from among all the candidate parses — requires a great deal of time if we calculate probabilities separately for each ambiguous parse. The following is a parsing procedure based on the Cocke-Kasami-Young (Aho & Ullman, 1972) bottom-up parsing algorithm, which can accomplish this task very efficiently. By using it, the most likely parse tree for a sentence will be obtained while the normal bottom-up parsing process is performed. It gives the maximum probability $\max_j P(t_j)$ as well as the total probability of all parses $\sum_j P(t_j)$ at the same time.

The Cocke-Kasami-Young parsing algorithm maintains a two-dimensional table called the Well-Formed-Substring Table (WFST). An entry in the table, $WFST(i, j)$, corresponds to a substring(i,j), j words in length, starting at the i-th word, of an input sentence (Aho & Ullman, 1972). The entry contains a list of triplets. An application of a rule $\alpha \rightarrow \beta\gamma$ will add an entry $(\alpha, \beta, \gamma)$ to the list. This triplet shows that a sequence of $\beta.\gamma$ which spans substring(i,j) is replaced with a non-terminal symbol $\alpha$. ($\beta$ is a pointer to another *WFST* entry that corresponds to the left subordinate structure of $\alpha$ and $\gamma$ is a pointer to the right subordinate structure of $\alpha$.)

In order to compute parse tree probabilities in parallel with this bottom-up parsing process, the structure of this WFST entry is modified as follows. Instead of having a one-level flat list of triplets, each entry of WFST is altered so as to hold a two-level list. The top level of the two-level list corresponds to a left-hand-side non-terminal symbol, called as LHS symbol hereinafter. All combinations of left and right subordinate structures are kept in the sub-list of the LHS symbol. For instance, an application of a rule $\alpha \rightarrow \beta\gamma$ will add $(\beta, \gamma)$ to the sub-list of $\alpha$.

In addition to the sub-list, a LHS symbol is associated with two variables — *MaxP* and *SumP*. These two variables keep the maximum and the total probabilities for the LHS symbol of all possible right hand side combinations. *MaxP* and *SumP* can be computed in the process of bottom-up chart parsing. When a rule $\alpha \rightarrow \beta\gamma$ is applied, *MaxP* and *SumP* are computed as:

$$MaxP(\alpha) = \overset{max}{\beta, \gamma} \left[ Pr(\alpha \rightarrow \beta\gamma) \times MaxP(\beta) \times Maxp(\gamma) \right]$$

$$SumP(\alpha) = \sum_{\beta,\gamma} \left[ Pr(\alpha \rightarrow \beta\gamma) \times SumP(\beta) \times SumP(\gamma) \right]$$

This procedure is similar to that of Viterbi algorithm (Forney, 1973) and maintains the maximum probability and the total probability in *MaxP* and *SumP* respectively. *MaxP/SumP* gives the maximum relative probability of the most likely parse.

## 10.3  Experiments

To demonstrate the capabilities of this modeling method, a few trials were made at disambiguating corpora of highly ambiguous phrases. Two of these experiments will be briefly described below. Details can be found elsewhere.

### 10.3.1  Disambiguation of English sentence parsing

As the basis of this experiment, a grammar developed by Prof. S. Kuno in the 1960's for the machine translation project at Harvard University (Kuno, 1966; Kuno & Oettinger, 1963; Oettinger, 1963) was used with some modification. The rules of the Kuno grammar, which are in Greibach Normal form, were translated into a form which is more favorable to our method. The 2118 original rules were reformulated into 7550 rules in Chomsky normal form (Aho & Ullman, 1972).

Training sentences were chosen from two corpora. One corpus is composed of articles from *Datamation* and *Reader's Digest* (average sentence length in words 10.85; average number of ambiguities per sentence 48.5) and the other from business correspondence (average sentence length in words 12.65; average number of ambiguities per sentence 13.5). A typical sentence from the latter corpus is shown below:

It was advised that there are limited opportunities at this time.

The 3582 sentences from the first corpus, and 624 sentences from the second corpus that were successfully parsed were used to train the 7550 grammar rules along with a set of lexical rules particular to each corpus.

Once the probabilities for rules were obtained in this manner, they were used to disambiguate sentences by the procedure described in Section 10.2.3.

Figure 10.1 shows the parsing result for the sentence "We do not utilize outside art services directly." which turned out to have three ambiguities.

As shown in the figure, ambiguities arise from the three distinct substructures, (A), (B) and (C), for the phrase "utilize outside art services." The derivation (C) corresponds to the most common interpretation while in (A) "art" and "outside" are regarded respectively as subject and object of the verb "services." In (B), "art service" is regarded as an object of the verb "utilize" and "outside" is inserted as a preposition. The numbers 0.356, 0.003 and 0.641 signify the relative probabilities of the three interpretations. As shown in this case, the correct parse (the third one) gets the highest relative probability, as was expected.

Some of the resultant probabilities obtained through the iteration process over both grammar and lexical rules are shown in Table 10.2.

The numbers in parentheses to the left of each rule denote probabilities estimated from the iteration process described in Section 10.2.3. For example, the probabilities that the words **believe** and **know** have the part of speech **IT**[6] are shown as 11.1% and 10.7% on Lines (a) and (b) respectively. Line (c) shows that the non-terminal SE (full sentence) rewrites as the sequence AAA (article and other adjective etc.), 4X (subject noun phrase), VX(predicate) and PD (period or post-sentential modifiers followed by period), with probability 21.6%. Line (d), on the other hand, shows that SE rewrites as the sequence PRN (pronoun), VX and PD with probability 15.3%. Such associations of probabilities with context-free rules are of obvious utility to language analysis.

Table 10.3 summarizes the experiments. Test 1 is based on the corpus of articles from *Datamation* and *Reader's Digest*, and Test 2 on the business correspondence. In both cases, the base Kuno grammar was successfully augmented with probabilities.

---

[1] Infinitive form of a "verb of belief" taking a noun-clause object.

[2] Infinitive form of a transitive verb taking both an object and an objective compliment.

[3] full sentence.

[4] predicate.

```
SENTENCE
  PRONOUN        ( we )
  PREDICATE
    AUXILIARY      ( do )
    INFINITE VERB PHRASE
      ADVERB TYPE1 ( not )
(A) 0.356 INFINITE VERB PHRASE
  :       VERB TYPE IT1( utilize )
  :       OBJECT
  :         NOUN            ( outside )
  :         ADJ CLAUSE
  :           NOUN            ( art )
  :           PRED. WITH NO OBJECT
  :             VERB TYPE VT1 ( services )
(B) 0.003 INFINITE VERB PHRASE
  :       VERB TYPE IT1( utilize )
  :       OBJECT
  :         PREPOSITION  ( outside )
  :         NOUN OBJECT
  :           NOUN            ( art )
  :         OBJECT
  :           NOUN            ( services )
(C) 0.641 INFINITE VERB PHRASE
  :       VERB TYPE IT1( utilize )
  :       OBJECT
  :         NOUN            ( outside )
  :         OBJECT MASTER
  :           NOUN            ( art )
  :           OBJECT MASTER
  :             NOUN            ( services )
  PERIOD
    ADVERB TYPE1 ( directly )
    PRD          ( . )
```

Figure 10.1. Parse tree for "We do not utilize ...."


## 10.3.2   Disambiguation of Japanese noun compounds

Analyzing the structure of noun compounds is difficult because such compounds by themselves usually fail to provide structural clues sufficient to enable the determination of their correct syntactic analysis (Finin, 1986). Particularly in the Japanese language, noun compounds are made up from just a few types of component, and pure syntactic analysis will result in many ambiguous parses. Some kind of mechanism which can handle inter-word analysis of the constituent words is needed to disambiguate them.

Table 10.2. Rule probabilities estimated by iteration.

| Rules for "IT6"[1] | | | Rules for "IT3"[2] | | |
|---|---|---|---|---|---|
| (a) | (0.111) | IT6 → BELIEVE | (0.161) | IT3 → GET |
| (b) | (0.107) | IT6 → KNOW | (0.124) | IT3 → MAKE |
| | (0.086) | IT6 → FIND | (0.120) | IT3 → HAVE |
| | (0.076) | IT6 → THINK | (0.081) | IT3 → SEE |
| | (0.035) | IT6 → CALL | (0.065) | IT3 → KEEP |
| | (0.033) | IT6 → REALIZE | (0.064) | IT3 → BELIEVE |

| Rules for "SE"[3] | | | Rules for "VX"[4] | | |
|---|---|---|---|---|---|
| (c) | (0.216) | SE → AAA 4X VX PD | (0.198) | VX → VT1 N2 |
| (d) | (0.153) | SE → PRN VX PD | (0.107) | VX → PRE NQ VX |
| | (0.153) | SE → NNN VX PD | (0.088) | VX → VI1 |
| | (0.120) | SE → AV1 SE | (0.075) | VX → AUX BV |
| | (0.047) | SE → PRE NQ SE | (0.055) | VX → AV1 VX |
| | (0.045) | SE → NNN AC VX PD | | |
| | (0.026) | SE → AV2 SE | | |

Table 10.3. Summary of English sentence parsing.

| CORPUS | TEST 1 | TEST 2 |
|---|---|---|
| Number of sentences used for training | 3582 | 624 |
| Number of sentences checked manually | 63 | 21 |
| Number of sentences with no correct parse | 4 | 2 |
| Number of sentences where highest prob. was given to the most natural parse | 54 | 18 |
| Number of sentences where highest prob. was not given to the right one | 5 | 1 |

We applied our probabilistic modeling method to the disambiguation of Japanese noun compounds. This was done by associating rule probabilities with basic construction rules for noun compounds. In order to make these rule probabilities reflect inter-word relationships among component words, words were grouped into finer categories $\{N_1, N_2, N_3, \ldots, N_m\}$. The base rules were replicated for each combination of right hand side word categories. Since we assumed that the right-most word of the right hand side transfers its category to the left-hand-side parent, a single $N \rightarrow NN$ rule was replicated to $m \times m$ rules. For these $m \times m$ rules, separate probabilities were prepared and estimated. The method described in Section 10.2.2 was used to estimate these probabilities from noun compounds actually observed in text.

Once probabilities for these rules were estimated, the parsing procedure described in Section 10.2.3 was used to compute the relative probability of each parse tree.

In this experiment, we categorized words via a conventional clustering technique which groups words according to neighboring word patterns. For example, "oil" and "coal" belong to the same category in our method because they frequently appear in similar word patterns such as "~ burner," "~ consumption," "~ resources." 31,900 noun compound words picked from abstracts of technical papers (MT for Electronics) were used for this categorization process. Twenty-eight categories were obtained through this process for 1000 high-frequency 2-character Kanji primitive words, eight categories for 200 single-character prefixes, and ten categories for 400 single-character suffixes (Nishno & Fujisaki, 1988). Base rules reflecting different combination of these 46 word categories expanded out to 5582 separate rules. These original base rules are displayed below.

<word> → <2 character Kanji primitive word>

<word> → <word> <word>

<word> → <prefix single character word> <word>

<word> → <word> <suffix single character word>

Conditional probabilities for these 5582 rules were estimated from 28,568 noun compounds.

Once the training had been carried out, 153 noun compounds were randomly chosen and parsed by the procedure shown in the Section 10.2.3, and the resulting parse trees were examined. In each case it was determined whether or not the correct parse had been assigned the highest probability among all the parses. Over the 153 test compounds, 22 were uniquely parsed and 131 were parsed with more than two different parse trees. Of these 131, 92 were such that the right parses were given the highest probabilities.

Shown below are parsing results for two sample noun compounds.

word 1: "medium scale integrated circuit."

word 2: "small scale electricity company."

(The word order is the same in English and Japanese).

In both of these cases, five different parse trees were obtained, and their relative probabilities computed (cf. Table 10.4). In the first case, the fifth parse tree, which is the most natural, got the highest probability (0.43). In the second case, the third parse tree, which is the most natural, got the highest probability (1.00).

# 10.4    Concluding remarks

The N-gram modeling technique (Shannon, 1951) has been proven to be a powerful and effective method of language modeling. It has successfully been used in several applications such as speech recognition, text segmentation,

Table 10.4. Parse trees and their probabilities.

| STRUCTURE OF PARSE TREE IN BRACKET NOTATION | MEANING CONVEYED | PROB. |
|---|---|---|
| WORD 1 "MEDIUM SCALE INTEGRATED CIRCUIT" | | |
| medium [[scale integrated] circuit] | a medium-sized "scale-integrated-circuit" | 0.17 |
| medium [scale [integrated circuit]] | a medium-sized integrated circuit which is scale (?) | 0.04 |
| [medium scale] [integrated circuit] | an integrated-circuit of medium-scale | 0.19 |
| [medium [scale integrated]] circuit | a circuit which is scale-integrated to a medium degree | 0.17 |
| [[medium scale] integrated] circuit | a circuit which is medium-scale integrated | 0.43 |
| WORD 2 "SMALL SCALE ELECTRICITY COMPANY" | | |
| small [[scale electricity] company] | a small company which provides scale-electricity | 0.00 |
| small [scale [electricity company]] | a company which is small, provides electricity, and has something to do with scale | 0.00 |
| [small scale] [electricity company] | a company which provides electricity and which is small scale | 1.00 |
| [small [scale electricity]] company | a company which provides small scale-electricity (?) | 0.00 |
| [[small scale] electricity] company | a company which provides small scale electricity (micro-electronics?) | 0.00 |

character recognition and others (Fujisaki, 1981, 1985; Jelinek, *et al.*, 1976; Raviv, 1967; Takeda & Fujisaki, 1987). At the same time, however, it has proved to be difficult to approximate language phenomena precisely enough when context dependencies expand over a long distance. A direct means to remedy the situation is (a) to increase $N$ in the N-gram or (b) to increase the length of the basic units utilized from a character to a word or to a phrase. If the vocabulary size is $M$, however, the number of statistical data needed to maintain the precision of the N-gram model increases in proportion to $M^N$. The situation is similar in (b). Increasing the length of the basic unit causes an exponential increase in vocabulary size. Hence an exponential increase in the volume of statistical data required follows in (b) as well. This shows that the N-gram model faces a serious data gathering problem given a task featuring long-context dependency. Obviously, the parsing of sentences creates this sort of problem.

On the other hand, the method introduced here aims to remedy this problem by combining a probabilistic modeling procedure with linguistic expertise. In this hybrid approach (Fujisaki, 1984, 1985), linguistic expertise provides the framework of a grammar, and the probabilistic modeling method augments the grammar quantitatively.

Since the probabilistic augmentation process is completely automatic, it is not necessary to rely on human endeavor which tends to be expensive, inconsistent, and subjective. Also the probabilistic augmentation of a grammar is adaptable for any set of sentences.

These two important features make the method useful for various problems in natural language processing. Besides its use for sentence disambiguation, the method can be used to customize a given grammar to a particular sub-language corpus. Namely, when a grammar designed for a general corpus is applied using this method, the rules and the lexical entries which are used less frequently in the corpus will automatically be given low or zero probabilities. In addition, the rules and the lexical entries which require more refinement will be given high probabilities. Thus the method helps us to tune a grammar in a top-down manner. The present method is also useful for improving performance in top-down parsing when used for obtaining hints for reordering rules according to rule probabilities.

Accordingly, although all its possible uses have not been explored, the method proposed in this paper has an enormous potential range of application, and the authors hope that a new natural language processing paradigm may emerge on its foundation.

Use of probability in natural language analysis may seem strange, but it is in effect but a simple generalization of common practice: the usual top-down parsing strategy forces a true or false (1 or 0) decision, i.e., the selection of one of a set of options at every non-deterministic choice point.

And most importantly, by the use of the proposed method, a grammar can be probabilistically augmented objectively and automatically from a set of sentences picked from an arbitrary corpus. On the other hand, the representation of semantic and pragmatic constraints in the form of the usual semantic networks, frame theory, etc., requires a huge amount of subjective human effort.

# Acknowledgments

The authors are indebted to Dr. B. Mercer and Dr. L. Bahl of the IBM Thomas J. Watson Research Center for their valuable technical suggestions and comments.

Prof. S. Kuno of Harvard University has not only given the senior author permission to use the Kuno grammar, but also has rendered him much valuable linguistic advice.

# References

Aho, A. V., & Ullman, J. D. (1972). *The theory of parsing, translation and compiling* (Vol. 1). Prentice-Hall.

Baker, J. K. (1982). *Trainable grammars for speech recognition* (Internal Memo).

Baum, L. E. (1970). A maximization technique occurring in the statistical analysis of probabilistic functions in Markov chains. *The Annals of Mathematical Statistics, 41, 1.*

Finin, T. W. (1986). Constraining the interpretation of nominal compounds in a limited context. In R. Grishman & R. Kittredge (Eds.), *Analysing language in a restricted domain*. Hillsdale, NJ: Lawrence Erlbaum Assoc.

Forney, G. D., Jr. (1973). The Viterbi algorithm. *Proceedings of IEEE, 61, 3.*

Fu, K. S. (1974). Syntactic methods in pattern recognition. *Mathematics in Science and Engineering, 112.* Academic Press.

Fujisaki, T. (1981). A scheme of separating and giving phonetic transcriptions to Kanji-kana mixed Japanese documents by dynamic programming (in Japanese). *Natural Language Workshop Report NL28-5.* Information Processing Society of Japan.

Fujisaki, T. (1984). An approach to stochastic parsing. *Proceedings of COLLING84.*

Fujisaki, T. (1985). *Handling of ambiguities in natural language processing* (in Japanese). Unpublished doctoral dissertation. University of Tokyo, Department of Information Science.

Harris, L. (1979). Experience with ROBOT in 12 commercial natural language database query applications. *Proceedings of the Sixth International Joint Conference on Artificial Intelligence.* Morgan Kaufmann.

Jelinek, F. (1983). *Notes on the outside/inside algorithm* (Internal Memo).

Jelinek, F., *et al.* (1976). Continuous speech recognition by statistical methods. *Proceedings of the IEEE, 64, 4.*

Kuno, S. (1966). The augmented predictive analyzer for context-free languages and its relative efficiency. *CACM, 9, 11.*

Kuno, S., & Oettinger, A. G. (1963). Syntactic structure and ambiguity of English. *Proceedings of FJCC.*

MT for Electronics. *Science and Technology Database, 26* (in tape form). Japanese Information Center for Science and Technology.

Martin, W. A., *et al.* (1979). *Preliminary analysis of a breadth-first parsing algorithm: Theoretical and experimental results* (Tech. Rep. No. TR-261). MIT LCS.

Nishno, T., & Fujisaki, T. (1988). Probabilistic parsing of Kanji compound words (in Japanese). *Journal of Information Processing Society of Japan, 29, 11.*

Oettinger, A. G. (1963). *Mathematical Linguistics and Automatic Translation* (Tech. Rep. No. NSF-8). Harvard University, The Computation Laboratory.

Raviv, J. (1967). Decision making in Markov chains applied to the problem of pattern recognition. *IEEE Trans. Information Theory, IT-3, 4.*

Shannon, C. E. (1951). Prediction and entropy of printed English. *Bell Sys. Tech. J, 30.*

Takeda, K., & Fujisaki, T. (1987). Segmentation of Kanji primitive word by a stochastical method (in Japanese). *Journal of Information Processing Society of Japan, 28, 9.*

Winograd, T. (1972). *Understanding natural language.* New York: Academic Press.

Winograd, T. (1983). *Language as a cognitive process: Syntax* (Vol. 1). Addison Wesley.

# 11. Towards a Uniform Formal Framework for Parsing

**Bernard Lang**

*INRIA*

## 11.1 Introduction

Many of the formalisms used to define the syntax of natural (and programming) languages may be located in a continuum that ranges from propositional Horn logic to full first order Horn logic, possibly with non-Herbrand interpretations. This structural parenthood has been previously remarked: it lead to the development of Prolog (Cohen, 1988; Colmerauer, 1978) and is analyzed in some detail in (Pereira & Warren, 1980) for Context-Free languages and Horn Clauses. A notable outcome is the parsing technique known as Earley deduction (Pereira & Warren, 1983).

These formalisms play (at least) three roles:

**descriptive:** they give a finite and organized description of the syntactic structure of the language,

**analytic:** they can be used to analyze sentences so as to retrieve a syntactic structure (i.e., a representation) from which the meaning can be extracted,

**generative:** they can also be used as the specification of the concrete representation of sentences from a more structured abstract syntactic representation (e.g., a parse tree).

The choice of a formalism is essential with respect to the descriptive role, since it controls the perspicuity with which linguistic phenomena may be understood and expressed in actual language descriptions, and hence the tractability of these descriptions for the human mind.

However, computational tractability is required by the other two roles if we intend to use these descriptions for mechanical processing of languages.

The aim of our work, which is partially reported here, is to obtain a uniform understanding of the computational aspects of syntactic phenomena within the continuum of Horn-like formalisms considered above, and devise general purpose algorithmic techniques to deal with these formalisms in practical applications.

To attain this goal, we follow a three-sided strategy:

- Systematic study of the lower end of the continuum, represented by context-free (CF) grammars (simpler formalisms, such as propositional Horn logic do not seem relevant for our purpose).

- Systematic study of the higher end of the continuum, i.e., first order Horn clauses,

- Analysis of the relations between intermediate formalisms and Horn clauses, so as to reuse for intermediate formalisms the understanding and algorithmic solutions developed for the more powerful Horn clauses.

This strategy is motivated by two facts:

- the computational properties of both CF grammars and Horn clauses may be expressed with the same computational model: the non-deterministic pushdown automaton,

- the two formalisms have a compatible concept of syntactic structure: the parse-tree in the CF case, and the proof-tree in the Horn clause case.

The greater simplicity of the CF formalism helps us in understanding more easily most of the computational phenomena. We then generalize this knowledge to the more powerful Horn clauses, and finally we specialize it from Horn clauses to the possibly less powerful but linguistically more perspicuous intermediate formalisms.

In this chapter we present two aspects of our work:

1. a new understanding of shared parse forests and their relation to CF grammars, and

2. a generalization to full Horn clauses, also called *Definite Clause (DC) programs*, of the push-down stack computational model developed for CF parsers.

## 11.2   Context-free parsing

Though much research has been devoted to this subject in the past, most of the practically usable work has concentrated on deterministic push-down parsing which is clearly inadequate for natural language applications and does not generalize to more complex formalisms. On the other hand there has been little formal investigation of general CF parsing, though many practical systems have been implemented based on some variant of Earley's algorithm.

Our contribution has been to develop a formal model which can describe these variants in a uniform way, and encompasses the construction of parse-trees, and more generally of parse-forests. This model is based on the *compilation paradigm* common in programming languages and deterministic parsing:

Table 11.1. A context-free grammar.

| (1) | S   | ::= | NP   | VP |
|-----|-----|-----|------|-----|
| (2) | S   | ::= | S    | PP |
| (3) | NP  | ::= | n    |    |
| (4) | NP  | ::= | det  | n  |
| (5) | NP  | ::= | NP   | PP |
| (6) | PP  | ::= | prep | NP |
| (7) | VP  | ::= | v    | NP |

we use the non-deterministic[1] *Pushdown Automaton (PDA)* as a virtual parsing machine which we can simulate with an Earley-like construction; variations on Earley's algorithm are then expressed as variations in the compilation schema used to produce the PDA code from the original CF grammar.[2] This uniform framework has been used to compare experimentally parsing schemata w.r.t. parser size, parsing speed and size of shared forest, and in reusing the wealth of PDA construction techniques to be found in the literature.

This work has been reported elsewhere (Billot & Lang, 1989; Lang, 1974, 1988a). An essential outcome, which is the object of this section, is a new understanding of the relation between CF grammars, parse-trees and parse-forests, and the parsing process itself. The presentation is informal since our purpose is to give an intuitive understanding of the concepts, which is our interpretation of the earlier theoretical results.

Essentially, we shall first show that both CF grammars and shared parsed forest may be represented by AND-OR graphs, with specific interpretations. We shall then argue that this representational similarity is not accidental, and that there is no difference between a shared forest and a grammar.

## 11.2.1   Context-free grammars

Our running example for a CF grammar is the pico-grammar of English, taken from (Tomita, 1987), which is given in Table 11.1.

In Figure 11.1 we give a graphical representation of this grammar as an AND-OR graph. The notation for this AND-OR graph is unusual and emphasizes the difference between AND and OR nodes. OR-nodes are represented by the non-terminal categories of the grammar, and AND-nodes are represented

---

[1] In this chapter, the abbreviation PDA always implies the possibility of non-determinism.

[2] Many variants of Earley's algorithm published in the literature (Bouckaert, Pirotte, & Snelling, 1975; Tomita, 1987), including Earley's own (Earley, 1970), could be viewed as special cases of that approach.

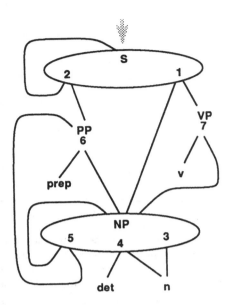

Figure 11.1. Graph of the grammar.

by the rules (numbers) of the grammar. There are also leaf-nodes corresponding to the terminal categories.

The OR-node corresponding to a non-terminal X has exiting arcs leading to
each AND-node n representing a rule that defines X. This arc is not explicitly
represented in the graphical formalism chosen. If there is only one such arc,
then it is represented by placing n immediately under X. This is the case for
the OR-node representing the non-terminal PP. If there are several such arcs,
they are implicitly represented by enclosing in an ellipse the OR-node X above
all its son nodes n, n', .... This is the case for the OR-node representing the
non-terminal NP.

The sons of an AND-node (i.e., a rule) are the grammatical categories found
in the right-hand-side of the rule, *in that order*. The arcs leading from an AND-
node to its sons are represented explicitly. The convention for orienting the
arcs is that they leave a node from below and reach a node from above.

This graph accurately represents the grammar, and is very similar to the
graphs used in some parsers. For example, LR(0) parsing uses a graph representation of the grammar that is very similar, the main difference being that
the sons of AND-nodes are linked together from left to right, rather than being
attached separately to the AND-node (Aho & Ullman, 1972; DeRemer, 1971).
More simply, this graph representation is very close to the data structures
often used to represent conveniently a grammar in a computer memory.

A characteristic of the AND/OR graph representing a grammar is that
all nodes have different labels. Conversely, any labeled AND/OR graph *such
that all node labels are different* may be read as — translated into — a CF

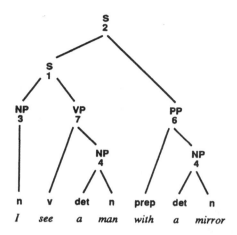

Figure 11.2. A parse tree.

grammar such that AND-node labels are rule names, OR-node labels represent non-terminal categories, and leaf-node labels represent terminal categories.

## 11.2.2   Parse trees and parse forests

Given a sentence in the language defined by a CF grammar, the parsing process consists in building a tree structure, *the parse tree*, that shows how this sentence can be constructed according to the grammatical rules of the language. It is however frequent that the CF syntax of a sentence is ambiguous, i.e., that several distinct parse-trees may be constructed for it.

Let us consider the grammar of Table 11.1.

If we take as example the sentence "I see a man with a mirror," which translate into the terminal sequence "n v det n prep det n," we can build the two parse trees given in Figures 11.2 and 11.3. Note that we label a parse tree node with its non-terminal category and with the rule used to decompose it into constituents. Hence such a parse tree could be seen as an AND-OR tree similar to the AND-OR grammar graph of Figure 11.1. However, since all OR-nodes are degenerated (i.e., have a unique son), a parse tree is just an AND-tree.

The number of possible parse trees may become very large when the size of sentences increases: it may grow exponentially with that size, and may even be infinite for cyclic grammars (which seem of little linguistic usefulness [Pereira & Warren, 1983; Tomita, 1985], except may-be for analyzing ill-formed sentences [Lang, 1988a]). Since it is often desirable to consider all possible parse trees (e.g., for semantic processing), it is convenient to merge as much as possible these parse trees into a single structure that allows them to share common

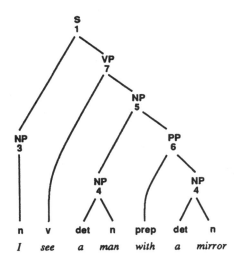

Figure 11.3. Another parse tree.

parts. This sharing save on the space needed to represent the trees, and also on the later processing of these trees since it may allows to share between two trees the processing of some common parts.[3] The shared representation of all parse trees is called *shared parse forest*, or just *parse forest*.

To analyze how two trees can share a (*connected*) part, we first notice that such a part may be isolated by cutting the tree along an edge (or arc) as in Figure 11.4. This actually gives us two parts: a *subtree* and a *context* (cf. Figure 11.4). Either of these two parts may be shared in forests representing two trees. When a subtree is the same for two trees, it may be shared as shown in Figure 11.5. When contexts are equal and may thus be shared, we get the structure depicted in Figure 11.6.

The sharing of context actually corresponds to ambiguities in the analyzed sentence: the ellipse in Figure 11.6 contains the head nodes for two distinct parses of the same subsentence $v$, that both recognize $v$ in the same non-terminal category NT. Each head node is labeled with the (number of the) rule used to decompose $v$ into constituents in that parse, and the common syntactical category labels the top of the ellipse. Not accidentally, this structure is precisely the structure of the OR-nodes we used to represent CF grammars. Indeed, an ambiguity is nothing but a choice between two possible parses of the same sentence fragment $v$ as the same syntactic category NT.

Using a combination of these two forms of sharing, the two parse trees of Figures 11.2 and 11.3 may be merged into the shared parse forest[4] of Fig-

---

[3]The direct production of such shared representation by parsing algorithms also corresponds to sharing in the parsing computation (Billot & Lang, 1989; Lang, 1974; Tomita, 1987).

[4]This graphical representation of shared forests is not original: to our knowledge it was

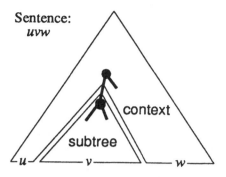

Figure 11.4. Context and subtree.

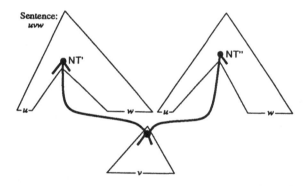

Figure 11.5. Two parses sharing a subtree.

ure 11.7. Note that, for this simple example, the only context being shared is the empty outer context of the two possible parse tree, that still states that a proper parse tree must belong to the syntactic category S.

In this representation we keep our double labeling of parse tree nodes with both the non-terminal category and the rule used to decompose it into its constituents. As indicated above, ambiguities are represented with context sharing, i.e., by OR-nodes that are the exact equivalent of those of Figure 11.1.

first used by Tomita (1987). However, we believe that its comparative understanding as context sharing, as AND-OR tree or as grammar has never been presented. Context sharing is called *local ambiguity packing* by Tomita.

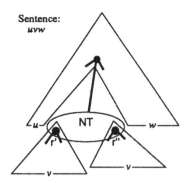

Figure 11.6. Two parses sharing a context.

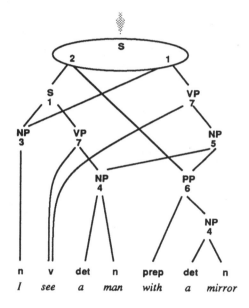

Figure 11.7. A shared parse forest.

Hence *a shared parse forest is an AND-OR graph*.[5] Note however that the same rule (resp. non-terminal) may now label several AND-nodes (resp. OR-nodes) of the shared parse forest graph.

If we make the labels distinct, for example by indexing them so as not to lose their original information, we can then read the shared forest graph of a sentence $s$ as a grammar $\mathcal{F}_s$. The language of this grammar contains only the sentence $s$, and it gives $s$ the same syntactic structure(s) — i.e., the same parse tree(s) and the same ambiguities — as the original grammar, up to the

---

[5] This graph may have cycles for infinitely ambiguous sentences when the grammar of the language is itself cyclic.

above renaming of labels.

It is easily shown that the space complexity of the shared forest representation is $\mathcal{O}(n^{p+1})$ where $n$ is the length of the sentence analyzed and $p$ is the length of the longest right-hand side of a rule. Hence, efficient representation requires a trivial transformation of the original grammar into a *2-size grammar*, i.e., a grammar such that the right-hand sides of rules have a length at most equal to 2. This generalizes/simplifies the use of *Chomsky Normal Form* (Pratt, 1975) or *2-form* (Sheil, 1976). Such a transformation amounts effectively to allowing two forest nodes to share a common sublist of their respective lists of sons.

This type of transformation is explicitly or implicitly performed/required by parsing algorithms that have $\mathcal{O}(n^3)$ complexity. For example in (Billot & Lang, 1989; Lang, 1974), the transformation is implicit in the construction of the PDA transitions.

## 11.2.3   Parse forests for incomplete sentences

Our view of parsing may be extended to the parsing of incomplete sentences (Lang, 1988a).

An example of incomplete sentence is "... see ... mirror." Assuming that we know that the first hole stands for a single missing word, and that the second one stands for an arbitrary number of words, we can represent this sentence by the sequence "?  v * n." The convention is that "?" stands for one unknown word, and "*" for any number of them.

Such an incomplete sentence $s$ may be understood as defining a sublanguage $\mathcal{L}_s$ which contains all the correct sentences matching $s$. Any parse tree for a sentence in that sublanguage may then be considered a possible parse tree for the incomplete sentence $s$. For example, the sentences "I see a man with a mirror" and "You see a mirror" are both in the sublanguage of the incomplete sentence above. Consequently, the two parse trees of Figures 11.2 and 11.3 are possible parse trees for this sentence, along with many others.

All parse trees for the sentence $s =$ "?  v * n" may be merged into a shared parse forest that is represented in Figure 11.8.

The graph of this forest has been divided into two parts by the horizontal grey line $\alpha - \beta$.

The terminal labels underscored with a "*" represent any word in the corresponding terminal category. This is also true for all the terminal labels in the bottom part of the graph.

The forest fragment below the horizontal line is a (closed) subgraph of the original grammar of Figure 11.1 (which we have completed in grey to emphasize the fact). It corresponds to parse trees of constituents that are completely undefined, within their syntactical categories, and may thus be any tree in that category that the grammar can generate. This occurs once in the forest for non-terminal PP at arc marked $\alpha$ and twice for NP at arcs marked $\beta$.

This bottom part of the graph brings no new information (it is just the part of the original grammar reachable from nodes PP and NP). Hence the forest could be simplified by eliminating this bottom subgraph, and labeling

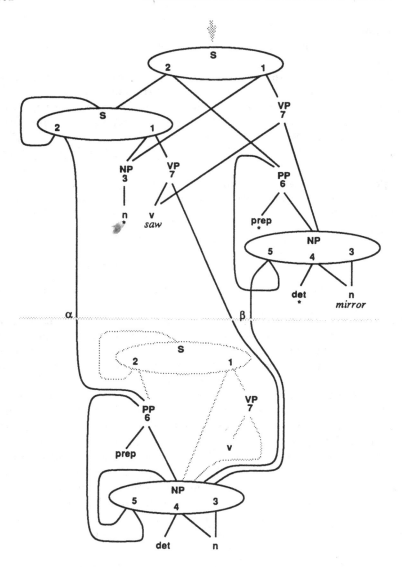

Figure 11.8. Full parse forest for an incomplete sentence.

the end node of the $\alpha$ (resp. $\beta$) arc with PP* (resp. NP*), meaning an arbitrary PP (resp. NP) constituent.

The complete shared forest of Figure 11.7 may be interpreted as a CF grammar $\mathcal{G}_s$. This grammar is precisely a grammar of the sublanguage $\mathcal{L}_s$ of all sentences that match the incomplete sentence $s$. Again, up to renaming of nonterminals, this grammar $\mathcal{G}_s$ gives the sentences in $\mathcal{L}_s$ the same syntactic structure as the original grammar of the full language.

If the sentence parsed is the completely unknown sentence $u = $ "$*$," then the corresponding sublanguage $\mathcal{L}_u$ is the complete language considered, and the parse forest for $u$ can be quite naturally the original grammar of the full language: *The grammar of a CF language is a parse-forest of the completely unknown sentence, i.e., the syntactic structure of all sentences in the language, in a non-trivial sense.* In other words, all one can say about a fully unknown sentence assumed to be correct, is that it satisfies the syntax of the language. This statement does take a stronger signification when shared parse forests are actually built by parsers, and when such a parser does return the original grammar for the fully unknown sentence.[6]

Parsing a sentence according to a CF grammar is just extracting a parse tree (or a sub-forest) fitting that sentence from the CF grammar considered as a parse forest.

Looking at these issues from another angle, we have the following consequence of the above discussion: given a set of parse trees (i.e., appropriately decorated trees), they form the set of parses of a CF language iff they can be merged into a shared forest that is finite.

In (Billot & Lang, 1989; Lang, 1988a) Billot and the author have proposed parsers that actually build shared forests formalized as CF grammar. This view of shared forests originally seemed to be an artifact of the formalization chosen in the design of these algorithms, and appeared possibly more obfuscatory than illuminating. It has been our purpose here to show that it really has a fundamental character, *independently of any parsing algorithm.*

This close relation between sharing structures and context-freeness actually hints to limitations of the effectiveness of sharing in parse forests defined by non-CF formalisms.

From an algorithmic point of view, the construction of a shared forest for a (possibly incomplete) sentence may be seen as a specialization of the original grammar to the sublanguage defined by that sentence. This shows interesting connections with the general theory of partial evaluation of programs (Futamura, 1988), which deals with the specialization of programs by propagation of known properties of their input.

In practice, the published parsing algorithms do not always give shared forest with maximum sharing. This may result in forests that are larger or more complex, but does not invalidate our presentation.

## 11.3  Horn clauses

The PDA based compilation approach proved itself a fruitful theoretical and experimental support for the analysis and understanding of general CF parsing à la Earley. In accordance with our strategy of uniform study of the "Horn continuum," we extended this approach to general Horn clauses, i.e., Definite Clause (DC) programs.

---

[6] However, if it does not produce optimal sharing in the forest, the parser may return a structurally equivalent, but larger grammar.

This lead to the definition of the *Logical Push-Down Automaton (LPDA)* which is an operational engine intended to play for Horn clauses the same role as the usual PDA for CF languages. Space limitations prevent giving here a detailed presentation of LPDAs, and we only sketch the underlying ideas. More details may be found in (Lang, 1988b, 1988c).

As in the CF case, the evaluation of a DC program may be decomposed into two phases:

- a compilation phase that translate the DC program into a LPDA. Independently of the later execution strategy, the compilation may be done according to a variety of evaluation schemata: top-down, bottom-up, predictive bottom-up, .... Specific optimization techniques may also be developed for each of these compilation schemata.

- an execution phase that can interpret the LPDA according to some execution technique: backtrack (depth-first), breadth-first, dynamic programming, or some combination (Tamaki & Sato, 1986).

This separation of concerns leads to a better understanding of issues, and should allow a more systematic comparison of the possible alternatives.

In the case of dynamic programming execution, the LPDA formalism uses to very simple structures that we believe easier to analyze, prove, and optimize than the corresponding direct constructions on DC programs (Pereira & Warren, 1983; Porter, 1986; Tamaki & Sato, 1986; Vieille, 1987), while remaining independent of the computation schema, unlike the direct constructions. Note that predictive bottom-up compilation followed by dynamic programming execution is essentially equivalent to Earley deduction as presented in (Pereira & Warren, 1983; Porter, 1986).

The next sections include a presentation of LPDAs and their dynamic programming interpretation, a compilation schema for building a LPDA from a DC program, and an example applying this top-down construction to a very simple DC program.

## 11.3.1 Logical PDAs and their dynamic programming interpretation

A LPDA is essentially a PDA that stores logical atoms (i.e., predicates applied to arguments) and substitutions on its stack, instead of simple symbols. The symbols of the standard CF PDA stack may be seen as predicates with no arguments (or more accurately with two argument similar to those used to translate CF grammars into DC in [Pereira & Warren, 1980]). A technical point is that we consider PDAs without "finite state" control: this is possible without loss of generality by having pop transitions that replace the top two atoms by only one (this is standard in LR(k) PDA parsers [Aho & Ullman, 1972]).

Formally a LPDA $\mathcal{A}$ is a 6-tuple: $\mathcal{A} = (\mathbf{X}, \mathbf{F}, \mathbf{\Delta}, \overset{\circ}{\$}, \$_f, \Theta)$ where $\mathbf{X}$ is a set of variables, $\mathbf{F}$ is a set of functions and constants symbols, $\mathbf{\Delta}$ is a set of stack predicate symbols, $\overset{\circ}{\$}$ and $\$_f$ are respectively the initial and final stack predicates, and $\Theta$ is a finite set of *transitions* having one of the following three forms:

*horizontal transitions:* $\quad B \mapsto C \qquad$ — replace B by C on top of stack

*push transitions:* $\qquad B \mapsto CB \qquad$ — push C on top of former stack top B

*pop transitions:* $\qquad BD \mapsto C \qquad$ — replace BD by C on top of stack

where B, C and D are $\Delta$-atoms, i.e., atoms built with $\Delta$, **F** and **X**.

Intuitively (and approximately) a pop transition $BD \mapsto C$ is applicable to a stack configuration with atoms A and A′ on top, iff there is a substitution $s$ such that $Bs = As$ and $Ds = A's$. Then A and A′ are removed from the stack and replaced by $Cs$, i.e., the atom C to which $s$ has been applied. Things are similar for other kinds of transitions. Of course a LPDA is usually non-deterministic w.r.t. the choice of the applicable transition.

In the case of dynamic programming interpretations, all possible computation paths are explored, with as much sub-computation sharing as possible. The algorithm proceeds by building a collection of *items* (analogous to those of Earley's algorithm) which are pairs of atoms. An item $<A \ A'>$ represents a stack fragment of two consecutive atoms (Lang, 1974, 1988a). If another item $<A' \ A''>$ was also created, this means that the sequence of atoms $AA'A''$ is to be found in some possible stack configuration, and so on (*up to the use of substitutions, not discussed here*). The computation is initialized with an initial item $\overset{\circ}{U} = \; < \overset{\circ}{\$} \dashv >$. New items are produced by applying the LPDA transitions to existing items, until no new application is possible (an application may often produce an already existing item). The computation terminates under similar conditions as specialized algorithms (Pereira & Warren, 1983; Tamaki & Sato, 1986; Vieille, 1987). If successful, the computation produces one or several *final items* of the form $<\$_f \; \overset{\circ}{\$} >$, where the arguments of $\$_f$ are an answer substitution of the initial DC program. In a parsing context, one is usually interested in obtaining parse-trees rather than "answer substitutions." The counterpart of CF a parse tree is here a proof tree corresponding to proofs with the original DC program. Such proof trees may be obtained by the same techniques that are used in the case of CF parsing (Billot, 1988; Billot & Lang, 1989; Lang, 1974), and that actually interpret the items and their relations as a shared parse forest structure.

Substitutions are applied to items as follows (we give as example the most complex case): a pop transition $BD \mapsto C$ is applicable to a pair of items $<A \ A'>$ and $<E \ E'>$, iff there is a unifier $s$ of $<A \ A'>$ and $<B \ D>$, and a unifier $s'$ of $A's$ and E. This produces the item $<Css' \ E's'>$.

## 11.3.2 Top-down compilation of DC programs into LPDAs

Given a DC program, *many different compilation schemata may be used to build a corresponding LPDA* (Lang, 1988c). We give here a very simple and unoptimized top-down construction. The DC program to be compiled is composed of a set of clauses $\gamma_k$: $A_{k,0}$ :- $A_{k,1}, \ldots, A_{k,n_k}$, where each $A_{k,i}$ is a logical literal. The query is assumed to be the head literal $A_{0,0}$ of the first clause $\gamma_0$.

The construction of the top-down LPDA is based on the introduction of new predicate symbols $\nabla_{k,i}$, corresponding to positions between the body literals of each clause $\gamma_k$. The predicate $\nabla_{k,0}$ corresponds to the position before the leftmost literal, and so on. Literals in clause bodies are refuted from left to right. The presence of an instance of a position literal $\nabla_{k,i}(t_k)$ in the stack indicates that the first $i$ subgoals corresponding to the body of some instance of clause $\gamma_k$ have already been refuted. The argument bindings of that position literal are the partial answer substitution computed by this partial refutation.

For every clause $\gamma_k$: $A_{k,0}$ :- $A_{k,1}, \ldots, A_{k,n_k}$, we note $t_k$ the vector of variables occurring in the clause. Recall that $A_{k,i}$ is a literal using some of the variables in $\gamma_k$, while $\nabla_{k,i}$ is only a predicate which needs to be given the argument vector $t_k$ to become the literal $\nabla_{k,i}(t_k)$.

Then we can define the top-down LPDA by the following transitions:

1. $\overset{\circ}{\$} \mapsto \nabla_{0,0}(t_0) \overset{\circ}{\$}$

2. $\nabla_{k,i}(t_k) \mapsto A_{k,i+1} \nabla_{k,i}(t_k)$ — *for every clause $\gamma_k$ and for every position $i$ in its body:* $0 \leq i < n_k$

3. $A_{k,0} \mapsto \nabla_{k,0}(t_k)$                              — *for every clause $\gamma_k$*

4. $\nabla_{k,n_k}(t_k) \nabla_{k',i}(t_{k'}) \mapsto \nabla_{k',i+1}(t_{k'})$[7]   — *for every pair of clauses $\gamma_k$ and $\gamma_{k'}$ and for every position $i$ in the body of $\gamma_{k'}$:* $0 \leq i < n_{k'}$

The final predicate of the LPDA is the stack predicate $\nabla_{0,n_0}$ which corresponds to the end of the body of the first "query clause" of the DC program. The rest of the LPDA is defined accordingly.

The following is an informal explanation of the above transitions:

1. *Initialization*: We require the refutation of the body of clause $\gamma_0$, i.e., of the query.

2. *Selection of the leftmost remaining subgoal*: When the first $i$ literals of clause $\gamma_k$ have been refuted, as indicated by the position literal $\nabla_{k,i}(t_k)$, then select the $i + 1^{st}$ literal $A_{k,i+1}$ to be now refuted.

3. *Selection of clause $\gamma_k$*: Having to satisfy a subgoal that is an instance of $A_{k,0}$, eliminate it by resolution with the clause $\gamma_k$. The body of $\gamma_k$ is now considered as a sequence of new subgoals, as indicated by the position literal $\nabla_{k,0}(t_k)$.

---

[7]If $k = k'$ then we rename the variable in $t_{k'}$ since the transition corresponds to the use of two distinct variants of the clause $\gamma_k$.

Note also that we need not define such a transition for all triples of integer $k$ $k'$ and $i$, but only for those triples such that the head of $\gamma_k$ unifies with the literal $A_{k',i+1}$.

Table 11.2. The definite clause program.

---

**Clauses:**   q(f(f(a))):-.

q(X1):-q(f(X1)).

**Query:**      q(X2)

---

4. *Return to calling clause* $\gamma_{k'}$: Having successfully refuted the head of clause $\gamma_k$ by refuting successively all literals in its body as indicated by position literal $\nabla_{k,n_k}(t_k)$, we return to the calling clause $\gamma_{k'}$ and "increment" its position literal from $\nabla_{k',i}(t_{k'})$ to $\nabla_{k',i+1}(t_{k'})$, since the body literal $A_{k',i+1}$ has been refuted as instance of the head of $\gamma_k$.

Backtrack interpretation of a LPDA thus constructed essentially mimics the Prolog interpretation of the original DC program.

### 11.3.3   A very simple example

The following example has been produced with a prototype implementation realized by Eric Villemonte de la Clergerie and Alain Zanchetta (1988). This example, as well as the top-down construction above, are taken from (Lang, 1988c).

The definite clause program to be executed is given in Table 11.2. Note that a search for all solutions in a backtrack evaluator would not terminate.

The solutions found by the computer are:   X2 = f(f(a))

X2 = f(a)

X2 = a

These solutions were obtained by first compiling the DC program into an LPDA according to the schema defined in Section 11.3.2, and then interpreting this LPDA with the general dynamic programming algorithm defined in Section 11.3.1.

The LPDA transitions produced by the compilation are in Table 11.3.

The collection of items produced by the dynamic programming computation is given in the Table 11.4.

In the transitions printout of Table 11.3, each predicate name nabla.i.j stands for our $\nabla_{i,j}$.

According to the construction of Section 11.3.2, the final predicate should be nabla.0.1. For better readability we have added a horizontal transition to a final predicate noted answer.

## 11.4   Other linguistic formalisms

Pereira and Warren (1980) have shown in their classical paper the link between CF grammars and DC programs. A similar approach may be applied to

Table 11.3. Transitions of the LPDA.

```
********* PUSH Transitions B->BC ***********
   predicate :nabla.2.0
nabla.2.0(X1) -> q(f(X1)) nabla.2.0(X1)
   predicate :nabla.0.0
nabla.0.0(X2) -> q(X2) nabla.0.0(X2)
   predicate :dollar0
dollar0() -> nabla.0.0(X2) dollar0()


********* Horizontal Transitions B->C ******
   predicate :q
q(f(f(a))) -> nabla.1.0()
q(X1) -> nabla.2.0(X1)
   predicate :query
query(X2) -> nabla.0.0(X2)
   predicate :nabla.0.1
nabla.0.1(X2) -> answer(X2)


********* POP Transitions BD->C ************
   predicate :nabla.2.1
nabla.2.1(X1) nabla.0.0(X2) -> nabla.0.1(X2)
nabla.2.1(X4) nabla.2.0(X1) -> nabla.2.1(X1)
   predicate :nabla.1.0
nabla.1.0() nabla.0.0(X2) -> nabla.0.1(X2)
nabla.1.0() nabla.2.0(X1) -> nabla.2.1(X1)
   predicate :nabla.0.1
nabla.0.1(X3) nabla.0.0(X2) -> nabla.0.1(X2)
nabla.0.1(X2) nabla.2.0(X1) -> nabla.2.1(X1)
```

more complex formalisms than CF grammars, and we have done so for Tree Adjoining Grammars (TAG) (Lang, in preparation).

By encoding TAGs into DC programs, we can specialize to TAGs the above results, and easily build TAG parsers (using at least the general optimization techniques valid for all DC programs). Furthermore, control mechanisms akin to the agenda of chart parsers, together with some finer properties of LPDA interpretation, allow to control precisely the parsing process and produce Earley-like left-to-right parsers, with a complexity $O(n^6)$.

We expect that this approach can be extended to a variety of other linguistic formalisms, with or without unification of feature structures, such as head grammars, linear indexed grammars, combinatory categorial grammars. This is indeed suggested by the results of Joshi, Vijay-Shanker and Weir that relate these formalisms and propose CKY or Earley parsers for some of them (Vijay-Shanker & Weir, in press; Vijay-Shanker, Weir, & Joshi, 1987).

Table 11.4. Items produced by the dynamic programming interpretation.

```
dollar0() , ()()
nabla.0.0(X5) , dollar0()
q(X6) , nabla.0.0(X6)
nabla.2.0(X7) , nabla.0.0(X7)
nabla.1.0() , nabla.0.0(f(f(a)))
q(f(X8)) , nabla.2.0(X8)
nabla.0.1(f(f(a))) , dollar0()
nabla.2.0(f(X9)) , nabla.2.0(X9)
nabla.1.0() , nabla.2.0(f(a))
nabla.2.1(f(a)) , nabla.0.0(f(a))
nabla.0.1(f(a)) , dollar0()
q(f(f(X10))) , nabla.2.0(f(X10)) *
nabla.2.1(f(a)) , nabla.2.0(a)
nabla.2.1(a) , nabla.0.0(a)
nabla.0.1(a) , dollar0()
answer(a) , dollar0()
answer(f(a)) , dollar0()
answer(f(f(a))) , dollar0()
* subsumed by: q(f(X8)),nabla.2.0(X8)
```

The parse forests built in the CF case correspond to proof forests in the Horn case. Such proof forests may be obtained by the same techniques that we used for CF parsing (Billot & Lang, 1989). However it is not yet fully clear how parse trees or derivation trees may be extracted from the proof forest when DC programs are used to encode non-CF syntactic formalisms. On the basis of our experience with TAGs, we conjecture that for non-CF formalisms, the proof forest obtained corresponds to derivation forests (i.e., containing derivation trees as defined in [Vijay-Shankar, Weir, & Joshi, 1987]) rather than to forest representing the possible superficial syntactic structure of object trees.

## 11.5 Concluding remarks

Our understanding of syntactic structures and parsing may be considerably enhanced by comparing the various approaches in similar formal terms, even though they may differ in power and/or superficial appearance. Hence we attempt to formally unify the problems in two ways:

- by considering all formalisms as special cases of Horn clauses

- by expressing all parsing strategies with a unique operational device: the pushdown automaton.

Systematic formalization of problems often considered to be pragmatic issues (e.g., structure and construction of parse forests) has considerably improved our understanding and has been an important success factor. It is our belief that such formalization is essential to harness the algorithmic intricacies of language processing, even if the expressive power of a formal system cannot not fully cover the richness of natural language constructions.

The links established with problems in other areas of computer science (e.g., partial evaluation, database recursive queries) could also be the source of interesting new approaches.

# Acknowledgments

This work has been partially supported by the Eureka Software Factory (ESF) Project.

# References

Aho, A. V., & Ullman, J. D. (1972). *The theory of parsing, translation and compiling*. Englewood Cliffs, NJ: Prentice-Hall.

Billot, S. (1988). *Analyseurs syntaxiques et non-déterminisme*. Unpublished doctoral dissertation. Orléans (France): Université d'Orléans la Source.

Billot, S., & Lang, B. (1989). The structure of shared forests in ambiguous parsing. *Proceedings of the 27th Annual Meeting of the Association for Computational Linguistics* (pp. 143–151). Vancouver, British Columbia. (Also INRIA Research Rep. No. 1038.)

Bouckaert, M., Pirotte, A., & Snelling, M. (1975). Efficient parsing algorithms for general context-free grammars. *Information Sciences, 8*, 1–26.

Cohen, J. (1988). A view of the origins and development of Prolog. *Communications of the ACM, 31*, 26–36.

Colmerauer, A. (1978). Metamorphosis grammars. In L. Bolc (Ed.), *Natural language communication with computers* (LNCS 63). Springer. First appeared as *Les Grammaires de Métamorphose* (Tech. Rep.). Groupe d'Intelligence Artificielle, Université de Marseille II, 1975.

DeRemer, F. L. (1971). Simple LR(k) grammars. *Communications ACM, 14*, 453–460.

Earley, J. (1970). An efficient context-free parsing algorithm. *Communications ACM, 13*, 94–102.

Futamura, Y. (Ed.) (1988). Proceedings of the workshop on partial evaluation and mixed computation. *New Generation Computing, 6, 2,3*.

Lang, B. (1974). Deterministic techniques for efficient non-deterministic parsers. *Proceedings of the 2nd Colloquium on Automata, Languages and Programming* (pp. 255–269). In J. Loeckx (Ed.) *Saarbrücken, Springer Lecture Notes in Computer Science 14*. (Also: Rapport de Recherche 72, IRIA-Laboria, Rocquencourt (France).)

Lang, B. (1988a). Parsing incomplete sentences. *Proceedings of the 12th International Conference on Computational Linguistics (COLING'88)* (Vol. 1, pp. 365–371). Budapest, Hungary.

Lang, B. (1988b). Datalog automata. *Proceedings of the 3rd International Conference on Data and Knowledge Bases* (pp. 389–404). Jerusalem, Israel: Morgan Kaufmann.

Lang, B. (1988c). *Complete evaluation of horn clauses: An automata theoretic approach* (Tech. Rep. No. 913). INRIA. (To appear in the *International Journal of Foundations of Computer Science.*)

Lang, B. (in preparation). *The systematic construction of Earley parsers: Application to the production of $O(n^6)$ Earley parsers for Tree Adjoining Grammars.*

Pereira, F. C. N., & Warren, D. H. D. (1980). Definite clause grammars for language analysis — A survey of the formalism and a comparison with augmented transition networks. *Artificial Intelligence, 13*, 231–278.

Pereira, F. C. N., & Warren, D. H. D. (1983). Parsing as deduction. *Proceedings of the 21st Annual Meeting of the Association for Computational Linguistics* (pp. 137–144). Cambridge, MA.

Porter, H. H., III. (1986). *Earley deduction* (Tech. Rep. No. CS/E-86-002). Beaverton: Oregon Graduate Center.

Pratt, V. R. (1975). LINGOL — A progress report. *Proceedings of the Fourth International Joint Conference on Artificial Intelligence* (pp. 422–428). Morgan Kaufmann.

Sheil, B. A. (1976). Observations on context free parsing. *Statistical methods in linguistics* (pp. 71–109) Stockholm, Sweden. *Proceedings of International Conference on Computational Linguistics (COLING-76).* Ottawa, Canada. (Also as Tech. Rep. No. TR 12-76, Cambridge, MA: Harvard University, Center for Research in Computing Technology, Aiken Computation Laboratory.)

Tamaki, H., & Sato, T. (1986). OLD resolution with tabulation. *Proceedings of 3rd International Conference on Logic Programming* (pp. 84–98). London, UK: Springer LNCS 225.

Tomita, M. (1985). *An efficient context-free parsing algorithm for natural languages and its applications.* Unpublished doctoral dissertation. Pittsburgh, PA: Carnegie Mellon University.

Tomita, M. (1987). An efficient augmented-context-free parsing algorithm. *Computational Linguistics, 13*, 31–46.

Vieille, L. (1987). *Recursive query processing: The power of logic* (Tech. Rep. No. TR-KB-17). Munich, West Germany: European Computer Industry Research Center (ECRC).

Vijay-Shanker, K., & Weir, D. J. (in press). Polynomial parsing of extensions of context-free grammars. *In this volume.*

Vijay-Shanker, K., Weir, D. J., & Joshi, A. K. (1987). Characterizing structural descriptions produced by various grammatical formalisms. *Proceedings of the 25th Annual Meeting of the Association for Computational Linguistics* (pp. 104–111). Stanford, CA.

Villemonte de la Clergerie, E., & Zanchetta, A. (1988). *Evaluateur de clauses de horn* (Rapport de Stage d'Option). Palaiseau, France: Ecole Polytechnique.

# 12. A Method for Disjunctive Constraint Satisfaction

## John T. Maxwell III and Ronald M. Kaplan

*Xerox Palo Alto Research Center*

## 12.1 Introduction

A distinctive property of many current grammatical formalisms is their use of feature equality constraints to express a wide variety of grammatical dependencies. Lexical-Functional Grammar (Kaplan & Bresnan, 1982), Head-Driven Phrase-Structure Grammar (Pollard & Sag, 1987), PATR (Karttunen, 1986a), FUG (Kay, 1979, 1985), and the various forms of categorial unification grammar (Karttunen, 1986b; Uszkoreit, 1986; Zeevat, Klein, & Calder, 1987) all require an analysis of a sentence to satisfy a collection of feature constraints in addition to a set of conditions on the arrangement of words and phrases. Conjunctions of equality constraints can be quickly solved by standard unification algorithms, so they in themselves do not present a computational problem. However, the equality constraints derived for typical sentences are not merely conjoined together in a form that unification algorithms can deal with directly. Rather, they are embedded as primitive elements in complex disjunctive formulas. For some formalisms, these disjunctions arise from explicit disjunction operators that the constraint language provides for (e.g., LFG) while for others disjunctive constraints are derived from the application of alternative phrase structure rules (e.g., PATR). In either case, disjunctive specifications help to simplify the statement of grammatical possibilities. Alternatives expressed locally within individual rules and lexical entries can appeal to more general disjunctive processing mechanisms to resolve their global interactions.

The computational problem, of course, is that processing disjunctive specifications is exponentially difficult in the worse case, even if conjunctions of primitive propositions can be solved very quickly, as is the case with equality. For example, the most direct way of dealing with a disjunctive formula is to convert it to disjunctive normal form and then separately solve each of the conjunctive subformulas in the result. There are in general exponentially many such subformulas to consider, hence the overall exponential complexity of the whole process. Despite its computational cost, the DNF strategy does have the significant advantage that it decouples the processing of disjunctions from any details of the primitive constraint formalism or of the conjunctive method for solving them. Grammatical constraint formulas can be solved by merely composing well-known DNF algorithms with equally well-known unification algorithms in a simple, modular implementation that is easy to understand and easy to prove correct.

The exponential time-bound does not reflect our naive intuitions about the intrinsic complexity of the natural language parsing problem. The number of alternatives that remain consistent for any given sentence is typically much, much smaller than the number that a DNF parsing algorithm would explore, and traces of such algorithms typically show enormous amounts of repetitive and irrelevant computation. Although disjunctive constraint satisfaction is known to be worst-case exponential, we and others have suspected that the disjunctive configurations that emerge from grammatical specifications may conform to certain restricted patterns that admit of more rapid solution algorithms. Karttunen (1984) observed that many grammatical disjunctions can be resolved locally among a limited number of morphological feature values and do not usually have the more global interactions that the DNF algorithm is optimized to handle. Kasper (1987a, b) suggested that many grammatical constraints lead to immediate inconsistencies and proposed an algorithm that noticed some of these inconsistencies before expanding to disjunctive normal form.

We have developed a contrasting set of intuitions. Working with Lexical-Functional Grammars, we have noticed that, as a grammar increases in its coverage, the number of disjunctions to be processed grows in rough proportion to the number of words in a sentence. However, we have not observed that elements of these disjunctions typically are mutually inconsistent. Rather, the most striking pattern is that disjunctions arising from words and phrases that are distant from each other in the string tend not to interact. A disjunction representing an ambiguity in the person or number of a sentence's subject, for example, tends to be independent of any ambiguities in, say, the complement's complements' object. That is, the constraint system is globally satisfiable no matter what choices are made from the two distant disjunctive branches. If disjunctions are independent, or free, of each other, it is not necessary to explore all combinations of their branches to determine the satisfiability of the entire system.

The algorithm we propose in this chapter is optimized for this common pattern of free disjunctions. Natural languages seem to have a certain locality property in that distant words and phrases usually contribute information about different grammatical functions and features. Distant disjunctions therefore tend to relate to different branches of the attribute-value matrix (functional structure in LFG terminology) that is characterized by the set of equality constraints. In essence, instead of multiplying disjunctions in advance of running a purely conjunctive unification algorithm, our algorithm embeds disjunctions underneath the particular attributes they are concerned with. Equality processing is then carried out on this disjunctive structure. Our method retains the important advantage of the DNF strategy of directly referencing the axioms of the conjunctive equality theory, and thus remains easy to understand and prove correct.

There are four main steps in our algorithm for processing disjunctive systems:

1. Turn the disjunctive system into an equi-satisfiable flat conjunction of contexted constraints;

2. Normalize the contexted constraints using extensions of standard techniques;

3. Extract and solve a propositional 'disjunctive residue;' and

4. Produce models for satisfiable systems.

Intuitively, the disjunctive residue represents the satisfiable combinations of disjuncts in a simple propositional form. Each of the transformations above preserves satisfiability, and so the original disjunctive system is satisfiable if and only if the disjunctive residue is satisfiable. If the disjunctions are relatively independent, then the disjunctive residue is significantly easier to solve than the original system.

The first four sections of this chapter cover the steps outlined above. The next section compares this approach with some other techniques for dealing with disjunctive systems of constraints. The last section discusses some of the things that we learned along the way.

# 12.2    Turning    disjunctions    into    contexted constraints

## 12.2.1    Basic lemma

Our method depends on a simple lemma for converting a disjunction into a conjunction of implications:

**Lemma 12.1** $\phi_1 \vee \phi_2$ *is satisfiable iff* $(p \rightarrow \phi_1) \wedge (\neg p \rightarrow \phi_2)$ *is satisfiable, where $p$ is a new propositional variable.*

Proof:

1. If $\phi_1 \vee \phi_2$ is satisfiable, then either $\phi_1$ is satisfiable or $\phi_2$ is satisfiable. Suppose that $\phi_1$ is satisfiable. Then if we choose $p$ to be true, then $p \rightarrow \phi_1$ is satisfiable because $\phi_1$ is satisfiable, and $\neg p \rightarrow \phi_2$ is vacuously satisfiable because its antecedent is false. Therefore $(p \rightarrow \phi_1) \wedge (\neg p \rightarrow \phi_2)$ is satisfiable.

2. If $(p \rightarrow \phi_1) \wedge (\neg p \rightarrow \phi_2)$ is satisfiable, then both clauses are satisfiable. One clause will be vacuously satisfiable because its antecedent is false and the other will have a true antecedent. Suppose that $p \rightarrow \phi_1$ is the clause with the true antecedent. Then $\phi_1$ must be satisfiable for $p \rightarrow \phi_1$ to be satisfiable. But if $\phi_1$ is satisfiable, then so is $\phi_1 \vee \phi_2$. Q.E.D.

Intuitively, the new variable $p$ is used to encode the requirement that at least one of the disjuncts be true. In the remainder of the chapter we use lower-case $p$ to refer to a single propositional variable, and upper-case $P$ to refer to a boolean combination of propositional variables. We call $P \rightarrow \phi$ a *contexted* constraint, where $P$ is the *context* and $\phi$ is called the *base* constraint.

(Note that this lemma is stated in terms of *satisfiability*, not logical equivalence. A form of the lemma that emphasized logical equivalence would be: $\phi_1 \vee \phi_2 \leftrightarrow \exists p : (p \rightarrow \phi_1) \wedge (\neg p \rightarrow \phi_2)$.)

## 12.2.2   Turning a disjunctive system into a conjunctive system

The lemma given above can be used to convert a disjunctive system of constraints into a flat conjunction of contexted constraints in linear time. The resulting conjunction is satisfiable if and only if the original system is satisfiable. The algorithm for doing so is as follows:

**Algorithm 12.1**

a) *push all of the negations down to the literals*

b) *turn all of the disjunctions into conjunctions using Lemma (12.1) above*

c) *flatten nested contexts with:* $(P_i \rightarrow (P_j \rightarrow \phi)) \Leftrightarrow (P_i \wedge P_j \rightarrow \phi)$

d) *separate conjoined constraints with:*

$$(P_i \rightarrow \phi_1 \wedge \phi_2) \Leftrightarrow (P_i \rightarrow \phi_1) \wedge (P_i \rightarrow \phi_2)$$

This algorithm is a variant of the reduction used to convert disjunctive systems to an equi-satisfiable formula in conjunctive normal form in the proof that the satisfiability problem for CNF is NP-complete (Hopcroft & Ullman, 1979). In effect, we are simply converting the disjunctive system to an implicational form of CNF (since $P \rightarrow \phi$ is logically equivalent to $\neg P \vee \phi$). CNF has the desirable property that if any one clause can be shown to be unsatisfiable, then the entire system is unsatisfiable.

## 12.2.3   Example

The functional structure $f$ of an uninflected English verb has the following constraints in the formalism of Lexical-Functional Grammar (Kaplan & Bresnan, 1982):

$$((f\,inf) = - \wedge (f\,tense) = pres$$
$$\wedge \neg[(f\,subj\,num) = sg \wedge (f\,subj\,pers) = 3]) \qquad (12.1)$$
$$\vee (f\,inf) = +$$

(In LFG notation, a constraint of the form $(f\,a) = v$ asserts that $f(a) = v$, where $f$ is a function, $a$ is an attribute, and $v$ is a value. $(f\,a\,b) = v$ is shorthand for $f(a)(b) = v$.) These constraints say that either an uninflected English verb is a present tense verb which is not third person singular, or it is infinitival. In the left column below this system has been reformatted so that it can be compared with the results of applying Algorithm 12.1 to it, shown on the right:

*reformatted:*                                *converts to:*

| | | | |
|---|---|---|---|
| ( | $(f\,inf) = -$ | $(p_1 \rightarrow$ | $(f\,inf) = -)\wedge$ |
| $\wedge$ | $(f\,tense) = pres$ | $(p_1 \rightarrow$ | $(f\,tense) = pres)\wedge$ |
| $\wedge \neg\,[$ | $(f\,subj\,num) = sg$ | $(p_1 \wedge p_2 \rightarrow$ | $(f\,subj\,num) \neq sg)\wedge$ |
| | $\wedge\,(f\,subj\,pers) = 3\,])$ | $(p_1 \wedge \neg p_2 \rightarrow$ | $(f\,subj\,pers) \neq 3)\wedge$ |
| $\vee$ | $(f\,inf) = +$ | $(\neg p_1 \rightarrow$ | $(f\,inf) = +)$ |

## 12.3   Normalizing the contexted constraints

A conjunction of contexted constraints can be put into an equi-satisfiable normalized form that makes it easy to identify all unsatisfiable combinations of constraints. The basic idea is to start with algorithms that determine the satisfiability of purely conjunctive systems and extend each rule of inference or rewriting rule so that it can handle contexted constraints. We illustrate this approach by modifying two conventional satisfiability algorithms, one based on deductive expansion and one based on rewriting.

### 12.3.1   Deductive expansion

Deductive expansion algorithms work by determining all the deductions that could lead to unsatisfiability given an initial set of clauses and some rules of inference. The key to extending a deductive expansion algorithm to contexted constraints is to show that for every rule of inference that is applicable to the base constraints, there is a corresponding rule of inference that works for contexted constraints. The basic observation is that base constraints can be conjoined if their contexts are conjoined:

**Lemma 12.2** $(P_1 \rightarrow \phi_1) \wedge (P_2 \rightarrow \phi_2) \Rightarrow (P_1 \wedge P_2 \rightarrow \phi_1 \wedge \phi_2)$

If we know from the underlying theory of conjoined base constraints that $\phi_1 \wedge \phi_2 \rightarrow \phi_3$, then the transitivity of implication gives us:

$$(P_1 \rightarrow \phi_1) \wedge (P_2 \rightarrow \phi_2) \Rightarrow (P_1 \wedge P_2 \rightarrow \phi_3) \qquad (12.2)$$

Equation (12.2) is the contexted version of $\phi_1 \wedge \phi_2 \rightarrow \phi_3$. Thus the following extension of a standard deductive expansion algorithm works for contexted constraints:

**Algorithm 12.2**

    *For every pair of contexted constraints $P_1 \rightarrow \phi_1$ and $P_2 \rightarrow \phi_2$ such that:*

        a) *there is a rule of inference $\phi_1 \wedge \phi_2 \rightarrow \phi_3$*

        b) $P_1 \wedge P_2 \neq FALSE$

c) *there are no other clauses* $P_3 \rightarrow \phi_3$ *such that* $P_1 \wedge P_2 \rightarrow P_3$

*add* $P_1 \wedge P_2 \rightarrow \phi_3$ *to the conjunction of clauses being processed.*

Condition (b) is based on the observation that any constraint of the form $FALSE \rightarrow \phi$ can be discarded since no unsatisfiable constraints can ever be derived from it. This condition is not necessary for the correctness of the algorithm, but may have performance advantages. Condition (c) corresponds to the condition in the standard deductive expansion algorithm that redundant constraints must be discarded if the algorithm is to terminate. We extend this condition by noting that any constraint of the form $P_i \rightarrow \phi$ is redundant if there is already a constraint of the form $P_j \rightarrow \phi$, where $P_i \rightarrow P_j$. This is because any unsatisfiable constraints derived from $P_i \rightarrow \phi$ will also be derived from $P_j \rightarrow \phi$. Our extended algorithm terminates if the standard algorithm for simple conjunctions terminates. When it terminates, an equi-satisfiable disjunctive residue can be easily extracted, as described in Section (12.4) below.

## 12.3.2   Rewriting

Rewriting algorithms work by repeatedly replacing conjunctions of constraints with logically equivalent conjunctions until a normal form is reached. This normal form usually has the property that all unsatisfiable constraints can be determined by inspection. Rewriting algorithms use a set of rewriting rules that specify what sorts of replacements are allowed. These are based on logical equivalences so that no information is lost when replacements occur. Rewriting rules are interpreted differently from logical equivalences, however, in that they have directionality: whenever a logical expression matches the left-hand side of a rewriting rule, it is replaced by an instance of the logical expression on the right-hand side, but not vice-versa. To distinguish the two, we will use $\leftrightarrow$ for logical equivalence and $\Leftrightarrow$ for rewriting rules. (This corresponds to our use of $\rightarrow$ for implication and $\Rightarrow$ for deduction above.)

A rewriting algorithm for contexted constraints can be produced by showing that for every rewrite rule that is applicable to the base constraints, there is a corresponding rewrite rule for contexted constraints. Suppose that $\phi_1 \wedge \phi_2 \Leftrightarrow \phi_3$ is a rewriting rule for base constraints. An obvious candidate for the contexted version of this rewrite rule would be to treat the deduction in (12.2) as a rewrite rule:

$$(P_1 \rightarrow \phi_1) \wedge (P_2 \rightarrow \phi_2) \Leftrightarrow (P_1 \wedge P_2 \rightarrow \phi_3) \qquad \text{(incorrect)} \qquad (12.3)$$

This is incorrect because it is not a logical equivalence: the information that $\phi_1$ is true in the context $P_1 \wedge \neg P_2$ and that $\phi_2$ is true in the context $P_2 \wedge \neg P_1$ has been lost as the basis of future deductions. If we add clauses to cover these cases, we get the logically correct:

$$\begin{aligned} (P_1 \rightarrow \phi_1) \wedge (P_2 \rightarrow \phi_2) \Leftrightarrow \\ (P_1 \wedge \neg P_2 \rightarrow \phi_1) \wedge (P_2 \wedge \neg P_1 \rightarrow \phi_2) \wedge (P_1 \wedge P_2 \rightarrow \phi_3) \end{aligned} \qquad (12.4)$$

This is the contexted equivalent of $\phi_1 \wedge \phi_2 \Leftrightarrow \phi_3$. Note that the effect of this is that the contexted constraints on the right-hand side have unconjoinable contexts (that is, the conjunction of the contexts is tautologically false). Thus, although the right-hand side of the rewrite rule has more conjuncts than the left-hand side, there are fewer implications to be derived from them.

Loosely speaking, a rewriting algorithm is constructed by iterative application of the contexted versions of the rewriting rules of a conjunctive theory. Rather than give a general outline here, let us consider the particular case of attribute value logic.

### 12.3.3  Application to attribute-value logic

Attribute-value logic is used by both LFG and unification-based grammars. We will start with a simple version of the rewriting formalism given in (Johnson, 1988). For our purposes, we only need two of the rewriting rules that Johnson defines (1988, pp. 38–39):

$$t_1 \approx t_2 \Leftrightarrow t_2 \approx t_1 \text{ when } \|t_1\| < \|t_2\|$$
$$(\|t_i\| \text{ is Johnson's norm for terms.)} \tag{12.5}$$

$$(t_2 \approx t_1 \wedge \phi) \Leftrightarrow (t_2 \approx t_1 \wedge \phi[t_2/t_1])$$
$$\text{where } \phi \text{ contains } t_2 \text{ and } \|t_2\| > \|t_1\| \tag{12.6}$$
$$(\phi[t_2/t_1] \text{ denotes } \phi \text{ with every occurrence of } t_2 \text{ replaced by } t_1.)$$

We turn Equation (12.6) into a contexted rewriting rule by a simple application of (12.3) above:

$$(P_1 \to t_2 \approx t_1) \wedge (P_2 \to \phi) \quad \Leftrightarrow \quad (P_1 \wedge \neg P_2 \to t_2 \approx t_1) \wedge$$
$$(\neg P_1 \wedge P_2 \to \phi) \wedge \tag{12.7}$$
$$(P_1 \wedge P_2 \to (t_2 \approx t_1 \wedge \phi[t_2/t_1]))$$

We can collapse the two instances of $t_2 \approx t_1$ together by observing that $(P \to A \wedge B) \Leftrightarrow (P \to A) \wedge (P \to B)$ and that $(P_i \to A) \wedge (P_j \to A) \Leftrightarrow (P_i \vee P_j \to A)$, giving the simpler form:

$$(P_1 \to t_2 \approx t_1) \wedge (P_2 \to \phi) \Leftrightarrow$$
$$(P_1 \to t_2 \approx t_1) \wedge (P_2 \wedge \neg P_1 \to \phi) \wedge (P_2 \wedge P_1 \to \phi[t_2/t_1]) \tag{12.8}$$

Formula (12.8) is the basis for a very simple rewriting algorithm for a conjunction of contexted attribute-value constraints:

**Algorithm 12.3**

  *For each pair of clauses $P_1 \to t_2 \approx t_1$ and $P_2 \to \phi$:*

   a) *if $\|t_2\| > \|t_1\|$, then set $x$ to $t_1$ and $y$ to $t_2$,*
      *else set $x$ to $t_2$ and $y$ to $t_1$*

   b) *if $\phi$ mentions $y$ then*

      *replace $P_2 \to \phi$ with $(P_2 \wedge \neg P_1 \to \phi) \wedge (P_2 \wedge P_1 \to \phi[y/x])$*

Notice that since $P_1 \to t_2 \approx t_1$ is carried over unchanged in (12.8), we only have to replace $P_2 \to \phi$ in Step (b). Note also that if $P_2 \wedge P_1$ is $FALSE$, there is no need to actually add the clause $(P_2 \wedge P_1 \rightarrow \phi[t_2/t_1])$ since no unsatisfiable constraints can be derived from it. Similarly if $P_2 \wedge \neg P_1$ is $FALSE$ there is no need to add $P_2 \wedge \neg P_1 \rightarrow \phi$. These modifications may or may not have performance advantages.

### 12.3.4  Proof of termination

We can prove that the contexted version of Johnson's algorithm terminates by extending his proof of termination (1988, pp. 38–40) to include contexted constraints. Johnson defines a norm on terms $\|t\|$ such that if $\|t_1\| < \|t_2\|$ and $\phi$ uses $t_2$, then $\|\phi[t_2/t_1]\| < \|\phi\|$ for all $\phi$. We do not need to know the details of this norm, except to note that $\|\phi_1 \wedge \phi_2\| = \|\phi_1\| \cdot \|\phi_2\|$.

We now define $\|P \rightarrow \phi\|$ to be $\|\phi\|^{\|P\|}$, where $\|P\|$ is the number of solutions that $P$ has in the truth table for all the propositional variables in the entire system. (In terms of a Venn diagram, $\|P\|$ is the size of the area covered by $P$.) One consequence of this definition is that $\|P_i\| = \|P_i \wedge P_j\| + \|P_i \wedge \neg P_j\|$ for all $P_i$ and $P_j$.

Using this definition, the norm for the left hand side of (12.8) is:

$$\|(P_1 \rightarrow t_2 \approx t_1) \wedge (P_2 \rightarrow \phi)\|$$
$$= \|(P_1 \rightarrow t_2 \approx t_1)\| \cdot \|(P_2 \rightarrow \phi)\| \qquad (12.9)$$
$$= \|t_2 \approx t_1\|^{\|P_1\|} \cdot \|\phi\|^{\|P_2\|}$$

and the norm for the right hand side is:

$$\|((P_1 \rightarrow t_2 \approx t_1) \wedge (P_2 \wedge \neg P_1 \rightarrow \phi) \wedge (P_2 \wedge P_1 \rightarrow \phi[t_2/t_1]))\|$$
$$= \|(P_1 \rightarrow t_2 \approx t_1)\| \cdot$$
$$\quad \|(P_2 \wedge \neg P_1 \rightarrow \phi)\| \cdot \qquad (12.10)$$
$$\quad \|(P_2 \wedge P_1 \rightarrow \phi[t_2/t_1])\|$$
$$= \|t_2 \approx t_1\|^{\|P_1\|} \cdot \|\phi\|^{\|P_2 \wedge \neg P_1\|} \cdot \|\phi[t_2/t_1]\|^{\|P_2 \wedge P_1\|}$$

We now show that (12.10) < (12.9) whenever $\|t_1\| < \|t_2\|$:

$$\|t_1\| < \|t_2\|$$
$$\rightarrow \quad \|\phi[t_2/t_1]\| < \|\phi\| \qquad \text{(by Johnson's definition)}$$
$$\rightarrow \quad \|\phi[t_2/t_1]\|^{\|P_2 \wedge P_1\|} < \|\phi\|^{\|P_2 \wedge P_1\|}$$
$$\rightarrow \quad \|\phi[t_2/t_1]\|^{\|P_2 \wedge P_1\|} \cdot \|\phi\|^{\|P_2 \wedge \neg P_1\|} < \|\phi\|^{\|P_2 \wedge P_1\|} \cdot \|\phi\|^{\|P_2 \wedge \neg P_1\|}$$
$$\rightarrow \quad \|\phi[t_2/t_1]\|^{\|P_2 \wedge P_1\|} \cdot \|\phi\|^{\|P_2 \wedge \neg P_1\|} < \|\phi\|^{\|P_2 \wedge P_1\| + \|P_2 \wedge \neg P_1\|} \qquad (12.11)$$
$$\rightarrow \quad \|\phi[t_2/t_1]\|^{\|P_2 \wedge P_1\|} \cdot \|\phi\|^{\|P_2 \wedge \neg P_1\|} < \|\phi\|^{\|P_2\|}$$
$$\quad \text{(by our definition of } \|P\|)$$
$$\rightarrow \quad \|t_2 \approx t_1\|^{\|P_1\|} \cdot \|\phi[t_2/t_1]\|^{\|P_2 \wedge P_1\|} \cdot \|\phi\|^{\|P_2 \wedge \neg P_1\|} <$$
$$\quad \|t_2 \approx t_1\|^{\|P_1\|} \cdot \|\phi\|^{\|P_2\|}$$

We can conclude from this that each application of (12.8) in Algorithm (12.3) will monotonically reduce the norm of the system as a whole, and hence the algorithm must terminate.

### 12.3.5 Example

The following example illustrates how this algorithm works. Suppose that (12.13) is the contexted version of (12.12):

$$[f_2 = f_1 \vee (f_1\, a) = c_1] \wedge [(f_2\, a) = c_2 \vee (f_1\, a) = c_3]$$
$$\text{where } c_i \neq c_j \text{ for all } i \neq j \tag{12.12}$$

$$
\begin{array}{ll}
a. & p_1 \rightarrow f_2 = f_1 \\
b. & \neg p_1 \rightarrow (f_1\, a) = c_1 \\
c. & p_2 \rightarrow (f_2\, a) = c_2 \\
d. & \neg p_2 \rightarrow (f_1\, a) = c_3
\end{array}
\tag{12.13}
$$

(For clarity, we omit the $\wedge$'s whenever contexted constraints are displayed in a column.) There is an applicable rewrite rule for Constraints (12.13a) and (12.13c) that produces three new constraints:

$$
\begin{array}{ll}
p_1 \rightarrow f_2 = f_1 & \quad p_1 \rightarrow f_2 = f_1 \\
p_2 \rightarrow (f_2\, a) = c_2 \quad \Leftrightarrow & \quad \neg p_1 \wedge p_2 \rightarrow (f_2\, a) = c_2 \\
& \quad p_1 \wedge p_2 \rightarrow (f_1\, a) = c_2
\end{array}
\tag{12.14}
$$

Although there is an applicable rewrite rule for (12.13d) and the last clause of (12.14), we ignore it since $p_1 \wedge p_2 \wedge \neg p_2$ is $FALSE$. The only other pair of constraints that can be rewritten are (12.13b) and (12.13d), producing three more constraints:

$$
\begin{array}{ll}
\neg p_1 \rightarrow (f_1\, a) = c_1 \quad \Leftrightarrow & \quad \neg p_1 \rightarrow (f_1\, a) = c_1 \\
\neg p_2 \rightarrow (f_1\, a) = c_3 & \quad p_1 \wedge \neg p_2 \rightarrow (f_1\, a) = c_3 \\
& \quad \neg p_1 \wedge \neg p_2 \rightarrow c_1 = c_3
\end{array}
\tag{12.15}
$$

Since no more rewrites are possible, the normal form of (12.13) is thus:

$$
\begin{array}{ll}
a. & p_1 \rightarrow f_2 = f_1 \\
b. & \neg p_1 \rightarrow (f_1\, a) = c_1 \\
c. & \neg p_1 \wedge p_2 \rightarrow (f_2\, a) = c_2 \\
d. & p_1 \wedge \neg p_2 \rightarrow (f_1\, a) = c_3 \\
e. & p_1 \wedge p_2 \rightarrow (f_1\, a) = c_2 \\
f. & \neg p_1 \wedge \neg p_2 \rightarrow c_1 = c_3
\end{array}
\tag{12.16}
$$

## 12.4  Extracting the disjunctive residue

When the rewriting algorithm is finished, all unsatisfiable combinations of base constraints will have been derived. But more reasoning must be done to determine from base unsatisfiabilities whether the disjunctive system is unsatisfiable. Consider the contexted constraint $P \rightarrow \phi$, where $\phi$ is unsatisfiable. In order for the conjunction of contexted constraints to be satisfiable, it must be the case that $\neg P$ is true. We call $\neg P$ a *nogood*, following TMS terminology (deKleer, 1986). Since $P$ contains propositional variables indicating disjunctive choices, information about which conjunctions of base constraints are unsatisfiable is thus back-propagated into information about the unsatisfiability of the conjunction of the disjuncts that they come from. The original system as a whole is satisfiable just in case the conjunction of all its nogoods is true. We call the conjunction of all of the nogoods the *residue* of the disjunctive system.

For example, Clause (12.16f) asserts that $\neg p_1 \wedge \neg p_2 \rightarrow c_1 = c_3$. But $c_1 = c_3$ is unsatisfiable, since we know that $c_1 \neq c_3$. Thus $\neg(\neg p_1 \wedge \neg p_2)$ is a nogood. Since $c_1 = c_3$ is the only unsatisfiable base constraint in (12.16), this is also the disjunctive residue of the system. Thus (12.12) is satisfiable because $\neg(\neg p_1 \wedge \neg p_2)$ has at least one solution (e.g., $p_1$ is true and $p_2$ is true).

Since each nogood may be a complex boolean expression involving conjunctions, disjunctions and negations of propositional variables, determining whether the residue is satisfiable may not be easy. In fact, the problem is NP complete. However, we have accomplished two things by reducing a disjunctive system to its residue. First, since the residue only involves propositional variables, it can be solved by propositional reasoning techniques (such as deKleer's ATMS [1986]) that do not require specialized knowledge of the problem domain. Second, we believe that for the particular case of linguistics, the final residue will be simpler than the original disjunctive problem. This is because the disjunctions introduced from different parts of the sentence usually involve different attributes in the feature structure, and thus they tend not to interact.

Another way that nogoods can be used is to reduce contexts while the rewriting is being carried out, using identities like the following:

$$\neg P_1 \wedge (\neg P_1 \wedge P_2 \rightarrow \phi) \Leftrightarrow \neg P_1 \wedge (P_2 \rightarrow \phi) \tag{12.17}$$

$$\neg P_1 \wedge (P_1 \wedge P_2 \rightarrow \phi) \Leftrightarrow \neg P_1 \tag{12.18}$$

$$P_1 \wedge \neg P_1 \Leftrightarrow FALSE \tag{12.19}$$

Doing this can improve the performance since some contexts are simplified and some constraints are eliminated altogether. However, the overhead of comparing the nogoods against the contexts may outweigh the potential benefit.

## 12.4.1   Complexity Analysis

The first part of our algorithm (converting the original constraints into contexted constraints) is linear in the number of constraints, since the number of transformations in Algorithm (12.1) is directly proportional to the number of operators in the original formula. In the particular case of unification, the second part (normalizing the constraints) can be made to run in polynomial time (although we have not given a proof of this). The third part, solving the disjunctive residue, contains the exponential that cannot be avoided. However, if the nogoods are mostly independent, then the complexity of this part will be closer to $k2^m$ than $2^n$, where $m \ll n$. This is because the disjunctive residue will break down into a number of independent problems each of which is still exponential, but with much smaller exponents.

### 12.4.2  Example

Let us assume that the following constraints represent the German words *die* and *Koffer*:

*die*:     $(f\,case) = nom \lor (f\,case) = acc$
   $\land [(f\,gend) = fem \land (f\,num) = sg] \lor (f\,num) = pl$

*Koffer*: $(f\,gend) = masc \land (f\,pers) = 3$
   $\land [(f\,num) = sg \land (f\,case) \neq gen] \lor [(f\,num) = pl \land (f\,case) \neq dat]$

If we convert to contexted constraints and sort by attributes we get the following:

$$
\begin{array}{lll}
a. & p_1 \rightarrow (f\,case) = nom & \\
b. & \neg p_1 \rightarrow (f\,case) = acc & \\
c. & p_3 \rightarrow (f\,case) \neq gen & \\
d. & \neg p_3 \rightarrow (f\,case) \neq dat & \\
e. & p_2 \rightarrow (f\,gend) = fem & \\
f. & true \rightarrow (f\,gend) = masc & (12.20) \\
g. & p_2 \rightarrow (f\,num) = sg & \\
h. & \neg p_2 \rightarrow (f\,num) = pl & \\
i. & p_3 \rightarrow (f\,num) = sg & \\
j. & \neg p_3 \rightarrow (f\,num) = pl & \\
k. & true \rightarrow (f\,pers) = 3 &
\end{array}
$$

Normalizing the constraints produces the following nogoods:

$$
\begin{array}{lll}
a. & p_2 & \text{(e and f)} \\
b. & p_2 \land \neg p_3 & \text{(g and j)} \qquad (12.21) \\
c. & \neg p_2 \land p_3 & \text{(h and i)}
\end{array}
$$

The conjunction of these nogoods has the solutions: $p_1 \land \neg p_2 \land \neg p_3$ and $\neg p_1 \land \neg p_2 \land \neg p_3$.

## 12.5  Producing the models

Assuming that there is a method for producing a model for a conjunction of base constraints, we can produce models from the contexted system. Every assignment of truth values to the propositional variables introduced in Lemma 12.1 corresponds to a different conjunction of base constraints in the original system, and each such conjunction is an element of the DNF of the original system. Rather than explore the entire space of assignments, we need only enumerate those assignments for which the disjunctive residue is true.

Given an assignment of truth values that is consistent with the disjunctive residue, we can produce a model from the contexted constraints by assigning the truth values to the propositional variables in the contexts, and then discarding those base constraints whose contexts evaluate to false. The minimal model for the remaining base constraints can be determined by inspection if the base constraints are in normal form, as is the case for rewriting algorithms. (Otherwise some deductions may have to be made to produce the model, but the system is guaranteed to be satisfiable.) This minimal model will satisfy the original disjunctive system.

### 12.5.1   Example

The residue for the system given in (12.20) is $\neg p_2 \wedge \neg[p_2 \wedge \neg p_3] \wedge \neg[\neg p_2 \wedge p_3]$. This residue has two solutions: $p_1 \wedge \neg p_2 \wedge \neg p_3$ and $\neg p_1 \wedge \neg p_2 \wedge \neg p_3$. We can produce models for these solutions by extracting the appropriate constraints from (12.20), and reading off the models. Here are the solutions for this system:

| solution: | constraints: | | model: |
|---|---|---|---|
| $p_1 \wedge \neg p_2 \wedge \neg p_3$ | $(f\,case) = nom \wedge$<br>$(f\,gend) = masc \wedge$<br>$(f\,num) = pl \wedge$<br>$(f\,pers) = 3$ | $f =$ | $\begin{bmatrix} case & nom \\ gend & masc \\ num & pl \\ pers & 3 \end{bmatrix}$ |
| $\neg p_1 \wedge \neg p_2 \wedge \neg p_3$ | $(f\,case) = acc \wedge$<br>$(f\,gend) = masc \wedge$<br>$(f\,num) = pl \wedge$<br>$(f\,pers) = 3$ | $f =$ | $\begin{bmatrix} case & acc \\ gend & masc \\ num & pl \\ pers & 3 \end{bmatrix}$ |

## 12.6   Comparison with other techniques

In this section we compare disjunctive constraint satisfaction with some of the other techniques that have been developed for dealing with disjunction as it arises in grammatical processing. These other techniques are framed in terms of feature-structure unification and a unification version of our approach would facilitate the comparisons. Although we do not provide a detailed specification of context-extended unification here, we note that unification can be thought of as an indexing scheme for rewriting. We start with a simple illustration of how such an indexing scheme might work.

### 12.6.1   Unification indexing

Regarding unification as an indexing scheme, the main question that needs to be answered is where to index the contexts. Suppose that we index the contexts with the values under the attributes. Then the attribute-value (actually, attribute-*context*-value) matrix for (12.22a) would be (12.22b):

a. $(f\,a) = c_1 \vee [(f\,b) = c_2 \vee (f\,a) = c_3]$    b. $\begin{bmatrix} a & \begin{bmatrix} p_1 & c_1 \\ \neg p_1 \wedge \neg p_2 & c_3 \end{bmatrix} \\ b & \begin{bmatrix} \neg p_1 \wedge p_2 & c_2 \end{bmatrix} \end{bmatrix}$ (12.22)

Since the contexts are indexed under the attributes, two disjunctions will only interact if they have attributes in common. If they have no attributes in common, their unification will be linear in the number of attributes, rather than multiplicative in the number of disjuncts. For instance, suppose that (12.23b) is the attribute value matrix for (12.23a):

a. $(f\,c) = c_4 \vee [(f\,d) = c_5 \vee (f\,e) = c_6]$    b. $\begin{bmatrix} c & \begin{bmatrix} p_3 & c_4 \end{bmatrix} \\ d & \begin{bmatrix} \neg p_3 \wedge p_4 & c_5 \end{bmatrix} \\ e & \begin{bmatrix} \neg p_3 \wedge \neg p_4 & c_6 \end{bmatrix} \end{bmatrix}$ (12.23)

Since these disjunctions have no attributes in common, the attribute-value matrix for the conjunction of (12.22a) and (12.23a) will be simply the *concatenation* of (12.22b) and (12.23b):

$$\begin{bmatrix} a & \begin{bmatrix} p_1 & c_1 \\ \neg p_1 \wedge \neg p_2 & c_3 \end{bmatrix} \\ b & \begin{bmatrix} \neg p_1 \wedge p_2 & c_2 \end{bmatrix} \\ c & \begin{bmatrix} p_3 & c_4 \end{bmatrix} \\ d & \begin{bmatrix} \neg p_3 \wedge p_4 & c_5 \end{bmatrix} \\ e & \begin{bmatrix} \neg p_3 \wedge \neg p_4 & c_6 \end{bmatrix} \end{bmatrix}$$ (12.24)

The DNF approach to this problem would produce nine f-structures with eighteen attribute-value pairs. In contrast, our approach produces one f-structure with eleven attribute-value and context-value pairs. In general, if disjunctions have independent attributes, then a DNF approach is exponential in the number of disjunctions, whereas our approach is linear. This independence feature is very important for language processing, since, as we have suggested, disjunctions from different parts of a sentence usually constrain different attributes.

## 12.6.2   Karttunen's disjunctive values

Karttunen (1984) introduced a special type of value called a "disjunctive value" to handle certain types of disjunctions. Disjunctive values allow simple disjunctions such as:

$(f\,case) = acc \vee (f\,case) = nom$ (12.25)

to be represented in the unification data structure as:

$\begin{bmatrix} case & \{nom\ acc\} \end{bmatrix}$ (12.26)

where the curly brackets indicate a disjunctive value. Karttunen's disjunctive values are not limited to atomic values, as the example he gives for the German article *die* shows:

$$die = \begin{bmatrix} infl & \begin{bmatrix} case & \{nom\ acc\} \\ agr & \left\{ \begin{bmatrix} gender & fem \\ number & sg \end{bmatrix} \\ \begin{bmatrix} number & pl \end{bmatrix} \right\} \end{bmatrix} \end{bmatrix} \qquad (12.27)$$

The corresponding attribute-context-value matrix for our scheme would be:

$$die = \begin{bmatrix} infl & \begin{bmatrix} case & \begin{bmatrix} p_1 & nom \\ \neg p_1 & acc \end{bmatrix} \\ agr & \begin{bmatrix} gender & \begin{bmatrix} p_2 & fem \end{bmatrix} \\ number & \begin{bmatrix} p_2 & sg \\ \neg p_2 & pl \end{bmatrix} \end{bmatrix} \end{bmatrix} \end{bmatrix} \qquad (12.28)$$

The advantage of disjunctive constraint satisfaction is that it can handle all types of disjunctions, whereas disjunctive values can only handle atomic values or simple feature-value matrices with no external dependencies. Furthermore, disjunctive constraint satisfaction can often do better than disjunctive values for the types of disjunctions that they can both handle. This can be seen in (12.28), where disjunctive constraint satisfaction has pushed a disjunction further down the *agr* feature than the disjunctive value approach in (12.27). This means that if *agr* were given an attribute other than *gender* or *number*, this new attribute would not interact with the existing disjunction.

However, disjunctive values may have an advantage of reduced overhead, because they do not require embedded contexts and they do not have to keep track of nogoods. It may be worthwhile to incorporate disjunctive values in our scheme to represent the very simple disjunctions, while disjunctive constraint satisfaction is used for the more complex disjunctions.

## 12.6.3   Kasper's successive approximation

Kasper (1987a, b) proposed that an efficient way to handle disjunctions is to do a step-wise approximation for determining satisfiability. Conceptually, the step-wise algorithm tries to find the inconsistencies that come from fewer disjuncts first. The algorithm starts by unifying the non-disjunctive constraints together. If the non-disjunctive constraints are inconsistent, then there is no need to even consider the disjunctions. If they are consistent, then the disjuncts are unified with them one at a time, where each unification is undone before the next unification is performed. If any of these unifications are inconsistent, then its disjunct is discarded. Then the algorithm unifies the non-disjunctive constraints with all possible pairs of disjuncts, and then all possible triples of disjuncts, and so on. (This technique is called "k-consistency" in the constraint satisfaction literature [Freuder, 1978].) In practice, Kasper noted that only the first two steps are computationally useful, and that once bad singleton disjuncts have been eliminated, it is more efficient to switch to DNF than to compute all of the higher degrees of consistency.

Kasper's technique is optimal when most of the disjuncts are inconsistent with the non-disjunctive constraints, or the non-disjunctive constraints are themselves inconsistent. His scheme tends to revert to DNF when this is not the case. Although simple inconsistencies are prevalent in many circumstances, we believe they become less predominate as grammars are extended to cover more and more linguistic phenomena. The coverage of a grammar increases as more options and alternatives are added, either in phrasal rules or lexical entries, so that there are fewer instances of pure non-disjunctive constraints and a greater proportion of inconsistencies involve higher-order interactions. This tendency is exacerbated because of the valuable role that disjunctions play in helping to control the complexity of broad-coverage grammatical specifications. Disjunctions permit constraints to be formulated in local contexts, relying on a general global satisfaction procedure to enforce them in all appropriate circumstances, and thus they improve the modularity and manageability of the overall grammatical system. We have seen this trend towards more localized disjunctive specifications particularly in our developing LFG grammars, and have observed a corresponding reduction in the number of disjuncts that can be eliminated using Kasper's technique. On the other hand, the number of independent disjunctions, which our approach does best on, tends to go up as modularity increases.

One other aspect of LFG grammatical processing is worth noting. Many LFG analyses are ruled out not because they are inconsistent, but rather because they are incomplete. That is, they fail to have an attribute that a predicate requires (e.g., the object is missing for a transitive verb). Since incomplete solutions cannot be ruled out incrementally (an incomplete solution may become complete with the addition of more information), completeness requirements provide no information to eliminate disjuncts in Kasper's successive approximation. These requirements can only be evaluated in what is effectively a disjunctive normal form computation. But our technique avoids this problem, since independent completeness requirements will be simply additive, and any incomplete contexts can be easily read off of the attribute-value matrix and added to the nogoods before solving the residue.

Kasper's scheme works best when disjuncts can be eliminated by unification with non-disjunctive constraints, while ours works best when disjunctions are independent. It is possible to construct a hybrid scheme that works well in both situations. For example, we can use Kasper's scheme up until some critical point (e.g., after the first two steps), and then switch over to our technique instead of computing the higher degrees of consistency.

Another, possibly more interesting, way to incorporate Kasper's strategy is to always process the sets of constraints with the fewest number of propositional variables first. That is, if $P_3 \wedge P_4$ had fewer propositional variables than $P_1 \wedge P_2$, then the rewrite rule in (12.30) should be done before (12.29):

$$(P_1 \rightarrow \phi_1) \wedge (P_2 \rightarrow \phi_2) \Rightarrow (P_1 \wedge P_2 \rightarrow \phi_5) \tag{12.29}$$

$$(P_3 \rightarrow \phi_3) \wedge (P_4 \rightarrow \phi_4) \Rightarrow (P_3 \wedge P_4 \rightarrow \phi_6) \tag{12.30}$$

This approach would find smaller nogoods earlier, which would allow combinations of constraints that depended on those nogoods to be ignored, since the contexts would already be known to be inconsistent.

### 12.6.4 Eisele and Dörre's techniques

Eisele and Dörre (1988) developed an algorithm for taking Karttunen's notion of disjunctive values a little further. Their algorithm allows disjunctive values to be unified with reentrant structures. The algorithm correctly detects such cases and "lifts the disjunction due to reentrancy." They give the following example:

$$
\begin{bmatrix} a: \left\{ \begin{bmatrix} b: + \\ c: - \end{bmatrix} \begin{bmatrix} b: - \\ c: + \end{bmatrix} \right\} \end{bmatrix}
\sqcup
\begin{bmatrix} a: \begin{bmatrix} b: \langle d \rangle \\ d: [] \end{bmatrix} \end{bmatrix}
=
\left\{
\begin{bmatrix} a: \begin{bmatrix} b: \langle d \rangle \\ c: - \end{bmatrix} \\ d: + \end{bmatrix}
\begin{bmatrix} a: \begin{bmatrix} b: \langle d \rangle \\ c: + \end{bmatrix} \\ d: - \end{bmatrix}
\right\}
\tag{12.31}
$$

Notice that the disjunction under the "a" attribute in the first matrix is moved one level up in order to handle the reentrancy introduced in the second matrix under the "b" attribute.

This type of unification can be handled with embedded contexts without requiring that the disjunction be lifted up. In fact, the disjunction is moved down one level, from under "a" to under "b" and "c":

$$
\begin{bmatrix} a: \begin{bmatrix} b: \begin{bmatrix} p_1 & + \\ \neg p_1 & - \end{bmatrix} \\ c: \begin{bmatrix} p_1 & - \\ \neg p_1 & + \end{bmatrix} \end{bmatrix} \end{bmatrix}
\sqcup
\begin{bmatrix} a: \begin{bmatrix} b: \langle d \rangle \\ d: [] \end{bmatrix} \end{bmatrix}
=
\begin{bmatrix} a: \begin{bmatrix} b: \langle d \rangle \\ c: \begin{bmatrix} p_1 & - \\ \neg p_1 & + \end{bmatrix} \end{bmatrix} \\ d: \begin{bmatrix} p_1 & + \\ \neg p_1 & - \end{bmatrix} \end{bmatrix}
\tag{12.32}
$$

### 12.6.5 Overall comparison

The major cost of using disjunctive constraint satisfaction is the overhead of dealing with contexts and the disjunctive residue. Our technique is quite general, but if the only types of disjunction that occur are covered by one of the other techniques, then that technique will probably do better than our scheme. For example, if all of the nogoods are the result of singleton inconsistencies (the result of unifying a single disjunct with the non-disjunctive part), then Kasper's successive approximation technique will work better because it avoids our overhead. However, if many of the nogoods involve multiple disjuncts, or if some nogoods are only produced from incomplete solutions, then disjunctive constraint satisfaction will do better than the other techniques, sometimes exponentially so. We also believe that further savings can be achieved by using hybrid techniques if the special cases are sufficiently common to warrant the extra complexity.

## 12.7    Concluding remarks

We set out to exploit a particular property of parsing (namely that constraints under different attributes tend not to interact) in order to obtain better average time performance for constraint satisfaction. Along the way, we have discovered a few strategies that we did not anticipate but in retrospect seem quite useful.

The first strategy is to *use the conjunctive theory to drive the disjunctive theory*. This is useful because in our case the conjunctive theory is polynomial and the disjunctive theory is exponential. Since the conjunctive theory can reduce the search space of the disjunctive theory in polynomial time, this saves the disjunctive theory exponential time. In general, it makes sense to use the more constrained theory to drive the less constrained theory. This is one of the major ways in which we differ from the ATMS (deKleer, 1986) work; the ATMS uses disjunctive information to guide the conjunctive theory, whereas we do it the other way around. We believe that it may be possible to gain more benefits by going even further in this direction.

The second strategy is to *use CNF rather than DNF*. This is because CNF allows for a compact representation of ambiguity. That is, a conjunction of independent disjunctions is much smaller than the equivalent formula expressed as a disjunction of conjunctions. This is particularly important for processing modular linguistic descriptions. In modular systems with separate specifications of syntax, semantics, pragmatics, etc., the syntactic component alone does not include all the constraints needed to determine the ultimately correct analysis of a sentence. It usually provides a set of possible outputs that are then filtered by the constraints of the more abstract modules, and these outputs are typically enumerated as a (possibly large) set of separate alternative structures. But in the absence of semantic or pragmatic constraints, many of the residual syntactic ambiguities appear as free or independent disjunctions, and these can be encoded efficiently using CNF. Thus, our approach to disjunction has the added advantage of reducing the performance penalty frequently associated with modular characterizations of linguistic information.

# Acknowledgments

The approach described in this chapter emerged from discussion and interaction with a number of our colleagues. We are particularly indebted to John Lamping, who suggested the initial formulation of Lemma 12.1, and to Bill Rounds for pointing out the relationship between our conversion algorithm and the NP completeness reduction for CNF. We are also grateful for many helpful discussions with Dan Bobrow, Johan deKleer, Jochen Dörre, Andreas Eisele, Pat Hayes, Mark Johnson, Lauri Karttunen, and Martin Kay.

# References

deKleer, J. (1986). An assumption-based TMS. *Artificial Intelligence, 28,* 127–162.

Eisele, A., & Dörre, J. (1988). Unification of disjunctive feature descriptions. *Proceedings of the 26th Annual Meeting of the ACL.* Buffalo, New York.

Freuder, E. C. (1978). Synthesizing constraint expressions. *Communications of the ACM, 21,* 958–966.

Hopcroft, J., & Ullman, J. (1979). *Introduction to automata theory, languages and computation* (pp. 328–330).

Johnson, M. (1988). *Attribute-value logic and the theory of grammar.* Unpublished doctoral dissertation. CA: Stanford University.

Kaplan, R., & Bresnan, J. (1982). Lexical functional grammar: A formal system for grammatical representation. In J. Bresnan (Ed.), *The mental representation of grammatical relations.* Cambridge, MA: MIT Press.

Karttunen, L. (1984). Features and values. *Proceedings of COLING 1984,* Stanford, CA.

Karttunen, L. (1986a). D-PATR: A development environment for unification-based grammars. *Proceedings of COLING 1986,* Bonn.

Karttunen, L. (1986b). Radical lexicalism. In M. Baltin & A Kroch (Eds.), *Alternative conceptions of phrase structures.* Chicago University Press.

Kasper, R. T. (1987a). *Feature structures: A logical theory with application to language analysis.* Unpublished doctoral dissertation. University of Michigan.

Kasper, R. T. (1987b). A unification method for disjunctive feature descriptions. *Proceedings of the 25th Annual Meeting of the ACL.* Stanford, CA.

Kay, M. (1979). Functional grammar. *Proceedings of the 5th Annual Meeting of the Berkeley Linguistic Society.*

Kay, M. (1985). Parsing in functional unification grammar. In D. Dowty, L. Karttunen, & A. Zwicky (Eds.), *Natural language parsing.* Cambridge University Press.

Pollard, C., & Sag, I. (1987). *Information-based syntax and semantics: Fundamentals* (Vol. 1). CSLI Lecture Note Series, Vol. 13, Center for the Study of Language and Information, Stanford University.

Uszkoreit, H. (1986). Categorial unification grammars. *Proceedings of COLING 1986,* Bonn.

Zeevat, H., Klein, E., & Calder, J. (1987). Unification categorial grammar. In N. Haddock, E. Klein, & G. Morrill (Eds.), *Categorial grammar, unification grammar, and parsing.* Scotland: University of Edinburgh.

# 13. Polynomial Parsing of Extensions of Context-Free Grammars

## K. Vijay-Shanker

*Department of Computer & Information Science, University of Delaware*

## David J. Weir

*Department of Electrical Engineering & Computer Science, Northwestern University*

## 13.1 Introduction

In (Joshi, Vijay-Shanker, & Weir, 1989; Vijay-Shanker, Weir, & Joshi, 1986; Weir & Joshi, 1988) we have shown that Combinatory Categorial Grammars (CCG), Head Grammars (HG), Linear Indexed Grammars (LIG), and Tree Adjoining Grammars (TAG) are weakly equivalent, i.e., they generate the same class of string languages. Although it is known that there are polynomial-time recognition algorithms for HG and TAG (Pollard, 1984; Vijay-Shanker & Joshi, 1985), there are no known polynomial-time recognition algorithms that work *directly* with CCG or LIG. In this chapter we present polynomial-time recognition algorithms for LIG and CCG that resemble the CKY algorithm for Context-Free Grammars (CFG) (Kasami, 1965; Younger, 1967). We also show how this approach can be adapted for TAG.

The tree sets derived by a CFG can be recognized by *finite state* tree automata (Thatcher, 1971).[1] This is reflected in CFL bottom-up recognition algorithms such as the CKY algorithm. Intermediate configurations of the recognizer can be encoded by the states of these finite state automaton (the nonterminal symbols of the grammar). The similarity of TAG, CCG, and LIG can be seen from the fact that the tree sets derived by these formalisms can be recognized by *pushdown* (rather than finite state) based tree automata. We give recognition algorithms for these formalisms by extending the CKY algorithm so that intermediate configurations are encoded using stacks. In (Pareschi & Steedman, 1987), a chart parser for CCG is given where copies

---

[1] A bottom-up finite state tree automaton reads a tree bottom-up. The state that the automaton associates with each node that it visits will depend on the states associated with the children of the node.

of stacks (derived categories) are stored explicitly in each chart entry. In Section 13.5, we show that storing separate copies of the entire stacks explicitly can lead to exponential run-time. In the algorithm we present here, the stack is encoded by storing its top element together with information about where the remainder of the stack can be found. Thus, we avoid the need for multiple copies of parts of the same stack through the sharing of common substacks. This reduces the number of possible elements in each entry in the chart and results in a polynomial time algorithm.

It is not necessary to independently derive separate algorithms for CCG, LIG, and TAG. In proving that these formalisms are equivalent, we developed constructions that map grammars between the different formalisms. We make use of these constructions to adapt an algorithm for one formalism into an algorithm for another. First, we present a discussion of the recognition algorithm for LIG in Section 13.2. We present the LIG recognition algorithm first since it appeared to be the clearest example involving the use of the notion of stacks in derivations. In Section 13.3, we give an informal description of how to map a CCG to an equivalent LIG. Based on this relationship, we adapt the recognition algorithm for LIG to one for CCG. We end by briefly describing how a new algorithm for TAG can be derived. The primary purpose of this chapter is to give a method by which formalisms that produce tree sets with context-free path sets can be efficiently parsed. For this reason we give a full algorithm only for LIG.

## 13.2   Linear indexed grammars

An Indexed Grammar (Aho, 1968) can be viewed as a CFG in which each nonterminal is associated with a stack of symbols. Productions, in addition to rewriting nonterminals, can have the effect of pushing or popping symbols on top of the stacks that are associated with each nonterminal. A LIG (Gazdar, 1985) is an Indexed Grammar in which the stack associated with the nonterminal of the LHS of each production can only be associated with one of the occurrences of nonterminals on the RHS of the production. Empty stacks are associated with other occurrences of nonterminals on the right-hand-side of the production. We write $A[\cdot\cdot]$ (or $A[\cdot\cdot\gamma]$) to denote the nonterminal $A$ associated with an arbitrary stack (or an arbitrary stack whose top symbol is $\gamma$). A nonterminal $A$ with an empty stack is written $A[\,]$.

**Definition 13.2.1**          A LIG, $G$, is denoted by $(V_N, V_T, V_S, S, P)$ where

   $V_N$ is a finite set of nonterminals,
   $V_T$ is a finite set of terminals,
   $V_S$ is a finite set of indices (stack symbols),
   $S \in V_N$ is the start symbol, and

$P$ is a finite set of productions, having one of the following forms.

$$A[\cdot\cdot\gamma] \rightarrow A_1[] \ldots A_i[\cdot\cdot] \ldots A_n[]$$
$$A[\cdot\cdot] \rightarrow A_1[] \ldots A_i[\cdot\cdot\gamma] \ldots A_n[]$$
$$A[] \rightarrow a$$

where $A, A_1, \ldots, A_n \in V_N$ and $a \in \{\epsilon\} \cup V_T$.

The relation $\underset{G}{\Longrightarrow}$ is defined as follows where $\alpha \in V_S^*$ and $\Upsilon_1, \Upsilon_2$ are strings of nonterminals with associated stacks.

- If $A[\cdot\cdot\gamma] \rightarrow A_1[] \ldots A_i[\cdot\cdot] \ldots A_n[] \in P$ then

$$\Upsilon_1 A[\alpha\gamma]\Upsilon_2 \underset{G}{\Longrightarrow} \Upsilon_1 A_1[] \ldots A_i[\alpha] \ldots A_n[]\Upsilon_2$$

- If $A[\cdot\cdot] \rightarrow A_1[] \ldots A_i[\cdot\cdot\gamma] \ldots A_n[] \in P$ then

$$\Upsilon_1 A[\alpha]\Upsilon_2 \underset{G}{\Longrightarrow} \Upsilon_1 A_1[] \ldots A_i[\alpha\gamma] \ldots A_n[]\Upsilon_2$$

In each of these two cases we say that $A_i$ is the **dependent** child of $A$ in the derivation.

- If $A[] \rightarrow a \in P$ then

$$\Upsilon_1 A[]\Upsilon_2 \underset{G}{\Longrightarrow} \Upsilon_1 a \Upsilon_2$$

The language generated by a LIG, $G$, is $L(G) = \{ w \mid S[] \underset{G}{\overset{*}{\Longrightarrow}} w \}$.

## 13.2.1  Recognition of LIG

In considering the recognition of LIG, we assume that the underlying CFG is in Chomsky Normal Form, i.e., either two nonterminals (with their stacks) or a single terminal can appear on the right-hand-side of a rule. We use an array $L$ consisting of $n^2$ elements where the string to be recognized is $a_1 \ldots a_n$. In the case of the CFG recognition algorithm, each array element $L_{i,j}$ contains that subset of the nonterminal symbols that can derive the substring $a_i \ldots a_j$. In the present algorithm the elements stored in $L_{i,j}$ will encode those nonterminals *and associated stacks* that can derive the string $a_i \ldots a_j$.

In order to obtain a polynomial algorithm we must encode the stacks efficiently. We store with each nonterminal only the top of its associated stack and an indication of the element in $L$ where the next part of the stack can be found. This is achieved by storing sets of tuples of the form $(A, \gamma, A', \gamma', p, q)$ in the array elements. Roughly speaking, a tuple, $(A, \gamma, A', \gamma', p, q)$, is stored in $L_{i,j}$ when

$$A[\alpha\gamma'\gamma] \overset{*}{\Longrightarrow} a_i \ldots a_j, \quad \text{and} \quad A'[\alpha\gamma'] \overset{*}{\Longrightarrow} a_p \ldots a_q$$

where $\alpha$ is a string of stack symbols and $A'$ is a *dependent descendent* of $A$ in the derivation of $a_i \ldots a_j$.

Note that tuples, as defined above, assume the presence of at least two stack symbols. We must also consider two other cases in which a nonterminal is associated with either a stack of a single element, or with the empty stack. Suppose that $A$ is associated with a stack containing only the single symbol $\gamma$. This case will be represented using tuples of the form $(A, \gamma, A', -, p, q)$ ($-$ indicates that an empty stack is associated with $A'$). When an empty stack is associated with $A$ we will use the tuple $(A, -, -, -, -, -)$.

The algorithm can be understood by verifying that at each step $(A, \gamma, A', \gamma', p, q)$ is in $L_{i,j}$ under the following conditions.

- If $\gamma' \in V_S$ (the stack associated with $A'$ is nonempty) $A, A' \in V_N$ and $(p, q) < (i, j)^2$ then

$$A[\gamma] \overset{*}{\Longrightarrow} a_i \ldots a_{p-1} A'[]a_{q+1} \ldots a_j \text{ and } A'[\alpha\gamma'] \overset{*}{\Longrightarrow} a_p \ldots a_q$$

  for some $\alpha \in V_S^*$ where $A'$ is a dependent descendent of $A$. Note that this implies that for all $\beta \in V_S^*$

$$A[\beta\gamma] \overset{*}{\Longrightarrow} a_i \ldots a_{p-1} A'[\beta]a_{q+1} \ldots a_j$$

  Thus, for $\beta = \alpha\gamma'$, $A[\alpha\gamma'\gamma] \overset{*}{\Longrightarrow} a_i \ldots a_{p-1} A'[\alpha\gamma']a_{q+1} \ldots a_j$ which implies $A[\alpha\gamma'\gamma] \overset{*}{\Longrightarrow} a_i \ldots a_j$.

- If $\gamma' = -$ then if $\gamma \in V_S$ (the stack associated with $A$ is not empty) $A, A' \in V_N$ and $p = q = -$ then

$$A[\gamma] \overset{*}{\Longrightarrow} a_i \ldots a_j \quad \text{and} \quad A'[] \overset{*}{\Longrightarrow} a_p \ldots a_q$$

  otherwise, $\gamma = -$ (the stack associated with $A$ is empty), $A \in V_S$ and $A = p = q = -$ in which case $A[] \overset{*}{\Longrightarrow} a_i \ldots a_j$.

We now describe how each entry $L_{i,j}$ is filled. As the algorithm proceeds, the gap between $i$ and $j$ increases until it spans the entire input. The input, $a_1 \ldots a_n$, is accepted if $(S, -, -, -, -, -) \in L_{1,n}$. New entries are added to the array elements according to the productions of the grammar as follows.

1. Suppose $A[] \to a$ is a production. This is used by the algorithm in the initialization of the array $L$. If the terminal symbol $a$ is the same as the $i^{th}$ symbol in the input string, i.e., $a = a_i$, then we include $(A, -, -, -, -, -)$ in the array element $L_{i,i}$.

---

[2]$(p, q) < (i, j)$ when $i \le p$ and $q \le j$ and $(p, q) \ne (i, j)$.

2. The production $A[\cdot\cdot\gamma] \rightarrow A_1[]A_2[\cdot\cdot]$ is used while filling the array element $L_{i,j}$ as follows. For every $k$ where $i \leq k \leq j$, check the previously completed array elements $L_{i,k}$ and $L_{k+1,j}$ for $(A_1, -, -, -, -, -)$ and some $(A_2, \gamma_2, A_3, \gamma_3, p, q)$, respectively. If these entries are found add $(A, \gamma, A_2, \gamma_2, k+1, j)$ to $L_{i,j}$. From these entries in $L_{i,k}$ and $L_{k+1,j}$ we know that $A_1[] \stackrel{*}{\Longrightarrow} a_i \ldots a_k$ and $A_2[\alpha] \stackrel{*}{\Longrightarrow} a_{k+1} \ldots a_j$ for some $\alpha \in V_S^*$. Thus, $A[\alpha\gamma] \stackrel{*}{\Longrightarrow} a_i \ldots a_j$.

   The production $A[\cdot\cdot\gamma] \rightarrow A_1[\cdot\cdot]A_2[]$ is handled similarly.

3. Suppose $A[\cdot\cdot] \rightarrow A_1[]A_2[\cdot\cdot\gamma]$ is a production. When filling $L_{i,j}$ we must check whether for some $k$ between $i$ and $j$ the tuple $(A_1, -, -, -, -, -)$ is in $L_{i,k}$ and some $(A_2, \gamma, A_3, \gamma_3, p, q)$ is in $L_{k+1,j}$. If we do find these tuples then we check in $L_{p,q}$ for some $(A_3, \gamma_3, A_4, \gamma_4, r, s)$. In this case we add $(A, \gamma_3, A_4, \gamma_4, r, s)$ to $L_{i,j}$.

   The above steps can be explained as follows.

   Case 1. The stack associated with $A_3$ is nonempty, i.e., $\gamma_3 \neq -$. We have for some $\alpha \in V_S^*$, $A_4[\alpha\gamma_4] \stackrel{*}{\Longrightarrow} a_r \ldots a_s$ a subderivation of $A_3[\alpha\gamma_4\gamma_3] \stackrel{*}{\Longrightarrow} a_p \ldots a_q$ (due to the entry in $L_{p,q}$) which in turn is a subderivation of $A_2[\alpha\gamma_4\gamma_3\gamma] \stackrel{*}{\Longrightarrow} a_{k+1} \ldots a_j$ (due to the entry in $L_{k+1,j}$). Combining this with $A_1[] \stackrel{*}{\Longrightarrow} a_i \ldots a_k$ we have $A[\alpha\gamma_4\gamma_3] \stackrel{*}{\Longrightarrow} a_i \ldots a_j$.

   Case 2. Stack associated with $A_3$ is empty, i.e., $\gamma_3 = -$. Then, $A_3[] \stackrel{*}{\Longrightarrow} a_p \ldots a_q$ is a subderivation of $A_2[\gamma] \stackrel{*}{\Longrightarrow} a_{k+1} \ldots a_j$. Combining this with $A_1[] \stackrel{*}{\Longrightarrow} a_i \ldots a_k$, we get $A[] \stackrel{*}{\Longrightarrow} a_i \ldots a_j$.

   Productions of the form $A[\cdot\cdot] \rightarrow A_1[\cdot\cdot\gamma]A_2[]$ are handled similarly.

## 13.2.2   Algorithm

We now give the complete recognition algorithm.

> For $i := 1$ to $n$ do
>
>   $L_{i,i} := \{(A, -, -, -, -, -) \mid A[] \rightarrow a_i\}$
>
> For $i := n$ to $1$ do
>   For $j := i$ to $n$ do
>     For $k := i$ to $j - 1$ do
>
>       *Step 1a.* For each production $A[\cdot\cdot\gamma] \rightarrow A_1[]A_2[\cdot\cdot]$
>       if $(A_1, -, -, -, -, -) \in L_{i,k}$ and
>       $(A_2, \gamma_2, A_3, \gamma_3, p, q) \in L_{k+1,j}$ for some $A_3, \gamma_3, p, q$
>       then $L_{i,j} := L_{i,j} \cup \{(A, \gamma, A_2, \gamma_2, k+1, j)\}$

*Step 1b.* For each production $A[\cdot\cdot\gamma] \to A_1[\cdot\cdot]A_2[]$
if $(A_1, \gamma_1, A_3, \gamma_3, p, q) \in L_{i,k}$ for some $A_3, \gamma_3, p, q$, and
$(A_2, -, -, -, -, -) \in L_{k+1,j}$
then $L_{i,j} := L_{i,j} \cup \{(A, \gamma, A_1, \gamma_1, i, k)\}$

*Step 2a.* For each production $A[\cdot\cdot] \to A_1[]A_2[\cdot\cdot\gamma]$
if $(A_2, \gamma, A_3, \gamma_3, p, q) \in L_{k+1,j}$ for some $A_3, \gamma_3, p, q$,
$(A_3, \gamma_3, A_4, \gamma_4, r, s) \in L_{p,q}$ for some $A_4, \gamma_4, r, s$, and
$(A_1, -, -, -, -, -) \in L_{i,k}$
then $L_{i,j} := L_{i,j} \cup \{(A, \gamma_3, A_4, \gamma_4, r, s)\}$

*Step 2b.* For each production $A[\cdot\cdot] \to A_1[\cdot\cdot\gamma]A_2[]$
if $(A_1, \gamma, A_3, \gamma_3, p, q) \in L_{i,k}$ for some $A_3, \gamma_3, p, q$,
$(A_3, \gamma_3, A_4, \gamma_4, r, s) \in L_{p,q}$ for some $A_4, \gamma_4, r, s$, and
$(A_2, -, -, -, -, -) \in L_{k+1,j}$
then $L_{i,j} := L_{i,j} \cup \{(A, \gamma_3, A_4, \gamma_4, r, s)\}$

If $(S, -, -, -, -, -) \in L_{1,n}$ then accept input string

## Complexity of the algorithm

Any array element, say $L_{i,j}$, is a set of tuples of the form $(A, \gamma, A', \gamma', p, q)$ where $p$ and $q$ are either integers between $i$ and $j$, or $i = j = -$. The number of possible values for $A, A', \gamma$, and $\gamma'$ are each bounded by a constant. Thus, the number of tuples in $L_{i,j}$ is at most $O((j - i)^2)$.

For a fixed value of $i, j, k$, Steps 1a and 1b will attempt to place at most $O((j - i)^2)$ tuples in $L_{i,j}$. Before adding any tuple to $L_{i,j}$ we first check whether the tuple is already present in that array element. This can be done in constant time on a RAM by assuming that each array element $L_{i,j}$ is itself an $(i + 1) \times (j + 1)$ array. A tuple of the form $(A, \gamma, A', \gamma', p, q)$ will be in the $\langle p, q \rangle^{th}$ element of $L_{i,j}$ and a tuple of the form $(A, -, -, -, -, -)$ will be in the $\langle 0, 0 \rangle^{th}$ element of $L_{i,j}$. Thus, these steps take at most $O((j - i)^2)$ time.

Similarly, for a fixed value of $i, j, k$, Steps 2a and 2b can add at most $O((j - i)^2)$ distinct tuples. However, in these steps $O((j - i)^4)$ not necessarily distinct tuples may be considered. There are $O((j - i)^4)$ such tuples because the integers $p, q, r, s$ can take values in the range between $i$ and $j$. Thus, steps 2a and 2b may each take $O((j - i)^4)$ time for a fixed value of $i, j, k$. Since we have three initial loops for $i, j$, and $k$, the time complexity of the algorithm is $O(n^7)$ where the length of the input is $n$. The algorithm can be modified slightly to be $O(n^6)$, however, for reasons of space we will not discuss this here.

# 13.3   Combinatory categorial grammars

Steedman and his colleagues (Ades & Steedman, 1982; Steedman, 1985, 1986) introduced CCG as an extension of Classical Categorial Grammars in which both function composition and function application are allowed. In addition, forward and backward slashes are used to place conditions concerning the relative ordering of adjacent categories that are to be combined. The definition of CCG that we adopt here is based on the version currently being used by Steedman.

**Definition 13.3.1**      A CCG, $G$, is denoted by $(V_T, V_N, S, f, R)$ where

$V_T$ is a finite set of terminals (lexical items),
$V_N$ is a finite set of nonterminals (atomic categories),
$S$ is a distinguished member of $V_N$,
$f$ is a function that maps elements of $V_T$ to finite subsets of $C(V_N)$, the set of categories, where $C(V_N)$ (the set of all categories build from $V_N$) is the smallest set such that $V_N \subseteq C(V_N)$ and $c_1, c_2 \in C(V_N)$ implies $(c_1/c_2), (c_1 \backslash c_2) \in C(V_N)$
$R$ is a finite set of combinatory rules.

There are four types of combinatory rules involving variables $x, y, z, z_1, \ldots$ over $C(V_N)$ and where $|_i \in \{\backslash, /\}$.[3]

1. forward application:          $(x/y) \quad y \rightarrow x$

2. backward application:          $y \quad (x \backslash y) \rightarrow x$
   For these rules we say that $(x/y)$ is the **primary** category and $y$ the **secondary** category.

3. generalized forward composition for some fixed $n \geq 1$:

$$(x/y) \quad (\ldots (y|_1 z_1)|_2 \ldots |_n z_n) \rightarrow (\ldots (x|_1 z_1)|_2 \ldots |_n z_n)$$

4. generalized backward composition for some $n \geq 1$:

$$(\ldots (y|_1 z_1)|_2 \ldots |_n z_n) \quad (x \backslash y) \rightarrow (\ldots (x|_1 z_1)|_2 \ldots |_n z_n)$$

For these rules $(x/y)$ is the primary category and $(\ldots (y|_1 z_1)|_2 \ldots |_n z_n)$ the secondary category.

Restrictions can be associated with the use of each combinatory rule in $R$. These restrictions take the form of constraints on the instantiations of variables in the rules.

1. The leftmost nonterminal (**target category**) of the primary category can be restricted to be in a given subset of $V_N$.

2. The category to which $y$ is instantiated can be restricted to be in a given finite subset of $C(V_N)$.

Derivations in a CCG, $G = (V_T, V_N, S, f, R)$, involve the use of the combinatory rules in $R$. Let $\underset{G}{\Longrightarrow}$ be defined as follows, where $\Upsilon_1, \Upsilon_2 \in (C(V_N) \cup V_T)^*$ and $c, c_1, c_2 \in C(V_N)$.

---

[3] There is no type-raising rule although its effect can be achieved to a limited extent since $f$ can assign type-raised categories to lexical items.

- If $R$ contains a combinatory rule that has $c_1 \, c_2 \to c$ as an instance then

$$\Upsilon_1 c \Upsilon_2 \underset{G}{\Longrightarrow} \Upsilon_1 c_1 c_2 \Upsilon_2$$

- If $c \in f(a)$ for some $a \in V_T$ and $c \in C(V_N)$ then

$$\Upsilon_1 c \Upsilon_2 \underset{G}{\Longrightarrow} \Upsilon_1 a \Upsilon_2$$

The string languages generated by a CCG, $G$, $L(G) = \{\, w \mid S \underset{G}{\overset{*}{\Longrightarrow}} w \mid w \in V_T^* \,\}$.

In order to simplify our presentation we assume that the categories are parenthesis-free. *The algorithm that we present can be adapted in a straightforward way to handle parenthesized categories.*

### 13.3.1   The LIG/CCG relationship

In this section, we describe the relationship between LIG and CCG by discussing how we can construct from any CCG a weakly equivalent LIG. The weak equivalence of LIG and CCG was established in (Weir & Joshi, 1988). The purpose of this section is to show how a CCG recognition algorithm can be derived from the algorithm given above for LIG.

Given a CCG, $G = (V_T, V_N, S, f, R)$, we construct an equivalent LIG, $G' = (V_T, V_N, V_N \cup \{/, \backslash\}, S, P)$, as follows. Each category in $c \in C(V_N)$ can be represented in $G'$ as a nonterminal and associated stack $A[\alpha]$ where $A$ is the target category of $c$ and $\alpha \in (\{/, \backslash\} V_N)^*$ such that $A\alpha = c$. Note that we are assuming that categories are parenthesis-free.

We begin by considering the function $f$ which assigns categories to each element of $V_T$. Suppose that $c \in f(a)$ where $c \in C(V_N)$ and $a \in V_T$. We should include the production $A[\alpha] \to a$ in $P$ where $c = A\alpha$. For each combinatory rule in $R$ we may include a number of productions in $P$. From the definition of CCG it can be seen that the length of all secondary categories in the rules $R$ is bounded by some constant. Therefore, there are a finite number of possible ground instantiations of the secondary category in each rule. Thus, we can remove all variables in secondary categories by expanding the number of rules in $R$. The rules that result will involve a secondary category $c \in C(V_N)$ and a primary category of the form $x/A$ or $x\backslash A$ where $A \in V_N$ is the target category of $c$. The rule may also place a restriction on the value of the target category of $x$. In the case of the primary categories of the combinatory rules there is no bound on their length and we cannot remove the variable that will be bound to the unbounded part of the category (the variable $x$ above). Therefore, the rules contain a single variable and are linear with respect to this variable, i.e., it appears once on either side of the rule.

It is straightforward to convert combinatory rules in this form into corresponding LIG productions. We illustrate how this can be done with an example. Suppose we have the following combinatory rule.

$$x/A \quad A/B\backslash C\backslash B \to x/B\backslash C\backslash B$$

where the target category of $x$ must be either $C$ or $D$. This is converted into the following two productions in $P$.

$$C[\cdots/B\backslash C\backslash B] \to C[\cdots/A] \quad A[/B\backslash C\backslash B]$$
$$D[\cdots/B\backslash C\backslash B] \to D[\cdots/A] \quad A[/B\backslash C\backslash B]$$

### 13.3.2  Recognition of CCG

Notice that the LIG productions described above do not correspond precisely to our earlier definition. We are pushing and popping more that one symbol on the stack and we have not associated empty stacks with all but one of the RHS nonterminals. Although this clearly does not affect weak generative power we must modify the earlier LIG recognition algorithm in order to produce a CCG algorithm. The algorithm will depend on a constant $k_1$ which is the largest $n$ such that the grammar contains one of the following rules.

$$x/y \quad y|_1 z_1|_2 \ldots |_n z_n \to x|_1 z_1|_2 \ldots |_n z_n$$
$$y|_1 z_1|_2 \ldots |_n z_n \quad x\backslash y \to x|_1 z_1|_2 \ldots |_n z_n$$

A second constant $k_2$ is also used which is the maximum of $k_1$ and the largest $m$ such that there is some $c \in f(a)$ where $c = A\alpha$ and $|\alpha| = m$.[4]

The recognition algorithm uses an array $L$ in which categories are stored. Since exponentially many categories can derive a string $a_i \ldots a_j$[5] it is necessary to store categories carefully. Note that application of a combinatory rule can depend on the entire secondary category (having length at most length $k_1$) and on the primary categories target category and suffix of length 1. Furthermore, when a combinatory rule is applied, a string of length at most $k_1$ replaces a string of length 1 in the encoding of the resulting category. Therefore, all categories that are introduced by lexical items or (because of their length) could be the secondary categories of a rule are encoded within a single array entry (see the first case below). All other categories are encoded with the sharing mechanism used in the LIG algorithm. However, since a rule introduces more than a single symbol, a string with length up to $k_1$ is stored locally giving the suffix of the encoded category (see the second case below).

An entry $(A, \alpha, \gamma, p, q)$ is included in $L[i, j]$ where $A \in V_N$ and $\alpha \in (\{\backslash, /\}V_N)^*$ when one of two cases holds. Either (1) $\gamma = p = q = -$ and $0 \leq |\alpha| \leq k_1 + k_2$ or (2) $\gamma \in \{\backslash, /\}V_N$, $(p, q) < (i, j)$ and $1 \leq |\alpha| \leq k_1$. The first case applies just in case $A\alpha \overset{*}{\underset{G}{\Longrightarrow}} a_i \ldots a_j$ ensuring that the complete secondary categories of a combinatory rules will be found in a single array entry. The second case holds when for some $\alpha' \in (\{\backslash, /\}V_N)^*$ we have the derivation $A\alpha'\gamma \overset{*}{\underset{G}{\Longrightarrow}} a_p \ldots a_q$. Furthermore, for all $\alpha' \in (\{\backslash, /\}V_N)^*$ if $A\alpha'\gamma \overset{*}{\underset{G}{\Longrightarrow}} a_p \ldots a_q$ then $A\alpha'\alpha \overset{*}{\underset{G}{\Longrightarrow}} a_i \ldots a_j$.

Next, we give the steps of the algorithm, where the input is $a_1 \ldots a_n$. The first step involves consideration of categories that can be assigned to the terminals in the input string. When $c \in f(a_i)$ ($1 \leq i \leq n$) for some category $c$, such

---

[4] If $\alpha \in (\{\backslash, /\}V_N)^n$ then the length of $\alpha$ $|\alpha|$ is equal to $n$.

[5] This is possible since the length of the category can be linear with respect to $j - i$.

that $c = A\alpha$, we include the tuple $(A, \alpha, -, -, -)$ in $L[i, i]$. The remaining steps involve the use of the forward application and composition combinatory rules. In the following discussion of the rule $x/y \ \ y|_1 z_1|_2 \cdots |_n z_n \rightarrow x|_1 z_1|_2 \cdots |_n z_n$ we allow for the possibility that $n = 0$ which corresponds to forward function application. Suppose there is an instance of this rule in which the primary category is $A\alpha'\alpha/B$, the secondary category is $B\beta$ with resulting category $A\alpha'\alpha\beta$ where $\alpha, \alpha', \beta \in (\{\backslash, /\}V_N)^*$. Notice that $|\beta| \le k_1$ and $|\alpha'\alpha|$ cannot be bounded. Thus, an encoding of the complete secondary category can be stored locally in a single array entry, whereas, only a bounded suffix $(\alpha/B)$ of the primary is stored locally together with an indication of where the remaining part of the category can be found. To establish which entries this rule permits us to add to $L[i, j]$ for each $i \le k \le j$, we look for $(B, \beta, -, -, -) \in L[k + 1, j]$ corresponding to the secondary category of the rule and we look for $(A, \alpha/B, \gamma, p, q) \in L[i, k]$ corresponding to the primary category of the rule. From these entries in $L$ we know that for some $\alpha'$ $A\alpha'\alpha/B \underset{G}{\overset{*}{\Longrightarrow}} a_i \ldots a_k$ and $B\beta \underset{G}{\overset{*}{\Longrightarrow}} a_{k+1} \ldots a_j$. Thus, by the combinatory rule given above we have $A\alpha'\alpha\beta \underset{G}{\overset{*}{\Longrightarrow}} a_i \ldots a_j$ and we should store and encoding of the category $A\alpha'\alpha\beta$ in $L[i, j]$. This encoding depends on $\alpha'$, $\alpha$, $\beta$, and $\gamma$.

- $\gamma = -$
  If $|\alpha\beta| \le k_2$ then add $(A, \alpha\beta, -, -, -)$ to $L[i, j]$. Otherwise, add $(A, \beta, /B, i, k)$ to $L[i, j]$.

- $\gamma \ne -$ and $n > 1$
  The new category is longer than the one found in $L[i, k]$. If $|\alpha| \ge 1$ then add $(A, \beta, /B, i, k)$ to $L[i, j]$, otherwise add $(A, \beta, \gamma, p, q)$ to $L[i, j]$.

- $\gamma \ne -$ and $n = 1$
  The new category has the same length as the one found in $L[i, k]$. Add $(A, \alpha\beta, \gamma, p, q)$ to $L[i, j]$.

- $\gamma \ne -$ and $n = 0$
  The new category has the a length one less than the one found in $L[i, k]$. If $|\alpha| \ge 1$ then add $(A, \alpha, \gamma, p, q)$ to $L[i, j]$. Otherwise, since $\alpha = \epsilon$ we have to look for part of the category that is not stored locally in $L[i, k]$. This may be found by looking in $L[p, q]$ for each $(A, \beta'\gamma, \gamma', r, s)$ where $(r, s) < (p, q)$ or $r = s = -$. We know that either $\gamma' = -$ or $\beta' \ne \epsilon$ and add $(A, \beta', \gamma', r, s)$ to $L[i, j]$. Note that for some $\alpha''$, $A\alpha''\beta'\gamma \underset{G}{\overset{*}{\Longrightarrow}}$ $a_p \ldots a_q$, $A\alpha''\beta'/B \underset{G}{\overset{*}{\Longrightarrow}} a_i \ldots a_k$, and thus by the combinatory rule above $A\alpha''\beta' \underset{G}{\overset{*}{\Longrightarrow}} a_i \ldots a_j$.

The rules for backward composition and application are treated in the same way, except that all occurrences of $i$ and $k$ are swapped with occurrences of $k + 1$ and $j$, respectively. This algorithm runs in time $O(n^7)$ and as in the LIG algorithm can be adapted to run in $O(n^6)$ time.

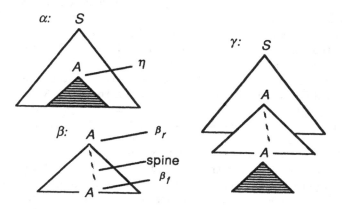

Figure 13.1. Elementary trees and ·adjunction.

## 13.4    Tree Adjoining Grammars

Tree Adjoining Grammars (TAG) (Joshi, 1985; Joshi, Levy, & Takahashi, 1975) are specified by a finite set of **initial** trees and a finite set of **auxiliary** trees. (An **elementary** tree is either an initial tree or an auxiliary tree.) An initial tree, that corresponds to the tree structure for a simple sentence, has its root labeled by the start symbol $S$ with the leaf nodes labeled by terminal symbols (as shown in the tree $\alpha$ in Figure 13.1). The root of an auxiliary tree is labeled by a nonterminal symbol ($A$ in the case of $\beta$ in Figure 13.1). Except for one leaf node, called the foot node, all leaf nodes are labeled by terminal symbols. The foot node of an auxiliary tree is labeled with the same nonterminal as the root. There is a single operation of composing trees called **adjoining**. This is shown in Figure 13.1 where the tree $\beta$ is adjoined in $\alpha$ at a node $\eta$ to give the tree $\gamma$.

### 13.4.1    Relationship between TAG and LIG

The relationship between LIG and TAG can be understood by considering the bottom-up recognition process. A bottom-up traversal begins with the recognition of terminal nodes of elementary trees. Movement up an elementary tree occurs when we have completed recognition of all of the children of some node at which point we can visit the parent. On reaching a node we consider adjunction by an auxiliary tree. Figure 13.1 corresponds to the case where adjoining takes place at a node addressed $\eta^6$ by an auxiliary tree $\beta$. In this example, when the traversal reaches the node $\eta$ we begin recognition of $\beta$ at its foot node $\beta_f$. When we have completed the traversal of $\beta$, (by recognizing

---

[6] We assume that there is some uniform way of addressing the nodes of an elementary tree that distinguishes between the different nodes in an elementary tree and between different elementary trees.

the root node $\beta_r$) the traversal resumes at the node $\eta$. Thus, it is necessary to keep track of the adjunction point $\eta$ while processing $\beta$. This information is passed between nodes on the path from the root to the foot node (the spine) of $\beta$. Since it is possible that additional adjunctions could take place at nodes on the spine of $\beta$ a stack is needed to store all adjunction points. This stack will be passed between nodes on the spines of auxiliary trees from the foot to the root of the tree. Adjunction points will be pushed on the stack when beginning the recognition of the foot of an adjoined tree, and popped from the stack when returning from an adjoined tree. This stacking of adjunction points can be simulated in an LIG.

It is necessary to distinguish between the point at which a node is first visited and the point at which we return to that node after adjunction. Therefore, for every node $\eta$ of an elementary tree we have two LIG nonterminals, $\eta^t$ and $\eta^b$. The nonterminal $\eta^b$ encodes the state at which we have reached $\eta$ but have not yet performed adjunctions. The nonterminal $\eta^t$ encodes the state at which we have returned to $\eta$ after adjunction has occurred. The adjunction shown in Figure 13.1 can be simulated in an LIG with the use of the following productions.

$$\beta_f^b[\cdot\cdot\eta] \rightarrow \eta^b[\cdot\cdot]$$

If we traverse the tree bottom-up and reach the node $\eta$ then this production predicts adjunction by the auxiliary tree $\beta$. Note that the production should be read right to left for a bottom-up derivation. The fact that we will have to return to $\eta$ is recorded on the stack.

$$\eta^t[\cdot\cdot] \rightarrow \beta_r^b[\cdot\cdot\eta]$$

In a bottom-up LIG derivation this production ensures that on reaching the root of $\beta$ we return to $\eta$ (the node where $\beta$ was adjoined).

For the case where there is no adjunction at $\eta$ we have the production

$$\eta^t[\cdot\cdot] \rightarrow \eta^b[\cdot\cdot]$$

The productions given above are used to simulate composition (using adjunction) of trees. To relate nodes within an elementary tree we have the following productions (for the different cases shown in Figure 13.2). Note that we are assuming that internal nodes either have two children labeled by nonterminals or a single child labeled by a terminal symbol.

$$\eta_1^b[\cdot\cdot] \rightarrow \eta_2^t[\cdot\cdot]\eta_3^t[\,]$$

This production is used when $\eta_1$ and its child $\eta_2$ are on the spine of the auxiliary tree. Notice that the stack of adjunction points is being propagated along the spine. A similar case arises when the right child of $\eta_1$ is on the spine.

$$\eta_4^b[\cdot\cdot] \rightarrow \eta_5^t[\cdot\cdot]\eta_6^t[\,]$$

This production is used when none of the nodes involved are on the spine. As in the case of $\eta_3$, when an node is not on the spine, initially the stack is empty.

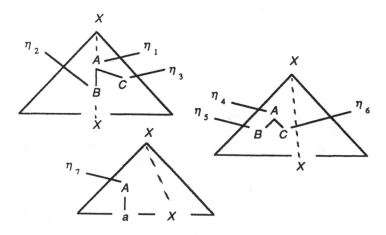

Figure 13.2. Nodes within elementary trees.

Hence although we have used $\eta_4^b[\cdot\cdot]$ (and $\eta_5^t[\cdot\cdot]$) to conform to productions of LIG, these stacks are empty.

$$\eta_7^b[] \to a$$

This production is used when $\eta_7$ has a single child labeled by the terminal symbol $a$.

## 13.4.2   Recognition of TAG

As we have seen, each case that must be considered in a bottom-up TAG recognition algorithm corresponds to a LIG production of the form considered in the recognition algorithm described in Section 13.2.2. It is, therefore, possible to give an recognition algorithm for TAG by making minor modifications to the LIG algorithm. For the TAG algorithm the tuples stored in an array entry indexed by the pair $(i, j)$ will have the form $(\eta, \eta', p, q)$ which indicates that we have reached $\eta$ (which spans the input $a_i \ldots a_j$) and that when the auxiliary tree to which $\eta$ belongs is completed we should return to the node $\eta'$ which before adjunction spanned the input sequence $a_p \ldots a_q$.

It turns out that adapting the LIG algorithm directly gives an inefficiency algorithm. It is possible for the stack to be popped more than once while completing a single array entry (i.e., without increasing the number of input symbols spanned). For example, this can occur when successive adjunction take place at the roots of auxiliary trees. When the root node of the last of these trees is completed and we return to the tree into which adjunction took place (another root node) we immediately pop the stack again. Removing symbols from the stack is expensive since it is necessary to search for all possible places where the remainder of the stack is stored. It is possible to address the problem of ensuring that only one symbol is popped at a time. However, we will not go into further details in this chapter.

## 13.5   Importance of linearity

The recognition algorithms given here have polynomial-time complexity because each array element contains a polynomial number (with respect to the difference between $j$ and $i$) of tuples. These tuples encode the top symbol of the stack (or top symbols of the category) together with an indication of where the next part of the stack (category) can be found. If we had stored the entire stack in the array elements,[7] then each array entry could include exponentially many elements giving exponential time complexity.

It is interesting to consider why it is not necessary to store the entire stack in the array elements. Suppose that $(A, \gamma, A', \gamma', p, q) \in L_{i,j}$. This indicates the existence of a tuple, say $(A', \gamma', A'', \gamma'', r, s)$, in $L_{p,q}$. Note that when we are adding the first tuple to $L_{i,j}$ we are not concerned about how the second tuple came to be put in $L_{p,q}$. This is because the productions in LIG (combinatory rules in CCG) are *linear* with respect to their unbounded stacks (categories). Hence the derivations from different nonterminals and their associated stacks (categories) are *independent* of each other. In Indexed Grammars, productions can have the form $A[\cdots\gamma] \rightarrow A_1[\cdots] A_2[\cdots]$. In such productions, there is more than one *dependent* child that inherits the unbounded stack from the nonterminal in the left hand side of the production. In a bottom-up recognition algorithm, using this form of production, the equality of the stacks associated with $A_1$ and $A_2$ has to be verified. This nullifies any advantage from the sharing of stacks since we would have to examine the complete stacks. A similar situation arises in the case of coordination schema used within the CCG framework to describe certain forms of coordination in Dutch. A coordination schema has been used (Steedman, 1985) that had the form $x$ *conj* $x \rightarrow x$ where the variable $x$ can be any category. With this schema we have to check the identity of two derived categories. This results in the loss of *independence* among paths in derivation trees. In (Vijay-Shanker, Weir, & Joshi, 1987), we have discussed the notion of independent paths in derivation trees with respect to a range of grammatical formalisms.

## 13.6   Concluding remarks

We have presented a general scheme for polynomial-time recognition of languages generated by a class of grammatical formalisms that are more powerful than CFG. This class of formalisms, which includes LIG, CCG, and TAG,

---

[7]In the chart parser for CCG given by Pareschi and Steedman (1987) the entire category is stored explicitly in each chart entry.

derive more complex trees than CFG due the use of an additional stack manipulating mechanism. Using the constructions used to show the equivalence of the formalisms (Joshi, Vijay-Shanker, & Weir, 1989; Weir & Joshi, 1988), we have described how a recognition algorithm we present for LIG can be adapted to give algorithms for CCG and TAG. Since the stacks can be exponentially large with respect to the size of the input we make crucial use of the sharing of substacks. The linearity of the composition operations in the above formalisms allows effective use of the sharing of stacks yielding polynomial algorithms.

# Acknowledgments

This work was partially supported by NSF grant IRI-8909810. We would like to thank Aravind Joshi, Michael Niv, Mark Steedman, and Kent Wittenburg for helpful discussions.

# References

Ades, A. E., & Steedman, M. J. (1982). On the order of words. *Ling. and Philosophy*, *3*, 517–558.

Aho, A. V. (1968) Indexed grammars — An extension to context free grammars. *J ACM*, *15*, 647–671.

Gazdar, G. (1985). *Applicability of indexed grammars to natural languages* (Tech. Rep. No. CSLI-85-34). Center for Study of Language and Information.

Joshi, A. K. (1985). How much context-sensitivity is necessary for characterizing structural descriptions — Tree Adjoining Grammars. In D. Dowty, L. Karttunen, & A. Zwicky (Eds.), *Natural language processing — Theoretical, computational and psychological perspectives*. New York: Cambridge University Press. (Originally presented in 1983.)

Joshi, A. K., Levy, L. S., & Takahashi, M. (1975). Tree adjunct grammars. *J Comput. Syst. Sci.*, *10*, *1*.

Joshi, A. K., Vijay-Shanker, K., & Weir, D. J. (1989). The convergence of mildly context-sensitive grammar formalisms. In T. Wasow & P. Sells (Eds.), *The processing of linguistic structure*. MIT Press.

Kasami, T. (1965). *An efficient recognition and syntax algorithm for context-free languages* (Tech. Rep. No. AF-CRL-65-758). Bedford, MA: Air Force Cambridge Research Laboratory.

Pareschi, R., & Steedman, M. J. (1987). A lazy way to chart-parse with categorial grammars. *25th Meeting Assoc. Comput. Ling.*

Pollard, C. (1984). *Generalized phrase structure grammars, head grammars and natural language*. Unpublished doctoral dissertation. CA: Stanford University.

Steedman, M. J. (1985). Dependency and coordination in the grammar of Dutch and English. *Language*, *61*, 523–568.

Steedman, M. (1986). Combinators and grammars. In R. Oehrle, E. Bach, & D. Wheeler (Eds.), *Categorial grammars and natural language structures.* Dordrecht: Foris.

Thatcher, J. W. (1971). Characterizing derivations trees of context free grammars through a generalization of finite automata theory. *J Comput. Syst. Sci., 5,* 365–396.

Vijay-Shanker, K., & Joshi, A. K. (1985). Some computational properties of Tree Adjoining Grammars. *23rd Meeting Assoc. Comput. Ling.* (pp. 82–93).

Vijay-Shanker, K., Weir, D. J., & Joshi, A. K. (1986). Tree adjoining and head wrapping. *11th International Conference on Comput. Ling.*

Vijay-Shanker, K., Weir, D. J., & Joshi, A. K. (1987). Characterizing structural descriptions produced by various grammatical formalisms. *25th Meeting Assoc. Comput. Ling.*

Weir, D. J., & Joshi, A. K. (1988). Combinatory categorial grammars: Generative power and relationship to linear context-free rewriting systems. *26th Meeting Assoc. Comput. Ling.*

Younger, D. H. (1967). Recognition and parsing of context-free languages in time $n^3$. *Inf. Control, 10,* 189–208.

# 14. Overview of Parallel Parsing Strategies

Anton Nijholt

*Faculty of Computer Science, University of Twente*

## 14.1 Introduction

In the early 1970's papers appeared in which ideas on parallel compiling for programming languages and parallel executing of computer programs were investigated. In these papers parallel lexical analysis, syntactic analysis (parsing) and code generation were discussed. At that time various multi-processor computers were introduced (CDC 6500, 7600, STAR, ILLIAC IV, etc.) and the first attempts were made to construct compilers which used more than one processor when compiling programs. Slowly, with the advent of new parallel architectures and the ubiquitous application of VLSI, interest increased and presently research on parallel compiling and executing is widespread.

Although more slowly, a similar change of orientation occurred in the field of natural language processing. However, unlike the compiler construction environment with its generally accepted theories, in natural language processing no generally advocated — and accepted — theory of natural language analysis and understanding is available. Therefore it is not only the desire to exploit parallelism for the improvement of speed but it is also the assumption that human sentence processing is of an inherently parallel nature which makes computer linguists and cognitive scientists turn to parallel approaches for their problems. For these reasons, in natural language processing many kinds of parallel approaches can be distinguished. While some researchers aim at cognitive simulation, others are satisfied with high performance language systems. The first-mentioned researchers may ultimately ask for numbers of processors and connections between processors that approximate the number of neurons and their connections in the human brain (that is, an order of $10^{11}$ neurons with $10^3 - 10^4$ connections each). They model human language processing with connectionist models and therefore they are interested in massive parallelism, distributed representation of knowledge and low degradation of overall behavior in the face of local errors. A more modest use of parallelism than offered by a connectionist model may also be useful. Any system used for understanding natural language sentences needs to distinguish different levels of analysis, e.g., analysis at the morphological, the lexical, the syntactic, the semantic and the referential level. For each level a different kind of knowledge has to be invoked. Therefore different tasks can be distinguished: the application of morphological knowledge, the application of lexical knowledge, etc. It is not necessarily the case that application of one type of knowledge is under control of one of the other types of knowledge. The tasks may interact and at times they can be performed simultaneously. Therefore processors which can work in parallel and which can communicate with each other may be assigned to these tasks in order to perform this interplay of multiple sources of knowledge. Hence, this task-oriented parallelism requires smart processors performing specialized functions.

Independently of a parallel nature that can be recognized in the domain of language processing, since operating in parallel with a collection of processors can achieve substantial speed-ups, designers and implementors of natural language processing systems consider the application of available parallel processing power for any task or subtask which allows that application. Designing parsing methods from the point of view of available or desired processor configurations has led to a variety of methods. Attacking the context-free parsing problem with more than one processor almost always means using identical processors, that is, processors that run the same software and compute the same function. In some cases this can amount to having several asynchronous parsers working on the same input string. Using more than one traditional parser is one way to attack the parsing problem. Another way is to re-investigate existing parsing methods to see whether they can be adapted to a parallel processing view. For the Earley and the Cocke-Younger-Kasami (CYK) parsing methods implementations have been designed for multiprocessor shared-memory computers, for pipelines of processors and for arrays of processors. In this view there exists an architecture (a configuration of physical processors) and algorithms are designed to make optimal use of this configuration. On the other hand, configurations can be designed to allow the use of certain algorithms. In high-level parallel programming languages parallelism (or concurrency) is introduced by the notion of processes. These languages offer concepts and language constructs to define processes which cooperate by communicating with each other using explicit communication instructions. The hardware, i.e., the physical processors, can remain hidden from the user of the language. Distinct processes may be distributed onto distinct processors, or they may be executed on a single processor. In the remainder of this chapter no distinction is made between processes and processors.

In the programming language point of view the starting point is the programming language and the problem of language analysis is programmed using the parallel concepts that are offered by the programming language. For instance, parallel logic programming languages such as GHC (Guarded Horn Clauses), Parlog and Concurrent Prolog invite us to approach the analysis problem from a parallel point of view. Many natural language processing systems based on these parallel logic programming languages have been built. In Matsumoto and Sugimura (1987) an example of this approach, using a left-corner method, can be found. In Tanaka and Numazaki (1989) GHC is used to implement a parallel version of Tomita's generalized LR parsing algorithm. In the paper of Matsumoto and Sugimora the terminal and nonterminal symbols are defined as parallel processes. In the paper of Tanaka and Numazaki each LR-table entry is defined as a process. Similarly, a parallel object-oriented point of view can be advocated, as is done by Yonezawa and Ohsawa (1988). They use the parallel object-oriented programming language ABCL/1 to implement a parsing system which is obtained by translating a collection of context-free grammar rules into a configuration of message passing, cooperating units (agents). Each occurrence of a terminal or nonterminal symbol in a grammar rule is represented as an agent in the system, the messages that are sent consist of control data or partial parse trees.

In this chapter various approaches to the problem of parallel parsing will be surveyed. We will discuss examples of parsing schemes which use more than one traditional parser, schemes where 'non-deterministic' choices during parsing lead to separate processes, schemes where the number of processes depends on the length of the sentence being parsed, and schemes where the number of processes depends on the grammar size rather than on the input length. Our aim is not to give a complete survey of methods that have been introduced in the area of parallel parsing. Rather we present some approaches that use ideas that seem to be characteristic for many of the parallel parsing methods that have been introduced.

## 14.2 From one to many traditional serial parsers

### 14.2.1 LR-parsers

As already mentioned in the introduction, many algorithms for parallel parsing have been proposed. Concentrating on the ideas that underlie these methods, some of them will be discussed here. For an annotated bibliography containing references to other methods see (Op den Akker *et al.*, 1989). Since we will frequently refer to *LR-parsing* a few words will be spent on this algorithm. The class of LR-grammars is a subclass of the class of context-free grammars. Each LR-grammar generates a *deterministic* context-free languages and each deterministic context-free language can be generated by an LR-grammar. From an LR-grammar an LR-parser can be constructed. The LR-parser consists of an LR-table and an LR-routine which consults the table to decide the actions that have to be performed on a pushdown stack and on the input. The pushdown stack will contain symbols denoting the *state* of the parser. As an example, consider the following context-free grammar:

1. S → NP VP
2. S → S PP
3. NP → *det *n
4. PP → *prep NP
5. VP → *v NP

With the LR-construction method the LR-table of Table 14.1 will be obtained from this grammar. It is assumed that each input string to be parsed will have an endmarker which consists of the $-sign.

Table 14.1. LR-parsing table for the example grammar.

| STATE | *DET | *N | *V | *PREP | $ | NP | PP | VP | S |
|-------|------|-----|-----|-------|-----|-----|-----|-----|-----|
| 0 | sh3 | | | | | 2 | | | 1 |
| 1 | | | | sh5 | acc | | 4 | | |
| 2 | | | sh6 | | | | | 7 | |
| 3 | | sh8 | | | | | | | |
| 4 | | | | re2 | re2 | | | | |
| 5 | sh3 | | | | | 9 | | | |
| 6 | sh3 | | | | | 10 | | | |
| 7 | | | | re1 | re1 | | | | |
| 8 | | | re3 | re3 | re3 | | | | |
| 9 | | | | re4 | re4 | | | | |
| 10 | | | | re5 | re5 | | | | |

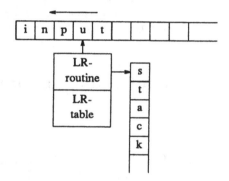

Figure 14.1. LR-parser.

An entry in the table of the form 'sh$n$' indicates the action 'shift state $n$ on the stack and advance the input pointer;' entry 're$n$' indicates the action 'reduce the stack using rule $n$.' The entry 'acc' indicates that the input string is accepted. The right part of the table is used to decide the state the parser has to enter after a reduce action. In a reduce action states are popped from the stack. The number of states that are popped is equal to the length of the right hand side of the rule that has to be used in the reduction. With the state which becomes the topmost symbol of the stack (0–10) and with the nonterminal of the left hand side of the rule which is used in the reduction ($S$, $NP$, $VP$, or $PP$) the right part of the table tells the parser what state to push next on the stack. In Figure 14.1 the usual configuration of an LR-parser is shown.

## 14.2.2   More than one serial parser

Having more than one processor, why not use two parsers? One of them can be used to process the input from left to right, the other can be used to process the input from right to left. Each parser can be assigned part of the input. When the parsers meet the complete parse tree has to be constructed from the partial parse trees delivered by the two parsers. Obviously, this idea is not new. We can find it in (Tseytlin & Yushchenko, 1977) and it appears again in (Loka, 1984). However, rather than having one or two parsers operating at the far left or the far right of the input, it is more interesting to see a number of parsers, where the number depends on the 'parallelism' the input string allows, working along the length of the input string. If there is a natural way to segment a string, then each segment can have its own parser. Examples of this strategy are the methods described in (Carlisle & Friesen, 1985; Fischer, 1975; Lincoln, 1970; Lozinskii & Nirenburg, 1986; and Mickunas & Schell, 1975). Here we confine ourselves to an explanation of Fischer's method. Fischer introduces 'synchronous parsing machines' (SPM) that LR-parse part of the input string. Each of the SPMs is a serial LR-parser which is able to parse any sentence of the grammar in the usual way from left to right. However, at least in theory, Fischer's method allows any symbol in the input string as the starting point of each SPM. For practical applications one may think of starting at keywords denoting the start of a procedure, a block, or even a statement. One obvious problem that emerges is, when we let a serial LR-parser start somewhere in the input string, in what state should it start? The solution is to let each SPM carry a set of states, guaranteed to include the correct one. In addition, for each of these states the SPM carries a pushdown stack on which the next actions are to be performed. An outline of the parsing algorithm follows.

For convenience we assume that the LR-parser is an LR(0) parser. No look-ahead is necessary to decide a shift or a reduce action. In the algorithm $M$ denotes the LR-parsing table and for any state $s$, $R(s)$ denotes the set consisting of the rule which has to be used in making a reduction in state $s$. By definition, $R(s) = \{0\}$ if no reduction has to be made in state $s$.

(1) *Initialization*

Start one SPM at the far left of the input string. This SPM has a single stack and it only contains $s_0$, the initial state. Start a number of other SPM's. Suppose we want to start an SPM immediately to the left of some symbol $a$. In the LR-parse table $M$ we can find which states have a non-empty entry for symbol $a$. For each of these states the SPM which will be started, possesses a stack containing this state only. Hence, the SPM is started with just those states that can validly scan the next symbol in the string.

(2) *Scan the next symbol*

Let $a$ be the symbol to be scanned. For each stack of the SPM, if state $s$ is on top, then

(a) if $M(s, a) = \text{sh}s'$, then push $s'$ on the stack;

(b) if $M(s,a) = \emptyset$, then delete this stack from the set of stacks this SPM carries. In the latter case the stack has been shown to be invalid. While scanning subsequent input symbols the number of stacks that an SPM carries will decrease.

(3) *Reduce?*

Let $Q = \{s_1, \ldots, s_n\}$ be the set of top states of the stacks of the SPM under consideration. Define

$$R(Q) = \bigcup_{s \in Q} R(s).$$

(a) if $R(Q) = \{0\}$, then go to Step 2; in this case the top states of the stacks agree that no reduction is indicated;

(b) if $R(Q) = \{i\}, i \neq 0$, and $i = A \rightarrow \gamma_i$, then, if the stacks of the SPM are deep enough to pop off $|\gamma_i|$ states and not be empty, then do reduction $i$;

(c) otherwise, if we have insufficient stack depth or not all top states agree on the same reduction, we stop this SPM (for the time being) and, if possible, we start a new SPM to the immediate right.

An SPM which has been stopped can be restarted. If an SPM is about to scan a symbol already scanned by an SPM to its immediate right, then a merge of the two SPM's will be attempted. The following two situations have to be distinguished:

- If the left SPM contains a single stack with top state $s$, then $s$ is the correct state to be in and we can select from the stacks of the right SPM the stack with bottom state $s$. Pop $s$ from the left stack and then concatenate the two. All other stacks can be discarded and the newly obtained SPM can continue parsing.

- If the left SPM contains more than one stack, then it is stopped. It has to wait until it is restarted by an SPM to its left. Notice that the leftmost SPM always has one stack and it will always have sufficient stack depth. Therefore there will always be an SPM coming from the left which can restart a waiting SPM.

In Step 3c we started a new SPM immediately to the right of the stopped SPM. What set of states and associated stacks should it be started in? We cannot, as was done in the initialization, simply take those states which allow a scan of the next input symbol. To the left of this new SPM reductions may have been done (or will be done) and therefore other states should be considered in order to guarantee that the correct state is included. Hence, if in Step 3 $|R(Q)| > 1$, then for each $s$ in $Q$, provided $R(s) = \{0\}$, we add $s$ to the set of states of the new SPM and in case $R(s) = \{i\}$ we add to the set of states that have to be carried by the new SPM also the states that can become topmost after a reduction using production rule $i$ (perhaps followed by other reductions). This concludes our explanation of Fischer's method. For more details and extensions of these ideas the reader is referred to (Fischer, 1975).

Table 14.2. LR-parsing table for grammar $G$.

| STATE | *DET | *N | *V | *PREP | $ | NP | PP | VP | S |
|---|---|---|---|---|---|---|---|---|---|
| 0 | sh3 | sh4 | | | | 2 | | | 1 |
| 1 | | | | sh6 | acc | | 5 | | |
| 2 | | | sh7 | sh6 | | | 9 | 8 | |
| 3 | | sh10 | | | | | | | |
| 4 | | | re3 | re3 | re3 | | | | |
| 5 | | | | re2 | re2 | | | | |
| 6 | sh3 | sh4 | | | | 11 | | | |
| 7 | sh3 | sh4 | | | | 12 | | | |
| 8 | | | | re1 | re1 | | | | |
| 9 | | | re5 | re5 | re5 | | | | |
| 10 | | | re4 | re4 | re4 | | | | |
| 11 | | | re6 | re6,sh6 | re6 | | 9 | | |
| 12 | | | | re7,sh6 | re7 | | 9 | | |

## 14.2.3 'Solving' parsing conflicts by parallelism?

To allow more efficient parsing methods restrictions on the class of general context-free grammars have been introduced. These restrictions have led to, among others, the classes of LL-, LR- and precedence grammars and associated LL-, LR- and precedence parsing techniques. The LR-technique uses, as discussed in the previous section, an LR-parsing table which is constructed from the LR-grammar.

If the grammar from which the table is constructed is not an LR-grammar, then the table will contain conflicting entries. In case of a conflict entry the parser has to choose. One decision may turn out to be wrong or both (or more) possibilities may be correct but only one may be chosen. The entry may allow reduction of a production rule but at the same time it may allow shifting of the next input symbol onto the stack. A conflict entry may also allow reductions according to different production rules. Consider the following example grammar $G$:

1.  S → NP VP          5.  NP → NP PP
2.  S → S PP           6.  PP → *prep NP
3.  NP → *n            7.  VP → *v NP
4.  NP → *det *n

The parsing table for this grammar, taken from (Tomita, 1985), is shown in Table 14.2.

Tomita's answer to the problem of LR-parsing of general context-free grammars is 'pseudo-parallelism.' Each time during parsing the parser encounters a multiple entry, the parsing process is split into as many processes as there are entries. Splitting is done by replicating the stack as many times as necessary and then continue parsing with the actions of the entry separately. The processes are 'synchronized' on the shift action. Any process that encounters a shift action waits until the other processes also encounter a shift action. Therefore all processes look at the same input word of the sentence.

Obviously, this LR-directed breadth-first parsing may lead to a large number of non-interacting stacks. So it may occur that during parts of a sentence all processes behave in exactly the same way. Both the amount of computation and the amount of space can be reduced considerably by unifying processes by combining their stacks into a so-called 'graph-structured' stack. Tomita does not suggest a parallel implementation of the algorithm. Rather his techniques for improving efficiency are aimed at efficient serial processing of sentences. Nevertheless, we can ask whether a parallel implementation might be useful. Obviously, Tomita's method is not a 'parallel-designed' algorithm. There is a master routine (the LR-parser) which maintains a data structure (the graph-structured stack) and each word that is read by the LR-parser is required for each process (or stack). In a parallel implementation nothing is gained when we weave a list of stacks into a graph-structured stack. In fact, when this is done, Tomita's method becomes closely related to Earley's method (see a next section) and it seems more natural — although the number of processes may become too large — to consider parallel versions of this algorithm since it is not restricted in advance by the use of a stack. When we want to stay close to Tomita's ideas, then we rather think of a more straightforward parallel implementation in which each LR conflict causes the creation of a new LR-parser which receives a copy of the stack and a copy of the remaining input (if it is already available) and then continues parsing without ever communicating with the other LR-parsers that work on the same string. On a transputer network, for example, each transputer may act as an LR-parser. However, due to its restrictions on interconnection patterns, sending stacks and strings through the network may become a time-consuming process. When a parser encounters a conflict the network should be searched for a free transputer whereas the stack and the remainder of the input should be passed through the network to this transputer. This will cause other processes to slow down and one may expect that only a limited 'degree of non-LR-ness' will allow an appropriate application of these ideas. Moreover, one may expect serious problems when on-line parsing of the input is required.

## 14.3   Translating grammar rules into process configurations

A simple 'object-oriented' parallel parsing method for ε-free and cycle-free context-free grammars has been introduced by Yonezawa and Ohsawa (1988). The method resembles the well-known Cocke-Younger-Kasami parsing method, but does not require that the grammars are in Chomsky Normal Form (CNF). Consider again our example grammar $G$:

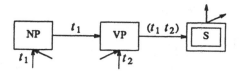

Figure 14.2. From rules to configuration.

1.  S → NP VP          5.  NP → NP PP
2.  S → S PP           6.  PP → *prep NP
3.  NP → *n            7.  VP → *v NP
4.  NP → *det *n

This set of rules will be viewed as a network of computing agents working concurrently. Each occurrence of a (pre-)terminal or a nonterminal symbol in the grammar rules corresponds with an agent with modest processing power and internal memory. The agents communicate with one another by passing subtrees of possible parse trees. The topology of the network is obtained as follows. Rule 1 yields the network fragment depicted in Figure 14.2.

In the figure we have three agents, one for *NP*, one for *VP* and a 'double' agent for *S*. Suppose the *NP*-agent has received a subtree $t_1$. It passes $t_1$ to the *VP*-agent. Suppose this agent has received a subtree $t_2$. It checks whether they can be put together (the 'boundary adjacency test') and, if this test succeeds, it passes $(t_1\ t_2)$ to the *S*-agent. This agent constructs the parse tree $(S\ (t_1\ t_2))$ and distributes the result to all computing agents in the network which correspond with an occurrence of *S* in a right hand side of a rule. The complete network for the rules of $G$ is shown in Figure 14.3. As can be seen in the network, there is only one of these *S*-agents. For this agent $(S\ (t_1\ t_2))$ plays the same role as $t_1$ did for the *NP*-agent. If the boundary adjacency test is not successful, then the *VP*-agent stores the trees until it has a pair of trees which satisfies the test.

As an example, consider the sentence *The man saw a girl with a telescope*. For this particular sentence we do not want to construct from a subtree $t_1$ for *a telescope* and from a subtree $t_2$ for *saw the girl* a subtree for *a telescope saw a girl*, although the rule $S \rightarrow NP\ VP$ permits this construction. Therefore, words to be sent into the network are provided with tags representing positional information and during construction of a subtree this information is inherited from its constituents. For our example sentence the input should look as

*(0 1 the)(1 2 man)(2 3 saw)(3 4 a)(4 5 girl)(5 6 with)(6 7 a)(7 8 telescope).*

Combination of tokens and trees according to the grammar rules and the positional information can yield a subtree *(3 5 (NP ((\*det a)(\*n girl))))* but not a subtree in which *(0 1 the)* and *(4 5 girl)* are combined. Each word accompanied with its tags is distributed to the agents for its (pre-)terminal(s) by a *manager agent* which has this information available.

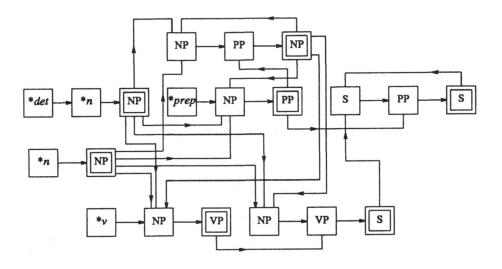

Figure 14.3. Computing agents for grammar $G$.

If the context-free grammar which underlies the network is ambiguous, then all possible parse trees for a given input sentence will be constructed. It is possible to pipe-line constructed subtrees to semantic processing agents which filter the trees so that only semantically valid subtrees are distributed to other agents. Another useful extension is the capability to unparse a sentence when the user of a system based on this method erases ('backspaces to') previously typed words. This can be realized by letting the agents send anti-messages that cancel the effects of earlier messages. It should be noted that the parsing of a sentence does not have to be finished before a next sentence is fed into the network. By attaching another tag to the words it becomes possible to distinguish the subtrees from one sentence from those of an other sentence. The method as explained here has been implemented in the object-oriented concurrent language ABCL/1. For the experiment a context-free English grammar which gave rise to 1124 computing agents has been used. Sentences with a length between 10 and 30 words and a parse tree height between 10 and 20 were used for input. Parallelism was simulated by time-slicing. From this simulation it followed that a parse tree is produced from the network in $O(n \times h)$ time, where $n$ is the length of the input string and $h$ is the height of the parse tree. Obviously, simple examples of grammars and their sentences can be given which cause an explosion in the number of adjacency tests and also in the number of subtrees that will be stored without ever being used. Constructs which lead to such explosions do not usually occur in context-free descriptions of natural language.

There are several ways in which the number of computing agents can be reduced. For example, instead of the three double $NP$-agents of Figure 14.3 it is possible to use one double $NP$-agent with the same function but with an

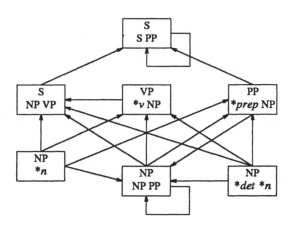

Figure 14.4. Agents for grammar rules.

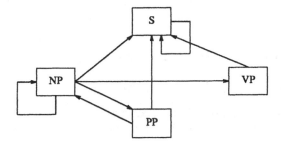

Figure 14.5. Agents for nonterminal symbols.

increase of parse trees that have to be constructed and distributed. The same can be done for the two $S$-agents. A next step is to eliminate all double agents and give their tasks to the agents which correspond with the rightmost symbol of a grammar rule. It is also possible to have one computing agent for each grammar rule. In this way we obtain the configuration of Figure 14.4. It will be clear what has to be done by the different agents.

Another configuration with a reduced number of computing agents is obtained if we have an agent for each nonterminal symbol of the grammar. For our example grammar we have four agents, the $S$-, the $NP$-, the $VP$-, and the $PP$-agent. We may also introduce agents for the pre-terminals or even for each word which can occur in an input sentence. We confine ourselves to agents for the nonterminal symbols and discuss their roles. In Figure 14.5 we have displayed the configuration of computing agents which will be obtained from the example grammar.

The communication between the agents of this network is as follows.

(1) The $S$-agent sends subtrees with root $S$ to itself; it receives subtrees from itself, the $PP$-agent, the $NP$-agent, and the $VP$-agent.

(2) The $NP$-agent sends subtrees with root $NP$ to itself, the $S$-agent, the $VP$-agent and the $PP$-agent; it receives subtrees from itself and from the $PP$-agent; moreover, input comes from the manager agent.

(3) The $VP$-agent sends subtrees with root $VP$ to the $S$-agent; it receives subtrees from the $NP$-agent; moreover, input comes from the manager agent.

(4) The $PP$-agent sends subtrees with root $PP$ to the $S$-agent and to the $NP$-agent; it receives subtrees from the $NP$-agent; moreover, it receives input from the manager agent.

The task of each of these nonterminal agents is to check whether the subtrees it receives can be put together according to the grammar rules with the nonterminal as left-hand side and according to positional information that is carried along with the subtrees. If possible, a tree with the nonterminal as root is constructed, otherwise the agent checks other trees or waits until trees are available.

## 14.4    From sentence words to processes

### 14.4.1    Cocke-Younger-Kasami's algorithm

Traditional parsing methods for context-free grammars have been re-investigated in order to see whether they can be adapted to a parallel processing view. First we consider the tabular Cocke-Younger-Kasami algorithm. The input grammar should be in CNF, hence, each rule is of the form $A \rightarrow BC$ or $A \rightarrow a$. This normal form allows the following bottom-up parsing method. For any string $x = a_1 a_2 \cdots a_n$ to be parsed an upper-triangular $(n+1) \times (n+1)$ recognition table $T$ is constructed. Each table entry $t_{i,j}$ with $i < j$ will contain a subset of $N$ (the set of nonterminal symbols) such that $A \in t_{i,j}$ if and only if $A \Rightarrow *a_{i+1} \cdots a_j$. Assume that the input string, if desired terminated with an endmarker, is available on the matrix diagonal. String $x$ belongs to $L(G)$ if and only if $S \in t_{0,n}$ when the construction of the table is completed.

(1) Compute $t_{i,i+1}$ as $i$ ranges from 0 to $n-1$, by placing $A$ in $t_{i,i+1}$ exactly when there is a production $A \rightarrow a_{i+1}$ in $P$.

(2) Set $d = 1$. Assuming $t_{i,i+d}$ has been formed for $0 \leq i \leq n-d$, increase $d$ with 1 and compute $t_{i,j}$ for $0 \leq i \leq n-d$ and $j = i+d$ where $A$ is placed in $t_{i,j}$ when, for any $k$ such that $i < k < j$, there is a production $A \rightarrow BC \in P$ with $B \in t_{i,j}$ and $C \in t_{k,j}$.

In a similar form the algorithm is usually presented (see e.g., Graham & Harrison, 1976). Figure 14.6 may be helpful in understanding a parallel implementation.

| | 0,1 | 0,2 | 0,3 | 0,4 | 0,5 |
|---|---|---|---|---|---|
| | | 1,2 | 1,3 | 1,4 | 1,5 |
| | | | 2,3 | 2,4 | 2,5 |
| | | | | 3,4 | 3,5 |
| | | | | | 4,5 |
| | | | | | |

Figure 14.6. The upper-triangular CYK-table.

Notice that after Step (1) the computation of the entries is done diagonal by diagonal until entry $t_{0,n}$ has been completed. For each entry of a diagonal only elements of preceding diagonals are used to compute its value. More specifically, in order to see whether a nonterminal should be included in an element $t_{i,j}$ it is necessary to compare $t_{i,k}$ and $t_{k,j}$, with $k$ between $i$ and $j$. The amount of storage that is required by this method is proportional to $n^2$ and the number of elementary operations is proportional to $n^3$. Unlike Yonezawa and Ohsawa's algorithm where positional information needs an explicit representation, here it is in fact available (due to the CNF of the grammar) in the indices of the table elements. For example, in $t_{1,4}$ we can find the nonterminals which generate the substring of the input between Positions 1 and 4. The algorithm can be extended in order to produce parse trees.

From the recognition table we can conclude a two-dimensional configuration of processes for the parallel approach. For each entry $t_{i,j}$ of the upper-triangular table there is a process $P_{i,j}$ which receives table elements (i.e., sets of nonterminals) from processes $P_{i,j-1}$ and $P_{i+1,j}$. Process $P_{i,j}$ transmits the table elements it receives from $P_{i,j-1}$ to $P_{i,j+1}$ and the elements it receives from $P_{i+1,j}$ to $P_{i-1,j}$. Process $P_{i,j}$ transmits the table element it has constructed to processes $P_{i-1,j}$ and $P_{i,j+1}$. Figure 14.7 shows the interconnection structure for $n = 5$. As soon as a table element has been computed, it is sent to its right and upstairs neighbor. Each process should be provided with a coding of the production rules of the grammar. Clearly, each process requires $O(n)$ time. It is not difficult to see that like similar algorithms suitable for VLSI-implementation, e.g., systolic algorithms for matrix multiplication or transitive closure computation (see (Guibas et al., 1979) and many others) the required parsing time is also $O(n)$. See (Nijholt, 1990b) for details. In (Chu & Fu, 1982) a VLSI design for this algorithm is presented.

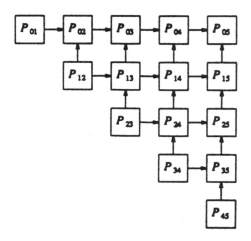

Figure 14.7. Process configuration for CYK's algorithm.

## 14.4.2   Earley's algorithm

The second algorithm we discuss in this section is the well-known Earley's method. It is not essentially different from the CYK algorithm. Since the method maintains information in the table entries about the righthand sides of the productions that are being recognized, the condition that the grammar should be in CNF is not necessary. For general context-free grammars Earley parsing takes $O(n^3)$ time. This time can be reduced to $O(n^2)$ or $O(n)$ for special subclasses of context-free grammars. Many versions of Earley's method exist. In (Graham & Harrison, 1976) the following tabular version can be found. For any string $x = a_1 a_2 \cdots a_n$ to be parsed an upper-triangular $(n + 1) \times (n+1)$ recognition table $T$ is constructed. Each table entry $t_{i,j}$ will contain a set of items, i.e., a set of elements of the form $A \rightarrow \alpha \cdot \beta$ (a dotted rule), where $A \rightarrow \alpha\beta$ is a production rule from the grammar and the dot $\cdot$ is a symbol not in $N \cup \sum$. The computation of the table entries goes column by column. The following two functions will be useful. Function PREDICT:$N \rightarrow 2^D$, where $D = \{A \rightarrow \alpha \cdot \beta | A \rightarrow \alpha\beta \in P\}$, is defined as

$$\text{PREDICT}(A) = \{B \rightarrow \alpha \cdot \beta | B \rightarrow \alpha\beta \in P,$$
$$\alpha \Rightarrow *\epsilon \text{ and } \exists \gamma \in V * \text{ with } A \Rightarrow *B\gamma\}.$$

Function PRED$(X)$:$2^N \rightarrow 2^D$ is defined as

$$\text{PRED}(X) = \bigcup_{A \in X} \text{PREDICT}(A).$$

Initially, $t_{0,0} = \text{PRED}(\{S\})$ and all other table entries are empty. Suppose we want to compute the elements of column $j$, $j > 0$. In order to compute $t_{i,j}$ with $i \neq j$ assume that all elements of the columns of the upper-triangular table to the left of column $j$ have already been computed and in column $j$ the elements $t_{k,j}$ for $i < k < j$ have been computed.

(1) Add $B \rightarrow \alpha a \beta \cdot \gamma$ to $t_{i,j}$ if $B \rightarrow \alpha \cdot a\beta\gamma \in t_{i,j-1}$, $a = a_j$ and $\beta \Rightarrow *\epsilon$.

(2) Add $B \rightarrow \alpha A \beta \cdot \gamma$ to $t_{i,j}$, if, for any $k$ such that $i < k < j$, $B \rightarrow \alpha \cdot A\beta\gamma \in t_{i,k}$, $A \rightarrow \omega \cdot \in t_{k,j}$ and $\beta \Rightarrow *\epsilon$.

(3) Add $B \rightarrow \alpha A \beta \cdot \gamma$ to $t_{i,j}$ if $B \rightarrow \alpha \cdot A\beta\gamma \in t_{i,i}$, $\beta \Rightarrow *\epsilon$ and there exists $C \in N$ such that $A \Rightarrow *C$ and $C \rightarrow \omega \cdot \in t_{i,j}$.

After all elements $t_{i,j}$ with $0 \le i \le j - 1$ of column $j$ have been computed then it is possible to compute $t_{j,j}$.

(4) Let $X_j = \{A \in N | B \rightarrow \alpha \cdot A\beta \in t_{i,j}, 0 \le i \le j - 1\}$. Then $t_{j,j} = \mathrm{PRED}(X_j)$.

It is not difficult to see that $A \rightarrow \alpha \cdot \beta \in t_{i,j}$ if and only if there exists $\gamma \in V*$ such that $S \Rightarrow *a_1 \cdots a_i A\gamma$ and $\alpha \Rightarrow *a_{i+1} \cdots a_j$. Hence, in $t_{0,n}$ we can read whether the sentence was correct. The algorithm can be extended in order to produce parse trees.

Various parallel implementations of Earley's algorithm have been suggested in the literature (see e.g., Chiang & Fu, 1984; Sijstermans, 1986; and Tan, 1983). The algorithms differ mainly in details on the handling of $\epsilon$-rules, preprocessing, the representation of data and circuit and layout design. The main problem in a parallel implementation of the previous algorithm is the computation of the diagonal elements $t_{i,i}$, for $0 \le i \le n$. The solution is simple. Initially all elements $t_{i,i}$, $0 \le i \le n$, are set equal to $\mathrm{PREDICT}(N)$, where $N$ is the set of nonterminal symbols. The other entries are defined according to the Steps (1), (2) and (3). As a consequence, we now have $A \rightarrow \alpha \cdot \beta \in t_{i,j}$ if and only if $\alpha \Rightarrow *a_{i+1} \cdots a_j$. In spite of weakening the conditions on the contents of the table entries the completed table can still be used to determine whether an input sentence was correct. Moreover, computation of the elements can be done diagonal by diagonal, similar to the CYK algorithm.

(1) Set $t_{i,i}$ equal to $\mathrm{PREDICT}(N)$, $0 \le i \le n$.

(2) Set $d = 0$. Assuming $t_{i,i+d}$ has been formed for $0 \le i \le n - d$, increase $d$ with 1 and compute $t_{i,j}$ for $0 \le i \le n - d$ and $j = i + d$ according to:

   (2.1) Add $B \rightarrow \alpha a \beta \cdot \gamma$ to $t_{i,j}$ if $B \rightarrow \alpha \cdot a\beta\gamma \in t_{i,j-1}$, $a = a_j$ and $\beta \Rightarrow *\epsilon$.

   (2.2) Add $B \rightarrow \alpha A \beta \cdot \gamma$ to $t_{i,j}$ if, for any $k$ such that $i < k < j$, $B \rightarrow \alpha \cdot A\beta\gamma \in t_{i,k}$, $A \rightarrow \omega \cdot \in t_{k,j}$ and $\beta \Rightarrow *\epsilon$.

   (2.3) Add $B \rightarrow \alpha A \beta \cdot \gamma$ to $t_{i,j}$ if $B \rightarrow \alpha \cdot A\beta\gamma \in t_{i,i}$, $\beta \Rightarrow *\epsilon$ and there exists $C \in N$ such that $A \Rightarrow *C$ and $C \rightarrow \omega \cdot \in t_{i,j}$.

VLSI designs or process configurations which implement this algorithm in such a way that it takes $O(n)$ time (with $O(n^2)$ cells or processes) can be found in (Chiang & Fu, 1982; Sijstermans, 1986; Tan, 1983) (see also Figure 14.7 and its explanation).

## 14.5   Connectionist parsing algorithms

Only few authors have considered context-free parsing in connectionist networks. Usually, in the connectionist approach we have a network of simple processing elements which function independently and in parallel. There is no central controller. The nodes of the network (i.e., the processing elements) have an activation level which is recomputed iteratively. The links between the nodes are weighted. Each node computes an output which is a function of its weighted inputs and the current activation level of the node. Initial activation of nodes in an input layer may spread to a pattern of activity at output nodes or may lead to the convergence of the network through cycles of spreading activation to a pattern of activity at a configuration of nodes which represents a solution of the problem for which the network has been built. Learning takes place through changes in the weights of the connections.

Among the papers that discuss connectionist context-free parsing are (Fanty, 1985), a straightforward and simple connectionist implementation of the CYK method, (Selman & Hirst, 1987), Boltzmann machine parsing, i.e., parsing which amounts to computation according to a parallel stochastic relaxation scheme using simulated annealing, (Howells, 1988), a relaxation algorithm which utilizes decay over time together with a competition for available activation, (Nakagawa & Mori, 1988), a parallel left-corner parser incorporated in a learning network, and (Charniak & Santos, 1987), not really connectionist, but ideas are borrowed from the connectionist approach. One theme which emerges in these papers is the finite size of networks. A parse tree is represented as a network of activated and connected nodes. Usually, these nodes represent syntactical categories (the so-called 'localist view'). Building a network in advance means that the length of a sentence that can be parsed is limited by the size of the network. In order to get round this problem some authors allow the building of the network during parsing. Although the above mentioned connectionist context-free parsing methods are interesting, it is not at all clear which approach should be chosen. None of them gives the impression that a connectionist approach is a 'natural' approach to context-free language parsing. This changes if we go beyond syntactic analysis. Especially in this area we see that the traditional methods of language analysis are replaced by strongly interactive distributed processing of word senses, case roles and semantic markers (see e.g., Cottrell & Small, 1984; McClelland & Kawamoto, 1986; Small, 1987; and Waltz & Pollack, 1985). It is also in this area that connectionism is used to explain human parsing mechanisms for natural language sentences. We confine ourselves to an explanation of Fanty's method since it fits rather naturally in the framework of parsing strategies we have considered in the previous sections. A connectionist Earley parsing algorithm can be found in (Nijholt, 1990a).

Fanty's strategy is that of the CYK parser. The nodes that will be part of the connectionist network are organized according to the positions of the entries of the upper-triangular recognition table. For convenience we first assume that the grammar is in CNF. The table's diagonal will be used for representing the input symbols. This representation will be explained later. For each

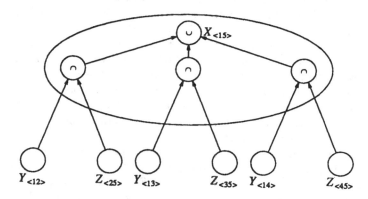

Figure 14.8. Bottom-up passing of activity.

nonterminal symbol each entry in the table which is not on the diagonal will represent a configuration of nodes. These nodes allow top-down and bottom-up passing of activity. We first explain the bottom-up pass. Consider a particular entry, say $t_{i,j}$ with $j - i \geq 2$, of the upper-triangular matrix. In the traditional algorithm a nonterminal symbol $X$ is added to the set of nonterminal symbols associated with the entry if there are symbols $Y \in t_{i,k}$ and $Z \in t_{k,j}$ such that $X \rightarrow YZ$ is in $P$. In the connectionist adaptation of the algorithm we already have a node for each nonterminal symbol in entry $t_{i,j}$. Therefore, rather than adding a symbol, here node $X$ at position $t_{i,j}$ is made active if node $Y$ at position $t_{i,k}$ and node $Z$ at position $t_{k,j}$ are active. In general there will be more ways to have a realization of the production $X \rightarrow YZ$ at position $t_{i,j}$. For example, a node for $X$ at entry $t_{1,5}$ can be made active for a production $X \rightarrow YZ$ if there is an active node for $Y$ at $t_{1,2}$ and for $Z$ at $t_{2,5}$, or for $Y$ at $t_{1,3}$ and for $Z$ at $t_{3,5}$, or for $Y$ at $t_{1,4}$ and for $Z$ at $t_{4,5}$. This separation is realized with the help of match nodes in the configuration of each entry of the table. The use of match nodes is illustrated in Figure 14.8 for a node for $X$ at position $t_{1,5}$ of a CYK-table. Here we have shown the three match nodes, one for each possible realization of $X \rightarrow YZ$, for this node at this particular position. For these match nodes to become active all of their inputs must be on. The node for $X$ becomes active when at least one of its inputs (coming from its match nodes) is on.

In the figure only match nodes for separate realizations of the same production are included. Obviously, match nodes should also be included at this position for all possible realizations of the other productions with lefthand side $X$. In this way all the inputs that can make the node for $X$ at this particular position active can be received in a proper way. Observe that if during the recognition of a sentence in an entry more than one match node for a nonterminal is active then the sentence is ambiguous.

In our explanation the assumption $j - i \geq 2$ for entry $t_{i,j}$ was made. We assume that there is a node for each terminal symbol in each position at the diagonal of the matrix. Since the grammar is in CNF we have realizations of productions of the form $X \rightarrow a$ in the entries $t_{i,j}$ with $j - i = 1$. Also in these entries match nodes are needed since different terminal symbols can have the same nonterminal as lefthand side. Parsing starts by activating the nodes which correspond with the input symbols. Then activation passes bottom-up through the network, first with realizations of productions of the form $X \rightarrow a$, next with realizations of productions of the form $X \rightarrow YZ$. The input is accepted as soon as the node for the start symbol in the topmost entry of the column of the last input symbol becomes active.

A straightforward construction of the network for a particular grammar can be performed as follows. We have to choose an $m$, the maximum length of the strings that can be processed by the network. For each entry $t_{i,j}$ with $i \leq j$ of an upper-triangular $(m + 1) \times (m + 1)$ table $T$ we have to introduce the nodes and the connections which allow the passing of activity we discussed above. This can be done diagonal by diagonal:

(0) For each $a \in \sum \cup \{\$\}$ introduce a node for $a$ in entry $t_{i,i}$, $0 \leq i \leq m$.

(1a) For each production rule $A \rightarrow a$ and for each entry $t_{i,j}$ of $T$ with $j - i = 1$ introduce a match node for $A$ in $t_{i,j}$ and connect it with the node for $a$ in $t_{i,i}$.

(1b) For each collection of match nodes in an entry $t_{i,j}$ with $j - i = 1$ that correspond with the same nonterminal introduce a node for that nonterminal in $t_{i,j}$ and connect it with its match nodes.

(2a) For each $k$, $i < k < j$, such that there is a node for $B$ in $t_{i,k}$, a node for $C$ in $t_{k,j}$ and a production rule $A \rightarrow BC$ in $P$ introduce a match node for $A$ in $t_{i,j}$ and connect it with the nodes for $B$ and $C$ in $t_{i,k}$ and $t_{k,j}$, respectively.

(2b) For each collection of match nodes in an entry $t_{i,j}$ that correspond with the same nonterminal introduce a node for that nonterminal in $t_{i,j}$ and connect it with its match nodes.

A more global look on the network learns us that in each entry of a particular diagonal the same collection of nodes and match nodes will be introduced. Since the set of nonterminals is finite we obtain a 'regular' pattern of diagonals. A node for a nonterminal $A$ is introduced in an entry $t_{i,j}$ if and only if $A$ can generate a string of length $j - i$. An appropriate name for building the network for a particular grammar should therefore be *meta-CYK-parsing*. Although we obtain in this way diagonals with entries that have nodes for the same set of nonterminals they can differ in the number of match nodes. As an example of meta-parsing consider the following context-free grammar in CNF. The symbol | separates the different alternatives of a nonterminal symbol.

$$S \rightarrow AB|AC \qquad C \rightarrow AB$$
$$A \rightarrow a \qquad\qquad D \rightarrow AB$$
$$B \rightarrow b|DE \qquad E \rightarrow b$$

| | | | | | | |
|---|---|---|---|---|---|---|
| *a b* | A B<br>E | S C<br>D | S B | S C<br>D | S B | S C<br>D |
| | *a b* | A B<br>E | S C<br>D | S B | S C<br>D | S B |
| | | *a b* | A B<br>E | S C<br>D | S B | S C<br>D |
| | | | *a b* | A B<br>E | S C<br>D | S B |
| | | | | *a b* | A B<br>E | S C<br>D |
| | | | | | *a b* | A B<br>E |
| | | | | | | *a b* |

Figure 14.9. Meta-CYK-Parsing.

In Figure 14.9 we show the nonterminals in the entries of the upper-triangular table for which nodes and match nodes will be introduced. On the second diagonal ($j - i = 1$) we have nodes for nonterminals with the property that they can generate strings of length 1, at the third diagonal ($j - i = 2$) those for strings of length 2, etc.

Until now we have discussed a network which accepts (or rejects) an input string. In order to obtain a representation of the parse tree or parse trees a second, top-down, pass of activity is necessary. To perform this top-down pass we assume that each node mentioned so far consists of a bottom-up and a top-down unit. The bottom-up units are used as explained above. In Figure 14.10 both bottom-up and top-down passing of activity is illustrated in a configuration of nodes for an entry $t_{i,j}$ with $j - i \geq 2$. Each node is represented as consisting of a leftmost or bottom-up and a rightmost or top-down unit.

A top-down unit becomes active when it receives input from its bottom-up counterpart and at least one external source. In order to activate the top-down unit of the node for the start symbol in the upper right corner of the table we assume that it receives input from its bottom-up counterpart and from the node at position $t_{n,n}$, where $n$ is the length of the input, which is used to represent endmarker $ of the input and which is made active when parsing starts. Hence, when the input is recognized this unit becomes active and it passes activity top-down. All top-down units which receive this activation and which receive activation from their bottom-up counterparts become active. In this way activity is passed down to the terminal nodes and the active top-down nodes of the network represent the parse tree(s). The parse in the connectionist network completes in $O(n)$ time. Above our assumption was that grammars are in CNF. This is not a necessary condition, but it facilitates the present discussion. See (Fanty, 1985) for possible relaxations of this condition and the

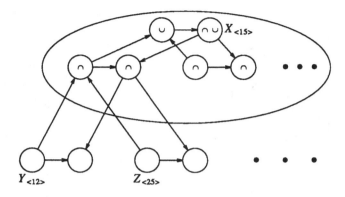

Figure 14.10. Top-down and bottom-up passing of activity.


consequences for the time complexity.


## 14.6   Concluding remarks

A survey of some ideas in parallel parsing has been presented. In the field
of natural language processing the Earley and CYK method are well known.
Sometimes closely related methods such as (active) chart parsing are used.
Because of this close relationship a parallel implementation along the lines
sketched above is possible. Chart parsing (and Earley parsing) can be done
with a more modest number of processors if an agenda approach is followed (see
e.g., Grishman & Chitrao, 1988; and Nijholt, 1990b). Earley's algorithm can be
modified to transition networks and extended to ATN's (see e.g., Chou & Fu,
1975). Therefore it is worthwhile to investigate a similar parallel approach to
the parsing of ATN's. No attention has been paid to ideas aimed at improving
upper bounds for the recognition and parsing of general context-free languages.
An introduction to that area can be found in Chapter 4 of (Gibbons & Rytter,
1988). Neither have we been looking here at the connectionist approaches to
parsing which go beyond context-free language parsing. More references to
papers on parallel parsing can be found in (Op den Akker *et al.*, 1989).


## Acknowledgments

I am grateful to P. R. J. Asveld for his comments on an earlier version of
this chapter and to Theo Vosse for drawing my attention to some papers on
connectionist parsing. Some discussions with Bart Van Acker and Bart De
Wolf have improved my understanding of parallel parsing methods.

# References

Carlisle, W. H., & Friesen, D. K. (1985). Parallel parsing using Ada. *Proceedings 3rd Annual National Conference on Ada Technology* (pp. 103–106).

Charniak, E., & Santos, E. (1987). A connectionist context-free parser which is not context-free, but then it is not really connectionist either. *Proceedings of the Ninth Annual Conference of the Cognitive Science Society* (pp. 70–77). Seattle, WA: Lawrence Erlbaum.

Chiang, Y. T., & Fu, K. S. (1984). Parsing algorithms and VLSI implementations for syntactic pattern recognition. *IEEE Transactions on Pattern Analysis and Machine Intelligence, PAMI-6, 3*, 302–314.

Chou, S. M., & Fu, K. S. (1975). *Transition networks for pattern recognition* (Tech. Rep. No. 75-39). West Lafayette, Indiana: School for Electrical Engineering, Purdue University.

Chu, K. H., & Fu, K. S. (1982). VLSI architectures for high-speed recognition of context-free languages and finite-state languages. *Proceedings of the Ninth Annual Symposium on Computer Architectures.* Also in *SIGARCH Newsletter, 10, 3*, 43–49.

Cottrell, G. W., & Small, S. L. (1984). Viewing parsing as word sense discrimination: A connectionist approach. In B. G. Bara & G. Guida (Eds.), *Computational models of natural language processing.* Elsevier Science Publishers, North-Holland.

Fanty, M. A. (1985). *Context-free parsing in connectionist networks* (Tech. Rep. No. TR 714). Computer Science Department, University of Rochester.

Fischer, C. N. (1975). *Parsing context-free languages in parallel environments* (Tech. Rep. No. 75-237). Unpublished doctoral dissertation. Ithaca, NY: Cornell University, Dept. of Computer Science.

Gibbons, A., & Rytter, W. (1988). Parallel recognition and parsing of context-free languages. In *Efficient parallel algorithms.* MA: Cambridge University Press.

Graham, S. L., & Harrison, M. A. (1976). Parsing of general context-free languages. In M. Yovits & M. Rubinoff (Eds.), *Advances in computers* (Vol. 14). New York: Academic Press.

Grishman, R., & Chitrao, M. (1988). Evaluation of a parallel chart parser. *Proceedings of the Second Conference on Applied Natural Language Processing* (pp. 71–76). Association for Computational Linguistics.

Guibas, L. J., Kung, H. T., & Thompson, C. D. (1979). Direct VLSI implementation of combinatorial algorithms. *Proceedings of the Conference on VLSI* (pp. 509–526). Caltech.

Howells, T. (1988). VITAL: A connectionist parser. *Proceedings of the Tenth Annual Conference of the Cognitive Science Society.* Lawrence Erlbaum.

Lincoln, N. (1970). Parallel programming techniques for compilers. *SIGPLAN Notices, 5, 10*, 18–31.

Loka, R. R. (1984). A note on parallel parsing. *SIGPLAN Notices, 19, 1*, 57–59.

Lozinskii, E. L., & Nirenburg, S. (1986). Parsing in parallel. *Computer Languages, 11*, 39–51.

Matsumoto, Y., & Sugimura, R. (1987). A parsing system based on logic programming. *Proceedings of the Tenth International Joint Conference on Artificial Intelligence* (pp. 671–674). Milan, Italy: Morgan Kaufmann.

McClelland J. L., & Kawamoto, A. H. (1986). Mechanism of sentence processing: Assigning roles to constituents of sentences. In D. E. Rumelhart & J. L. McClelland (Eds.), *Parallel distributed processing* (Vol. 2). Cambridge, MA: The MIT Press.

Mickunas, M. D., & Schell, R. M. (1978). Parallel compilation in a multiprocessor environment. *Proceedings ACM Annual Conf.* (pp. 241–246).

Nakagawa, H., & Mori, T. (1988). A parser based on a connectionist model. *Proceedings of the Twelfth International Conference on Computational Linguistics* (COLING 88) (pp. 454–458). Budapest.

Nijholt, A. (1988). *Computers and languages: Theory and practice.* Studies in computer science and artificial intelligence. Amsterdam: North-Holland, Elsevier Science Publishers.

Nijholt, A. (1990a). Meta-parsing in neural networks. *Tenth European Meeting on Cybernetics and Systems Research.* Austrian Society for Cybernetic Studies, Vienna: World Scientific Publishing Corporation.

Nijholt, A. (1990b). Parallel approaches to context-free language parsing. In U. Hahn & G. Adriaens (Eds.), *Parallel models of natural language computation.* Norwood, NJ: Ablex.

Op den Akker, R., Alblas, H., Nijholt, A., & Oude Luttighuis, P. (1989). *An annotated bibliography on parallel parsing* (Memo. Info. No. 89-67). Twente University.

Selman, B., & Hirst, G. (1987). Parsing as an energy minimization problem. In *Genetic algorithms and simulated annealing: Research notes in AI.* Los Altos, CA: Morgan Kaufmann.

Sijstermans, F. W. (1986). *Parallel parsing of context-free languages* (Doc. No. 202). Eindhoven: Philips Research Laboratories, Esprit Project 415, Subproject A: Object-oriented language approach.

Small, S. L. (1987). A distributed word-based approach to parsing. In L. Bolc (Ed.), *Natural language parsing systems.* Berlin: Springer-Verlag.

Tan, H. D. A. (1983). *VLSI-algoritmen voor herkenning van context-vrije talen in lineaire tijd* (Tech. Rep. No. IN 24/83). Amsterdam: Stichting Mathematisch Centrum.

Tanaka, H., Numazaki, H. (1989). Parallel generalized LR parsing based on logic programming. *Proceedings of the International Workshop on Parsing Technologies* (pp. 329–338). Pittsburgh, PA: Carnegie Mellon University.

Tomita, M. (1985). *Efficient parsing for natural language.* Boston, MA: Kluwer Academic Publishers.

Tseytlin, G. E., & Yushchenko, E. L. (1977). Several aspects of theory of parametric models of languages and parallel syntactic analysis. In A. Ershov & C. H. A. Koster (Eds.), *Methods of algorithmic language implementation* (Lect. Notes Comp. Sci. 47). Berlin: Springer-Verlag.

Waltz, D. L., & Pollack, J. B. (1985). Massively parallel parsing: A strongly interactive model of natural language interpretation. *Cognitive Science, 9*, 51–74.

Yonezawa, A., & Ohsawa, I. (1988).  Object-oriented parallel parsing for context-free grammars. *Proceedings of the 12th International Conference on Computational Linguistics* (COLING'88) (pp. 773–778). Budapest.

# 15. Chart Parsing for Loosely Coupled Parallel Systems

Henry S. Thompson

*Human Communication Research Centre, Department of Artificial Intelligence, Centre for Cognitive Science, University of Edinburgh*

## 15.1  Introduction

Of the parallel systems currently available, far and away the most common are loosely coupled collections of conventional processors, and this is likely to remain true for some time. By loosely coupled I mean that the processors do not share memory, so that some form of stream or message-passing protocol is required for processor-processor communication. It follows that in most cases the programmer must make explicit appeal to communication primitives in the construction of software which exploits the available parallelism. Even in shared-memory systems, the absence of parallel constructs from available programming languages may mean that appeal to a similar communication model may be necessary, at least in the short term.

Although not ideally suited to loosely coupled systems, the general problem of parsing for speech and natural language is of sufficient importance to merit investigation in the parallel world. This paper reports on explorations of the computation/communication trade-off in parallel parsing, together with the development of an portable parallel parser which will enable the comparison of a variety of parallel systems.

## 15.2  Parsing for loosely coupled systems

Given the prevalence of loosely coupled systems, although one might suppose that shared-memory parallelism offers greater scope for the construction of parallel parsing systems, and parallel chart parsers in particular, none-the-less it is a good idea to look at what can be done in the loosely coupled case.

Loosely coupled parallel systems can be expected to do best, that is, show a nearly linear (inverse) relationship between solution time and number of processors, when the problem at hand is (isomorphic to a) tree-search problem with large initial fan-out and compact specifications of sub-problems and results. In such problems, the ratio of communication to computation is low, so the loose coupling does not significantly impede linear speed-up. Large problems can be broken down into as many pieces as there are processors, cheaply distributed to them, and the results cheaply returned.

Parsing of single sentences is not obviously suited to loosely coupled parallel systems. Whether one attacks single-sentence parsing by some form of left-to-right breadth-first parse, or by some form of all-at-once bottom-up breadth-first parse, very high communication costs would seem to be involved. The only hope would seem to be to pursue the latter route nevertheless, and see whether the communication costs can be brought down to an acceptable level. There are a number of different dimensions along which one might try to parallelize the parsing process, but insofar as they involve the distribution of sub-problems, they are highly likely to require the representation of partial solutions. Since this is a primary characteristic of the active chart parsing methodology, my investigations have focussed on parallel implementations of active chart parsers.

## 15.3   Parallelism and the chart

We start with the observation that chart parsing seems a natural technique to base a parallel parser on. Its hallmarks are the reification of partial hypotheses as active edges, and the flexibility it allows in terms of search strategy, and it would seem straight-forward to adapt a chart parser doing pseudo-parallel breadth-first bottom-up parsing into a genuinely parallel parser. Indeed with a shared-memory parallel system, the BBN Butterfly$^{TM}$, I have done just that, and the result exhibits the expected linear speed-up. The approach used was simply to allow multiple processors to remove entries from the queue of hypothesised edges and add them to the chart in parallel, performing the associated parsing tasks and thereby in some cases hypothesising further edges onto the queue. Locks were of course required to prevent race conditions in updating the chart and edge queue, but instrumentation suggested that there was rarely contention for these locks and they had little adverse impact on performance.

Clearly this approach would not be appropriate in the loosely coupled case. One could of course use some system which supports virtual shared memory to implement a shared chart and edge queue. But this would defeat the whole purpose, as the parser would be serialized by the processor responsible for maintaining the shared structures. What I have explored instead is retaining the same granularity of parallelism, namely the edge, but accepting that at least some of the chart itself will have to be distributed among the processors.

## 15.4   Distributing the chart

I have explored the approach of distributing the chart among the processors in several implementations of a chart parser for the Intel Hypercube$^{TM}$, a loosely coupled system, and for a network of Lisp workstations. A memory-

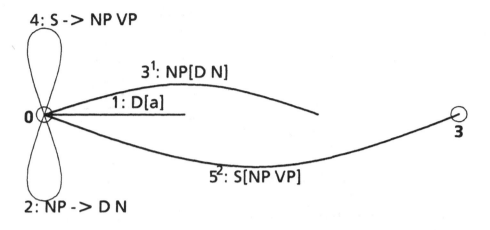

Figure 15.1. Chart portion resident on Processor 0.

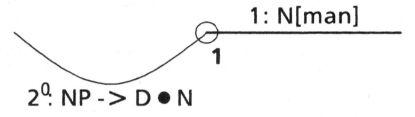

Figure 15.2. Chart portion resident on Processor 1.

independent representation of the chart is used, allowing edges to be easily encoded for transmission between processors. The chart is distributed among the processors on a vertex by vertex basis. Vertices are numbered and assigned to processors in round-robin fashion. Edges 'reside' on the processor which holds their 'hot' vertex, that is, their right-hand vertex if active, left-hand if inactive. From this it can be seen that once a new edge is delivered to its 'home' processor, that processor has all the edges required to execute the fundamental rule with respect to that new edge. Each processor also has a copy of the grammar, so it can perform rule invocation as necessary, and a copy of the dictionary, so that once the input sentence is distributed, pre-terminal edge creation can proceed in parallel.

The following three figures illustrate the distribution of vertices and edges for a simple example sentence and grammar, assuming a three processor system.

Vertices are numbered circles. Edges are thin if active, thick if inactive, and

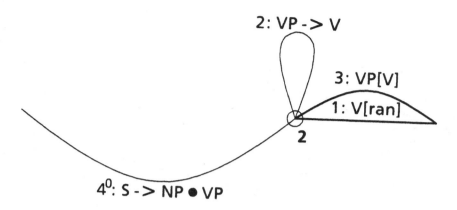

Figure 15.3. Chart portion resident on Processor 2.

their contents are noted. They are numbered on a per processor basis. Those with superscripts, e.g., 40, are ones which originated on another processor, whose number is given by the superscript. Of the eleven edges, four had to be transmitted from where they were created by the action of the fundamental rule to where they belonged.

Transmission of edges, as noted above, requires a memory-independent representation. This is accomplished by flattening the structure of the edges, by making all their contents indirect references. Thus where in the single processor or shared memory parallel processor versions edges contained their endpoint vertices and label elements (category, dotted rules, daughters), in the loosely coupled version edges name their endpoint vertices, and index their label elements relative to appropriate baselines.

Note that this means that when parsing is completed, a complete parse is not available on any single processor. If it is required, then it will have to be assembled by requesting sub-parses from appropriate processors, recursively.

## 15.5  Communication vs. computation — Results for the Hypercube$^{\text{TM}}$

Testing to date has been confined to a two processor system. The edge distribution scheme described above was installed into an existing serial chart parser. Considerable care has been taken within the limits imposed by the host system communications primitives to keep communication bandwidth to a minimum (approximately 100 bits/edge in a single packet). Even with a relatively trivial grammar and lexicon and simple sentences of limited ambiguity, two processors are faster than one under some circumstances. In order to explore the computation/communication trade-off, and to simulate the oper-

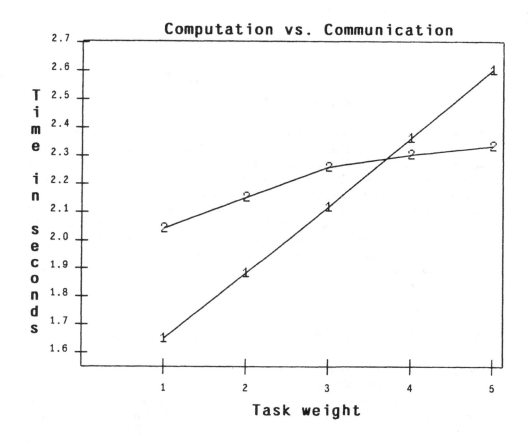

Figure 15.4. Graph of results of two processor Hypercube[TM] experiment.

ation of the system with more complex grammatical formalisms which would require substantially greater per-edge computation, a parameterized wait-loop was added to the function implementing the fundamental rule. As the duration of that loop increased, the parse-time increased less rapidly for the two processor case than for the single-processor case, so that although in the initial, un-slowed, condition, a single processor parsed faster than two, when the fundamental rule was slowed by a factor of around four, two processors were faster than one. Figure 15.4 illustrates this for the sentence "The orange saw saw the orange saw with the orange saw" with a standard grammar which allows for PP attachment ambiguity and a lexicon in which orange is ambiguous between N and A and saw is ambiguous between N and V. The times plotted are to the discovery of the second parse, as the termination detection algorithm described below had not yet been implemented.

It is hoped that further experimentation with larger cubes will shortly be possible.

## 15.6   Towards   wider   comparability   —   The abstract parallel agenda

With an eye to allowing an easy extension of this work to other systems, and more principled comparison between systems, I have gone back to the original serial chart parser (Thompson, 1983) from which the Hypercube$^{TM}$ system was constructed, and produced an abstract parallel version. The original parser was based on a quite general agenda mechanism, and the abstraction was largely performed at this level. A multi-processor agenda system, allowing the programmer to schedule the evaluation of any memory-independent form on any processor at a specified priority level is provided, together with a novel means of synchronization and termination. Implemented in Common Lisp, all this agenda system requires for porting to a new system is the provision of a simple 'remote funcall' primitive.

## 15.7   Termination and Synchronization

Termination detection in distributed systems is a well-known problem. It arises obtrusively in any parallel approach to chart parsing, since this depends on an absence of activity to detect the completion of parsing. The abstract parallel agenda mechanism which underlies the portable parallel parser uses a new (we think — see (Thompson, Crowe, & Roberts, in press) for discussion) algorithm for effective synchronization of task execution (of which termination is a special case). It is thus possible to reconstruct not only the prioritization function of an agenda (run this in preference to this), but also the ordering function (run this only if that is finished). Unlike some existing termination algorithms, this one is particular appropriate where no constraints can be placed on processor connectivity (any processor may, and usually does, send messages to any other processor). It requires only a modest increase in the number of primitive operations which must be supported to port the agenda system — all that is required is a simple channel for FIFO queuing of control messages between a designated 'boss' processor and the rest. The overhead imposed by the scheme on normal operation is effectively zero — communication remains asynchronous until near to a synchronization point. Essentially the scheme operates by each processor keeping track of the number of tasks created vs. the number of tasks run locally. When a processor is idle waiting for synchronization, it sends its counts to the boss. When the boss has a complete set of counts which tally, it requests them again. If they haven't changed, synchrony is signaled. Thus in the best case 4*n fixed length messages are required to synchronize n processors.

Table 15.1. Sentences used in the network experiments.

| SENTENCE | | ACTIVE EDGES | INACTIVE EDGES | PARSES |
|---|---|---|---|---|
| a. | The orange saw saw the orange saw. | 46 | 22 | 1 |
| b. | The orange saw saw the orange saw with the orange saw. | 88 | 43 | 2 |
| c. | The orange saw saw the orange saw with the orange saw with the orange saw. | 166 | 82 | 5 |
| d. | The front-end consists of those phases that depend primarily on the source-language. | 285 | 58 | 0 |

## 15.8  Testing the portable system — Results of network experiment

For this experiment four Xerox 1186 processors running Interlisp-D and connected by a 10MB Ethernet were used, running the parallel system on top of the abstract parallel agenda. Communication for the implementation of the agenda was via the Courier$^{TM}$ remote procedure call mechanism, whose hallmark is reliability, not speed. Results were obtained during a period of low network loading, and three trials were performed. The times used in the figures are the fastest times obtained over the trials, which were quite consistent from one to the next. Figure 15.5 shows processing time versus number of processors for each of three sentences, using the same grammar and lexicon as in the previous experiment, and for a fourth sentence, using a much larger and more realistic grammar with 70 rules and an appropriate lexicon (the failure to find any parses was caused by a typing error in the grammar, detected too late for correction). Table 15.1 gives the sentences, the number of active and inactive edges involved and the number of parses found.

Clearly not much encouragement can be taken from this experiment. Although there is some speed-up from two to three processors in some cases, overall the pattern is one where communication costs clearly dominate, so no advantage is gained. With slower processors and/or faster networks, we might hope to see better results, especially given the results in Section 15.5, but the appropriateness of this approach to networked systems must remain in doubt in the absence of better evidence.

## 15.9  Alternative patterns of edge distribution

One possible alternative decomposition of the task, which might offer some hope of improving the computation/communication trade-off, would be to

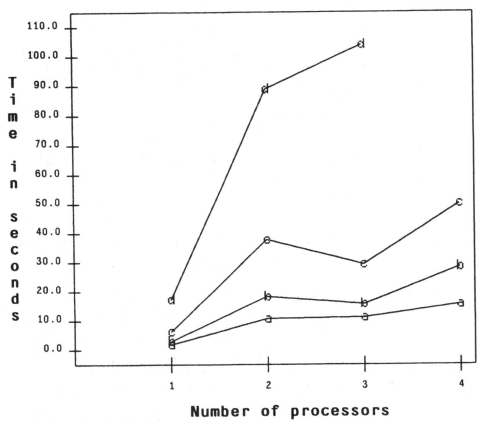

Figure 15.5. Graph of results of network experiment.

transmit only inactive edges, but to send them to all processors. Then every processor would have the complete inactive chart, and could run active edges from start to finish without ever sending them anywhere. In order to distribute the computational load, rule invocation would be distributed on a per vertex basis. That is, each processor would only do bottom up rule invocation for those inactive edges which began at a vertex owned by that processor. The plus side of this route is that it sends only inactive edges around, which are simpler to encode, that the final result is available on a single processor, indeed on all processors, without having to be assembled, and that active edge processing is more efficient. The minus side is that the inactive edges have to be sent to all processors. In the simple example given in Figures 15.1, 15.2, and 15.3, this actually balances out — four edges in the original implementation, two edges twice in the alternative one. A further experiment with the network system was conducted to explore this approach. The same sentences as before were used, but this time with the new edge distribution pattern.

Table 15.2. Edges processed locally versus transmitted for two edge distribution patterns.

| No. of Processors | Active | | Inactive | | Total | |
|---|---|---|---|---|---|---|
| | Local | Xmtd | Local | Xmtd | Local | Xmtd |
| 2 | 59\|88 | 29\|0 | 26\|36 | 17\|25 | 85\|124 | 46\|25 |
| 3 | 57\|88 | 31\|0 | 29\|54 | 14\|50 | 86\|142 | 45\|50 |
| 4 | 47\|88 | 41\|0 | 23\|72 | 20\|75 | 70\|160 | 61\|75 |

Table 15.2 compares Sentence b from Table 15.1, "The orange saw saw the orange saw with the orange saw," in terms of the number of edges of each type processed locally and transmitted under the two patterns for different numbers of processors. In each case, the figures are given as a|b, where a is the number for the original pattern, and b is the number in the inactive-edge-only pattern.

The increase in local edges is somewhat artifactual, coming in part from the replication of lexical edge construction across all processors. Clearly only for small numbers of processors is there a net gain in number of edges transmitted. The effect this has on processing time is pretty much as one would expect. Figure 15.6 shows the times for Sentence b for both patterns. The curve with points labeled "o" is for the original pattern, that with points labeled "i" is for the alternative, inactive-edge-only pattern.

As expected, only in the two processor case do we see an advantage to the alternative approach.

# 15.10   Concluding remarks

In general it is clear that the principal determinate of processing time is number of edges transmitted — the overhead in the network communication dominates all other factors. The obvious conclusion is that, particularly as processors speeds increase, it will take very high bandwidth inter-processor communication, perhaps only achievable with special purpose architectures, to make at least this edge-distribution approach to parallel parsing worthwhile. This in turn leads one to reconsider just where parallel parsing might be expected to be required. For many applications where high-speed parsing is desirable, the volume of material to be processed is the main source of pressure for speed. If this volume is not itself arising in real time (e.g., from a news wire), then simple data parallelism offers a much more obvious route to exploitation of loosely coupled systems. In a simple experiment using a central controller running in Common Lisp on a workstation and using UNIX$^{TM}$ remote shell commands to distribute sentences from a text one at a time to other workstations running a serial parser and monitor (but *not* collect) results, nearly linear speed-up was observed.

The theoretical investigation of parallel parsing is obviously worth pursuing in its own right: it remains to be seen whether implementations on non-shared memory systems will be of practical use. The work reported here suggests that

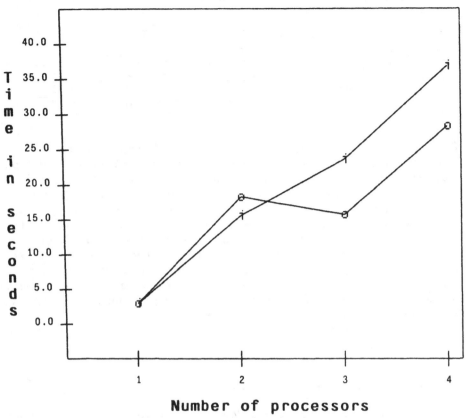

Figure 15.6. Graph of alternative distribution strategies for parsing Sentence b.

on current hardware at any rate the communications/computation tradeoff militates against achieving any practical advantage in parsing by parallelizing the task at a low level.

# Acknowledgments

The work described in this paper was made possible in part by the use of equipment made available by the Rank Xerox University Grants Programme, BBN Labs Inc., Artificial Intelligence Ltd., Xerox Palo Alto Research Center and Intel Scientific Corp. — to all of them my thanks. None of them are in any way responsible for the opinions expressed here.

# References

Thompson, H. S. (1983). MCHART: A flexible, modular, chart parsing system. *Proceedings of the National Conference on Artificial Intelligence* (pp. 408–410). Washington, D.C.: AAAI Press.

Thompson, H. S., Crowe, A., & Roberts, G. (in press). *Termination and synchronisation in distributed event systems.*

MCHART is available via electronic mail in both serial and parallel versions, implemented in a relatively installation-independent Common Lisp.

Requests to hthompson@uk.ac.edinburgh (JANET), hthompson%edinburgh.ac.uk@nsfnet-relay.ac.uk (ARPANet).

# 16. Parsing with Connectionist Networks

Ajay N. Jain and Alex H. Waibel

*School of Computer Science, Carnegie Mellon University*

## 16.1 Introduction

Traditional methods employed in parsing natural language have focused on developing powerful formalisms to represent syntactic and semantic structure along with rules for transforming language into these formalisms. The builders of such systems must accurately anticipate and model all of the language constructs that their systems will encounter. In loosely structured domains such as spoken language the task becomes very difficult. Connectionist networks that learn to transform input word sequences into meaningful target representations may be useful in such cases.

Application of connectionist computational models to language tasks is not a new idea. Some researchers have used connectionist networks to implement formal grammar systems for use in syntactic parsing (Charniak & Santos, 1987; Fanty, 1986; Howells, 1988; Selman & Hirst, 1985). In such networks, the grammar is built in. Other work has focused on semantics and has not addressed the problem of grammar acquisition (Cottrell, 1985, 1989; McClelland & Kawamoto, 1986; Waltz & Pollack, 1985). Connectionist networks have also been applied in building statistical language models for use in speech recognition (Nakamura & Shikano, 1989). However, such language models do not produce traditional parses of sentences; they seek to use statistical regularities in language structure and word usage directly for recognition tasks.

This chapter presents a connectionist network architecture which learns its own "grammar rules" through training on example sentences. A trained network transforms an input sequence of words into a syntactic/semantic target representation. At each point in time, a parsing network produces hypotheses of sentences structure and confirms or revises hypotheses as more information is processed. This type of parser is robust in the face of noisy input sentences. The work is a first step in learning to build connectionist networks for parsing which will be useful in realistic natural language domains.

## 16.2    Incremental parsing

Language is inherently sequential. Interpreting a sequence of words requires the incorporation of right context information into an evolving representation of meaning. Connectionist networks have been applied to many types of static recognition problems, but problems such as language interpretation require complex dynamic behavior over time. The following sentences illustrate the point:

- A snake ate the girl.

- A snake was given to the dog by Peter.

In the first sentence, "a snake" acts as an agent, but in the second sentence, "a snake" is a patient. It is not possible to determine the proper role of a noun phrase based on left context information alone — right context is needed. Processing sentences whole instead of one word at a time alleviates this problem but is undesirable especially in spoken language processing.

Below, a parsing task is presented. It is designed to see if connectionist networks can learn the dynamical behavior necessary to process sentences incrementally. Following that is a brief overview of the connectionist architecture used along with its temporal performance on the first sentence given above. The remaining sections of the report describe the details of the network formalism and architecture and its performance.

### 16.2.1    Task description

The domain for this experiment consists of active and passive sentences consisting of up to three noun phrases and two verb phrases each. There are up to three roles for nouns to fill for each verb — agent, patient, and recipient. The lexicon consists of 40 words. The emphasis of the experiment is on single clause sentences. Two clause sentences are present to suggest extensibility.

The input for the network is sequential. Words are presented to the network one at a time. The network must learn to parse the input stream into noun and verb blocks consisting of head words and their modifiers. Further, noun phrases must be assigned an appropriate role or attached to another noun phrase. Subordinate and relative clauses and their relationships must be identified.

### 16.2.2    Overview of network architecture

Figure 16.1 gives a high-level picture of the network architecture along with the target representation for "John gave a bone to the old dog." There are three levels to the network: Word, Phrase, and Structure. The Word level contains the representation for the current input word. A word is presented to the network by stimulating its associated word unit for a short period. This evokes a pattern of activation across the feature units which represents the meaning of the word. The Phrase level learns to use the time-varying word representation to build noun and verb blocks that represent the phrasal

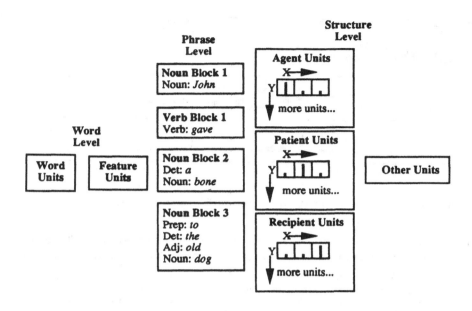

Figure 16.1. High-Level Network Architecture.

structure of the input sentence. The Structure level learns to assign roles to noun phrases and identify phrasal/clausal relationships.

The sentence shown in Figure 16.1 is broken up into four blocks in the Phrase level: "[NB1 John] [VB1 gave] [NB2 a bone] [NB3 to the old dog]." The groups of units in the Structure level show the role assignment for this simple single clause sentence. A high activation level of a unit X,Y in the group of units marked Agent indicates that the network believes that Noun Block X is the agent of Verb Block Y. The units in the groups marked Patient and Recipient have analogous meanings. In the diagram, "John" is labeled as the agent, "a bone" the patient, and "to the old dog" the recipient. The other groups of units will be discussed later.

Recall the first example sentence given at the beginning of this section, "A snake ate the girl." It is a simple active sentence with an Agent/Patient role structure. For this sentence, the behavior of the Structure units corresponding to the roles of Verb Block 1 in a trained network are shown in Figure 16.2. Each small box of vertical lines corresponds to the activation level of a single unit through time (long lines for high activity, time proceeds from left to right). The unit activation pattern in the upper left box indicates the hypothesis that Noun Block 1 functions as the Agent in the sentence. Activation patterns that form columns correspond to the label at the top of the uppermost box. Rows

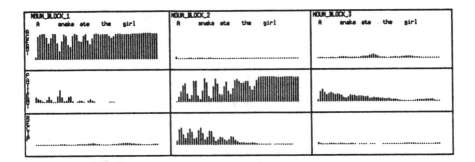

Figure 16.2. Performance of the network on, "A snake ate the girl."

of activation patterns correspond to the label in the leftmost box. There are three columns — corresponding to the three noun blocks. There are three rows — corresponding to the role values.

During presentation of the first word, the unit representing the hypothesis that Noun Block 1 is the Agent (Row 1, Column 1) becomes quite active. The network "expects" that the sentence is active (due to a high proportion of active sentences in the training set). However, since the task includes passive structures, the network cannot decisively make any role assignments at this point. The indecision is manifested as oscillating activation values. The patient unit for the second noun block (Row 2, Column 2) also oscillates and competes with the recipient unit for the second noun block (Row 3, Column 2). When the verb "ate" is presented, the agent unit corresponding to Noun 1 fires strongly since it is now clear that the sentence is not a passive construction. Similarly, the patient unit for Noun 2 becomes more active since "ate" is transitive, and the recipient unit for Noun 2 loses activation since "ate" does not take a recipient. The last part of the sentence further verifies the correct representation. This complex dynamic behavior emerged spontaneously. The units of the Structure level are predictive, but they postpone final decisions until sufficient information has been processed to make correct ones. The network's performance on a passive example sentence is shown in a later section.

## 16.3   Connectionist network formalism

The task described above requires some special considerations in constructing a network formalism:

- Notions of time and sequentiality should be inherent.

- Units should be able to distinguish static and dynamic behavior.

- Atomic symbols should be represented and manipulated in a natural way.

This section briefly outlines a network formalism which has these properties.

The most common type of deterministic connectionist network is an error back propagation network (Rumelhart, Hinton, & Williams, 1986). Processing units are connected to each other, and each connection has an associated weight. Connections are unidirectional. Units have an activity value and an output value (a sigmoidal function of the activity). For a connection from unit A to unit B, we define the stimulation along the connection to be the output value of unit A multiplied by the weight associated with the connection. A unit's activity is simply the sum of the stimulation along each of its input connections. A network learns input/output mappings by iteratively updating its weight values using a gradient descent technique. Such networks can learn complex internal representations that combine many types of information. However, standard back propagation is not well suited to sequential tasks such as language processing. Recently, some recurrent extensions to back propagation where sequences of connections can form cycles have been proposed (Elman, 1988; Jordan, 1986). Such networks can learn certain types of simple sequential tasks, but they do not fulfill all of the criteria desired.

The networks discussed here explicitly account for time in the processing units and also allow for special structures that can manipulate atomic symbols.[1] Units have activities which decay during each discrete time step by a constant factor. Thus, the activation of a unit can be built up over time from repetitive weak stimulation. Activity values are also damped to prevent unstable behavior. By gently "integrating" activities, the network has time to adapt to new information smoothly.

The activity of a unit is passed through a sigmoidal function to produce an output value as in standard back propagation. In addition, a value called the *velocity* is calculated. It is the rate of change of the output of a unit. Each connection in the network has two weights associated with it — one for the output value and one for the velocity value. The velocity values are important in learning dynamic behavior which depends on changes in activation as opposed to absolute activation.

In order to manipulate symbolic structures efficiently, units are allowed to *gate* connections between other units. In Figure 16.3, imagine that the pattern of activation across the lower set of units represents a word. Assume that the connection weights are set such that the top slot takes on the activity pattern of the bottom slot when no gating unit is present. The gate functions as a control on assignment of the word in the bottom slot to the top slot. When the gate is on (has high output), the word is assigned. When the gate is off, the word is "locked" into the top slot (no stimulation can flow nor can the units of the top slot decay). This type of assignment behavior would be difficult to learn for a connectionist network by gradient descent. By architecturally constraining a network using this type of device, networks can manipulate symbol structures efficiently.

---

[1] For a more detailed presentation of the network formalism and learning procedure, see (Jain & Waibel, 1990).

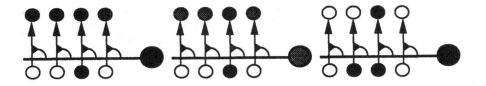

Figure 16.3. Slots of units with a gate.

These networks learn by iterative weight changes during a supervised training phase. An input pattern is presented to the network, and the network is
allowed to process it. The behavior of the network is compared with the desired behavior, and the weights are modified so as to minimize the difference
between actual and desired behavior.

## 16.4    Parsing network architecture

The parsing architecture is modular, recurrent, and hierarchical. This section
will proceed bottom up from the Word level to the Structure level and give
the details of the architecture that were omitted earlier. Then the procedure
used to construct and train the parsing network will be explained.

### 16.4.1    Word level

The meanings of words are represented as microfeature patterns much the
same way as in (McClelland & Kawamoto, 1986). The representations are not
learned. In this architecture, each word in the lexicon is assigned to a single
unit in the network, and the microfeature representation of a word is encoded
in fixed output connections from the unit corresponding to the word. Words
are divided into seven classes: nouns, verbs, adjectives, adverbs, auxiliaries,
prepositions, and determiners. Each class has a set of feature units with fixed
connections from word units. There are two parts to a word's representation:
the feature part and the identification part, as shown in Figure 16.4. The
feature part contains both syntactic and semantic information. The identification part serves to distinguish between words which have identical feature
parts (e.g., Peter and John). The units in the network that learn do not have
any input connections from the identification parts of words. This has the very
convenient effect of allowing new individuals to be added to a network without
additional training as long as they are not syntactically/semantically distinct
from old ones.

A word is presented to the network by artificially stimulating its associated
word unit. This causes the representation for a word to appear gradually
during the course of a few time steps across one (possibly more) set of feature
units. The pattern of activation across a single set of feature units constitutes

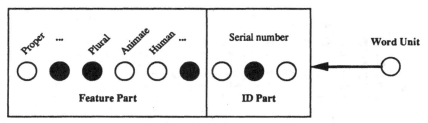

Figure 16.4. Word Representation.

a symbol which should not be modified during further processing; however, it may be moved around from slot to slot.

It should be noted that it is possible for connectionist networks to learn internal representations of words from their usage in sentences (Miikkulainen & Dyer, 1989). However, the focus of this task is on dynamic parsing behavior, not on acquisition of lexical information. Also, in more realistic domains with larger vocabularies, some degree of prewiring lexical information is a pragmatic design choice for the construction of large-scale systems.

## 16.4.2  Phrase level

Phrases are represented as head words with modifiers (called blocks). For example, "the big old house" would be represented as the noun "house" modified by the determiner "the" and the adjectives "big" and "old." Figure 16.5 shows the structure of noun and verb blocks. A noun block has slots for a noun, two adjectives, a preposition, and a determiner. A verb block has slots for a verb, an auxiliary, and an adverb. Each word slot of each block has fixed connections from one set of feature units. The connections for each slot share a single gating unit (see Figure 16.3). These gating units completely control the behavior of the slots in the blocks. When the gating unit for a particular slot is active, the pattern of activation on the feature units becomes active on the units of the slot.

Figure 16.6 depicts the network's detailed structure. In the diagram, the units shown in thick lined boxes have modifiable input connections — they learn their behavior. The gating units at the Phrase level share a group of hidden units. These hidden units have connections from the feature units, the noun and verb blocks, and the gating units themselves. The Phrase level forms a recurrent subnetwork. It is recurrent in two ways. One, there is direct recurrence arising from the connections among the gates and the hidden layer. Each has modifiable weights to the other. Two, the hidden layer has input

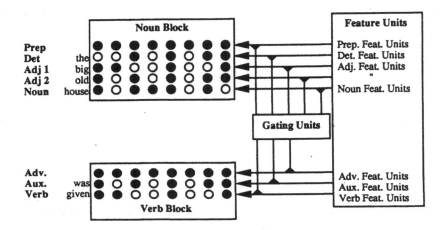

Figure 16.5. Phrase Representation.

connections from the noun and verb blocks that are completely controlled by the gating units. Both types of recurrence are important in the behavior of the gating units.

### 16.4.3  Structure level

The units in the Structure level describe the relationships between the phrases in the Phrase level the clauses they make up. There are six relationships possible (see Figure 16.6). If the unit at position X,Y of a (rectangularly organized) group is active, it means the following:

- Agent Group: Noun block (NB) X is the agent of verb block (VB) Y. Group of 3 by 2 units.

- Patient Group: NB X is patient of VB Y. Group of 3×2.

- Recipient Group: NB X is recipient of VB Y. Group of 3×2.

- Prepositional Modification Group: NB X modifies other NB Y. Group of 3×3.

- Relative Clause Group: VB X modifies NB Y. Group of 2×3.

- Subordinate Clause Group: VB X subordinate to VB Y. Group of 2×2.

The units of the Structure level also share a set of hidden units. These hidden units "see" all that the other set of hidden units see but have connections from

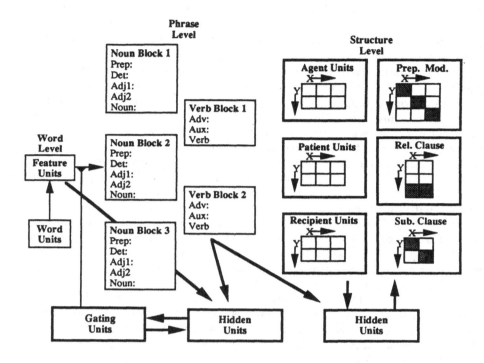

Figure 16.6. Detailed Network Architecture.

the structure representation units instead of connections from the gating units. The Structure level forms a recurrent subnetwork as did the Phrase level.

## 16.4.4   Training

A network with this architecture is trained in two phases. First, the gating units in the Phrase level that are responsible for the behavior of the slots of the noun and verb blocks are trained. Their behavior is quite complex. They must learn to turn on when a word appears across the feature units for their slot (and their slot is supposed to be filled), stay on until the word disappears (even after the word has been assigned to the slot), turn off sharply, and stay off even when another word appears across their feature units. They must also learn to overwrite or empty out incorrectly assigned slots. Words are assigned incorrectly when they have representations in more than one class and there is insufficient information to disambiguate the usage. The word "was" has representations both as a verb and as an auxiliary verb. The network must assign it to both the auxiliary and the verb slots of the current verb block, and disambiguate the assignment when the next word comes in by either overwriting the verb slot with the real verb or emptying out the auxiliary slot.

The next phase involves adding the Structure level and training the structure representation units. The targets for the structure units are set at the beginning of a sentence and remain the same for the whole sentence. This forces the units to try to make decisions about sentence structure as early as possible; otherwise, they accumulate error signals during the initial part of the presentation of the input pattern. An interpretation is considered successful if the structure units are in the appropriate states at the *end* of the input. On the surface, it may seem that these units should have more or less monotonic behavior. However, the sentences in this domain do not necessarily contain sufficient information at word presentation time to make accurate decisions about the word's function. This coupled with the network's attempt to make decisions early causes the structure units to have surprisingly complicated activation patterns over time.

A set of nine sentences was used to train the gating units of the Phrase level of a network. They were selected to be the smallest set of sentences which would cover a reasonably rich set of sentences for training the Structure units. The network generalized very well to include "compositions" of sentence types from the initial set of nine. From this network, the Structure units were added. Eighteen sentences which were correctly processed at the Phrase level were chosen to train the Structure level. A variety of sentences was included. There were more active constructions than passive, more single clause than two clause sentences. Many different role structures were present in the training set. The network learned the set successfully. In what follows, references to "the network" or to substructures of a network are referring to the network described here.

## 16.5   Parsing network performance

It should be noted here that the goals of this task are to see if:

- The network architecture "works."

- It can learn intricate dynamic behavior.

- It can learn to incorporate previously unseen right context into an evolving representation.

- It generalizes.

- It is robust with respect to noisy ill-formed input.

The goal is not to posit a theory of human language processing. There are three aspects of performance which will be characterized. First, the dynamic behavior of the network will be discussed. The ability of the network to generalize will follow. Lastly, network performance on noisy input will be explored.

## 16.5.1 Dynamic behavior

The units of the Structure level in the trained network display several interesting properties during the parsing process:

- They attempt to be predictive.

- They quickly respond to violations of predicted behavior when incorporating new right context information.

- They oscillate during periods of uncertainty.

- They show strong competitive effects which are learned via the recurrent connections.

These aspects of the network's behavior will be illustrated with some example sentences.

The performance of the key Structure level units on, "A snake ate the girl," was shown in Figure 16.2. On this simple sentence, the network's dynamic behavior was still somewhat complex. The role representation units were predictive but postponed final decisions until they could be made with confidence. Periods of indecision were marked by oscillations among competing units. Ultimately, the expectations of the network were confirmed.

The behavior of the network on passive sentences is more involved. A passive sentence with Patient/Recipient/Agent role structure is shown in Figure 16.7. The behavior of the units is similar to the previous sentence in the beginning. When the passive construction is detected, several things happen. The agent unit for Noun 1 loses activity. The recipient and patient units for Nouns 1 and 2 show modest activity — anticipating the likely possible role structures. Also, the agent unit for Noun 3 anticipates the distant terminal phrase. When the preposition "to" is presented, the units quickly respond and indicate that Noun 1 is the patient and Noun 2 is the recipient. The lingering activation of the agent unit for Noun 3 finally becomes most active when the phrase "by Peter" confirms the unit's expectation. The role structure is assigned correctly.

This strongly predictive behavior would be undesirable if it were not possible to train the network to respond correctly to exceptions in generally prevalent structures. One sentence with a Patient/Agent/Recipient role structure was present in the training set. Figure 16.8 shows the network's behavior on that type of sentence. During the early part of the sentence, the network detects the passive construction, and the agent unit for Noun 1 loses activation. Since, "bone" is inanimate, the patient unit for Noun 1 is able to quickly assign "bone" the role of patient. It quickly achieves a steady high activation, and the competing patient unit settles into a steady low activation. However, the network expects Noun 2 to be the recipient since that is the most common construction in the training set. The preposition "by" violates the default

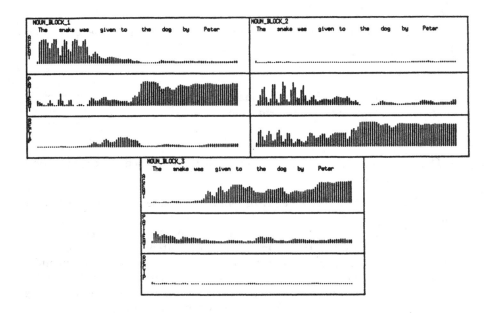

Figure 16.7. Performance of the network on, "The snake was given to the dog by Peter."

expectation of the network, and the units adjust accordingly. The recipient units for Nouns 2 and 3 invert their respective activities. The agent unit for Noun 2 quickly responds. The network was able to learn to react quickly to this sharp exception to the network's default expectations. The competing units behave sensibly, showing partial or oscillating activation for expectations, and responding quickly when right context information disambiguates the role assignment.

## 16.5.2  Generalization

The previous section discussed dynamic behavior of the network on sentences which it "expected" to see, but a very important aspect of network behavior is its ability to generalize to include well formed sentences which are *not* explicitly learned among those sentences which can be successfully processed. Two types of generalization will be discussed here: automatic generalization, and generalization to truly novel well formed sentences.

Automatic generalization is built into the network through the representation of words. For example, if the network successfully learns to parse "Peter

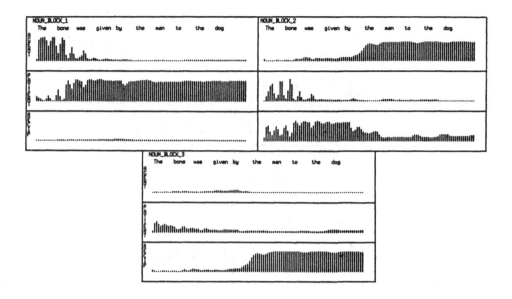

Figure 16.8. Performance of the network on, "The bone was given by the man to the dog."

gave the bone to the dog," it will know how to parse "Jim promised the mitt to the boy." This may appear to be a mere trick, but if one really wants to build connectionist networks to operate over domains with large vocabularies, techniques such as this which minimize training costs while producing better generalization will be useful. This type of generalization is important, but isn't particularly surprising — it is built into the network.

The other type of generalization is where a novel sentence is processed correctly by the network. A novel sentence is any sentence that is not isomorphic to a sentence in the training set modulo the identification bits of the words in the sentence. Generalization to novel sentences is clearly important if one hopes to have manageable training sets. One cannot expect the network to generalize to the point where it would correctly process a sentence with a role structure not present in the training set. However, if the network is able to tolerate variations in phrase structure and variations in the features of words, the necessary training set can be greatly reduced. Since the task is very restricted, it is difficult to measure this type of generalization meaningfully; however some examples will be instructive.

Figure 16.9 shows a variation of the sentence shown in Figure 16.8 that is

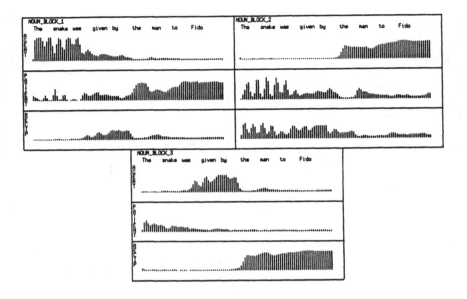

Figure 16.9. Performance of the network on, "The snake was given by the man to Fido."

similar to the sentence in Figure 16.7. Recall that only one sentence with a Patient/Agent/Recipient role structure was in the training set. The sentence, "The snake was given by the man to Fido," differs from the training sentence in two respects: "snake" is animate and the terminal noun phrase has a proper noun. The fact that "snake" is animate is quite significant since it is possible for animate nouns to be recipients. If the network simply memorized the single exceptional exemplar from the training set, this new sentence would not be processed properly. Figure 16.9 shows that the network behaves correctly. Initially the structure units behave as they did in Figure 16.7. The expectation is for Noun 3 to be the agent. There is considerable uncertainty about the role of Noun 1 since it can be either a patient or a recipient (unlike the sentence in Figure 16.8). When the phrase "by the man" is presented, the network reacts quickly and ultimately assigns the correct role structure although the path to the assignment is different from the path taken on the training sentence. In this example, the network treats the novel input as it would its closest exemplar from the training set.

A more difficult situation occurs when the most similar sentence from the training set does *not* have the correct role structure. Rather, the detailed features of the words must dominate the role assignment. The sentence, "A snake was given an apple by John," was in the training set. It has a Recipient/Patient/Agent role structure. A similar sentence given by, "A bone was given the dog by John," receives a Patient/Recipient/Agent role structure by the network, as is desired. Here, the network must combine several different types of evidence to come up with the correct answer. It appears to be expressing a heuristic such as "Inanimate objects are preferred as patients over animate ones." Soft rules like this are combined with other knowledge about word order and sentence structure to parse novel sentences.

## 16.5.3 Noise

In spoken language systems, there are many sources of noise. Two prominent ones are potential errors in the incoming word hypotheses and the user. Since it is not possible to achieve perfect performance from either the speech recognition system or the speaker, the higher level systems must be able to tolerate such problems.

In a tightly coupled system where the parsing level feeds back to the speech level, variations in word duration must not degrade performance. Despite being trained using a constant word duration, the network handled a thirty percent variation in duration with no performance loss. Inter-word silences also had no effect.

Determiners and other short function words often are poorly articulated. This is a persistent problem for speech recognition systems as it leads to word deletions. Despite such deletions, the network makes appropriate role assignments with such sentences as "Snake ate girl." The role assignment is Agent/Patient as in the uncorrupted sentence. Random deletion of determiners from sentences does not lead to serious misinterpretation (an incorrect role assignment) ninety percent of the time.

Non-speech interjections are also possible as in, "A snake (ahh) ate the girl." A speech recognition system can easily interpret the non-speech "ahh" as "a." In this case, the network puts the non-speech "a" in the determiner slot of the second noun block, and then overwrites it with "the." The result is a good parse of the ill-formed sentence. Interjections of "ahh" before verb phrases do not interfere with proper role assignments. Some errors in the noun phrases do occur, but all content words are stored in the correct blocks.

Multi-word repetition in noun phrases such as, "John gave a bone to the to the dog," occur in spontaneous speech. The network responds most often by re-assigning the repeated portion of the phrase to the appropriate block. This has the effect that sentences like, "John gave a bone to the ... to a dog," are usually handled by overwriting the old phrase with the modified one — a desirable effect. Also, ungrammatical sentences such as, "We was happy," are generally treated by the network in the same manner as their closest grammatical counterpart.

### 16.5.4   Summary

It is important to note that this domain is so small that these results can only be suggestive of potential performance in larger, more realistic domains where performance is easier to quantify. However, the goals of the experiment have been met. The network was able to successfully learn to combine syntactic, semantic, and word order information effectively. The network displays complex dynamic behavior and is able to confirm or revise hypotheses based on right context information. It generalizes well and is robust with respect to noise.

## 16.6   Extensions

With the encouraging results obtained from the experiment discussed above, an experiment much larger in scope has been attempted. A network was successfully trained to parse sentences with up to three clauses. The training corpus contained over 200 sentences including sentences with passive constructions and complex center embedded clauses. Given sequential word input, the network does phrase parsing, role assignment, relative and subordinate clause identification, and prepositional attachment. Details of this enhanced parsing architecture can be found in (Jain & Waibel, 1990).

Future work will focus on building real spoken language systems using networks of this type. Networks which provide feedback to word recognition systems for perplexity reduction will be explored. Networks which incorporate prosodic information at the parsing level are also of interest.

## 16.7   Concluding remarks

Connectionist formalisms that have the ability to manipulate symbols through a time sequence show promise in helping to solve some difficult problems in spoken language processing and other domains. There are three central strengths of the connectionist approach. Networks learn their behavior. The rules that are learned are not rigid or formal and hence tend to generalize and be resistant to noise. Networks can learn to incorporate information from multiple knowledge sources and input modalities. Connectionist networks should become increasingly important in language processing.

## Acknowledgments

This research was funded by grants from ATR Interpreting Telephony Research Laboratories and the National Science Foundation under grant number EET-8716324.

The authors thank David Touretzky for his valuable technical suggestions and comments.

# References

Charniak, E., & Santos, E. (1987). A connectionist context-free parser which is not context-free but then it is not really connectionist either. *Proceedings of the Ninth Annual Conference of the Cognitive Science Society* (pp. 70–77). Seattle, WA: Lawrence Erlbaum.

Cottrell, G. W. (1985). Connectionist parsing. *Proceedings of the Seventh Annual Conference of the Cognitive Science Society* (pp. 201–211). Irvine, CA: Lawrence Erlbaum.

Cottrell, G. W. (1989). *A connectionist approach to word sense disambiguation.* San Mateo, CA: Morgan Kaufmann.

Elman, J. L. (1988). *Finding structure in time* (Tech. Rep. No. 8801). San Diego: University of California, Center for Research in Language.

Fanty, M. (1986). Context-free parsing with connectionist networks. In J. S. Denker (Ed.), *AIP Conference Proceedings No. 151.* New York: American Institute of Physics.

Howells, T. (1988). VITAL: A connectionist parser. *Proceedings of the Tenth Annual Conference of the Cognitive Science Society* (pp. 18–25). Lawrence Erlbaum.

Jain, A. N. (1989). *A connectionist architecture for sequential symbolic domains* (Tech. Rep. No. CMU-CS-89-187). Pittsburgh, PA: Carnegie Mellon University, School of Computer Science.

Jain, A. N., & Waibel, A. H. (1990). Incremental parsing by modular recurrent connectionist networks. In D. S. Touretzky (Ed.), *Advances in neural information processing systems 2.* San Mateo, CA: Morgan Kaufmann.

Jordan, M. I. (1986). *Serial order: A parallel distributed processing approach* (Tech. Rep. No. 8604). San Diego: University of California, Institute for Cognitive Science.

McClelland, J. L., & Kawamoto, A. H. (1986). Mechanisms of sentence processing: Assigning roles to constituents. In J. L. McClelland & D. E. Rumelhart (Eds.), *Parallel distributed processing* (Vol. 2). MIT Press.

Miikkulainen, R., & Dyer, M. G. (1989). Encoding input/output representations in connectionist cognitive systems. *Proceedings of the 1988 Connectionist Models Summer School* (pp. 347–356). Morgan Kaufmann.

Nakamura, M., & Shikano, K. (1989). A study of English word category prediction based on neural networks. *Proceedings of the 1989 IEEE International Conference on Acoustic, Speech, and Signal Processing* (Vol. S) (pp. 731–734).

Rumelhart, D. E., Hinton, G. E., & Williams, R. J. (1986). Learning internal representations by error propagation. In D. E. Rumelhart & J. L. McClelland (Eds.), *Parallel distributed processing* (Vol. 1). The MIT Press.

Selman, B., & Hirst, G. (1985). A rule-based connectionist parsing system. *Proceedings of the Seventh Annual Conference of the Cognitive Science Society* (pp. 212–221). Irvine, CA: Lawrence Erlbaum.

Waltz, D., & Pollack, J. (1985). Massively parallel parsing: A strongly interactive model of natural language interpretation. *Cognitive Science, 9*, 51–74.

# 17. A Broad-Coverage Natural Language Analysis System

Karen Jensen

*IBM*

## 17.1 Introduction

A broad-coverage goal requires a robust and flexible natural language processing base, one that is adaptable to linguistic needs and also to the exigencies of computation. The Programming Language for Natural Language Processing (PLNLP: Heidorn, 1972) is well suited for this task. PLNLP provides a general programming capability, including a rule-writing formalism and algorithms for both parsing ("decoding") and generation ("encoding"). Although linguistic scholarship and linguistic intuitions motivate our system strongly, we have chosen not to commit our computational formalism to any of the reigning linguistic theories. To quote Ron Kaplan:

> the problem is that, at least in the current state of the art, (linguists) don't know which generalizations and restrictions are really going to be true and correct, and which are either accidental, uninteresting or false. The data just isn't in ... (Kaplan, 1985, p. 5)

So our work is experimental, descriptive, and data-driven. This does not mean that it has no theoretical implications. Any functioning unit of this size is an embodiment of some theory.

This chapter discusses the three components of our broad-coverage natural language analysis system, as they appear at this time.

1. The PLNLP English Grammar (PEG) makes an initial syntactic analysis for each input sentence (Jensen, 1986).

2. The reattachment component takes syntactically consistent, but semantically inaccurate, parses, and then reattaches constituents, when necessary, based on information gained from a rich semantic data base (Jensen & Binot, 1987).

3. The paragraph modeling component receives sentence parses and, for connected text, builds them into logically consistent and coherent models of the chunks of discourse that are typically called paragraphs (Zadrozny & Jensen, 1989).

Hand-in-hand with each of these components goes a separate dictionary access.

1. The first dictionary access (for PEG) is to a lexicon that is essentially just a glorified word list. However, it is a word list that, when coupled with morphological rules and a default strategy provided by the access mechanism, aims at supplying an entry for every word of the language, including neologisms. We started with the full online Webster's Seventh New Collegiate Dictionary (W7). We have modified this word list somewhat, but only to enlarge it — never to reduce its scope. Although the word coverage is great, the amount of information per word is small. Only reduced, streamlined feature information is available in each entry; subcategorization, or valency, information is not distinguished by word senses.

2. The second dictionary access (for reattachment) consults a far richer source than before. For English, we make central use of online dictionary entries — both their definitions and their example sentences. W7 and the Longman Dictionary of Contemporary English (LDOCE) are available to us. We can parse the definitions and examples with PEG, and use the syntactic information that PEG provides in order to bootstrap our way into semantics. The amount of information per word obtainable during this second access is huge — much greater than what is typically described, even for lexicalist systems.

3. The third access (for paragraph modeling) again includes full natural language text. Since this component is only at a very early stage, there is not much to be said about it. We envision a NL knowledge base that contains information from every available source, from word lists to dictionaries and beyond, to encyclopedias.

It is interesting that the purposes of the separate components divide so neatly along linguistic levels: syntax, semantics, discourse. We do not mean to insist that the ultimate version of this system would need to have it components so cleanly divided. Neither has separation of the components been done for reasons of theoretical elegance or symmetry, but simply because the necessities of broad-coverage NLP have brought it about.

# 17.2  A syntactic sketch: PEG

PEG is an augmented phrase structure grammar which has been useful in a number of different settings — text critiquing and machine translation, to name two. PEG's significant characteristics include:

- binary rules, in most cases (Jensen, 1987);

- a wealth of conditions on the operation of the rules — conditions that range from those that are strongly general, and express real grammatical patterns of the language, to those that are quite specific, and are intended to filter out certain semantically anomalous parses;

- a "relaxed" or "textual" approach to parsing, which means that we consistently avoid the use of selectional ("semantic") information to condition the parse, and that we also try, in so far as possible, to avoid, or at least to soften, the use of subcategorization (valency) information for that purpose. We assume for example, that almost any verb can have a sense which will fit almost any frame; and that almost any noun might be used as an argument to almost any verb; and that the job of a computational parsing grammar is not to separate grammatical and ungrammatical sentences, but to provide the most reasonable analysis for any input string. The system is certainly able to distinguish grammatical from ungrammatical input, but this can be done by commenting on, rather than by failing to accept, an ungrammatical string.

The lexicon that supports this initial syntactic parse started out, in 1981, as a list of all the main entries in W7 — minus, of course, morphological variants that could be productively described by rules. W7 claims to have 130,000 entries; after morphological variants were subtracted, the list contained 63,850 entries. That number has been increased from time to time; it now stands at roughly 70,000. As stated earlier, the goal of this lexicon is to supply useful syntactic information for every word of the language, including neologisms.

Because it contains so many entries, this lexicon provides very broad coverage. However, for each entry it contains only very limited information. The information is for parts of speech, morphology (tense, number, etc.), and word class features (transitive, ditransitive, factive, etc). The features are mostly binary (present or absent), but include some lists, such as lists of verbal particles.

Word class features are valency features — granted. But both the presentation and the use of these features are different from what is described for most other parsing systems. First, no attempt is made to specify the nature of the valency arguments. Second, although different parts of speech for a single word are listed and marked separately, all other sense distinctions, within each part of speech, are collapsed. One lexical item might have many, often contradictory, feature markings. The word "go," for example, appears in the lexicon as follows:

go(NOUN SING)

go(VERB COPL INF PLUR PRES TRAN)

The first definition of "go," as a SINGular NOUN, collapses two different noun entries for "go" in W7. One is the Japanese game; the other has seven subsenses, including "the act or manner of going"; "the height of fashion"; etc. The definition of "go" as a VERB collapses 19 intransitive or COPLulative senses (e.g., "to go crazy"), and six TRANsitive senses (e.g., "to go his way," "to go bail for").

The work "know" also has two entries:

know(NOUN SING)

know(VERB INF NPTOV PLUR PRES THATCOMP TRAN WH-COMP)

This means that "know" can be a singular noun ("in the know") or a verb. If it is a verb, besides being INfinitive, PLURal, and PRESent, it might be expected, with fair frequency, to have one of the following complementation types:

NPTOV: We know him to be a good man.

THATCOMP: We know that he is here.

TRAN: We know him.

WHCOMP: We know what he wants.

The great advantage to this collapsing strategy (affectionately known as "smooshing") is that it helps to avoid multiple parses in a simple, straightforward way. And this is no trivial accomplishment: a broad-coverage, bottom-up parallel parser can easily strangle on proliferating parses. With simple lexical information, however, we can expect a manageable number of parses, even in the worst case. We aim for a single parse that carries forward all of the necessary data. We like to think of this as a syntactic sketch; we have also called it an "approximate parse." The techniques for writing this kind of grammar are varied, and use all sorts of syntactic and morphological hooks. We can exploit the presence of valency features; but we try to blunt their force, using them to favor one situation over another, rather than as strict necessary conditions for the success of a certain rule.

The result of the operation of PEG's augmented phrase structure rules, coupled with the streamlined lexicon just described, is an attribute-value data structure (in PLNLP terms, a "record structure"). Table 17.1 lists a somewhat pared-down example of the top-level record produced from the simple input sentence, "Geometry is a very old science."

Attribute names are in the left-hand column; their values are to the right. The attributes SEGTYPE and SEGTYP2 refer to different labelings of the topmost node; STR has as its value the character string covered by this node; and RULES contains a list of rule numbers, a derivational history for the parse at this level. POS indicates the possible parts of speech of the BASE; the INDICator features are fairly self-explanatory. Most of the values in Table 17.1 are actually pointers to other records. For example, the value of the PRMODS attribute is a pointer to the noun phrase (NP1) which covers the noun "geometry."

All of the analysis information is carried in the record structure. For ease of recognition, however, we also display a variant of the standard parse tree:

Note that the start node presents the value of the SEGTYP2 attribute from Table 17.1, plus a number (each node is numbered for easy reference). The other, fairly standard, node names are the values of the SEGTYP2 attributes in their corresponding records. Trees are produced by a routine that uses just five attributes from the record structure: PRMODS, HEAD, PSMODS,

Table 17.1. PLNLP record for "Geometry is a very old science."

| SEGTYPE | 'SENT' |
|---------|--------|
| SEGTYP2 | 'DECL' |
| STR | "geometry is a very old science" |
| RULES | 4000 4080 5080 7200 |
| BASE | 'BE' |
| POS | VERB |
| INDIC | SING PRES COPL PERS3 |
| PRMODS | NP1 "geometry" |
| HEAD | VERB1 "is" |
| PSMODS | NP2 "a very old science" |
| PSMODS | PUNC1 "." |
| SUBJECT | NP1 "geometry" |
| PREDNOM | NP2 "a very old science" |
| TOPIC | NP1 "geometry" |

```
DECL1    NP1      NOUN1*    "geometry"
         BERB1*   "is"
         NP2      DETP1    ADJ1*    "a"
                  AJP1     AVP1     ADV1*    "very"
                           ADJ2*    "old"
                  NOUN2*   "science"
         PUNC1    "."
```

Figure 17.1. Parse tree for the same sentence.

SEGTYP2, and STR. Since such a tree is conventionally said to depict phrase- or constituent-structure, it might be said that these five attributes make up the constituent structure for the parse.

More than constituent structure is contained in the records, however. During the operation of the grammar rules, attributes are assigned that point to subject, object, indirect object, predicate nominative, etc. In other parlance, these might be assigned by "... a function that goes from the nodes of a tree into f-structure space" (Kaplan, 1985, p. 11). Table 17.1 shows two examples, SUBJECT and PREDNOM. Such attributes, and their values, could be said to present the functional structure. The TOPIC of the sentence is also computed, based on some exploratory work done in (Davison, 1984). Other attributes will be added during further processing, and these attributes will define higher levels of analysis. Progress in the analysis seems not to involve jumping between levels, but rather a smooth accumulation (and sometimes an erasing) of attributes and values.

Now, some people might object that the same analysis could be obtained by using subcategorization frames (together, perhaps, with selectional features on NPs), either as conditions on the rules or, within a lexicalist framework, as statements within the dictionary, to be honored by the rules. According to this way of thinking, we would control multiple parses by exercising valency information, not by ignoring it. From experience, we have found this to be a dangerous path, for several reasons. The most forceful reason is that real text (at least, real English text) just does not behave in the well-disciplined fashion that such specifications would require. If we really want to do broad-coverage parsing, then we have to be prepared for many imaginative uses of words to occur; and strict subcategorization does not allow for that.

Strict subcategorization expects, for example, that verbs will occur in well-defined contexts. "Give" should be either transitive or ditransitive, surely not intransitive. But what about the sentence "I gave at the office?" It's no good saying that there is an "understood" NP; if the computational grammar depends on the presence of a least one object in context, then this sentence will fail to parse. And even though there are subcategorizational differences between "go" and "know" (by our own earlier definitions), it is possible to use "go" with a that-complement, as in:

I said, no. And then he goes, "See you later."

or with a wh-complement, as in:

We'll go whatever amount (i.e., bail) is necessary.

These real-life facts of language tend in one direction: stated in extreme form, any word can, and might, be used in any context. But to mark every verb in the lexicon with every possible subcategorization frame would be absurd, of course. And to add some sort of "recovery" procedures into the grammar would be costly. The most sensible way to regard subcategorization (valency frames) is as codified frequency information. A verb that is marked transitive is quite frequently used in its transitive sense — that's all.

This does not mean that we ignore the semantic implications of valencies. On the contrary, what we do is postpone the differentiation of word senses until after the initial syntactic sketch is completed. This strategy allows us to get our hands on any input string, assign it some (reasonable, we hope) structure, and then interpret the input, whatever it might be. Before making the interpretation, however, the parse may have to pass through the reattachment component.

# 17.3   Semantic readjustment

No matter how clever the grammarian's exploitation of word order, word class, and morphological hooks is, there are many analyses in English that just will not yield a correct analysis from syntax alone. Among these are the correct attachment of prepositional phrases and of relative and other embedded clauses; the optimal structure of complex noun phrases; and the degree of structural

```
DECL2 NP6     DETP7 ADJ1* "this"
                    NOUN9* "re-measuring"
                    PP1   PP2   PREP1* "of"
                          DETP2 ADJ2* "the"
                          NOUN1* "land"
              VERB2* "was"
              AJP1  ADJ3* "necessary"
                    PP3   PP4   PREP2* "due to"
                          DETP3 ADJ4* "the"
                          AJP2  ADJ5* "annual"
                          NOUN2* "overflow"
                          PP5   PP6   PREP3* "of"
                                NP2   DETP4 ADJ6* "the"
                                      NP3   NOUN3* "river"
                                      NOUN4* "Nile"
                          ?     CONJ1* "and"
                                NP4   DETP5 ADJ7* "the"
                                      AJP3  ADJ8* "consequent"
                                      NOUN5* "destroying"
                                      PP7   PP8   PREP4* "of"
                                      DETP6 ADJ9* "the"
                                      NOUN6* "boundaries"
                                      PP9   PP10  PREP5* "of"
                                            NP5   NOUN7* "farm"
                                      NOUN8* "lands"
       PUNC1  "."
```

Figure 17.2. Parse tree for a sentence with structural ambiguity.

ambiguity exhibited by coordinated elements (Langendoen, p.c.). There are no markers, in English, that serve to disambiguate these constructions; the plain fact is that semantic (or even broader, contextual) information is required.

Consider the following parse, summarized in Figure 17.2 by its tree structure. Where the correct structure cannot be determined by syntax, attachment is arbitrarily made to the closest available node, encouraging right branching.

The question mark indicates doubt about the acceptability of the coordinate NP inside PP5: "the river Nile and the consequent destroying of the boundaries of farm lands." Should NP4, "the consequent destroying . . . ," be and-ed with NP2, "the river Nile," or with the NP in PP3, "the annual overflow . . . ?"

Question marks are placed at various points in the parse tree by a routine that is sensitive to problematic constructions in English. We could have produced two separate analyses; but, given the large number of such attachment

situations, this approach would have led straight to the fatal trap of proliferating parses. The questions marks, in effect, collapse different possible parses,
and allow for efficient handling of ambiguities (Jensen, 1986, pp. 22–23).

Human readers of the sentence will not hesitate to say that the NP attachment shown in PP3 of Figure 17.2 is not the intended one; the attachment
indicated by the question mark is what we want. Our problem is how to enable
the computer to determine that.

The sort of information that enables the right decision to be made, in
this and similar cases, generally falls under the rubric of "background" or
"common sense" knowledge. The usual method for making such knowledge
available to a computer program has been to hand-code the relevant concepts,
in whatever format. Although some hand-coding will undoubtedly be necessary
and valuable, we approach the problem from another angle.

Written text is itself a rich source of information. It can be viewed as
a knowledge base; the language that it is written in, even though this is a
natural language, is a knowledge representation language. In particular, reference works like dictionaries actually contain a storehouse of common sense
knowledge. We can parse the entries in an online dictionary with a syntactic
grammar, and retrieve a surprising amount of the information that is necessary
to resolve syntactic ambiguities, like the one displayed in Figure 17.2 (Binot
& Jensen, 1987; Jensen & Binot, 1988).

The problem presented in Figure 17.2 reduces to a question: which of the
following pairs in more likely?

- overflow and destroying

- Nile and destroying

Bearing in mind the old adage that "likes conjoin," we will consider that pair
more likely whose terms can be more easily related through dictionary entries
— including both definitions and example sentences. (Das Gupta, 1987 also
uses dictionary entries for interpreting conjoined words.)

Decisions on where to start these search procedures will ultimately be important, but here we avoid them. Assume that we start with the first pair,
first word. The noun definition for "overflow" in W7 begins:

overflow ... n 1: a flowing over: INUNDATION

Here "inundation" is asserted to be a synonym for "overflow." The noun
"inundation" has no definition of its own, but is merely listed under the verb
"inundate:"

inundate ... vt ...: to cover with a flood: OVERFLOW

The circularity of the synonym definitions is no problem; because now we can
infer something new about "overflow:" it involves the act of covering by means
of a flood. The definition of "flood" in W7 is not much help, but in LDOCE,
the first example sentence quoted in the entry for the noun "flood," when
analyzed by PEG, takes us right where we want to go:

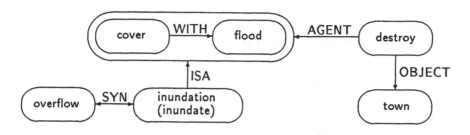

Figure 17.3. Network connecting "overflow" to "destroying."

flood ... n ... 1 ... The town was destroyed by the floods after the storm.

Focusing on only the relevant information, these dictionary entries depicted in Figure 17.3 present a small part of a conceptual network, and the path from "overflow" to "destroying" is clear in three steps.

Any attempt to connect "Nile" with "destroying" is bound to take longer. We can link "Nile" with "river" (this link is actually present in W7, in the Pronouncing Gazetteer); but we still have to get from "river" to "water," and then from "water" to "flood," and from "flood" to "destroy" (a total of four steps). The link between "water" and "flood" is also likely to incur a penalty, since moving from "water" to "flood" is difficult (i.e., "flood" does not appear in the definition of "water"), although moving in the reverse direction is easy ("water" does appear in the definition of "flood"). On this basis, we revise the analysis of the sentence in Figure 17.2 to reflect the more likely coordinate structure depicted in Figure 17.4.

We have not yet implemented this particular disambiguation, although it is similar to work reported on in (Jensen & Binot, 1987). Many technical issues remain to be investigated. For one example, there is the problem of how to combine two (or more) dictionaries — in this case, W7 and LDOCE — in a way that allows for efficient access to, and processing of, all the information that they contain. We want to set such problems aside for the moment, and assume that they will be solved. The point is that vast, rich, and potentially rewarding networks of information exist in written text, and much of that information is of the hitherto elusive "common sense" sort.

This is our second dictionary access. The amount of information available at this stage of processing is immense and complexly structured. It is, needless, to say, much greater that what is afforded by any of the current lexicalist frameworks. It avoids the pitfalls of straight hand-coding — incompleteness, and time required — and it points to a new way of looking at knowledge bases. The prospect of a system that uses natural language in order to understand natural language is pleasingly recursive. Words may yet prove to be the most adequate knowledge representation tools.

```
DECL2 NP6   DETP7 ADJ1* "this"
            NOUN9* "re-measuring"
            PP1   PP2     PREP1* "of"
                  DETP2   ADJ2* "the"
                  NOUN1*  "land"
      VERB2* "was"
      AJP1  ADJ3* "necessary"
            PP3   PP4     PREP2* "due to"
                  NP2     DETP3   ADJ4* "the"
                          AJP2    ADJ5* "annual"
                          NOUN2*  "overflow"
                          PP5     PP6     PREP3* "of"
                                  NP3     DETP4   ADJ6* "the"
                                          NP4             NOUN3* "river"
                                          NOUN4* "Nile"
            CONJ1* "and"
            NP5     DETP5   ADJ7* "the"
                    AJP3    ADJ8* "consequent"
                    NOUN5*  "destroying"
                    PP7     PP8     PREP4* "of"
                            DETP6   ADJ9* "the"
                            NOUN6*  "boundaries"
                            PP9     PP10    PREP5* "of"
                                    NP6             NOUN7* "farm"
                                    NOUN8* "lands"
      PUNC1 "."
```

Figure 17.4. Readjusted parse for sentence in Figure 17.2.

# 17.4   The paragraph as a discourse unit

Beyond the semantic readjustment component lies the whole world of connected text processing. This area is generally referred to as "discourse." We take the paragraph (loosely defined) to be the first formal unit of discourse. It is the smallest reasonable domain of anaphora resolution, and the smallest domain in which topic and coherence can be reliably defined (Zadrozny & Jensen, 1989, p. 1, pp. 4ff).

The sentences in Figures 17.1 and 17.2 are actually part of a paragraph taken from a reading comprehension exercise in a well-known series used by countless prospective college students who want to prepare for the standard Scholastic Aptitude Test (Brownstein *et al.*, 1987, pp. 144–5). Table 17.2 lists the complete text.

If we are going to make discourse sense of this text, however, we need

Table 17.2. Paragraph from Barron's, *How to prepare for the SAT.*

---

Geometry is a very old science. We are told by Herodotus, a Greek historian, that geometry had its origin in Egypt along the banks of the river Nile. The first record we have of its study is found in a manuscript written by Ahmes, an Egyptian scholar, about 1550 B.C. This manuscript is believed to be a copy of a treatise which dated back probably more than a thousand years, and describes the use of geometry at that time in a very crude form of surveying or measurement. In fact, geometry, which means "earth measurement," received its name in this manner. This re-measuring of the land was necessary due to the annual overflow of the river Nile and the consequent destroying of the boundaries of farm lands. This early geometry was very largely a list of rules or formulas for finding the areas of plane figures. Many of these rules were inaccurate, but, in the main, they were fairly satisfactory.

---

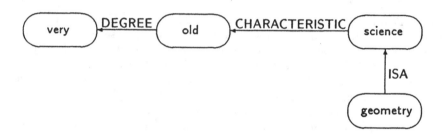

Figure 17.5. A network representation for "Geometry is a very old science."

something more than a linear concatenation of syntactic sentence parses — just as, in order to make syntactic sense out of a sentence, we need something more than a linear concatenation of words. A popular and effective way of modeling this non-linear set of sentence relationships is as a network with nodes connected by arcs (e.g., Sowa, 1984). We can label the nodes with content words and the arcs with function (or relation) names, for a simple beginning. For now, we can use a fairly intuitive set of relation names, rather than take the time to explain precisely how each arc gets labeled.

The basic network for one sentence derives not directly from the surface syntactic structure, but from the underlying predicate-argument structure, which itself is derived from the surface structure, after all necessary readjustments have been made (Jensen forthcoming). Figure 17.5 depicts a network representation, or model, for the first sentence in the geometry paragraph.

To build a model for an entire paragraph (a P-model), the trick now is to map the network for each consecutive sentence onto the network for the preceding sentence or sentences, joining nodes whenever possible. Stated simply, nodes can be joined when they "mean" the same thing. To a first approximation, sameness of meaning can be defined by:

1. use of the same word;

2. use of a synonym or paraphrase;

3. use of a pronoun reference;

4. use of zero anaphora (e.g., ellipsis in coordination).

Identification of "same word" is easy enough, and syntax will suffice to determine the referents for most cases of zero anaphora, and for many pronouns. However, there are also many pronoun referents that cannot be syntactically resolved, and nothing in syntax will identify synonyms and paraphrases. This fact has prevented the development of a formal discourse model (Bond & Hayes, 1983, p. 16).

For a solution to the problems of pronoun reference and synonym identification, we turn again to reference works written in natural language. Dictionaries and thesauri are full of such information.

Figure 17.6 depicts part of the model that can be build for the paragraph in Figure 17.2. It included information from only the first, second, fifth, and sixth sentences in that paragraph. Even so, many details have been left out.

In order to build the link between "necessary" and "geometry," we have to know that "re-measuring of the land" is a paraphrase for "geometry." We are told that "earth measurement" is a synonym for "geometry" in the fifth sentence. Syntax allows us to say that "NOUN measurement" and "measurement of NOUN" are possible equals. If we can establish that "earth measurement" and "land re-measuring" are equals, then the problem is solved. "Measurement" and "re-measuring" are transparently related, so the problem reduces to finding a link between "earth" and "land."

This, of course, is quite easy to find in dictionaries and thesauri. In LDOCE, one definition of "earth" contains "land" as a synonym, and vice versa (actually, the first four definitions for "land" contain the word "earth" in a critical position in the parse). Similar conditions exist in W7. Roget's Thesaurus (RT) lists "land" as a synonym for "earth" and "earth" as a synonym for "land." Q.E.D.

The intended purpose for paragraphs like the one we have been playing with, of course, is to test a reader's comprehension ability by requiring sensible answers to questions based on the information in the paragraph. In Brownstein *et al.*, the first test concerning our paragraph is:

(1) The title below that best expresses the ideas of this passage is

and the possible solutions are

(A) Plane Figures

(B) Beginnings of Geometry

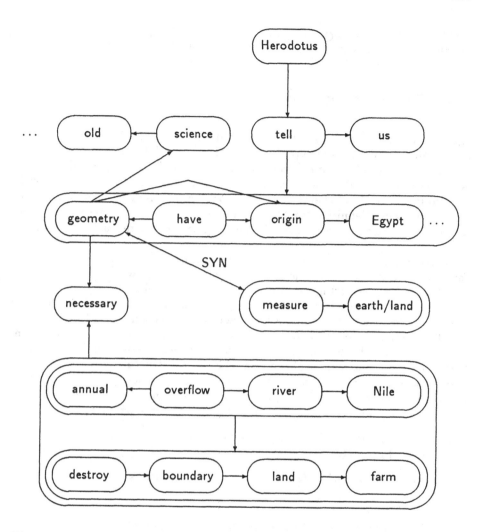

Figure 17.6. Partial P-model for the text in Figure 17.2.

(C) Manuscript of Ahmes

(D) Surveying in Egypt

(E) Importance of the Study of Geometry

It is tempting to ask whether a program that is able to build and manipulate the P-model in Figure 17.6 could also answer (1) successfully.

Without going into any formal explanation of topic definition, let's assume that we can identify the node labeled "geometry" as the main idea, or topic, of the paragraph. (Note that it occupies a central position in the network.) So we discard all possible answers to (1) except for those that contain the word

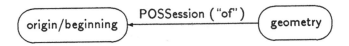

Figure 17.7. Network for the answer to (1).

"geometry." This leaves us with two candidates, (B) and (E). We then search the graph around the "geometry" node, looking for related nodes that express either "beginnings" or "importance of the study of." The latter alternative is not easy to find. But the "origin" node can be immediately identified with "beginnings." In W7, the entry for "beginning" has "origin" as a synonym, and the second sense definition for "origin" is "rise, beginning, or derivation from a source ..." Furthermore, "origin" and "beginning" are mutual synonyms in RT.

Resolving the referent for the possessive pronoun "its" in the second sentence of our test paragraph allowed us to draw the arc between the "geometry" and "origin" nodes in Figure 17.6, which we now label as in Figure 17.7. In this subgraph, the preferred answer to Question (1) is clear: The title that best expresses the ideas in the test passage is (B), "Beginnings of Geometry."

Obviously a tremendous amount of important detail has been left out in order to produce this blueprint for a formal model of a discourse unit. The challenges of implementation lie ahead. But the general structure seems promising, and most promising of all is the possibility of finding a repository of background knowledge, already coded for us, in online natural language sources.

Here is another comprehension question on the same paragraph:

(2) It can be inferred that one of the most important factors in the development of geometry as a science was

An answer must be picked from the following alternatives:

(A) Ahmes' treatise

(B) the inaccuracy of the early rules and formulas

(C) the annual flooding of the Nile Valley

(D) the destruction of farm crops by the Nile

(E) an ancient manuscript copied by Ahmes

We suggest that the preferred answer to (2) can also be found by using the P-model in Figure 17.6, in conjunction with a good dictionary and thesaurus; and we leave this as an exercise for the interested reader.

## 17.5   Concluding remarks

This chapter contains an overview of our broad-coverage NL analysis system, including components that already exist, that are currently being worked on,

and that are projected for the future. Some aspects of our system that differentiate it from other NL analysis systems are:

- It is not modeled along the lines of any currently accepted linguistic
  theory; rather it is highly experimental and data-driven.

- Separate components are emerging from this experimental process; they
  coincide roughly with the accepted linguistic levels: syntax, semantics,
  discourse.

- Each component makes its own dictionary access or accesses, and the
  dictionaries associated with different components will differ in the type
  and amount of information they contain.

- The written text of standard reference works is used as a repository for
  much of the background or common sense knowledge that is necessary
  to solve many analysis problems. This knowledge base can be accessed
  with the syntactic parser that forms one component of the system.

# Acknowledgments

Thanks are due to Joel Fagan, George Heidorn, Lee Schwartz, and Lucy Van-
derwende, who provided helpful comments and criticism. Any errors remain
the author's responsibility.

# References

Binot, J.-L., & Jensen, K. (1987). A semantic expert using an online standard
dictionary. *Proceedings of the Tenth International Joint Conference on
Artificial Intelligence* (pp. 709–714). Milan, Italy: Morgan Kaufmann.

Bond, S. J., & Hayes, J. R. (1983). *Cues people use to paragraph text* (Tech.
Rep.). Pittsburgh, PA: Carnegie Mellon University, Dept. of Psychology.

Brownstein, S. C., Weiner, M., & Green, S. W. (1987). *How to prepare for
the Scholastic Aptitude Test*. New York: Barron's.

Das-Gupta, P. (1987). Boolean interpretation of conjunctions for document
retrieval. *Journal of the American Society for Information Science, 38,
4*, 245–254.

Davison, A. (1984). Syntactic markedness and the definition of sentence topic.
*Language, 60, 4*, 797–846.

Heidorn, G. E. (1972). *Natural language inputs to a simulation programming
system*. Unpublished doctoral dissertation. Yale University.

Jensen, K. (1986). *PEG 1986: A broad-coverage computational syntax of
English*. Unpublished paper.

Jensen, K. (1987). Binary rules and non-binary trees. In A. Manaster-Ramer
(Ed.), *Mathematics of Language*. Amsterdam: John Benjamins.

Jensen, K. (forthcoming). *PEGASUS: Deriving predicate-argument structures from a syntactic parse*.

Jensen, K., & Binot, J.-L. (1987). Disambiguating prepositional phrase attachments by using on-line dictionary definitions. *CL*, *13*, *3–4*, 251–60.

Kaplan, R. (1985). Three seductions of computational psycholinguistics. In P. Whitclock, M. M. Woods, H. L. Somers, R. Johnson, & P. Bennett (Eds.), *Linguistic theory and computer applications*. London: Academic Press.

*Longman dictionary of contemporary English* (1978). Harlow and London, Longman Group Limited.

*Roget's thesaurus of English words and phrases* (1962). New York: St. Martin's Press.

Sowa, J. F. (1984). *Conceptual structures: Information processing in mind and machine*. Reading, MA: Addison-Wesley.

*Webster's seventh new collegiate dictionary* (1967). Springfield, MA: G. & C. Merriam Co.

Zadrozny, W., & Jensen, K. (1989). *Semantics of paragraphs*. Unpublished paper.

# 18. Parsing 2-Dimensional Language

## Masaru Tomita

*School of Computer Science and Center for Machine Translation*
*Carnegie Mellon University*

### Abstract

2-Dimensional Context Free Grammar (2D-CFG) for 2-dimensional input text is introduced and efficient parsing algorithms for 2D-CFG are presented. In 2D-CFG, a grammar rule's right hand side symbols can be placed not only horizontally but also vertically. Terminal symbols in a 2-dimensional input text are combined to form a rectangular *region*, and regions are combined to form a larger region using a 2-dimensional phrase structure rule. The parsing algorithms presented in this chapter are 2D-Earley algorithm and 2D-LR algorithm, which are a 2-dimensionally extended version of Earley's algorithm and the Generalized LR algorithm, respectively.

## 18.1 Introduction

Existing grammar formalisms and formal language theories, as well as parsing algorithms, deal only with one-dimensional strings. However, 2-dimensional layout information plays an important role in understanding a text. It is especially crucial for such texts as title pages of articles, business cards, announcements and formal letters to be read by an optical character reader (OCR). A number of projects (Akiyama & Masuda, 1986; Inagaki, Kato, Hiroshima, & Sakai, 1984; Kubota, *et al.*, 1984; Wong, Casey, & Wahl, 1982), most notably by Fujisawa *et al.* (1988), try to analyze and utilize the 2-dimensional layout information. Fujisawa *et al.*, unlike others, uses a procedural language called Form Definition Language (FDL) (Higashino, Fujisawa, Nakano, & Eijiri, 1986; Yashiro, *et al.*, 1989) to specify layout rules. On the other hand, in the area of image understanding, several attempts have been also made to define a language to describe 2-dimensional images (Fu, 1977; Watanabe, 1972).

This chapter presents a formalism called 2 Dimensional Context Free Grammar (2D-CFG), and two parsing algorithms to parse 2-dimensional language with 2D-CFG. Unlike all the previous attempts mentioned above, our approach is to extend existing well-studied (one dimensional) grammar formalisms and parsing techniques to handle 2-dimensional language. In the rest of this section, we informally describe the 2-dimensional context free grammar (2D-CFG) in comparison with the 1-dimensional traditional context free grammar.

Input to the traditional context free grammar is a string, or *sentence*; namely a one-dimensional array of terminal symbols. Input to the 2-dimensional context free grammar, on the other hand, is a rectangular block of symbols, or *text*; namely, a 2-dimensional array of terminal symbols.

In the traditional context free grammar, a non-terminal symbol represents a *phrase*, which is a substring of the original input string. A grammar rule is applied to combine adjoining phrases to form a larger phrase. In the 2-dimensional context free grammar, on the other hand, a non-terminal represents a *region*, which is a rectangular sub-block of the input text. A grammar rule is applied to combine two adjoining regions to form a larger region. Rules like

(1) $A \rightarrow B \; C$

are used to combine horizontally adjacent regions. In addition, rules like

$$(2) \quad A \quad \rightarrow \quad \begin{matrix} B \\ C \end{matrix}$$

can be used in the 2-dimensional context free grammar to combine vertically adjacent regions.

A region can be represented with a non-terminal symbol and four positional parameters: x, y, X, and Y, which determine the upper-left position and the lower-right position of the rectangle (assuming that the coordinate origin is the upper-left corner of the input text).

Horizontally adjacent regions, $(B, x_B, y_B, X_B, Y_B)$ and $(C, x_C, y_C, X_C, Y_C)$, can be combined only if

- $y_B = y_C$,
- $Y_B = Y_C$, and
- $X_B = x_C$.

The first two conditions say that B and C must have the same vertical position and the same height, and the last condition says that B and C are horizontally adjoining.

Similarly, vertically adjacent regions, B and C, can be combined only if

- $x_B = x_C$,
- $X_B = X_C$, and
- $Y_B = y_C$.

A new region, $(A, x_B, y_B, X_C, Y_C)$, is then formed. Figure 18.1 shows examples of adjacent regions, and Figure 18.2 shows the results of combining them using Rules (2) and (1).

Let G be a 2D-CFG $(G(N), G(S), P_H, P_V, S)$, where

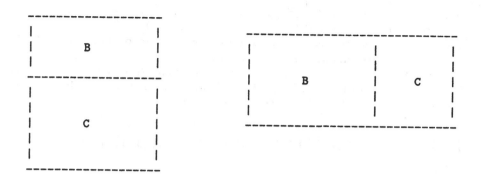

Figure 18.1. Examples of adjacent regions.

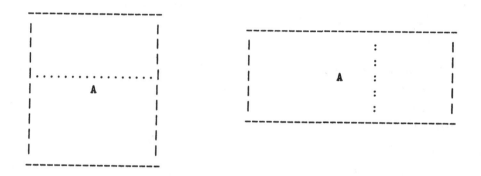

Figure 18.2. After applying Rule (2) and (1), respectively.

N: a set of non-terminal symbols

G(S): is a set of terminal symbols

$P_H$: a set of horizontal production rules

$P_V$: a set of vertical production rules

S: start symbol

Let LEFT(p) be the left hand side symbol of p. Let RIGHT(p, i) be the i-th right hand side symbol of p. Without loss of generality, we assume each rule in $P_H$ is either in the form of

A → B C or A → b

and each rule in $P_V$ is in the form of

A    →    B
          C

Where A,B,C $\in$ N and b $\in$ G(S). This form of grammar is called *2-dimensional Chomsky Normal Form (2D-CNF)*, and an arbitrary 2D-CFG can be converted into 2D-CNF. The conversion algorithm is very similar to the standard CNF conversion algorithm, and we do not describe the algorithm in this chapter.

The subsequent two sections present two efficient 2D parsing algorithms, 2D-Earley and 2D-LR, based on Earley's algorithm (1970) and the Generalized LR algorithm (Tomita, 1985, 1987), respectively.

## 18.2    The 2D-Earley parsing algorithm

### Input:

2D-CFG G = (G(N), G(S), $P_H$, $P_V$, S) and an input text

$a_{11}$ $a_{21}$ $\cdots$ $a_{n1}$

$a_{12}$ $a_{22}$ $\cdots$ $a_{n2}$

$\cdots$

$a_{1m}$ $a_{2m}$ $\cdots$ $a_{nm}$

where $a_{ij} \in$ G(S).

### Output:

A parse table

$I_{00}$ $I_{10}$ $\cdots$ $I_{n0}$

$I_{01}$ $I_{11}$ $\cdots$ $I_{n1}$

$\cdots$

$I_{0m}$ $I_{1m}$ $\cdots$ $I_{nm}$

$I_{ij}$ is a set of *items*, and each item is (p, d, x, y, X, Y), where p is a rule in $P_H$ or $P_V$, d is an integer to represent its dot position ($0 \leq d \leq |p|$, where $|p|$ represents the length of p's left hand side). The integers x and y represent the item's origin (x,y) or the upper-left corner of the region being constructed by the item. The integers X and Y represent its perspective lower-right corner, and the parser's horizontal (vertical) position should never exceed X (Y) until the item is completed.

### Method:

For each p $\in$ $P_H \cup P_V$ such that LEFT(p) = S, add an item (p, 0, 0, 0, n, m) to $I_{00}$.

For each item (p, d, x, y, X, Y) in $I_{ij}$,

If d = |p|, do COMPLETOR

If RIGHT(p, d+1) $\in$ G(N), do PREDICTOR

If RIGHT(p, d+1) $\in$ G(S), do SHIFTER

## PREDICTOR:

For all q $\in$ $P_H \wedge P_V$ such that LEFT(q) = RIGHT(p, d+1), add an item (q, 0, i, j, X, Y) to $I_{ij}$.

## SHIFTER:

If $a_{i+1, j+1}$ = RIGHT(p, d+1), and if i<X $\wedge$ j<Y, then add an item (p, d+1, i, j, X, j+1) to $I_{i+1, j}$.

## COMPLETOR:

For all item (p', d', x', y', X', Y') in $I_{xy}$ such that RIGHT(p', d'+1) = LEFT(p), do the following:

- **Case 1.** $p \in P_H \wedge p' \in P_H$ — Add an item (p', d'+1, x', y' X', Y) to $I_{ij}$, if Y'=Y $\vee$ d'=0.

- **Case 2.** $p \in P_V \wedge p' \in P_H$ — Add an item (p', d'+1, x', y' X', Y) to $I_{Xy}$, if Y'=Y $\vee$ d'=0.

- **Case 3.** $p \in P_H \wedge p' \in P_V$ — Add an item (p', d'+1, x', y' X, Y') to $I_{xY}$, if X'=X $\vee$ d'=0.

- **Case 4.** $p \in P_V \wedge p' \in P_V$ — Add an item (p', d'+1, x', y' X, Y') to $I_{ij}$, if X'=X $\vee$ d'=0.

# 18.3   The 2D-LR parsing algorithm

A 2D-LR(0) parsing table consists of three parts: ACTION, GOTO-RIGHT and GOTO-DOWN. Table 18.2 is a 2D-LR(0) table obtained from the grammar in Table 18.1.

As in Standard LR parsing, the runtime parser performs shift-reduce parsing with a stack guided by this 2D-LR table. Unlike standard LR(0), however, each item in the stack is represented as (s, x, y, X, Y), where s is an LR state number, and (x,y) represents the current position in the input text. X and Y represent right and lower limits, respectively, and no positions beyond these limits should never be explored until this state is popped off from the stack.

Initially the stack has an item (0, 0, 0, n, m), where n and m are the number of columns and rows in the input text, respectively.

Now let the current elements in the stack be

$\dots$ — $(s_3, x_3, y_3, X_3, Y_3)$ — $B_2$ — $(s_2, x_2, y_2, X_2, Y_2)$ — $B_1$ — $(s_1, x_1, y_1, X_1, Y_1)$

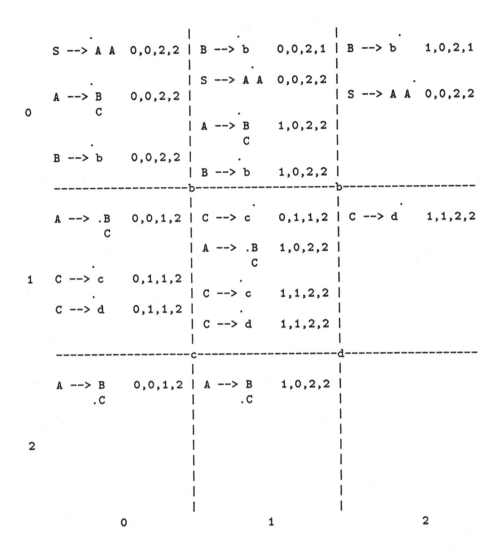

Figure 18.3. An example of 2D Earley parsing.

where the right most element is the top of the stack. Also assume that the current input symbol $a_{ij}$ is b, where $i = x_1+1$ and $j = y_1+1$. According to the parsing table, we perform SHIFT, REDUCE or ACCEPT.

## SHIFT:

If ACTION($s_1$, b) = sh $s_0$, then if $x_1 < X_1 \land y_1 < Y_1$, push b and ($s_0$, $x_1+1$, $y_1$, $X_1$, $y_1+1$) onto the stack.

Table 18.1. Example grammar and text.

| GRAMMAR RULES | | | | | | TEXT | |
|---|---|---|---|---|---|---|---|
| (1) | S | $\rightarrow$ | A A | (4) | C | $\rightarrow$ | c | b | b |
| | | | | | | | | c | d |
| (2) | A | $\rightarrow$ | B | (5) | C | $\rightarrow$ | d | | |
| | | | C | | | | | | |
| (3) | B | $\rightarrow$ | b | | | | | | |

Table 18.2. A 2D-LR parsing table.

| ST | ACTION | | | | GOTO-RIGHT | | | | GOTO-DOWN | | | |
|---|---|---|---|---|---|---|---|---|---|---|---|---|
| | b | c | d | $ | S | A | B | C | S | A | B | C |
| 0 | sh3 | | | | 8 | 1 | | | | 4 | | |
| 1 | sh3 | | | | | 2 | | | | 4 | | |
| 2 | re1 | re1 | re1 | re1 | | | | | | | | |
| 3 | re3 | re3 | re3 | re3 | | | | | | | | |
| 4 | | sh6 | sh7 | | | | | | | | | 5 |
| 5 | re2 | re2 | re2 | re2 | | | | | | | | |
| 6 | re4 | re4 | re4 | re4 | | | | | | | | |
| 7 | re5 | re5 | re5 | re5 | | | | | | | | |
| 8 | | | | acc | | | | | | | | |

## REDUCE:

If $ACTION(s_1, b) = re\ p$, then let k be $|p|+1$ and do the following:

- **Case 1.** $p \in P_H$ and $GOTO\text{-}RIGHT(s_k, LEFT(p)) = s_0$ — If $Y_{k-1} = Y_1$ then pop $2*\text{—}p\text{—}$ elements from the stack, and push $LEFT(p)$ and $(s_0, x_1, y_1, X_k, Y_1)$.

- **Case 2.** $p \in P_H$ and $GOTO\text{-}DOWN(s_k, LEFT(p)) = s_0$ — If $Y_{k-1} = Y_1$ then pop $2*\text{—}p\text{—}$ elements from the stack, and push $LEFT(p)$ and $(s_0, x_k, Y_1, x_1, Y_k)$.

- **Case 3.** $p \in P_V$ and $GOTO\text{-}RIGHT(s_k, LEFT(p)) = s_0$ — If $X_{k-1} = X_1$ then pop $2*\text{—}p\text{—}$ elements from the stack, and push $LEFT(p)$ and $(s_0, X_1, y_k, X_k, y_1)$.

- **Case 4.** $p \in P_V$ and $GOTO\text{-}DOWN(s_k, LEFT(p)) = s_0$ — If $X_{k-1} = X_1$ then pop $2*\text{—}p\text{—}$ elements from the stack, and push $LEFT(p)$ and $(s_0, x_1, y_1, X_1, Y_k)$.

Figure 18.4 shows an example trace of 2D-LR parsing with the grammar in Table 18.1.

```
(0,0,0,2,2)
(0,0,0,2,2)   b   (3,0,1,2,1)
(0,0,0,2,2)   B   (4,0,1,1,2)
(0,0,0,2,2)   B   (4,0,1,1,2)   c   (6,1,1,1,2)
(0,0,0,2,2)   B   (4,0,1,1,2)   C   (5,0,2,2,2)
(0,0,0,2,2)   A   (1,1,0,2,2)
(0,0,0,2,2)   A   (1,1,0,2,2)   b   (3,2,0,2,1)
(0,0,0,2,2)   A   (1,1,0,2,2)   B   (4,1,1,2,2)
(0,0,0,2,2)   A   (1,1,0,2,2)   B   (4,1,1,2,2)   d   (7,2,1,2,2)
(0,0,0,2,2)   A   (1,1,0,2,2)   B   (4,1,1,2,2)   C   (5,1,2,2,2)
(0,0,0,2,2)   A   (1,1,0,2,2)   A   (2,2,0,2,2)
(0,0,0,2,2)   S   (8,2,0,2,2)
```

Figure 18.4. Example trace of 2D-LR parsing.

The example given in this section is totally deterministic. In general, however, a 2D-LR table may have multiple entries, or both GOTO-DOWN and GOTO-RIGHT may be defined from an identical state with an identical symbol. Such nondeterminism can be also handled efficiently using a *graph-structured stack* as in Generalized LR parsing (Tomita, 1985, 1987).

## 18.4   More interesting 2D grammars

This section presents a couple of more interesting example grammars and texts. Example Grammar I (see Table 18.3 and Figure 18.5) generates nested rectangles of b's and c's, one after the other. In the grammar, B1 represents vertical bars (sequences) of b's, and B2 represents horizontal bars of b's. Similarly, C1 and C2 represent vertical and horizontal bars of c's, respectively. A1 then represents rectangles surrounded by c's. A2 represents rectangles surrounded by c's which are sandwiched by two vertical bars of b's. A3 further sandwiches A2 with two horizontal b bars, representing rectangles surrounded by b's. Similarly, A4 sandwiches A3 with two vertical c bars, and A1 further sandwiches A4 with two horizontal c bars, representing rectangles surrounded by c's.

A similar analysis can be made for Grammar II (see Table 18.4 and Figure 18.6), which generates triangles of b's and c's.

Grammar III (see Figure 18.7) generates all rectangles of a's which have exactly 2 b's somewhere in them. Xn represents horizontal lines of a's with n b's. Thus, X0, X1 and X2 represent lines of a's, keeping track of how many b's inside. Yn then combines those lines vertically, keeping track of how many a's have been seen thus far (n being the number of b's). Therefore, Y2 contains exactly two b's.

Table 18.3. Example Grammar I.

| START → A1 | | | | | | | | |
|---|---|---|---|---|---|---|---|---|
| A1 | → | c | B1 | → | b | C1 | → | c |
| A1 | → | C2 A4 C2 | B1 | → | b B1 b | C1 | → | c C1 c |
| A2 | → | B1 A1 B1 | B2 | → | b | C2 | → | c |
| A3 | → | B2 A2 B2 | B2 | → | b B2 b | C2 | → | c C2 c |
| A4 | → | C1 A3 C1 | | | | | | |

```
                                              ccccccccccccc
                                              cbbbbbbbbbbbc
                          ccccccccc           cbccccccccccbc
              bbbbbbb     cbbbbbbbc           cbcbbbbbbbbcbc
      ccccc   bcccccb     cbccccccbc          cbcbccccccbcbc
  bbb cbbbc   bcbbbcb     cbcbbbcbc           cbcbcbbbbcbcbc
c bcb cbcbc   bcbcbcb     cbcbcbcbc           cbcbcbcbcbcbc
  bbb cbbbc   bcbbbcb     cbcbbbcbc           cbcbcbbbcbcbc
      ccccc   bcccccb     cbccccccbc          cbcbccccccbcbc
              bbbbbbb     cbbbbbbbc           cbcbbbbbbbbcbc
                          ccccccccc           cbccccccccccbc
                                              cbbbbbbbbbbbc
                                              ccccccccccccc
```

Figure 18.5. Example text for Grammar I.

## 18.5   Formal property of 2D-CFG

Very little is known about 2D-CFG's formal/mathematical properties. Each column or row of a text forms a string. It is easy to show that such strings can get as complex as context-free. Interestingly enough, however, the author recently found that such strings can get even more complex than context-free. The grammar in Table 18.6 will generate texts like those in Figure 18.8 whose rows form a context-sensitive language, $a^n b^n c^n$. In the grammar, it is easy to see from the rules with A1, A2 and A3 that the non-terminal, A, represents a square of a's. Similarly, the non-terminal B represents a square of b's and C represents a square of c's. When we combine these three squares using the

Table 18.4. Example Grammar II.

| START | → | A1 | A1 | → | c | B1 | → | b | C1 | → | c |
|-------|---|----|----|----|----|----|----|----|----|----|----|
| | | | | | | | | b | | | c |
| | | A1 | → | A4 | | B1 | → | B1 | C1 | → | C1 |
| | | | | C2 | | | | | | | |
| | | A2 | → | A1 B1 | | B2 | → | b | C2 | → | c |
| | | | | B2 | | | | | | | |
| | | A3 | → | A2 | | B2 | → | b B2 | C2 | → | c C2 |
| | | A4 | → | C1 A3 | | | | | | | |

```
                                              cbbbbbbbbbbbb
                                              ccbbbbbbbbbbb
                            cbbbbbbbb          cccbbbbbbbbbb
                cbbbbbb      ccbbbbbbb          ccccbbbbbbbbb
         cbbbb  ccbbbbb      cccbbbbbb          cccccbbbbbbbb
   cbb   ccbbb  cccbbbb      ccccbbbbb          ccccccbbbbbbb
c  ccb   cccbb  ccccbbb      cccccbbbb          cccccccbbbbbb
   ccc   ccccb  cccccbb      ccccccbbb          ccccccccbbbbb
   ccccc        cccccccb     cccccccbb          cccccccccbbbb
                ccccccc       ccccccccb          ccccccccccbbb
                             ccccccccc           cccccccccccbb
                                                 ccccccccccccb
                                                 cccccccccccc
```

Figure 18.6. Example text for Grammar II.

```
aaaaaaaaaaaa          aaa          aaaaaaa
aaabaaaaaaaa          aaa          aaaabaa
aaaaaaaaaaaa          bba          aabaaaa
aaaaaaaaaaab          aaa
aaaaaaaaaaaa          aaa
                      aaa
                      aaa
                      aaa
```

Figure 18.7. Example text for Grammar III.

last rule, all the three squares are forced to have the same height due to the adjoining constraint. If all three squares have the same height, say n, then all

Table 18.5. Example Grammar III.

| START | → | Y2 | X0 | → | [empty] | Y0 | → | [empty] |
|---|---|---|---|---|---|---|---|---|
| | | | X0 | → | X0 a | Y0 | → | Y0 X0 |
| | | | X1 | → | X0 b | Y1 | → | Y0 X1 |
| | | | X1 | → | X1 a | Y1 | → | Y1 X0 |
| | | | X2 | → | X1 b | Y2 | → | Y0 X2 |
| | | | X2 | → | X2 a | Y2 | → | Y1 X1 |
| | | | | | | Y2 | → | Y2 X0 |

Table 18.6. Example Grammar IV.

| S | → | A B C | | | | | | | | | |
|---|---|---|---|---|---|---|---|---|---|---|---|
| A | → | a | A | → | A3 A2 | A1 | → | a | A1 | → | A1 a |
| A2 | → | a | A2 | → | A2 a | A3 | → | A A1 | | | |
| B | → | b | B | → | B B2 | B1 | → | b | B1 | → | B1 b |
| B2 | → | b | B2 | → | B2 b | B3 | → | B B1 | | | |
| C | → | c | C | → | C C2 | C1 | → | c | C1 | → | C1 c |
| C2 | → | c | C2 | → | C2 c | C3 | → | C C1 | | | |

the three squares must have the same width, n. Thus, each row string of S is in the language, $a^n b^n c^n$.

Exactly how complex row (or column) strings can get is unknown. There appear to be many other interesting problems like this behind the theory of 2D-CFG.

```
                            aaaaaaaaabbbbbbbbbbccccccccc
                            aaaaaaaaabbbbbbbbbbccccccccc
                            aaaaaaaaabbbbbbbbbbccccccccc
                            aaaaaaaaabbbbbbbbbbccccccccc
aaabbbccc                   aaaaaaaaabbbbbbbbbbccccccccc
aaabbbccc                   aaaaaaaaabbbbbbbbbbccccccccc
aaabbbccc                   aaaaaaaaabbbbbbbbbbccccccccc
                            aaaaaaaaabbbbbbbbbbccccccccc
                            aaaaaaaaabbbbbbbbbbccccccccc
```

Figure 18.8. Example text for Grammar IV.

## 18.6   Concluding remarks

In this chapter, 2D-CFG, 2-dimensional context free grammar, has been introduced, and two efficient parsing algorithms for 2D-CFG have been presented. Traditional one-dimension context free grammars are well studied and well understood (e.g., Aho & Ullman, 1972), and Many of their theorems and techniques might be extended and adopted for 2D-CFG, as we have done for Earley's algorithm and LR parsing in this chapter.

## Acknowledgments

This research was supported by National Science Foundation under the contract IRI-8858085.

## References

Aho, A. V., & Ullman, J. D. (1972). *The theory of parsing, translation and compiling.* Englewood Cliffs, NJ: Prentice-Hall.

Akiyama, T., & Masuda, I. (1986). A method of document-image segmentation based on projection profiles, stroke density and circumscribed rectangles. *Trans. IECE, J69-D*, 1187–1196.

Earley, J. (1970). An efficient context-free parsing algorithm. *Communications of ACM, 6*, 94–102.

Fu, K. S. (1977). *Syntactic pattern recognition.* Springer-Verlag.

Fujisawa, H., *et al.* (1988). Document analysis and decomposition method for multimedia contents retrieval. *Proceedings of the Second International Symposium on Interoperable Information Systems* (p. 231).

Higashino, J., Fujisawa, H., Nakano, Y., & Ejiri, M. (1986). A knowledge-based segmentation method for document understanding. *Proceedings of the Eighth International Conference on Pattern Recognition* (pp. 745–748).

Inagaki, K., Kato, T., Hiroshima, T., & Sakai, T. (1984). MACSYM: A hierarchical image processing system for event-driven pattern understanding of documents. *Pattern Recognition, 17*, 85–108.

Kubota, K., *et al.* (1984). Document understanding system. *Proceedings of the Seventh International Conference on Pattern Recognition* (pp. 612–614).

Tomita, M. (1985). *Efficient parsing for natural language.* Boston, MA: Kluwer.

Tomita, M. (1987). An efficient augmented-context-free parsing algorithm. *Computational Linguistics, 13*, 31–46.

Watanabe, S. (Ed.) (1972). *Frontiers of pattern recognition.* Academic Press.

Wong, K., Casey, R., Wahl, F. (1982). Document analysis system. *IBM J. Research and Development, 26*, 647–656.

Yashiro, H., *et al.* (1989). A new method of document structure extraction. *Proceedings of the International Workshop on Industrial Applications of Machine Intelligence and Vision (MIV-89)* (p. 282).

# Index